Authorisation and decision-making in native title

Authorisation and decision-making in native title

Nick Duff
Goldfields Land and Sea Council

First published in 2017 by AIATSIS Research Publications

Australian Institute of Aboriginal and Torres Strait Islander Studies (AIATSIS)

GPO Box 553, Canberra ACT 2601
Phone: (61 2) 6246 1111
Fax: (61 2) 6261 4285
Email: researchpublications@aiatsis.gov.au
Web: www.aiatsis.gov.au

National Library of Australia Cataloguing-in-Publication entry

Creator: Duff, Nick, author.

Title: Authorisation and decision-making in native title / Nick Duff.

ISBN: 9781922102614 (paperback)
9781922102607 (ebook)
9781922102638 (ePub)

Subjects: Native title (Australia)
Land tenure--Law and legislation--Australia.
Aboriginal Australians--Land tenure.
Culture and law--Australia.
Australian

Other Creators/Contributors:
Australian Institute of Aboriginal and Torres Strait Islander Studies

Typeset in Garamond

Contents

Summary

Native title involves an interface between the Australian legal system and Indigenous legal, cultural and political systems. In Australia, traditional Indigenous rights in land are necessarily recognised and managed at the group level, even in contexts where some rights can be held individually. At the same time, the Australian legal system generally demands hard-edged decisions, with legal consequences that are concrete, final and binding rather than fluid, contextual and renegotiable. In this setting, native title law must regulate complex and contested interactions between the Australian legal system and sometimes large and disparate groups of Indigenous people. In doing so, the law faces a twin challenge: how to remain neutral in the face of competing claims about legitimate Indigenous authority, while ensuring that internal disagreements do not make collective agency impossible.

The Australian legal system addresses this challenge by imposing a centralised representative structure on Indigenous group decision-making. During the native title claims process and compensation claims, this is done by requiring groups to appoint one or more individuals to act as the 'applicant' in the Federal Court. After native title is formally recognised, a new representative structure is mandated – the 'registered native title body corporate'. In both cases, the law sets out rules that both govern the process by which the group authorises the representative and define the scope of the representative's power to make decisions on behalf of the group without prior consultation. Together, these rules can broadly be referred to as the 'law on authorisation'.

In the more than 20 years since the first native title claim, a vast and complex body of law and practice has developed, covering everything from the legal duties owed by representatives to their constituencies, to the minutiae of how to advertise and run a claim group meeting. This book describes the law on authorisation as it applies to all stages of the native title process: authorising an applicant; replacing the applicant; making decisions during the conduct of a claim; changing the composition of the claim group; making agreements with third parties; and the appointment and management of registered native title bodies corporate. Referring to relevant legislation and case law, the book explains the fundamental legal principles as well as their application to particular circumstances. It identifies the areas in which the law is unclear, unsettled, or in need of reform.

The book also addresses some key practical, ethical and political dimensions of native title decision-making. For example, what logistical arrangements are necessary to give all members of a claim group a reasonable opportunity to participate? And what are the implications for Indigenous self-determination if the cost and complexity of these arrangements are beyond the capacity of grassroots Indigenous leaders? How can native title advocates balance their mission of securing recognition of native title against the imperative to remain impartial within intra-Indigenous politics? And what should be done when a group cannot agree on the decision-making process they should use?

This book will be useful for lawyers, judges and anyone involved in the practical aspects of native title advocacy and governance – including, of course, native title holders themselves. The factual and theoretical material may also benefit future academic work on the broader ethical, political and anthropological dimensions of Indigenous governance.

Abbreviations

AIATSIS	Australian Institute of Aboriginal and Torres Strait Islander Studies
ALRC	Australian Law Reform Commission
CATSI Act	*Corporations (Aboriginal and Torres Strait Islander) Act 2006* (Cth)
CLR	*Commonwealth Law Reports*
FCA, also Federal Court	Federal Court of Australia
FCR	*Federal Court Reports*
Federal Court Regulations	Native Title (Federal Court) Regulations 1998
Federal Court Rules	Federal Court Rules 2011
HCA	High Court of Australia
ILC	Indigenous land corporation
ILUA	Indigenous land use agreement
ILUA Regulations	Native Title (Indigenous Land Use Agreement) Regulations 1999
NNTTA	National Native Title Tribunal of Australia
NTA, also Native Title Act	*Native Title Act 1993* (Cth)
NTRB	native title representative body
ORIC	Office of the Registrar of Aboriginal Corporations
PBC	prescribed body corporate
PBC Regulations	Native Title (Prescribed Bodies Corporate) Regulations 1999
RTN	right to negotiate
RTNBC	registered native title body corporate
YAC	Yindjibarndi Aboriginal Corporation

Acknowledgments

Many people have contributed in a range of ways to this book. It could not have been written without the support of the Australian Institute of Aboriginal and Torres Strait Islander Studies (AIATSIS), nor the guidance, encouragement and assistance of Lisa Strelein, Toni Bauman, Rob Powrie and Pauline McGuire. I am very grateful for the time and patience of all those native title practitioners who have shared their knowledge and experience with me, including Tina Jowett, Vance Hughston, John Southalan, Angus Frith, Greg McIntyre, Tim Wishart, Jacki Cole, Graham and Malcolm O'Dell, Michael Meegan, Mishka Holt, Tessa Herrmann, Gemma Wheeler-Carver, Michael Pagsanjan, Greg Young, Wendy Gilbert, Craig Reiach, Kelly Thomas-Greer, Tony McAvoy, Daniel Jacobs, Monica Franz, Joe Fardin, Matthew Moharich, Mark Rumler, Marnie Parkinson, Louahna Lloyd, Rob Houston, Nick Testro, Tony Kelly, Hema Hanrihan and many others. I'm grateful for the input and assistance of AIATSIS colleagues Tran Tran, Claire Stacey, Gabrielle Lauder, Pamela McGrath, Donna Bagnara and Christine Deng. Thank you to Valerie Cooms for bringing me along to my very first authorisation meeting. Lastly, I must thank my brilliant and beautiful wife for tolerating the many weekends and evenings I have spoiled by working on this manuscript, and whose own academic writing has given me a model of clarity and succinctness to which I can only aspire.

1. Introduction

'Authorisation' is an area of native title law about how the views and intentions of native title claimants or holders are translated into legally effective decisions and actions.[1] This book sets out the legal rules and some practical considerations relating to authorisation in four broad areas: native title determination applications, native title agreement-making, post-determination decision-making, and compensation applications.

Before amendments were made to the *Native Title Act 1993* (Cth) in 1998, authorisation was an informal process. Courts essentially left the matter of authorisation to the claimants themselves and generally took at face value the word of the applicant(s) that they were the right person(s) to bring the claim. As French J explained in a 2002 case:

> Prior to the 1998 amendments there was no requirement under the *Native Title Act* that an applicant have such authority. The absence of that requirement led, in some cases, to conflicting and overlapping claims all carrying with them the statutory right to negotiate in respect of the grant of mineral tenements and the compulsory acquisition by Commonwealth or State Governments of native title rights and interests. Although many aspects of the 1998 amendments were the subject of controversy in the public and parliamentary debates that preceded their enactment, the need for communal authorisation of claims was largely a matter of common ground.[2]

Similarly in debates preceding the 1998 amendments, government MP Sharman Stone said:

> The core of the problem at the moment is that virtually no threshold tests are in place: any individual or group can walk in and make a claim. That has caused a great amount of tension.[3]

---

1 In this book the term 'native title holders' refers to people who have been determined by the Federal Court of Australia to hold native title rights and interests in a particular area. 'Native title claimants' refers to people on whose behalf a native title claim has been made, when that claim has not yet been determined. 'Claim' refers to a native title determination application. Note that the term 'registered native title claimant' has a special technical meaning and is to be distinguished from the more colloquial 'native title claimant'. Note also that, in cases where native title is held on trust by a prescribed body corporate (PBC), that corporation is technically the 'native title holder' and the people who would otherwise be the native title holders are called the 'common law holders of native title': ss 224 and 56(2)(a), NTA. This ungainly use of language will be avoided in this book wherever possible.

2 *Daniel v Western Australia* [2002] FCA 1147 [11].

3 Australia, House of Representatives 1998, *Debates*, 11 March 1998, p. 968 (see <http://parlinfo.aph.gov.au/parlInfo/search/search.w3p;adv=yes>).

As this book will explain, since 1998 the individuals named as applicant on a native title application are legally required to demonstrate the basis of their authorisation by the broader claim group. This increased legislative emphasis on authorisation has been well noted by the courts. Justice Finn stated in one case: 'It is difficult to overstate the centrality of the requirement of "authorisation" in the scheme laid down by the Act for the making of a native title application.'[4] Justice Lindgren described 'proper authorisation' as 'the foundation for the institution and maintenance of a native title claimant application'.[5] Drawing attention to the rationale behind this centrality, French J said:

> It is of central importance to the conduct of native title determination applications and the exercise of the rights that flow from their registration, that those who purport to bring such applications and to exercise such rights on behalf of a group of asserted native title holders have the authority of that group to do so.[6]

In an earlier case, French J described the authorisation requirements of the *Native Title Act* as 'a matter of considerable importance and fundamental to the legitimacy of native title determination applications [which] acknowledges the communal character of traditional law and custom which grounds native title'.[7] Elsewhere, Wilcox J put the matter as follows:

> It is important that those who come to the Court asserting a native title right, with all this involves in terms of effort and expense to other parties and the Court itself, should be properly authorised to make the claim.[8]

There are at least four primary reasons for authorisation's importance in the legislative scheme:

- **Internal legitimacy** — protecting the interests of native title claimants by ensuring that the claim is brought truly on their behalf, that the litigation is conducted in accordance with the group's wishes and that decisions made about the litigation are made using processes that are understood by the group as being legitimate.[9]

---

4 *Kokatha People v South Australia* [2007] FCA 1057 [18].

5 *Harrington-Smith on behalf of the Wongatha People v Western Australia (No. 9)* [2007] FCA 31 [1171], quoting M Perry & S Lloyd, *Australian native title law*, Thomson Lawbook Co., Pyrmont, NSW, 2003, p. 439 at [3.140]. In *Quall v Risk* [2001] FCA 378 [67] O'Loughlin J described the proper identification of the native title claim group as going to the heart of a native title determination application.

6 *Daniel v Western Australia* [2002] FCA 1147 [11]. On 'central importance' see also *Landers v South Australia* [2003] FCA 264 [35].

7 *Strickland v Native Title Registrar* [1999] FCA 1530 [57].

8 *Moran v Minister for Land and Water Conservation (NSW)* [1999] FCA 1637 [48].

9 In his introductory summary to the *Wongatha* trial judgment (not forming part of the formal reasons), Lindgren J said 'It may seem unfortunate that, in circumstances where there is no internal challenge to authorisation, it should be able to be challenged by third parties, at least in the circumstances of this case. However, the requirement of s. 61(1) is strict, and I was obliged to

- **Procedural rights pending finalisation of the claim** — ensuring that the procedural rights afforded by the *Native Title Act* to native title holders pending the resolution of their claims (including the right to participate in decisions about development on the land and, potentially, to receive benefits from such development) are enjoyed by the entire group rather than just a few individuals, or at least that there is transparency and agreement within the group about the application of benefits.[10]
- **External legitimacy and predictability** — related to the last point, authorisation also provides confidence to external parties (such as mining companies) that the people with whom they are negotiating can speak authoritatively for the broader group.
- **Efficiency** — avoiding the confusion, expense and time wasting that are generated by overlapping or otherwise weak claims.

Related to the first of these is an additional consideration: the need to ensure that the ultimate determination is made in favour of the 'right people for country'. Although in contested litigation the court will make its own findings about who has native title based on the evidence, in practice the statutory framework encourages native title claims to be settled by agreement, avoiding the need for a full hearing on the evidence.[11] So, whereas in contested hearings courts may sort through disagreements about which groups hold native title and which do not, in consent determinations parties are expected to agree on facts and issues to limit the extent to which the court is required to make its own findings of fact.[12] And even in contested hearings, courts are expected to make inferences where appropriate.[13] In that context, courts will be more confident in making a determination of native title if they can be assured that the applicants

deal with the question'. *Harrington-Smith on behalf of the Wongatha People v Western Australia (No. 9)* [2007] FCA 31. See also *Edward Landers v South Australia* [2003] FCA 264 [38].

10 See Explanatory Memorandum, Native Title Amendment Bill 1997 at 29.27 in relation to s. 190C(4).

11 See e.g. *Clarrie Smith v Western Australia* [2000] FCA 1249 [22]–[24]; *Ward v Western Australia* [2006] FCA 1848 [8]; *Hunter v Western Australia* [2012] FCA 690; *Hoolihan on behalf of the Gugu Badhun People #2 v Queensland* [2012] FCA 800; *Archer on behalf of the Djungan People #1 v Queensland* [2012] FCA 801 [3]; *Close on behalf of the Githabul People v Minister for Lands* [2007] FCA 1847 [6]; *Payi Payi on behalf of the Ngururrpa People v Western Australia* [2007] FCA 2113 [6].

12 *North Ganalanja Aboriginal Corporation v Queensland* [1996] HCA 2; (1996) 185 CLR 595 [26]. See also *Nangkiriny v Western Australia* [2004] FCA 1156 [15]; *Munn for and on behalf of the Gunggari People v Queensland* [2001] FCA 1229 [29]–[30]; *Nelson v Northern Territory* (2010) 190 FCR 344 [14]. Cf. *Wik and Wik Way Native Title Claim Group v Queensland* [2009] FCA 789 [16]–[17]; *Kowanyama People v Queensland* [2009] FCA 1192 [24]; *Kuuku Ya'u People v Queensland* [2009] FCA 679 [12]. See also *Delaney on behalf of the Quandamooka People v Queensland* [2011] FCA 741; *Wonga on behalf of the Wanyurr Majay People v Queensland* [2011] FCA 1055.

13 *Members of the Yorta Yorta Aboriginal Community v Victoria* 214 CLR 422; [2002] HCA 58 [80]–[82]; *Daniel v Western Australia* [2003] FCA 666 [149], [366], [428]; *Alyawarr, Kaytetye, Warumungu, Wakay Native Title Claim Group v Northern Territory* [2004] FCA 472 [74], [100]–[112].

represent all of the people who claim to hold rights and interests in the claim area. Without the legal requirement to demonstrate authorisation, this assurance would be lacking.

1.1 What this book is about

This book is primarily intended for native title legal practitioners. It sets out a range of legal issues that must be considered in acting for native title claim groups, as well as some associated practical considerations. The book is also intended to have some broader relevance to other stakeholders in the native title system. That is because the law on authorisation governs the interface between the Australian legal system and the decision-making processes of Indigenous polities. The fine legal details and technicalities have real consequences for how Indigenous politics works in practice. They determine the extent to which individuals and subgroups have a voice and the extent to which native title claims and future act decisions can proceed in the face of internal disagreement. Although this book does not deal directly with these broader policy issues, it is intended to articulate the legal foundation on which such analysis can be developed.

1.2 What is authorisation?

Under the *Native Title Act*, litigation and agreement-making are done by single individuals or small groups of individuals on behalf of larger groups of people. This is a matter of clear necessity — it would be unmanageable for each member of a native title claim group to be a party to a court proceeding or a contract. And given that births and deaths are constantly altering the composition of a claim group, there would always be uncertainty as to whether the group was accurately captured. So the law provides for representative 'applicants' to conduct the litigation and sign agreements on behalf of the broader group[14] and requires applicants to demonstrate that they are authorised by the broader group to do so.

In one sense, authorisation is simply a part of the Australian legal system — a set of statutory rules specifying certain requirements for native title claimants to follow if they are to succeed in their claim. In another sense, though, authorisation constitutes a point of interface between the Australian legal system and Indigenous political and legal systems. It is the means by which an unincorporated group of people, defined by a commonality of rights and interests under

14 Native title claims are prosecuted by way of representative proceedings where the applicant litigates on behalf of a broader group of people: *Tigan v Western Australia* [2010] FCA 993 [10]; *Butchulla People v Queensland* [2006] FCA 1063 [39]; *Ankamuthi People v Queensland* [2002] FCA 897 [7]; *Bullen v Western Australia* [2010] FCA 900 [50] (not disturbed on appeal); *Augustine v Western Australia* [2013] FCA 338 [10]; *Doolan v Native Title Registrar* [2007] FCA 192 [62]; *Close on behalf of the Githabul People #2 v Queensland* [2010] FCA 828 [2], [25]; *Levinge on behalf of the Gold Coast Native Title Group v Queensland* [2012] FCA 1321 [47]; *Weribone on behalf of the Mandandanji People v Queensland* [2011] FCA 1169; *Roe on behalf of the Goolarabooloo and Jabirr Jabirr Peoples v Western Australia* [2011] FCA 421 [36].

traditional law and custom, is able to make joint decisions that are legally effective in the *Australian* legal system. Importantly, it represents an attempt (however imperfect) by the Australian legal system to give effect to Indigenous legal, customary and political systems.

The term 'authorisation' has two meanings under the *Native Title Act*:

- the authorisation granted by a group to an applicant to make a native title determination application or compensation application and to deal with matters arising in relation to the application;[15]
- the decision by a group to enter into an Indigenous land use agreement (ILUA).[16]

In addition, there is a third concept under the *Native Title Act* that serves many of the same basic functions but is not called 'authorisation'. After a formal determination of native title is made, the native title rights and interests are held or managed by a registered native title body corporate (RNTBC). There are some things the RNTBC cannot do without first consulting with the native title holders and obtaining their consent.[17] As will be seen, the process for obtaining this consent is similar to the other forms of authorisation, though with some important differences.

Authorisation in the claims process

Under the *Native Title Act* a native title determination application can only be made by a person or persons who are authorised by the native title claim group.[18] This rule is relevant to several different points in the native title claims process:

- applying the registration test (s. 190A□F, *Native Title Act*);
- determining strike-out applications that allege a lack of proper authorisation;
- responding to assertions by claim group members under s. 84D, *Native Title Act* that the applicant is not authorised, or not authorised to do a particular thing;
- deciding whether a person purporting to act on behalf of a group of native title holders should be joined as a respondent;
- dealing with an application to replace the applicant;
- deciding whether a determination of native title should be made.[19]

---

15 As we shall see below in Section 7.2 at 'The role and autonomy of the applicant in s. 31 agreements', this arguably covers so-called 's. 31 agreements' in relation to future acts.

16 Sections 24CG(3), 203BE, 251A, NTA.

17 Regs 3 and 8, PBC Regulations.

18 Section 61(1), NTA. Applications can also be made by the holders of non–native title interests, as well as state, territory and Commonwealth ministers.

19 Anecdotally, it appears that respondent parties such as governments or mining companies will also sometimes request evidence of proper authorisation. While such requests may be prudent from the respondent's perspective, and while the applicant may find it useful to comply with the request, the legislation contains no requirement for the applicant to satisfy the respondents of its authorisation.

The Federal Court of Australia or the National Native Title Tribunal may also require information about an applicant's authorisation when the applicant proposes to take some step in the proceedings. For example, where the court must decide whether to grant leave to amend[20] or discontinue[21] an application, or where the court or tribunal is asked to make a determination by consent[22], it may seek confirmation that the applicant is acting with the authority of the broader claim group. (All these scenarios are discussed in more detail below in Section 2.2, 'When and why is it necessary to establish authorisation?')

Authorisation in the agreement-making process

There are two main mechanisms through which native title claim groups and native title holders can make agreements in relation to their native title rights and interests: ILUAs and so-called 'future act agreements' or 's. 31 agreements'. Each of these has different authorisation requirements and each gives different roles to the applicants, discussed below in Chapter 7.

The *Native Title Act* sets out strict procedural requirements for authorising ILUAs, discussed below in Section 7.1 ('Entering and authorising ILUAs'). In relation to 's. 31 agreements', the process is not spelled out in the legislation but practices have developed within native title representative bodies (NTRBs), mining companies, governments and the tribunal that somewhat mirror the processes for ILUAs. These are discussed below in Section 7.2 ('Entering and authorising s. 31 agreements').

Authorisation after the determination

After a determination of native title is made by the Federal Court, the native title rights and interests are either held on trust or managed on an agency basis by an RNTBC. In one sense this makes day-to-day questions of 'authorisation' somewhat simpler, since a corporation is a fixed, stable entity with its own legal personality, capable of acting in its own right. The native title holders can control and influence the corporation's activities through voting (in their capacity as members of the corporation) for directors at general meetings.

Yet for certain types of decision, the RNTBC must comply with 'consultation and consent' procedures that effectively mirror the authorisation process for claim groups.[23] And in addition to these statutorily prescribed rules, native title holders can creatively design their RNTBC's decision-making rules to provide the best cultural 'fit'. Post-determination decision-making and authorisation structures will be discussed below in Chapter 8.

---

20 *Lovett on behalf of the Gunditjmara People v Victoria (No. 3)* [2011] FCA 867 [4].

21 *Gorringe on behalf of the Mithaka People v Queensland* [2010] FCA 716 [24]; *Levinge on behalf of the Gold Coast Native Title Group v Queensland* [2012] FCA 1321 [43]–[50].

22 E.g. *Wik and Wik Way Native Title Claim Group v Queensland* [2009] FCA 789 [37]; *Cheinmora v Western Australia (No. 2)* [2013] FCA 768 [20]. In the tribunal, see e.g. *Western Australia/Arthur Dimer & Ors on behalf of the WA Mirning People/R A Higgins & T F Higgins* [2013] NNTTA 46.

23 Reg. 8 and 8A, PBC Regulations; s. 24CG(3), NTA.

Authorisation for compensation applications

The final aspect of authorisation to be addressed in this book, albeit quite briefly, is the way in which applications for native title compensation may be made in the Federal Court. That issue is addressed below in Chapter 9.

2. Authorisation in native title determination applications

2.1 What is an applicant?

The *Native Title Act* sets out a scheme for the recognition and protection of native title rights and interests. In order to secure such recognition and protection, a native title determination application must be filed in the Federal Court. This commences a process of litigation in which the native title claimants have to prove the existence of their traditional rights and interests in the claim area. This will be done either through a trial process in which witnesses' testimony and other evidence is put before the judge to assess, or else through a negotiated process in which the claimants provide their evidence directly to the respondent parties to consider. If the claimants succeed in convincing the judge (in contested proceedings) or the respondent parties (in a negotiated settlement) that they hold the rights and interests claimed, the court will make a determination of native title recognising those rights and interests.[24]

So the starting point for the claims process is the filing of a native title determination *application* under ss 13 and 61 of the *Native Title Act*. This term refers to both the court *proceeding* and the *document* filed in court to commence the proceeding. The first concept, referring to the litigation as a whole, is often simply called the 'claim'; the second concept is colloquially called the 'Form 1'.[25]

Every Federal Court application is filed by an *applicant*. The applicant is a party to the proceeding — the other parties are called respondents.[26] Section 61(2) of the *Native Title Act* states that 'in the case of a native title determination application made by a person or persons authorised to make the application by a native title claim group…the person is, or the persons are jointly, the applicant; and…none of the other members of the native title claim group…is the applicant.'[27]

The core proposition about authorisation in the native title claims process is set out in s. 61(1): that applications can only be made by applicants who are *authorised* by the native title claim group.

---

24 Sections 94A and 225, NTA.

25 Reg. 5, Federal Court Regulations requires a native title determination application to be made using Form 1 in the schedule to those regulations.

26 Section 84(2), NTA.

27 Note that s. 253 states not that 'applicant' is *defined* in s. 61(2) but that the term 'has a meaning affected by s. 61(2)'. Note also that native title determination applications can be made by people other than native title claimants: if a person holds a non–native title interest in an area of land, they can apply for a determination of native title (including a determination that no native title exists). State, territory and Commonwealth ministers can also make applications. In these so-called non-claimant applicants, the applicant would be whichever party is making the application and the people who assert that they hold native title rights would be respondents.

A native title applicant is one or more persons who have commenced proceedings in the Federal Court,[28] and is no different from any other person or corporation who sues someone else in court, except that:

a) The proceedings are representative in nature — the applicant sues on behalf of a larger group of people.[29]

b) Native title applicants have a unique joint-but-unincorporated nature, explained below.

c) In order to be an applicant or a member of the applicant, an individual must be a member of the native title claim group.

d) The applicant must have been authorised by the native title claim group in a way prescribed by the legislation.

Point (a) is generally relevant to the whole of the law of authorisation but is particularly pertinent to the discussion of applicants' powers and duties below in Chapter 4. Point (d) is similarly all-encompassing and will be the subject of discussion below in Section 2.2 ('When and why is it necessary to establish authorisation?') and Chapter 3. Point (c) will be addressed briefly within Section 2.1 at 'Eligibility to be named applicant' and Section 6.2 ('Authorisation by proposed amended claim group'). Point (b) is explained immediately below.

Applicants are joint but not incorporated

As mentioned, the definition of 'applicant' in s. 61(2) contains the phrase: 'the person is, or the persons are jointly, the applicant.' This use of language is somewhat unfamiliar to an Australian lawyer — in general, two or more individuals may only sue (and be sued) *as separate individuals* unless they are incorporated into a company or association.[30]

In *Doolan* Spender J observed that '[i]n some instances, the term "*the applicant*" is used in the Act to refer to the group of people who, as a group, are deemed to be "the applicant" for the purposes of bringing and prosecuting the claim. In other circumstances, it is used to refer to each person (who must be a member of the claim group) who has been authorised to be an applicant.'[31] As an example of the latter, Spender J pointed to s. 62(1)(a), which requires a native title application to be accompanied by 'an affidavit sworn by the applicant'. He said:

> As a matter of language (and in fact of practice), the requirements of s 62 are satisfied by the filing of affidavits by each of the persons who constitute 'the applicant' deposing to the

---

28 Or, as we shall see below in Chapter 5, a person or persons who have (under s. 66B) replaced the person or persons who originally brought the application.

29 Beyond native title, representative proceedings or 'class actions' have been commonly used in consumer law and negligence matters.

30 See *Taff Vale Railway v Amalgamated Society of Railway Servants* [1901] AC 426 at 429, cited in *QGC Pty Limited v Bygrave (No. 2)* [2010] FCA 1019 [71].

31 *Doolan v Native Title Registrar* [2007] FCA 192 [65].

> specified beliefs. It is not meaningful to speak of an affidavit sworn by a group of persons, or an affidavit deposing to what that group of persons believes.[32]

To account for this ambiguity, the practice has developed among native title lawyers to speak of 'named applicants' or 'members of the applicant' to refer to the individuals who together constitute *the applicant*.[33]

What does it mean, then, for a number of individuals to constitute the applicant 'jointly'? Certainly it does not mean that the legislation creates a new separate legal entity. The case law clearly establishes that the named applicants are suing in their individual capacities (albeit jointly with other named applicants and on a representative basis) rather than as part of some entity having its own distinct corporate character.[34] This complex hybridity is evident in Collier J's summary in *Anderson on behalf of the Wulli Wulli People*:

> [W]hile the persons authorised to comprise the applicant are each authorised in their personal capacity, they are nonetheless 'jointly' the applicant. They are not authorised separately as multiple applicants in respect of the determination application (cf *Butchulla*

---

32 ibid. [67]. Similarly, Spender J pointed (at [75]–[76]) to the requirement in s. 190C(4) that 'the applicant' be a member of the claim group — something that could not apply to the group of persons who jointly make up the applicant.

33 Occasionally the term 'applicant group' is used to refer to all of the named applicants — this can be confusing, however, since some might understand it to refer to the native title claim group on whose behalf the application is made. Note also that in non–native title proceedings in the Federal Court it is quite usual to have more than one applicant: for example one company might be 'first applicant' and another may be 'second applicant'. In such cases there are truly *multiple applicants* in a way that there are not in a single native title application. Of course, multiple native title applications may be heard together in a single proceeding (particularly where the claims are overlapping); in such a case there may well be a multiplicity of compound applicants and so the distinction between 'applicants' and 'members of the applicant' becomes crucial.

34 *Butchulla People v Queensland* [2006] FCA 1063 [39]; *Chapman on behalf of the Wakka Wakka People 2 v Queensland* [2007] FCA 597 [9]; *Lennon v South Australia* [2010] FCA 743 [27]; *Anderson on behalf of the Wulli Wulli People v Queensland* [2011] FCA 1158 [54]. Even though Spender J in Doolan said 'the applicant will usually be the group as a single entity rather than one or more of the persons who comprise the group' (at [62]), it is clear from the context that his Honour did not mean that the applicant constitutes a separate legal entity; indeed, the decision in that case rested on the opposite conclusion (cf. the interpretation of *Doolan* in *QGC v Bygrave (No. 2)* [2010] FCA 1019 [76]). Justice Siopis's comment in *Sambo v Western Australia* [2008] FCA 1575 [29] that '[t]he decisions in the cases of Butchulla People, Chapman and Doolan have been superseded by the [2007] amendments' should be taken to refer to those cases' position on the mechanisms available for replacing the applicant, rather than to their assessment of whether a distinct legal entity is created under the NTA.

at [39], *Lennon v South Australia* [2010] FCA 743 at [6]) — they are one applicant, acting together and in common.[35]

There is disagreement among judges about the implications of this situation for the following questions:

- Is the applicant a party or is each of the named applicants a party to the proceedings (or is the party the native title claim group)?
- Who is the client of the lawyers; who gives instructions and has other rights and powers as a client?
- Where the applicant is composed of multiple individuals, are there any legal constraints on its decision-making process? For example, must the applicant act by the unanimous decision of the named applicants or can it act by majority?
- Under what circumstances can or will a named applicant cease to be part of the applicant?

The second of these questions is beyond the scope of this book and is dealt with in detail in a paper by Tim Wishart, Principal Legal Officer at Queensland South Native Title Services.[36] The third is discussed below in Chapter 4 and the fourth in Section 2.1 at 'Eligibility to be named applicant', Chapter 5 and Section 6.2 ('Authorisation by proposed amended claim group'). The answer to the first question, which is somewhat dependent on one's view of the fourth question, can be dealt with briefly here.

In determining whether each named applicant is a party or whether all the individuals together constitute a single party, the purpose or context is crucial. There have been cases in which the court has considered individual named applicants to be 'parties' in their own right, in the specific context of deciding that individual named applicants can be removed as parties under O. 6 r. 9 of the old Federal Court Rules (now r. 9.08 of the Federal Court Rules 2011).[37] In *Butchulla People* Kiefel J considered that the term 'party' refers to each of the persons who together make up the applicant, 'since the "*applicant*" referred to in the NTA is not an entity itself capable of suing'.[38] However, in *Que Noy*, Mansfield J noted that s. 66B of the *Native Title Act* refers to the 'replacement' of the applicant, even if only one of many named applicants is

---

35 *Anderson on behalf of the Wulli Wulli People v Queensland* [2011] FCA 1158 [59].

36 T Wishart, 'The multifaceted statutory responsibilities faced by representative body lawyers', address to the 4th Annual Native Title Summit, convened by Lexus Nexus, Brisbane, 11–12 July 2012, available at <http://www.qsnts.com.au/publications/TheMultifacetedStatutoryResponsibilitesFacedByRepresentativeBodyLawyersandWhatThisCouldMeanForYou.pdf>, viewed 15 August 2016.

37 *Central West Goldfields People v Western Australia* [2003] FCA 467 [10]; *Button v Chapman on behalf of the Wakka Wakka People* [2003] FCA 861 [7]–[10]; *Butchulla People v Queensland* [2006] FCA 1063 [44]–[45]; *Doolan v Native Title Registrar* [2007] FCA 192 [72]–[74]; *Chapman on behalf of the Wakka Wakka People (No. 2) v Queensland* [2007] FCA 597 [14], [17].

38 *Butchulla People v Queensland* [2006] FCA 1063 [44].

added, removed or replaced.[39] This suggests that 'the applicant' is a single party constituted by a number of individuals. In *Sambo*, Siopis J considered that Kiefel J's approach had been superseded by amendments to the *Native Title Act* that meant the only way to remove a named applicant is by an order under s. 66B replacing the applicant as a whole.[40] The substance of this debate about s. 66B versus the Federal Court Rules 2011 is addressed below in Section 5.1 ('How can the composition of the applicant be changed?'). The important point for present purposes is that the question about whether each individual named applicant is a 'party' was subsidiary to the operative question, which was whether named applicants could be removed without an order under s. 66B.

In other contexts, the question of who is 'the party' to the proceedings may have different implications and perhaps different answers.[41] For example, where a costs order is made against an applicant (noting that this is a rare occurrence by reason of s. 85A, *Native Title Act*)[42] it is necessary to know who has to pay and whether liability is joint, several, or joint and several. In the costs decision of *Birri-Gubba (Cape Upstart)*, Rares J decided that 'a fair allocation of the costs burden would be that the *Birri Gubba people* pay 50% of the costs of the State' (emphasis added).[43] His Honour ordered that '*[t]he applicant* pay 50% of the costs of the State' (emphasis added).[44] The former version would suggest that every member of the claim group would be liable, whereas the latter restricts liability to the applicant. There is nothing in Rares J's judgment or orders to indicate how liability was to be apportioned between the five named applicants, but it seems plausible that liability would be joint and several. Similarly, in *Levinge* Rares J awarded costs against 'the applicant' but stayed the order 'having regard to the personal and financial circumstances of those members of the applicant, who put on evidence'.[45] The implied intention was for the individual named applicants, rather than the group at large, to bear liability for costs. Again, there was no explicit consideration of apportionment of liability between the named applicants. However, the decision was based on the unreasonable conduct of 'the applicant' as a whole rather than any individual applicant, which suggests that 'the applicant' as a whole was the relevant party rather than each named applicant.[46]

Similarly, the question of who is 'the party' will be relevant to issues of estoppel and *res judicata.* Once a court makes a final decision in litigation, the parties to the proceedings cannot later dispute or re-agitate the subject matter of that decision in later proceedings.[47] This basic rule is simple enough in cases where the court has made a determination that native title does *not* exist in a

---

39 *Que Noy v Northern Territory* [2007] FCA 1888 [8]. See also *Daniel v Western Australia* [2002] FCA 1147 [5].

40 *Sambo v Western Australia* [2008] FCA 1575 [1], [15], [29]–[30].

41 *Doolan v Native Title Registrar* [2007] FCA 192 [74], citing *Butchulla People v Queensland* [2006] FCA 1063 [36].

42 See generally *Oil Basins Limited v Watson* [2014] FCAFC 154 and cases cited therein.

43 *Birri-Gubba (Cape Upstart) People v Queensland* [2008] FCA 659 [40].

44 ibid.

45 *Levinge on behalf of the Gold Coast Native Title Group v Queensland* [2013] FCA 634 [65].

46 See *Levinge on behalf of the Gold Coast Native Title Group v Queensland* [2013] FCA 634 [61]. In *A.D. (deceased) on behalf of the Mirning People v Western Australia* [2013] FCA 565 a costs order was made against one named applicant out of many. But this was in respect of an interlocutory application filed by him personally.

47 *Blair v Curran* (1939) 62 CLR 464 at 531–33.

particular area — the determination binds the world at large as a judgment *in rem* and no person will be able to bring another claim over the same area.[48] But if a claim is merely *dismissed* it will not be a judgment in rem and will only bind the *parties* to the proceedings. An applicant will be prevented from lodging a new claim over an area in which their previous claim has been dismissed[49] (or, perhaps, only where the dismissal is on substantive grounds).[50] Further, an applicant will be prevented from making factual assertions about their claim group that have already been rejected in previous proceedings, even if those proceedings concerned a different geographical area.[51] But do these restrictions affect the *claim group* or just the particular named applicants? And is each named applicant bound in future proceedings or only the specific combination of named applicants? In *Levinge*[52] Rares J declined to make an in-rem determination that no native title existed in the claim area but considered it appropriate to dismiss the application on a final basis. His Honour said that this would 'create a *res judicata* preventing the *present applicant* from bringing any further proceedings on the same subject matter' (emphasis added).[53] His Honour's intention was to prevent 'this litigant' from resurrecting the claim in future.[54] It seems implicit that the particular applicant was the relevant 'party' estopped from prosecuting future proceedings; otherwise the dismissal would have the same effect as a negative determination of native title.[55] However, the matter was not dealt with explicitly and has not been the subject of express judicial consideration to date. This is an area in

---

48 *Wik Peoples v Queensland* [1994] FCA 967; *Jango v Northern Territory* [2007] FCAFC 101 [85]; *Dale v Western Australia* [2011] FCAFC 46 [92]. However, the Commonwealth, state or Native Title Registrar could apply for a variation/revocation application under s. 13(1)(b): see s. 61(1), NTA.

49 *Quall v Northern Territory* [2009] FCAFC 157.

50 Note the absence of any concluded view on this in *Western Australia v Fazeldean on behalf of the Thalanyji People (No. 2)* [2013] FCAFC 58.

51 *Dale v Western Australia* [2011] FCAFC 46. In that case the applicant was prevented from making a claim in one area when a previous claim over a different area had been decided against them on the basis that they do not represent a group capable of holding native title. This factual finding from the previous judgment bound them as against the other respondents who were also parties to the previous proceedings.

52 *Levinge on behalf of the Gold Coast Native Title Group v Queensland* [2013] FCA 634.

53 ibid. [56].

54 ibid. [53].

55 In *Fazeldean*, Barker J held that the Thalanyji people were not precluded from claiming certain areas that had been deliberately excluded from a previous consent determination. The parties had agreed that the claim, insofar as it related to these areas, would be dismissed on the basis that the state did not consider the evidence strong enough to consent: *Fazeldean on behalf of the Thalanyji People (No. 2) v Western Australia* [2012] FCA 1163. Interestingly, none of the arguments in that case raised the fact that the named applicants in the new claim were completely different from those in the original claim. Rather, the case appears to have been conducted on the basis that the claim group, not just the applicant, would be stopped from bringing a new claim. And on appeal the State argued just this — that the consensual dismissal of the previous claim meant that 'the same claim under the NTA could not be brought by the same claim group': *Western Australia v Fazeldean on behalf of the Thalanyji People (No. 2)* [2013] FCAFC 58 [18]. Ultimately the Full Court on appeal declined to determine the issue on

which future legal developments are likely as areas that have been previously claimed and dismissed are brought back before the courts.

Ultimately, the question of who is 'the party' for any particular purpose will be resolved by reference to standard rules of statutory interpretation, drawing on the beneficial intent and 'facultative' purpose of the *Native Title Act*.[56] That has been the approach taken for the analysis of s. 66B (see Chapter 5 below) and also for the analysis of the ILUA requirements (see Chapter 7 below). Therefore there is no single answer for all purposes.

Eligibility to be named applicant

To fully appreciate the concept of 'applicant' under the *Native Title Act* scheme, it is necessary to consider how the *definition* of an applicant interacts with the *eligibility criteria* to be applicant.

A person *is* an applicant (or a number of people *are* an applicant) if they file an application in the Federal Court in their name (or names) and it is accepted for filing. Until they do, they are not an applicant.[57] A person or persons are also an applicant if they have successfully obtained an order under s. 66B of the *Native Title Act* to replace the previous applicant. A person *is eligible*

---

a summary basis and the proceedings were later terminated for unrelated reasons, so there was no final resolution of the question: *Fazeldean on behalf of the Thalanyji People v Western Australia* [2014] FCA 234.

56 *Project Blue Sky Inc. v Australian Broadcasting Authority* [1998] HCA 28; (1998) 194 CLR 355 at 384; *Daniel v Western Australia* [2002] FCA 1147 [16]. For another situation in which the question of the applicant's status as party has had to be addressed, see *Placer (Granny Smith) Pty Ltd and Granny Smith Mines Limited/Western Australia/Ron Harrington-Smith & Ors on behalf of the Wongatha people* [2000] NNTTA 75.

57 In *Doolan* two out of the 18 people who had been authorised to bring a claim withdrew before the filing of the application. Justice Spender was required to determine whether this withdrawal created a defect in the authorisation of the 16 remaining named applicants. In the course of that decision Spender J drew attention to the dependence of 'applicant' status on the actual filing of an application: 'Until the Form 1 application for a claimant determination has been filed with the Court, there is not an application for the purposes of the Act.': *Doolan v Native Title Registrar* [2007] FCA 192 [62].

to be an applicant if (a) they are a member of the native title claim group,[58] and (b) they are authorised by the native title claim group to make the application.[59]

How does a deficiency in these eligibility criteria (whether resulting from a change in circumstances or an initial defect) affect the *current status* of the applicant *as applicant*? That is, if a person has filed an application and later it transpires that they are not a member of the claim group (e.g. because the claim group description has been amended[60] or because newly discovered facts cast doubt on their descent from an apical ancestor),[61] do they cease to be an applicant at that point? Similarly, if the person is found never to have been properly authorised or if their authorisation is later revoked, does that automatically affect their current status as applicant?

The answer to both of these questions is 'no'. Section 66B of the *Native Title Act* sets out a mechanism for changing the composition of the applicant. That mechanism is available where a named applicant: (a) consents to their removal from the applicant, (b) dies or becomes incapacitated, (c) is no longer authorised by the claim group, or (d) has exceeded their authority.[62] As discussed below in Chapter 5, judges currently disagree about whether s. 66B

58 An additional eligibility criterion is that the named applicant must be a natural person and not a corporation. See *De Rose v South Australia* [2013] FCA 988 [13]. This follows from the requirement that the applicant be a member of the claim group (all the persons who hold rights and interests in relation to land and water under traditional law and custom). See e.g. *Far West Coast Native Title Claim v South Australia* [2011] FCA 24. (Note in *Western Australia v Lane* [1995] FCA 1484 the court declined to rule out the possibility of a corporate applicant but the decision was made prior to the 1998 amendments that strengthened the authorisation requirements. Note that a corporation may be the applicant for a compensation claim, so long as it is the RNTBC for the relevant area: see Chapter 9 below (cf. *Wintawari Guruma Aboriginal Corporation RNTBC v Western Australia* [2015] FCA 1053). It may also be inferred that an additional eligibility condition is that the named applicant be alive.

59 Note that while s. 251B defines the process a person must go through in order to be authorised to make an application and to 'deal with matters arising in relation to it', and while s. 62(1)(a) requires each applicant to file an affidavit stating that they are authorised to make the application and to 'deal with matters arising in relation to it', in fact s. 61(1) and (2) only imposes a requirement that the applicant be authorised to make the claim. (Section 62A clarifies that the applicant 'may deal with all matters arising under this Act in relation to the application'.) This appears to be an inconsistency in the drafting of the Act — s. 66B, by contrast, specifically requires replacement applicants to be authorised to make the application and to deal with matters arising in relation to it. The registration test requirement in s. 190C(4)(b) uses the same language.

60 Ineligibility as a consequence of an amendment is considered below in Section 6.2 at 'Where amended claim group authorises replacement applicant'.

61 E.g. in *Dann v Western Australia* [2011] FCA 99 a claim group member objected to the appointment of one of the named applicants on the grounds that the named applicant was not descended from any of the relevant apical ancestors. Justice Barker at [46] held that the initial anthropological evidence was sufficient to support the named applicant's continued status as named applicant and any further issues could be resolved at the final hearing of the matter.

62 Note that prior to the 2007 amendments, grounds (a) and (b) were not listed in s. 66B — a factor contributing to some judges considering that s. 66B was not intended to 'cover the field' in

is the *only* mechanism available for changing the composition of the applicant. Regardless of this, the terms of s. 66B assume that a named applicant who meets any of the four criteria listed above is still part of the applicant unless and until an order under s. 66B is made.[63] That is, merely meeting one of those criteria is not sufficient for the removal of a named applicant. If no application is made to replace the applicant, or the proposed replacement applicant is not (properly) authorised,[64] or the court exercises its discretion to refuse the replacement application, the applicant will remain unchanged despite the fact that some of its members are deceased, unwilling to act, or no longer authorised.[65] And even those judges who consider that named applicants can be removed under the Federal Court Rules (rather than s. 66B) assume that the *exercise of that power* is necessary to effect a change in the composition of the applicant.[66] If removal was an automatic consequence of a named applicant's death, unwillingness or de-authorisation then the question of whether such a power existed would not arise.

The Full Court of the Federal Court held, in *FQM*, that the legislative framework established by the *Native Title Act* requires that the applicant continue to exist even if its sole or last remaining member dies.[67] Firstly, as mentioned, s. 66B would have no work to do otherwise — upon the death of the only named applicant, there would no longer be any applicant to replace under that section.[68] Further, the objectives of the future act provisions and the claims process more generally would be frustrated if a new application needed to be filed upon the

---

relation to changing the composition of the applicant. See Section 5.1 ('How can the composition of the applicant be changed?') below.

63 *P.C. (name withheld) on behalf of the Njamal People v Western Australia* [2007] FCA 1054 [48].

64 In *Mandandanji People v Queensland* [2013] FCA 255 [55], Rares J found that recent events had deprived the current applicant of its authorisation without authorising a new one. This meant there was 'no longer an applicant authorised by the claim group to make or prosecute the existing application and deal with matters arising in relation to it. A new meeting of the claim group must be held to authorise a replacement applicant'. His Honour made orders protecting the status quo pending a new s. 66B application.

65 E.g. *Sambo v Western Australia* [2008] FCA 1575; *Doctor on behalf of the Bigambul People v Queensland (No. 2)* [2013] FCA 746. Deceased persons remained listed as named applicants right through to determination in e.g. *W.F. (deceased) on behalf of the Wiluna People v Western Australia* [2013] FCA 755 and *Akiba v Queensland (No. 2)* [2010] FCA 643 [55].

66 See e.g. *Chapman on behalf of the Wakka Wakka People #2 v Queensland* [2007] FCA 597, dealing with the death of one named applicant and the non-participation or unwillingness of two others.

67 *FQM Australia Nickel Pty Ltd v Bullen* [2011] FCAFC 30 [26]–[40] per North, McKerracher and Jagot JJ. Cf. *Doolan v Native Title Registrar* [2007] FCA 192 [74]; *Butchulla People v Queensland* [2006] FCA 1063 [36]; *Chapman v Queensland* [2007] FCA 597 [12]. Although FQM dealt with the concept of the 'registered native title claimant' for the purpose of the 'right to negotiate' regime, the discussion in that case deals equally with the concept of 'applicant' for the purposes of a native title determination application.

68 The court also highlighted at [31] the use in s. 66B of the term 'current applicant' to describe the person or persons who are to be replaced as a consequence of the death. That language assumes that a deceased person remains the 'current applicant'.

death of the sole or last-surviving applicant.[69] Extrapolating from the Full Court's reasoning, it can be seen that the objectives of the legislation would be similarly frustrated if the other kinds of ineligibility had the automatic and immediate effect of taking away a person's status as applicant. Some further step, whether under s. 66B or the Federal Court Rules 2011, is necessary for a person to cease being applicant.

Similar considerations apply to situations in which authorisation is found to be defective from the beginning. In some (but certainly not all) cases where respondents have sought to have claims struck out on this basis, the court has found or assumed that authorisation was defective but nevertheless allowed the hearing to proceed (particularly under s. 84D(4)(a), *Native Title Act*).[70] This shows that the applicants' non-eligibility has not prevented them from holding the formal status of applicant and performing the functions of the applicant.[71]

All of this simply supports the proposition that the 'applicant' is defined by the fact of having made a native title application in the Federal Court (or having successfully replaced a previous applicant). The status of the applicant is not directly affected by the non-fulfilment of the eligibility criteria. Rather, non-fulfilment of those criteria merely provide *grounds* for replacing the applicant or striking out the application (as discussed below in Section 5.1 at 'Grounds for removal and replacement' and Section 2.2 at 'Strike-out, dismissal and "show cause" orders'). Nevertheless, just because a named applicant remains a named applicant despite their lack or loss of authorisation, unwillingness, incapacity, or their death, this does not necessarily mean that the applicant as a whole can continue to act as normal. A change

---

69 A number of native title determinations and other judgments have been made in respect of applicants whose members include deceased individuals: e.g. *W.F. (deceased) on behalf of the Wiluna People v Western Australia* [2013] FCA 755; A.D. *(deceased) on behalf of the Mirning People v Western Australia (No. 2)* [2013] FCA 1000; B.P. *(deceased) v Western Australia* [2013] FCA 760. This constitutes further support for the proposition that death does not automatically cause a person to cease to be a named applicant. Interestingly, it seems that claims in Western Australia often retain deceased named applicants (with the name replaced by initials) whereas in Queensland the practice is generally to remove the names of the deceased named applicants.

70 E.g. *Sandy on behalf of the Yugara/Yugarapul People v Queensland* [2012] FCA 978 [47]–[48]; *Akiba on behalf of the Torres Strait Islanders of the Regional Seas Claim Group v Queensland (No. 2)* [2010] FCA 643 [55], [916]–[918].

71 A number of cases have dealt with situations where the parties have agreed to a consent determination that recognises a native title holding group that is differently described from that which was originally listed in the Form 1, without any amended Form 1 being filed. Assuming the 'new' group is the right one, this means that the applicant was never authorised by the 'native title claim group' in its strict sense. (See Section 3.1 ('The "native title claim group": conceptualising the authorising constituency') below.) In those circumstances, courts have been willing to allow the consent determination notwithstanding this defect in authorisation, pursuant to s. 84D(4)(a). See *Cheinmora v Western Australia (No. 3)* [2013] FCA 769; *Sharpe v Western Australia* [2013] FCA 599; *Barunga v Western Australia* [2011] FCA 518; *Goonack v Western Australia* [2011] FCA 516; *Smirke on behalf of the Jurruru People v Western Australia* [2015] FCA 939.

may be required in order to continue to prosecute the claim effectively. That separate issue is considered below in the introduction to Chapter 5.

Summary: What is an applicant?

Two key points can be drawn from the discussion above. First, the term 'applicant' has two distinct meanings in the *Native Title Act* — in some places it refers to each individual 'named applicant' separately, and in others it refers to them collectively (though without imparting on them a separate corporate legal personality).

Second, the applicant (in either sense) is defined by the contents of the court file: a person is a named applicant if their name is entered on the court file as an applicant and they remain so until their name is removed. Even if they later die or have their authority rescinded, or if they were ineligible from the beginning by reason of defective authorisation or non-membership of the native title claim group, they will continue to be part of the applicant until they are removed.

2.2 When and why is it necessary to establish authorisation?

At the start of this chapter we saw that the fundamental legal requirement for authorisation in the claims process is contained in s. 61(1) of the *Native Title Act*. That provision states that a native title determination application can only be made on behalf of a native title claim group by an applicant authorised by that claim group. But this does not tell us anything about the circumstances in which the applicant may be required to prove their authorisation. The next seven sections of this book will set out the different situations in which an applicant's authorisation may need to be established during the native title claims process. As mentioned in Chapter 1, authorisation is also relevant to situations outside the claims process; these will be dealt with separately in chapters 7 to 9.

Originating application — Form 1

The very first step in any claim is the filing of the application at the Federal Court registry. The Native Title (Federal Court) Regulations 1998 (Federal Court Regulations) specifies the form of application that must be used — the Form 1 (attached as a schedule to the regulations). The Form 1 requires the applicant to make a statement that 'the applicant is a member of the native title claim group and is authorised to make the application, and deal with matters arising in relation to it, by all the other persons in the native title claim group.'[72] The applicant must also state 'the grounds on which the [Native Title Registrar] should consider that the statement is correct'.

Similarly, s. 62 of the *Native Title Act* requires the Form 1 to be accompanied by an affidavit sworn by each named applicant[73] stating that 'the applicant is authorised by all the persons in the native title claim group to make the application and to deal with matters arising in relation to it.' The affidavit must also set out 'details of the process of decision-making complied with in authorising the applicant to make the application and to deal with matters arising in relation to it'.

In general, the Federal Court registry will accept the Form 1 for filing if it is in the correct form, accompanied by the relevant affidavits and the relevant fee. The registry staff do not make any substantive inquiry into authorisation. So although it will be important *later* in the process for the Form 1 and s. 62 affidavits to clearly establish the applicant's authorisation, the actual filing of the documents is not a step that involves any assessment by the court of authorisation issues.

Registration test

The Native Title Registrar is required to assess every determination application against criteria listed in s. 190B and C of the *Native Title Act*.[74] This is called the 'registration test' and it has two important consequences. Firstly, passing the registration test is necessary to obtain procedural

---

72 Schedule R, Form 1, Federal Court Regulations.

73 *Doolan v Native Title Registrar* [2007] FCA 192 [66]–[67]; *Anderson on behalf of the Wulli Wulli People v Queensland* [2011] FCA 1158 [54].

74 Section 190A, NTA.

rights in relation to future acts and has implications for making ILUAs.[75] Secondly, failing the registration test is a ground for dismissing an application.[76]

Among other things, the registration test requires the registrar to be satisfied *either* that the applicant is 'authorised to make the application, and deal with matters arising in relation to it, by all the other persons in the native title claim group', *or* that the relevant NTRB has certified the application under s. 203BE. NTRB certification in turn requires the NTRB to be satisfied that the applicant has been authorised by all the persons in the native title claim group.[77] If an application is not certified and the registrar is not satisfied that the applicant is properly authorised, the registrar must refuse to register the application.[78]

So the registration test is the first point in the claims process where the applicant's authorisation will be considered in any substantive way. However, the level of detail required to pass the registration test is less than may be required at later stages, such as in a strike-out application (discussed below). For registration of an uncertified application, the application must 'briefly [set] out the grounds on which the Registrar should consider that [the authorisation requirement] has been met'.[79] That does not necessarily require 'any detailed explanation of the process by which authorisation is obtained'.[80]

In *Strickland* the application stated that the applicants were authorised by the claim group 'in accordance with a traditional custom acknowledged by the members of the native title claim group of younger generations respecting elder generations and elder generations having authority to make decisions and deal with matters relating to traditional interests in land and waters on their own behalf and on behalf of younger generations'.[81] The state complained that the registrar should not have been satisfied on this basis because 'it does not reveal whether any process of consultation has taken place and, if so, whether that process complied with the process of decision-making customarily used by the group.'[82] That argument was rejected by French J and by the Full Court on appeal. Justice French said that although the statement in the application could be criticised for being too brief, 'neither the Registrar nor this Court is in a position to reject the contention that all relevant authority is vested in the elders of the relevant native title claim group and that the applicants fall into that category.'[83]

---

75 Sections 24CD and 25–44, NTA.

76 Section 190F(6), NTA.

77 Section 203BE(5), NTA.

78 Section 190A(6B) and C(4)(b), NTA.

79 Section 190C(5), NTA.

80 *Strickland v Native Title Registrar* [1999] FCA 1530 [57], approved on appeal by the Full Court in *Western Australia v Strickland* [2000] FCA 652 [75]–[78].

81 *Strickland v Native Title Registrar* [1999] FCA 1530 [56].

82 *Western Australia v Strickland* [2000] FCA 652 [75].

83 *Strickland v Native Title Registrar* [1999] FCA 1530 [57]. See also the registrar's approach in *Ashwin on behalf of the Wutha People v Western Australia* [2010] FCA 206 [24]–[25].

The registrar can consider a range of material in determining whether the application is authorised and is not limited to considering just the application and accompanying affidavits.[84] That means that the registrar is not required to assume that the statements in the application and affidavits are true, but may weigh them against other information.[85] As will be seen, this is a different process to that employed in determining strike-out applications.

Three points should be made regarding the option of having an application certified by the NTRB under s. 203BE:

a) If the NTRB certifies the authorisation of an application, the registrar is not required (nor allowed) to make its own decision about authorisation — for the purposes of the registration test, certification is conclusive on the issue of authorisation.[86]

b) Certification by the NTRB is not an *alternative* to authorisation by the claim group, it is an alternative *way of establishing* authorisation for the purposes of the registration test. The claim must still have been authorised by whatever process would have been followed pursuant to s. 251B; certification merely confirms that proper authorisation has occurred.[87]

c) Passing the registration test, whether by certification or by directly satisfying the registrar, does not determine the substantive question of authorisation later in the proceedings. To succeed in court an applicant must still be able to demonstrate that they have in fact been authorised by the claim group.[88]

Jurisdiction

As mentioned, s. 61(1) of the *Native Title Act* states that only a person or persons authorised by the native title claim group can make an application for a native title determination.[89] This requirement has been interpreted in the past as imposing a threshold condition for the exercise of the court's jurisdiction. Some judges have taken the view that a defect in authorisation deprives the court

---

84 *Strickland v Native Title Registrar* [1999] FCA 1530 [70]; *Wiri People v Native Title Registrar* [2008] FCA 574 [17]. Note that this position is different from that regarding s. 190C(2) (relating to the description of the claim group, among other things): see *Wiri People v Native Title Registrar* [2008] FCA 574 [30]–[31].

85 *Wiri People v Native Title Registrar* [2008] FCA 574 [20]–[21]. Cf. *Gudjala People # 2 v Native Title Registrar* [2008] FCAFC 157 [92] in relation to s. 190B(5).

86 *Northern Territory v Doepel* [2003] FCA 1384 [80]–[81]; *Wakaman People #2 v Native Title Registrar and Authorised Delegate* [2006] FCA 1198.

87 See s. 203BE(2) and (5), NTA.

88 *Akiba (Torres Strait Islanders) v Queensland (No. 2)* [2010] FCA 643 [926]. Note in *Landers v South Australia* [2003] FCA 264 [27]–[28], Mansfield J refused to strike out an application for want of authorisation. His Honour was careful to say that he placed no reliance on the registrar's decision to register the application and only a little reliance on the fact that the NTRB had seen fit to certify the applicant.

89 It should be added that non-claimant applications can be made and these do not need to be authorised: s. 61(1), NTA.

of jurisdiction to hear the application.[90] Contrary to that position, Graham Hiley (prior to his appointment as a judge) has argued that on a proper construction of the legislation, the court still has jurisdiction to hear and determine an application even if it was not properly authorised.[91] Hiley's reasoning rests in part on the observation (which will be explained below in Section 3.2, 'Authorisation by "all the persons" in the native title claim group') that s. 61 requires an application to be authorised by all of the persons 'who, according to their traditional laws and customs, hold the common or group rights and interests comprising the particular native title claimed' — and not merely the people who claim to hold such rights and interests.[92] Accordingly, in order to determine whether an application is properly authorised or not, it will be necessary to determine the ultimate fact in issue in the proceedings — namely, whether native title exists or not and, if so, who holds it.[93] It would be strange if the legislation were interpreted as imposing a threshold jurisdictional condition that could only be conclusively determined at the very end of the proceedings!

This question had not been conclusively settled in the courts by the time amendments to the *Native Title Act* were introduced in 2007.[94] In 2007, s. 84D(4)(a) was introduced to expressly allow the court to hear and determine an application despite a defect in authorisation.[95] In determining whether or not to do so, the court must balance 'the need for due prosecution of the application and the interests of justice'.[96] The existence of this discretion seems to put to rest the previous debate about authorisation's status as a jurisdictional condition: if the court has the power to continue the proceedings in spite of a defect in authorisation, it must be concluded that such a defect does not deprive the court of jurisdiction.

---

90 *Harrington-Smith on behalf of the Wongatha People v Western Australia (No. 9)* [2007] FCA 31 [1170]–[1175], [1269]–[1270]; also *Fesl v Queensland* [2005] FCA 120 [2]–[3]. For the question of whether a native title determination can be made in favour of people on whose behalf no application has been made at all, see *Commonwealth v Clifton* [2007] FCAFC 190; *A.B. (deceased) (on behalf of the Ngarla People) v Western Australia (No. 4)* [2012] FCA 1268 [109]–[117]; *Moses v Western Australia* [2007] FCAFC 78 [18]; cf. *Billy Patch on behalf of the Birriliburu People v Western Australia* [2008] FCA 944 [18].

91 G Hiley, 'How important is authorisation?', *Native Title News*, vol. 7, no. 5, pp. 83–87, October 2005.

92 ibid., citing *Landers v South Australia* [2003] FCA 264; *Williams v Grant* [2004] FCAFC 178; *Bodney v Bropho* [2004] FCAFC 226.

93 Admittedly, it is possible to identify a patent lack of authorisation well before the proper native title claim group has been identified — it is really a positive finding of authorisation that must wait for such identification. See *Davidson v Fesl* [2005] FCAFC 183 [3].

94 In *Davidson v Fesl* [2005] FCAFC 183 [22] French, Finn and Hely JJ expressed 'serious doubts' that the legislature intended that an initial defect in authorisation could not be remedied, though they did not consider it necessary to come to a concluded view on the matter. Note the discussion of jurisdiction in *Billy Patch on behalf of the Birriliburu People v Western Australia* [2008] FCA 944 [18]; *Western Australia v Ward* [2000] FCA 191 [191]–[192]; *A.B. (deceased) (on behalf of the Ngarla People) v Western Australia (No. 4)* [2012] FCA 1268 [114]–[117]; *Rubibi v Western Australia* [2002] FCA 876 [17]–[18]; *Commonwealth v Clifton* [2007] FCAFC 190 [40]–[61].

95 E.g. *Sharpe v Western Australia* [2013] FCA 599 [20]–[21]; *Barunga v Western Australia* [2011] FCA 518 [20]–[21].

96 Section 84D(4), NTA.

Strike-out, dismissal and 'show cause' orders

The conclusion above about jurisdiction does not mean that the courts do not take defective authorisation seriously. On the contrary: under s. 84C of the *Native Title Act*, any party may apply to the court to strike out an application for failure to comply with ss 61, 61A or 62 — including lack of authorisation.[97] Many applications have been struck out or dismissed[98] on the grounds that they are not properly authorised (or that they have failed the registration test for reasons including defective authorisation).[99] These cases have occurred both before and after the 2007 amendments — which means that judges do not regard the insertion of s. 84D(4)(a) as relaxing the general requirement for authorisation so much as allowing departures from the general rule in exceptional circumstances.[100] Such exceptional circumstances may include: the discovery or assertion of the defect coming late in the proceedings (particularly if the matter has already come to trial); evidence that the group's authorisation has been given in substance even if the form or evidence is inadequate; lack of any dispute from within the claim group about authorisation;[101] or substantive evidentiary or anthropological issues that would need to be resolved before the issue of authorisation could be determined.[102]

Striking out or dismissing an application can have significant consequences. In addition to the frustration and disappointment and the loss of the time and money that may have been put into the application, there are specific consequences relating to the future acts regime. Applicants may have entered agreements under which the payment of benefits is contingent on the continued existence of the registered claim (or a determination). Further, without a registered claim the right to negotiate will no longer be available for negotiating new agreements in future.

---

97 Note that there is also a summary dismissal power under the Federal Court Rules — an example of this (using O. 20 r. 2 of the pre-2011 rules) is *Moran v Minister for Land and Water Conservation (NSW)* [1999] FCA 1637. See also *Walker on behalf of the Noonukul of Minjerrabah v Queensland* [2007] FCA 967 [16]–[17].

98 Note there is a distinction between strike-out and summary dismissal, with potentially important procedural consequences. Nevertheless, the two processes are often treated as serving equivalent functions: *Walker on behalf of the Noonukul of Minjerrabah v Queensland* [2007] FCA 967 [16]–[17]; *Williams v Grant* [2004] FCAFC 178 [58].

99 Note that strike-out on authorisation grounds is available under s. 84C and dismissal (where the defect in authorisation had caused the application to fail the registration test) under s. 190F(6), NTA.

100 E.g. *Velickovic v Western Australia* [2012] FCA 782; *Laing v South Australia (No. 2)* [2012] FCA 980; *Brown v South Australia* [2009] FCA 206; *Hazelbane v Northern Territory* [2008] FCA 291. See discussion of the Explanatory Memorandum for the amendments in *Akiba on behalf of the Torres Strait Islanders of the Regional Seas Claim Group v Queensland (No. 2)* [2010] FCA 643 [917]–[918].

101 *Barunga v Western Australia* [2011] FCA 518 [15]–[19]; *Akiba v Queensland (No. 2)* [2010] FCA 643 [55], [918], [930]–[931]. Note that in Akiba the court had to determine this question after a full contested hearing, rather than on an interlocutory strike-out application. See also *A.B. (deceased) (on behalf of the Ngarla People) v Western Australia (No. 4)* [2012] FCA 1268 [115]–[117].

102 *Sandy on behalf of the Yugara/Yugarapul People v Queensland* [2012] FCA 978.

Because of these consequences, the power to strike out must be exercised 'sparingly and with caution, and only when the Court is satisfied that the moving party has made out a clear case that the applicant has not complied with the relevant section and cannot, by amending the application, comply'.[103] Courts should only dismiss an application summarily where the claim as it is expressed is untenable on the version of the evidence most favourable to the applicant.[104] There is no requirement that the defect be obvious — substantive argument may be necessary to establish that the application is clearly untenable.[105] In some cases, a considerable amount of evidence may be required to determine whether or not the application is properly authorised — in such cases, judges may decide to determine the authorisation issue application at the same time as the main determination hearing,[106] or else they may decide to hear and determine the authorisation issue as a separate question. The merit of this latter option will depend on the extent to which the evidence about authorisation overlaps with the evidence relating to the main issues in the primary claim.[107]

The case law shows that an initial defect in authorisation, even an obvious one, will not necessarily mean that strike-out or dismissal is appropriate. It is true that some judges may have assumed that a lack of initial authorisation cannot be remedied and so an inadequately authorised application is doomed to failure.[108] Yet even before the 2007 amendments, there were doubts about this.[109] In any case, once s. 84D(4)(a) was introduced in 2007 to expressly allow a claim to be heard and determined in spite of a flaw in its authorisation, courts have been open to the possibility that defects may be remedied — either by replacing the applicant under s. 66B or by amending the claim group description. Often the opportunity to fix an authorisation problem is given as part of a 'springing' or 'guillotine' order — an order that the application will stand dismissed unless particular action is taken (such as the holding of a new authorisation meeting or the production of certain evidence).[110] Section 84D(4)(b) has been regarded as a source of

---

103 *Williams v Grant* [2004] FCAFC 178 [49].

104 *Bodney v Bropho* [2004] FCAFC 226 [11], [48]–[49], citing *Edward Landers v South Australia* [2003] FCA 264 [7]. See also *McKenzie v South Australia* [2005] FCA 22 [26]. In *Harrington-Smith on behalf of the Wongatha People v Western Australia (No. 9)* [2007] FCA 31 [1192], Lindgren J said 'the striking out remedy is available once it clearly appears that, if the application were to succeed according to its own terms, the applicants would not have been authorised by all those persons the Court would determine to be the actual holders of the particular native title claimed.'

105 *Bodney v Bropho* [2004] FCAFC 226 [49].

106 See *Bodney v Western Australia* [2003] FCA 890 [45]; *Harrington-Smith on behalf of the Wongatha People v Western Australia (No. 9)* [2007] FCA 31 [1264] and generally.

107 *Hazelbane v Northern Territory* [2008] FCA 291 [15]–[16].

108 E.g. *Booth v Queensland* [2003] FCA 418; *Van Hemmen on behalf of the Kabi Kabi People 3 v Queensland* [2007] FCA 1185.

109 *Davidson v Fesl* [2005] FCAFC 183 [22].

110 E.g. *Hazelbane v Northern Territory* [2008] FCA 291; *Roe v Kimberley Land Council Aboriginal Corporation* [2010] FCA 809 [44]–[45], [53].

power for ordering such other actions, though it has been suggested that the court's general powers under the *Federal Court of Australia Act 1976* would be sufficient to ground such orders.[111]

The following examples indicate some factors that have influenced courts in deciding that applicants should not be given the opportunity of remedying a defect in authorisation and that the applications should be struck out:

- The application overlapped another claim and was filed late in the course of determining that other claim, and/or the application would cause unreasonable detriment to other parties if it were allowed to continue.[112]
- The proposed amendment to the application would still not remedy the defect.[113]
- The evidence shows disagreements within the claim group (or between the claim group and an overlapping claim group) such that the necessary amendments or re-authorisation are unlikely to happen, at least not without substantial negotiation and mediation.[114]
- The claim group description reflects a misconception of the requirements of the *Native Title Act* such that proper authorisation is unlikely to occur without entirely reconceiving the basis of the claim. (This is particularly relevant where the history of the claim shows a number of unsuccessful attempts to amend.)[115]
- The lack of prejudice to the claim group in the sense that they can file a new application later without serious repercussions for their procedural rights.[116]

Where a question has been raised in relation to the authorisation of an application but the application is not so clearly problematic as to justify strike-out, the court has the express power to order the applicant to produce evidence of its authorisation. This power arises under s. 84D(1), also introduced in the 2007 amendments, and can be exercised on the court's own motion, on the application of a party to the proceedings, or on the application by any member of the native title claim group.[117] That means that claim group members who challenge the applicant's

---

111 *Roe v Kimberley Land Council Aboriginal Corporation* [2010] FCA 809 [53]; *Doctor on behalf of the Bigambul People v Queensland (No. 2)* [2013] FCA 746.

112 *Laing v South Australia (No. 2)* [2012] FCA 980; *Velickovic v Western Australia* [2012] FCA 782.

113 *Laing v South Australia (No. 2)* [2012] FCA 980.

114 *Roe v Kimberley Land Council Aboriginal Corporation* [2010] FCA 809 [55]; *Hazelbane v Northern Territory* [2008] FCA 291 [34]–[35]; *Tilmouth v Northern Territory* [2001] FCA 820; *Moran v Minister for Land and Water Conservation (NSW)* [1999] FCA 1637 [49]. A similar point was made in *Wiri People v Native Title Registrar* [2008] FCA 574, although in that case strike-out was under s. 190F for failing the registration test on authorisation grounds rather than under s. 84C.

115 *Strickland v Western Australia* [2013] FCA 677; *Reid v South Australia* [2007] FCA 1479; *Kite v South Australia* [2007] FCA 1662; *Worimi v Minister for Lands (NSW)* [2006] FCA 1770.

116 *Hillig as Administrator of Worimi Local Aboriginal Land Council v Minister for Lands (NSW) (No. 2)* [2006] FCA 1115 [81]–[83]; *Strickland v Western Australia* [2013] FCA 677 [15]. Note in *Velickovic v Western Australia* [2012] FCA 782 the future act repercussions were seen to be insufficient to justify allowing the claim to continue.

117 Section 84D(2), NTA.

authorisation can do so under s. 84D(1) without becoming respondent parties in their own right. (They would need to join as respondents if they wished to seek a strike-out order under s. 84C.)[118] An order under s. 84D(1) may be thought of as an order to 'show cause' — that is, to show how the application *does* satisfy the legislative authorisation requirements. In this sense it may be a precursor to a strike-out application or a way of settling a dispute about authorisation.[119]

Joinder

Sometimes Indigenous persons seek to be joined as respondent parties to an existing native title claim. There are two scenarios where this might happen:

- The person is a member of the native title claim group described in the application but feels that their interests are not being adequately promoted by the applicant.
- The person is not a member of the claim group described in the application but asserts that they have native title rights and interests in the claim area.

This latter situation potentially raises an authorisation issue, while the former is more relevant to the discussion of applicant decision-making (discussed below in Section 4.1 at 'Disagreement between applicant and some members of the claim group'). A non–claim group member may seek to assert that the primary application does not cover all of the claim area's native title holders. This assertion might be made by an individual in their own capacity or in a representative capacity on behalf of a group of people said to hold native title in the area. An individual-based joinder application, which does not seek to obtain a determination of native title in its own right,[120] will not require any proof of authorisation:

> [W]here a person is seeking to be joined as a respondent to native title proceedings on the basis that he or she claims to hold native title rights and interests in an area of land or waters that may be affected by a determination in those proceedings, that person may only do so if he or she wishes to pursue a personal claim or interest in defensively asserting those native title rights and interests or, in other words, to protect them from erosion, dilution or discount…[121]

By contrast, if the person wishes to assert the existence of native title rights and interests in order to obtain a determination of native title on behalf of others, they must file a s. 61 application

---

118 *Corunna on behalf of the Swan River People v Western Australia* [2010] FCA 1113 [22]. Native title lawyers have commented on the irony of this situation: a claim group member has standing to seek orders requiring the applicant to prove their authorisation but lacks standing to seek orders addressing an absence of authorisation.

119 E.g. *Ashwin on behalf of the Wutha People v Western Australia* [2010] FCA 206; *Corunna on behalf of the Swan River People v Western Australia* [2010] FCA 1113.

120 See *Kokatha Native Title Claim v South Australia* [2005] FCA 836 [24]–[25]; *Worimi Local Aboriginal Land Council v Minister for Lands (NSW)* [2007] FCA 1357 [29]–[30].

121 *Isaacs on behalf of the Turrbal People v Queensland (No. 2)* [2011] FCA 942 [18]. See also *Bonner on behalf of the Jagera People #2 v Queensland* [2011] FCA 321.

authorised by those other persons.[122] This is because the *Native Title Act* prescribes a set of procedural requirements for making claims, the objective of which would be frustrated if groups could circumvent the formal route by joining as respondents.[123]

Replacing the existing applicant

Another important point in the native title process in which a person may be required to demonstrate their authorisation is where that person seeks to replace the existing applicant for a native title claim. As will be explained below in Chapter 5, the proposed replacement applicant must demonstrate (among other things) that they are authorised to bring the application and deal with matters arising in relation to it. Otherwise, the objectives of the authorisation provisions would be defeated.

Note that if a person wishing to replace the current applicant produced convincing evidence that the current applicant is no longer authorised, but failed to establish that the replacement applicant was properly authorised, the court may consider striking out the claim or ordering the holding of a new authorisation meeting. (See Section 5.2 below, 'Consequences of a failed s. 66B application'.)

Taking steps in the proceedings

Finally, the court may seek to be satisfied about an applicant's authority to take particular steps in the proceedings — such as amending the application (particularly the claim group description or claim boundary description), merging claims with other claimants, appointing new lawyers, discontinuing the claim or agreeing to a consent determination. The court has the power under s. 84D(1)(b) to order applicants to produce evidence about their authorisation to deal with a particular matter in the proceedings. This evidence may be relevant to the exercise of the court's discretion to allow the applicant to take the particular step proposed. This issue is dealt with in more detail below in Chapter 4.

---

122 *Isaacs on behalf of the Turrbal People v Queensland (No. 2)* [2011] FCA 942 [18]–[19]; *Moses v Western Australia* [2007] FCAFC 78. Note in *Far West Coast Native Title Claim v South Australia* [2011] FCA 24 a corporation whose members were restricted to a certain subset of the broader claim group was refused joinder as a respondent to the claim. The corporation was not found to have a sufficient interest in the proceedings even though its members may have.

123 *Commonwealth v Clifton* [2007] FCAFC 190 [49]–[61]; *Kokatha People v South Australia* [2007] FCA 1057 [48]; *Kokatha Native Title Claim v South Australia* [2005] FCA 836 [23]; *Kanak v Minister for Land and Water Conservation* [2000] FCA 1105 [11]. Note that Finn J in *Kokatha People* rejected the view of Beaumont and von Doussa JJ in *Western Australia v Ward* [2000] FCA 191 [190]–[194] that the court was empowered and indeed obliged to make a determination in favour of whomever held native title, regardless of whether they had filed their own application under s. 61. Justice Merkel in *Rubibi v Western Australia* [2002] FCA 876 [12]–[17] held that the court had power to join individuals as respondents even if they were asserting native title rights and interests in a representative capacity; his Honour (at [18]) did not decide whether the court's jurisdiction would also extend to making a determination in favour of those respondents in the absence of a duly authorised application under s. 61.

2.3 Legal, political and social importance of the applicant

The above analysis demonstrates the applicant's centrality in the legal processes surrounding a native title claim. Chapter 4 will elaborate on the applicant's legal role in native title decision-making. Before continuing with the legal analysis, however, it is worth pausing to reflect on some of the broader political, social and symbolic meanings that are sometimes associated with the applicant. It is important for lawyers and others assisting native title claim groups to be aware of these other dynamics.

In some cases, claim group members may perceive the applicant to be an important representative office and may therefore seek to ensure that this status is shared between all of the constituent subgroups such as clans, 'families', estate groups, descent groups, political factions or previously overlapping claims that have now been combined. On this logic, any given candidate for applicant will not be solely or even primarily representing the claim group as a whole but rather the individual's own subgroup. If that understanding prevails, each subgroup may seek to ensure its own representation and to prevent any other subgroup from 'taking over'. Linked to this impulse may be a desire to create formal recognition of the group's internal structure, as a demonstration of the ongoing vitality of traditional culture.[124] Where claim groups hold these related concerns, they may seek to ensure that there is one member of the applicant for each subgroup. In some cases this could result in a large number of named applicants — in some cases numbering 20[125] or even 79.[126] Importantly, the *Native Title Act* is silent on this sub-representative function of the applicant — it neither requires nor prohibits it, leaving the matter entirely to the internal processes and cultural politics of the claim group.[127] (Further, see Section 4.3 below, 'Obligations of the applicant'.)

A slightly different tendency may appear where claim group members feel that the applicant's function involves a more substantive role in 'speaking for' the claim area so as to engage traditional customary authority structures. One result of this is that 'elders' or 'law bosses' may be chosen as applicants — even if this carries the risk that they may fall ill or pass away during the course of proceedings. Another risk is that such people may have difficulty communicating in English and understanding the technical Australian legal processes. There may also be controversy amongst the group about *who* holds the relevant authority under traditional law and custom.[128]

---

124 E.g. a claim group with six constituent estate groups may consider it important for those six clans to be represented by six members of the applicant, out of respect for the traditions and structure of the group.

125 E.g. *Ward v Northern Territory* [2002] FCA 171.

126 *Bennell v Western Australia* [2006] FCA 1243.

127 Cf. *Butchulla People v Queensland* [2006] FCA 1063 [41].

128 In *Starkey*, for example, Mr Reid sought to be joined as a respondent to the Kokatha Uwankara native title application on the grounds that only he was qualified to be the applicant. He claimed to be the 'sole Kokatha Custodian who possesses the traditional Kokatha native title rights and interests' having 'prime responsibility for upholding the Law, and protecting it for cultural survival': *Starkey v South Australia* [2011] FCA 456 [23]–[24].

A third possible dynamic may involve a belief that whoever is chosen to be applicant will gain some additional personal status and access to financial or other resources. There is some basis for this, in that applicants may in some circumstances receive sitting fees or travel allowance for various meetings and may gain access to networking opportunities through their role. Beyond this, claim group members may suspect that the applicants can manipulate future act negotiations and heritage clearance procedures to benefit themselves or their families financially. These beliefs may not be correct but may in any event lead to strong individual- or subgroup-based competition over applicant appointments. Just how far an applicant can go in making autonomous decisions without the sanction of the broader claim group is discussed in Section 4.1 below ('Extent of applicant autonomy'). In general, out of prudence, legal representatives will generally treat the claim group as the primary decision-maker unless the claim group has clearly delegated such power to the applicant or there are well-established cultural norms giving substantive decision-making power to the individuals who constitute the applicant.[129] To the extent that there is any ambiguity in this area, legal representatives may wish to discuss the matter explicitly with the claim group and invite the group to give explicit directions about the circumstances in which they are content for the applicant to provide instructions directly.

More broadly, disagreements over who should be applicant may be directly linked to substantive debates about the best way to respond to the pressures of litigation and agreement-making. Claim groups are likely to contain some people who are reluctant to allow mining and other development, and others who seek to embrace the opportunities that development may bring. There will be some who are willing to compromise with overlapping claimants or respondent parties, and others who are not. In such situations, authorisation processes can serve as proxy referenda for disputed issues. (See Section 4.1 below at 'Disagreement between applicant and some members of the claim group'.)

Finally, applicants often have an important role in communicating information about the claim (and about native title agreements) to the broader claim group and, conversely, communicating any concerns of the claim group to external parties such as the claim lawyers, mining companies, the court or the tribunal. Groups may seek to replace applicants who are perceived as not performing this role well — particularly if they are seen as keeping some or all of the claim group 'in the dark'.[130]

---

129 J Southalan, 'Authorisation of native title claims: problems with a "claim group representative body"', *Australian Resources and Energy Law Journal*, vol. 29, no. 1, pp. 49–59, April 2010, p. 59.

130 E.g. *Johnson, in the matter of Lawson v Lawson* [2001] FCA 894 [31].

3. Authorising an applicant

The previous chapter explained why an applicant must be authorised. This chapter explains how authorisation occurs. It will outline the legal requirements for the valid authorisation of an applicant and some practical issues that lawyers may face in the process. The first section deals with the complex conceptual task of identifying the relevant decision-making constituency for authorisation — the native title claim group. The following sections summarise the law that determines what constitutes a legally effective decision by that constituency.

3.1 The 'native title claim group': conceptualising the authorising constituency

The core authorisation requirement is in s. 61(1), which states that a native title determination application may (only) be made by a:

> person or persons authorised by all the persons (*the native title claim group*) who, according to their traditional laws and customs, hold the common or group rights and interests comprising the particular native title claimed, provided the person or persons are also included in the native title claim group… (emphasis added)

The immediate thing to notice is that the native title claim group is not defined as the group of people who *claim* to hold native title. Instead it is the group of people who *really do* hold native title.[131] Justice Lindgren said in the *Wongatha* trial judgment:

> The expression ['native title claim group'] is commonly and understandably used to refer to the group on whose behalf a native title determination application — claimant application is made…But there is no escaping the fact that the 'native title claim group'…is a group constituted by all the actual holders...of the common or group rights or interests comprising the particular native title claimed.[132]

131 See *Risk v National Native Title Tribunal* [2000] FCA 1589 [60], cited in *Worimi Local Aboriginal Land Council v Minister for Lands (NSW)* [2007] FCA 1357 [20]. Note the definition of 'native title claim group' in s. 253 simply refers back to s. 61(1). Interestingly, the definition of 'compensation claim group' in s. 61(1) does not follow this wording — instead, it refers to 'all the persons…who claim to be entitled to the compensation' (emphasis added).

132 *Harrington-Smith v Western Australia (No. 9)* [2007] FCA 31 [72].

His Honour noted that this 'odd use of language' was introduced in the 1998 amendments and appears to have been part of the move towards limiting spurious or competing claims.[133] Justice Lindgren interpreted s. 61(1) as requiring a perfect overlap between three categories:

a) the actual holders of the native title rights and interests under traditional law and custom (defined in s. 61 as the 'native title claim group');

b) the group described as the 'native title claim group' in the Form 1 filed to commence the proceedings (which I will call the 'application group'[134] for the purposes of this book);

c) the people who authorised the making of the application (this may be called the 'authorising group').[135]

---

133 ibid. [1189]. Justice Lindgren said that the specification of actual, rather than claimed, native title holders was 'not accidental'. His Honour observed that the original version of the 1998 amendment bill required applications to be authorised by 'the persons (the native title claim group) who claim to hold [native title]'. The later version that was eventually passed 'altered the description of permissible applicants by introducing the word "all" and relocating the "claiming" concept from "claim to hold" to "particular native title claimed"' (at [1188]). This change was not carried through to the final bill's Explanatory Memorandum, although that was perhaps an oversight by the drafters: <http://www.austlii.edu.au/au/legis/cth/bill_em/ntab1997237/memo2.html> at [25.16], viewed 15 August 2016.

134 The use of the word 'group' does not necessarily imply or require a 'group' in the sense of a self-identifying, coherent unit. Some Western Desert claim groups are not understood in those terms but rather as collections of individuals holding rights and interests in country.

135 *Harrington-Smith v Western Australia (No. 9)* [2007] FCA 31 [1216]. Note that although s. 61(1) sets out the general requirement for authorisation, s. 84D(4)(a) now means that a defect in authorisation is not necessarily fatal. For an example of a claim allowed to proceed despite a mismatch between the application group and the authorising group: *Sandy on behalf of the Yugara/Yugarapul People v Queensland* [2012] FCA 978. For examples of mismatches between application group and actual holders: *Sharpe v Western Australia* [2013] FCA 599 [20]–[21]; *Barunga v Western Australia* [2011] FCA 518 [20]–[21]; *Goonack v Western Australia* [2011] FCA 516 [18]. These cases cited *Billy Patch on behalf of the Birriliburu People v Western Australia* [2008] FCA 944 [17]–[18] for the proposition that the court is not limited to making a determination in the form originally sought in the application. It should be noted that in *Birriliburu* (and also in *Cheinmora v Western Australia (No. 2)* [2013] FCA 768 [19]–[28]) the discrepancy in the claim group descriptions as between the Form 1 and the ultimate determination did not produce any actual change in the composition of the claim group. In *Sharpe* and *Barunga*, by contrast, there was a substantive change. In *Thudgari People v Western Australia* [2009] FCA 1334 [8]–[12] there was also a substantive change but that case did not deal with authorisation issues, since the application was filed before the 1998 amendments. In both *Banjima People v Western Australia (No. 2)* [2013] FCA 868 and *Western Australia v Graham on behalf of the Ngadju People* [2013] FCAFC 143, an apical ancestor was found not to be a person who held native title in the claim area and so their descendants were not included in the ultimate description of the native title holders. This late change was not taken by the court in either case to affect the quality of the original authorisation.

The difficulty in applying this test of authorisation at an early stage in the proceedings is immediately apparent: without hearing all the evidence and deciding who the actual native title holders are, how can the court say for sure whether or not the authorising group, the application group and the native title claim group are all the same group of people?[136]

Of course, where the application has not even been authorised by the *application group*, the question of who comprises the native title claim group never arises. If the authorising group is not the same as (or at least does not include)[137] the application group, the application is not authorised. Similarly, if there was some obvious flaw in the authorisation process (e.g. inadequate notification or an inappropriate decision-making process — see below) then the particular group that was involved is immaterial.

But these limited cases of obvious non-authorisation do not solve the larger question of how a threshold issue (authorisation by the native title claim group) can be determined at the beginning of the claim, when it depends on the ultimate issue in the proceedings (i.e. who are the native title holders?)

The answer is to conduct a hypothetical exercise.[138] The court asks whether the applicant's authorisation *would be* valid *assuming the applicant's own version of the facts*.[139] This is not the same as simply asking whether the applicant is authorised by the application group described in the Form 1 — that would be to ignore Lindgren J's emphasis on the particular form of words chosen by the legislature for s. 61(1). Rather, the court examines *all* the material brought forward by the applicant in support of their claim, including:[140]

---

136 *Bodney v Western Australia* [2003] FCA 890 [45]; *Harrington-Smith on behalf of the Wongatha People v Western Australia (No. 9)* [2007] FCA 31 [1264].

137 Some cases have suggested that a meeting will be invalid if non-members of the claim group attend and participate in voting (e.g. *Weribone on behalf of the Mandandanji People v Queensland* [2013] FCA 255 [43]–[44]). But it is not clear that this result necessarily flows from s. 61(1), which requires only that authorisation be given by all of the people in the native title claim group. Certainly if there is a close majority then the participation of non–claim group members will have to be examined to determine whether it affected the outcome. In *Dodd on behalf of the Wulli Wulli People v Queensland (No. 2)* [2009] FCA 1180 [14] the court examined the voting record to determine whether an overly inclusive meeting could still give valid authorisation. See Section 3.2 below at 'Will the participation of non–claim group members at a meeting void the authorisation given?'

138 *Harrington-Smith on behalf of the Wongatha People v Western Australia (No. 9)* [2007] FCA 31 [1192]–[1193], [1253], [2433], [2747], [3387]; *Kite v South Australia* [2007] FCA 1662 [21].

139 It was in this sense that Mansfield J used the term 'native title claim group' to mean 'the persons on whose behalf a grant of native title should be made if the native title determination application is successful': *Dieri People v South Australia* [2003] FCA 187 [56]. Other judges have used the phrase 'alleged claim group' — one could even use the term 'claimed claim group' but I will continue to use the term 'application group' for this purpose.

140 In *Moran v Minister for Land and Water Conservation (NSW)* [1999] FCA 1637 [32], Wilcox J said 'In order to decide whether that requirement is satisfied, it is first necessary for the Court to

- the entire Form 1[141] (including, in some cases, previous versions of the Form 1);[142]
- any supplementary pleadings (such as Points of Claim or Statement of Facts Issues and Contentions) and any proposed amended pleadings;[143]
- any written or oral submissions made on behalf of the applicant;
- any evidence brought on behalf of the applicant[144] (which, in the context of a strike-out application, should be interpreted as favourably to the applicant as possible).[145]

---

determine who constitutes the "claim group". This must be done by reference to the document or documents making the claim.'

141 Note in *Doctor on behalf of the Bigambul People v Queensland (No. 2)* [2013] FCA 746 [48] and *Weribone on behalf of the Mandandanji People v Queensland* [2013] FCA 255 [43]–[44] the claim group was treated as being dependent on the outcome of a validly constituted community meeting, rather than on the state of the Form 1.

142 Previous iterations of the claim group description were considered as relevant to the applicant's 'case' in *Risk v National Native Title Tribunal* [2000] FCA 1589; *McKenzie v South Australia* [2005] FCA 22; *Worimi v Minister for Lands (NSW)* [2006] FCA 1770; *Harrington-Smith on behalf of the Wongatha People v Western Australia (No. 9)* [2007] FCA 31 [1222], [2751]; *Hazelbane v Northern Territory* [2008] FCA 291. It must be noted, however, that amendments to the Form 1 will not invariably make it impossible to prove that the newer application group is properly authorised. Apical ancestors can be successfully removed without the implication that only the previously larger group is the 'real' native title claim group: *Harrington-Smith on behalf of the Wongatha People v Western Australia (No. 9)* [2007] FCA 31 [3387]–[3388]. See Chapter 6 below.

143 *Velickovic v Western Australia* [2012] FCA 782 [16], [20], [39]–[40].

144 See *Hillig as Administrator of Worimi Local Aboriginal Land Council v Minister for Lands (NSW) (No. 2)* [2006] FCA 1115 [55]; *Tucker on behalf of the Narnoobinya Family Group v Western Australia* [2011] FCA 1232 [16], [42]. In *Wiri People v Native Title Registrar* [2008] FCA 574 the registrar was found to have acted correctly in considering a range of evidence for and against the version of the native title claim group put forward in the applicant's Form 1. However, this seems to be unique to the context of registration test decisions (at [23]). See also *Brown v South Australia* [2009] FCA 206 [20]. One perplexing example is *Worimi v Minister for Lands (NSW)* [2006] FCA 1770 where the court found that the application was not properly authorised because there were people not covered by the Form 1 who nevertheless fell within the 'native title claim group'. But these excluded people had given explicit evidence that they did not hold any native title rights in the area and indeed the ultimate determination was that nobody held any native title rights in the area: *Worimi Local Aboriginal Land Council v Minister for Lands (NSW) (No. 2)* [2008] FCA 1929. So the assessment of authorisation was conducted solely on the applicant's own case, although it ultimately found against the express assertions of the applicant.

145 *Kite v South Australia* [2007] FCA 1662; *McKenzie v South Australia* [2005] FCA 22 [26].

If, on the basis of all of this material, the court concludes that the application group as described in the Form 1 is not the 'native title claim group', the authorisation must be defective.[146] That is, if the applicant's material implies or concedes that other people beyond the application group also hold the 'particular native title rights and interests claimed',[147] then on the applicant's own case they do not represent the entire native title claim group. Perhaps surprisingly, such concessions are not uncommon.[148] Where, however, the applicant's case is consistent in asserting that only those persons listed in the Form 1 hold native title in the claim area, they will generally be taken at their word and the question of authorisation will be decided by asking whether those people described in the Form 1 have authorised the claim.[149]

The native title claim group might be found to be different from the application group despite the applicant's explicit protestations to the contrary. This is possible where the applicant's pleadings or anthropological evidence set out particular criteria for group membership and these criteria appear to apply to a broader set of people than those listed in the Form 1. The court may find on the evidence that there are people who satisfy the criteria who are not included in the application group, even if the applicant or the people in question deny (when asked) that those people are so included.[150]

---

146 *Risk v National Native Title Tribunal* [2000] FCA 1589 [62]; *Hillig as Administrator of Worimi Local Aboriginal Land Council v Minister for Lands (NSW) (No. 2)* [2006] FCA 1115 [47]; *Bodney v Western Australia* [2003] FCA 890 [36] and, on appeal, *Bodney v Bropho* [2004] FCAFC 226 [31], [90]–[91]; *McKenzie v South Australia* [2005] FCA 22; *Hazelbane v Northern Territory* [2008] FCA 291.

147 There is an issue, discussed below, about whether an applicant can be validly authorised if it recognises that other people hold *different* rights and interests in the same area. See later in Section 3.1 at 'Subgroups and shared country'.

148 Applicants in all of the following cases admitted, either in their Form 1 or in other documents or evidence, that there are, or may be, other people who hold native title rights and interests in the claim area: *Risk v National Native Title Tribunal* [2000] FCA 1589; *Tilmouth v Northern Territory* [2001] FCA 820; *Edward Landers v South Australia* [2003] FCA 264; *Dieri People v South Australia* [2003] FCA 187; *McKenzie v South Australia* [2005] FCA 22; *Worimi v Minister for Lands (NSW)* [2006] FCA 1770; *Kite v South Australia* [2007] FCA 1662; *Brown v South Australia* [2009] FCA 206; *Velickovic v Western Australia* [2012] FCA 782; *Strickland v Western Australia* [2013] FCA 677; *Hazelbane v Northern Territory* [2008] FCA 291; *Laing v South Australia (No. 2)* [2012] FCA 980.

149 See particularly *Risk v National Native Title Tribunal* [2000] FCA 1589 [62]; *Colbung v Western Australia* [2003] FCA 774; *Bodney v Bropho* [2004] FCAFC 226; *Stock v Native Title Registrar* [2013] FCA 1290 [85]–[101]. In *Tucker on behalf of the Narnoobinya Family Group v Western Australia* [2011] FCA 1232 [41] Marshall J suggested that the applicant may have been able to resist an attack on their authorisation if they had asserted that their application group exclusively held rights in the claim area. In the event, however, the applicant had conceded under cross-examination that members of a broader group did in fact hold some rights in the area. Accordingly an assertion to the contrary could not be maintained in good faith.

150 E.g. *Harrington-Smith on behalf of the Wongatha People v Western Australia (No. 9)* [2007] FCA 31 [2967]; *Worimi v Minister for Lands (NSW)* [2006] FCA 1770 [46]; *Strickland v Western Australia* [2013] FCA 677; see also *McKenzie v South Australia* [2005] FCA 22 where the problem was that no criteria could be discerned.

A final point to be addressed is the extent to which the composition of the 'native title claim group' might be dependent on *choice* — either the choice of the persons said to be part of the claim group or the choice of an authorising group in a meeting. Claim group descriptions that are based on a principle of 'self-selection' have been doubted by courts in a number of cases. Such groups are seen to lack coherent principles of traditional law and custom that determine who holds native title and who does not. That is so particularly if the composition of the group appears to fluctuate significantly over time.[151] In *McKenzie* the application defined the claim group by listing its currently living members (and later including their descendants in the description). The applicant said that the list reflected all of the people 'who have chosen to identify as Kujani and who claim an interest in the Kujani claim area'.[152] The list was amended a number of times, reflecting the applicant's changing understanding of who was Kujani and also the fact that some named individuals no longer wished to make a claim to the Kujani claim area. Justice Finn was unable to 'divine the descriptive criteria that makes [sic] the named persons members of the native title claim group', concluding that this meant the application did not describe the claim group sufficiently clearly.[153] Similarly, in *Wongatha* Lindgren J did not consider that individual choice about which *application group* to join was relevant to the definition of the *native title claim group* under traditional law and custom.[154] In *Wyman* Jagot J was not persuaded by evidence to the effect that group membership could be determined by the decisions of a single elder.[155]

By contrast, at least two cases have treated the *decisions* of community meetings as being potentially determinative of the composition of the native title claim group for the purposes of deciding whether the applicant is properly authorised. In *Weribone* a meeting was held to authorise an amendment to the claim group description and a second meeting was held to allow the amended claim group to authorise a replacement applicant.[156] The first meeting was found to have been ineffective because its notification was defective. As a consequence, the second meeting was said not to have been a meeting of the native title claim group because the first meeting had failed in its attempt to change the composition of the claim group.[157] Similarly, in *Doctor on behalf of the Bigambul People* the notification for a meeting was held to be defective such that the meeting 'was not competent to make any changes to the constitution of the [native title claim group]'.[158] These cases are interesting because they suggest a greater emphasis on the group's *decisions* than on the *evidence* adduced in support of the claim.[159] Of course, the anthropological evidence may

---

151 E.g. *Velickovic v Western Australia* [2012] FCA 782 [40]; *Brown v South Australia* [2009] FCA 206.

152 *McKenzie v South Australia* [2005] FCA 22 [19].

153 ibid. [44].

154 *Harrington-Smith on behalf of the Wongatha People v Western Australia (No. 9)* [2007] FCA 31 [909], [3070], [3262], [3424]; cf. [916], [1219].

155 *Wyman on behalf of the Bidjara People v Queensland (No. 2)* [2013] FCA 1229 [566]–[567].

156 *Weribone on behalf of the Mandandanji People v Queensland* [2013] FCA 255.

157 ibid. [43]–[44].

158 *Doctor on behalf of the Bigambul People v Queensland (No. 2)* [2013] FCA 746 [55].

159 Note the reference to *Aplin on behalf of the Waanyi Peoples v Queensland* [2010] FCA 625 in *Doctor on behalf of the Bigambul People v Queensland (No. 2)* [2013] FCA [64].

well establish that acceptance by the broader group is objectively a criterion that must be satisfied in order to hold native title rights under traditional law — in such a case the group's opinion about an individual may be determinative.[160]

Subgroups and shared country

The discussion above describes the various material that will be used by the court to determine whether the native title claim group aligns with the authorisation group and the application group. But what about that content of that material? How does the court determine the extent of the claim group and what will cause the court to conclude that the claim group has been misconceived?

It is best to begin by distinguishing between three situations:[161]

a) Two distinct neighbouring groups make separate claims which overlap in some areas. They may disagree with each other on the exact location of the border between their territories, or perhaps the overlap area is mutually acknowledged as 'shared country'. There is no suggestion that one group subsumes the other.

b) An application is made on behalf of a local-level landholding group and the anthropology suggests that this group forms part of a larger regional group — perhaps a language group, cultural bloc or nation.

c) An application is made on behalf of a particular group of people or on the basis of a particular criterion for holding rights under traditional law and it transpires that not all of the people belonging to that group or satisfying that criterion are included in the application group or authorisation group.

In the first situation, courts routinely make determinations recognising the rights of two distinct groups that have lodged their own applications, even if each applicant has conceded that the other group may also have rights in some areas.[162] The logical basis for this was outlined by Lindgren J in *Wongatha*.[163] There, the government respondents argued that any acknowledgment of shared rights amounted to a concession that the applicants were not authorised by the entire native title claim group. They argued that 'where an application itself acknowledges that native

---

160 *Aplin on behalf of the Waanyi Peoples v Queensland* [2010] FCA 625.

161 See *Northern Territory v Doepel* [2003] FCA 1384 [43], [46] and *Harrington-Smith v Western Australia (No. 9)* [2007] FCA 31 [1195], [1202], [1205].

162 In *Hunter v Western Australia* [2012] FCA 690 two separate applications were filed in respect of an area of 'shared country'. Neither application in its terms recognised the rights of the other group and neither application group authorised the other group's application. In *James on behalf of the Martu People v Western Australia* [2002] FCA 1208 a determination was made in favour of the Martu people (the principal claim group) and also the Ngurrura people. The Ngurrura people had a separate application, which they had amended to exclude the overlap area. They were then joined as a respondent to the Martu people's application pursuant to an agreement reached between Ngurrura and Martu. The consent determination was made in respect of both groups even though the Martu application did not refer to (and was not authorised by) the Ngurrura people. See also *Ward v Western Australia* [1998] FCA 1478 and comments in *Northern Territory v Doepel* [2003] FCA 1384 [43].

163 *Harrington-Smith v Western Australia (No. 9)* [2007] FCA 31.

title rights and interests in the claim area or part of it are also held by persons who are not claimants on whose behalf the application is made, authorisation by them is also required.'[164] Justice Lindgren rejected this argument on the grounds that s. 61(1) only requires an application to be authorised by the people who hold 'the particular native title claimed'. An application may explicitly recognise that another group of people hold some *different* set of rights and interests, without needing to be authorised by those other people.[165]

The same logic can also apply to the second situation described above, but not necessarily.[166] In *Colbung* a group known as the 'Harris family' made a native title application whose accompanying material recognised that other members of the broader regional Noongar society/language-group may also hold some rights in the area.[167] Justice Finn rejected an argument that the Harris family claim should be struck out because it was not authorised by the entire Noongar super-group:

> While the group does not claim that it alone has native title rights in the claim area, I do not consider that the application asserts other than that the particular rights and interests claimed by the Harris family group are held in virtue of their membership of that group and that group alone. [...] And it may be that the Harris' are able to establish their rights to those lands (or to part thereof) where others who are Noongar cannot.[168]

So it seems that the set of rights asserted at the local level may have been different from the rights that may have existed at the regional level. Therefore it was open for the applicant to argue that the native title claim group, for the purposes of authorisation, was the local group. Similarly, in one of the earlier *Wongatha* decisions Lindgren J held that it was not necessary for the *entire* Western Desert Cultural Bloc to authorise a particular desert claim. Although the application group shares laws and customs with other people, those other people do not necessarily hold rights and interests in the claim area and are therefore not in the native title claim group.[169]

This ability of subgroups to authorise and prosecute their own claims depends on their clear assertion of a difference in the rights held by the subgroup versus the broader group. Where an applicant recognises that they represent a subgroup but do not assert that the subgroup holds special or different rights to the broader group, the court is likely to find that the applicant is not authorised by the 'native title claim group'.[170] The application group will be seen as a 'mere subgroup' incapable of giving proper authorisation. This appears to have been

164 ibid. [1195].

165 ibid. [1202], [1205].

166 *Hillig as Administrator of Worimi Local Aboriginal Land Council v Minister for Lands (NSW) (No. 2)* [2006] FCA 1115 [58]–[62]; *Stock v Native Title Registrar* [2013] FCA 1290 [85]–[101].

167 *Colbung v Western Australia* [2003] FCA 774.

168 ibid. [22]–[24].

169 *Harrington-Smith on behalf of the Wongatha People v Western Australia (No. 5)* [2003] FCA 218 [52]–[53].

170 *Hillig as Administrator of Worimi Local Aboriginal Land Council v Minister for Lands (NSW) (No. 2)* [2006] FCA 1115 [60]; *Brown v South Australia* [2009] FCA 206 [19]–[20]; *Walker on behalf of the Noonukul of Minjerrabah v Queensland* [2007] FCA 967 [36].

the result in *Tilmouth*, although in that case the question of differential rights was not raised for consideration. Justice O'Loughlin had to answer the following question: 'Can the Yirra Bandoo, an acknowledged subgroup of the Larrakia people and authorised only by members of the Yirra Bandoo, prosecute a claim for native title of Larrakia land in respect of which the Yirra Bandoo has a special interest?' His Honour's answer was: 'as a matter of law, no'.[171] The reasons for this decision suggest that larger 'communal' claims should be pursued if available, in preference to estate-by-estate claims.[172] As a blanket proposition, such a view would not seem to be consistent with *Wongatha* and *Colbung*; it would overlook the question of whether the 'particular native title claimed' by the subgroup was the same as that held by the broader group. It may be that the evidence in *Tilmouth* indicated (or the parties assumed) that there was no difference between the rights of the Yirra Bandoo and those of the Larrakia. But it is not necessary for the purposes of determining authorisation to postulate the existence of a 'true' or 'authentic' scale of native title group; all that is required is that the rights claimed in the Form 1 are not enjoyed on the same basis by a broader set of people.

As a matter of policy or prudence it may often be preferable for native title claims to be cast at the broadest feasible level and leave the intramural allocation of rights for the native title holders to work out amongst themselves.[173] It may also be that, as a matter of traditional law and custom in a particular case, the rights and interests really are held at a broad communal level even if there are smaller estate groups with particular interests or responsibilities for particular areas.[174]

---

171 *Tilmouth v Northern Territory* [2001] FCA 820 [4].

172 ibid.

173 *Neowarra v Western Australia* [2003] FCA 1402; *Northern Territory v Alyawarr, Kaytetye, Warumungu, Wakaya Native Title Claim Group* [2005] FCAFC 136 [78]–[112]; *Gumana v Northern Territory* [2007] FCAFC 23 [154]–[163]; *Akiba on behalf of the Torres Strait Islanders of the Regional Seas Claim Group v Queensland (No. 2)* [2010] FCA 643 [245]; *Starkey v South Australia* [2011] FCA 456 [62], [65]; *A.B. (deceased) (on behalf of the Ngarla People) v Western Australia (No. 4)* [2012] FCA 1268 [838]; *Western Australia v Ward* [2000] FCA 191 [202]–[206]. In the bulk of these cases the court was defending these larger claims against assertions by government respondents that the claims should have been made at the smaller scale — effectively saying that the super-group can validly make a claim. The converse proposition that the subgroup cannot make and authorise a claim was expressly adopted in *Tilmouth* but I was unable to identify any other cases articulating that position. See also D Lavery, *The recognition level of the native title claim group: a legal and policy perspective*, Lands, Rights, Laws: Issues of Native Title, vol. 2, no. 30, *Native Title Research Unit, AIATSIS, 2004* and L Strelein, *Native title-holding groups and native title societies: Sampi v State of Western Australia [2005]*', Lands, Rights, Laws: Issues of Native Title, vol. 2, no. 30, Native Title Research Unit, AIATSIS, 2005. The question of how native title will be managed by one or more RNTBCs post-determination may also favour broader claims at a policy level.

174 *Western Australia v Ward* [2000] FCA 191 [202]–[206]; *Sampi v Western Australia* [2005] FCA 777 [1069]; *Sampi on behalf of the Bardi and Jawi People v Western Australia* [2010] FCAFC 26 [63]–[80]. See also *Hayes v Northern Territory* [1999] FCA 1248 [31]–[33] for a discussion of how Western Desert relationships to land may be accommodated in this framework. By contrast, Lindgren J

So after a full hearing of the evidence, the court may well find that since only one determination may be made for any given area, the determination should only recognise the broader community as the native title holders.[175] But for the purposes of determining authorisation as a threshold issue at the outset of proceedings, it seems that smaller estate groups are legally able to pursue their own claims — so long as they can articulate how the rights that they claim differ from those of the broader group.[176]

The third situation described above is a fairly common basis on which native title claims have been struck out or otherwise found to be defective in their authorisation.[177] Typically, two or more applications are made in respect of the same area of land on the basis of essentially the same traditional source of rights. This will often occur because of personal, political or ideological disagreements between the respective applicants, or because of disputes about whether particular individuals or families should be recognised as native title holders. Or the applicants may simply interpret the native title claims process as one in which individuals or families can 'register' their interests in land without reference to others who may also hold native title in the same area.[178] Whatever the explanation, authorisation will be defective in any case where an application group claims to hold rights and interests on the basis of their satisfaction of certain criteria (such as descent from a particular set of ancestors) and it transpires that there are other people who also satisfy those criteria.[179]

One particularly striking instance of this issue arises when claim group descriptions are framed deliberately to conform with s. 190C(3) of the *Native Title Act*. Section 190C sets out some of the conditions that must be satisfied before an application can be registered (thereby

---

in *Wongatha* considered that the various application groups in that case were inappropriate to the Western Desert rules of land-holding since they were cast in terms of descent groups — see *Harrington-Smith on behalf of the Wongatha People v Western Australia (No. 9)* [2007] FCA 31 [880]–[932], [1145], [1933].

175 *Neowarra v Western Australia* [2003] FCA 1402 [387], [389]. See s. 68, NTA.

176 See *Risk v National Native Title Tribunal* [2000] FCA 1589 [55], [69]. In that case the application was found not to be authorised because it was not authorised by all members of the Danggalaba clan; the further contention that Danggalaba was a mere subset of the Larrakia people was held not to be determinative of the question of authorisation.

177 *Risk v National Native Title Tribunal* [2000] FCA 1589; *Edward Landers v South Australia* [2003] FCA 264; *Dieri People v South Australia* [2003] FCA 187; *Harrington-Smith v Western Australia (No. 9)* [2007] FCA 31; *Worimi Local Aboriginal Land Council v Minister for Lands (NSW)* [2007] FCA 1357; *Hazelbane v Northern Territory* [2008] FCA 291; *Wiri People v Native Title Registrar* [2008] FCA 574; *Brown v South Australia* [2009] FCA 206; *Strickland v Western Australia* [2013] FCA 677; *Laing v South Australia (No. 2)* [2012] FCA 980 [30]–[32].

178 This appears to have been the case in the *Wongatha* proceedings: *Harrington-Smith v Western Australia (No. 9)* [2007] FCA 31. See also *McKenzie v South Australia* [2005] FCA 22; *Brown v South Australia* [2009] FCA 206.

179 *Harrington-Smith on behalf of the Wongatha People v Western Australia (No. 9)* [2007] FCA 31 [2967]; *Worimi v Minister for Lands (NSW)* [2006] FCA 1770 [46]; *Strickland v Western Australia* [2013] FCA 677.

giving the claimants procedural rights in relation to ILUAs and future acts). Subsection 3 prevents a claim from being registered if another, already registered claim over the same area includes any of the same people in the application group. So applicants have been known to specifically exclude particular families or individuals from the claim group description in order to avoid failing the registration test on this account. Alternatively, the claim group description might simply exclude the entire category of 'persons falling within s. 190C(3)'. Although this may be sufficient to satisfy s. 190C it is also likely to pose serious problems from an authorisation perspective.[180] For example, in *Wongatha* the Wongatha people's claim group description was framed in terms of descent from particular ancestors but excluded particular descendants by name. In written submissions the applicants contended that native title was held by the 'Wongatha people', defined as 'those persons of the [Western Desert Cultural Bloc] who pursuant to [their] laws and customs, have rights and interests in the land and waters covered by the application'.[181] Justice Lindgren found that the excluded individuals were left out of the claim group description not because they did not meet these criteria or because they were not 'Wongatha', but instead because they had filed their own claim and the applicants did not wish their claim to fail the registration test.[182] Accordingly, on the Wongatha people's own case, the claim group description did not describe all of the alleged native title holders and the application was not authorised by them.[183] Similarly, the anthropologist giving evidence in the *Wongatha* trial for the Koara group had stated that there were people who met the membership criteria listed in the Points of Claim for the Koara application, who were not listed in the claim group description for that claim. Justice Lindgren said:

---

180 *Edward Landers v South Australia* [2003] FCA 264; *Dieri People v South Australia* [2003] FCA 187. Note authorisation is also a necessary part of the registration process: s. 190C(4). In *Champion v Western Australia (No. 3)* [2014] FCA 280 a claim was dismissed because it had failed the registration test a number of times. One of the reasons for these failures was that the native title claim group was found not to be properly reflected in the Form 1 claim group description. The Form 1 stated that it was brought on behalf of 'those persons who are specifically excluded from other claims which have previously passed the registration test, namely the following persons…' The registrar concluded that this clearly did not describe all of the people who hold native title in the relevant area: <http://www.nntt.gov.au/searchRegApps/NativeTitleClaims/RegistrationDecisionDocuments/DECEMBER%202009/WC97_100%2011122009.pdf>, viewed 17 August 2016.

181 *Harrington-Smith on behalf of the Wongatha People v Western Australia (No. 9)* [2007] FCA 31 [1222].

182 ibid. [1222]–[1223], and at [2013]: 'All Claims are made by reference to Western Desert laws and customs. How can it be, in relation to the Wongatha/MN overlap, that one GLSC claimant is a Wongatha claimant and another, an MN claimant? The MN Claim group acknowledges that there are Wongatha claimants who satisfy these criteria, and the Wongatha Claim group acknowledges that there are MN claimants who satisfy the comparable Wongatha criteria.'

183 See also the converse finding — that the Cosmo application was unauthorised because it excluded some Wongatha people: *Harrington-Smith on behalf of the Wongatha People v Western Australia (No. 9)* [2007] FCA 31 [2967], [3012].

> [T]he conclusion is inescapable that these other persons are part of the hypothetical holders of the particular native title claimed, and that their authorisation of the Koara application was required by s 61(1).[184]

Accordingly the arbitrary or artificial[185] exclusion of people who otherwise fulfilled the same criteria as pleaded by the applicants was found to be fatal to the authorisation of the application.[186] An exception to this general position appears to have arisen in the more recent case of *Martin (deceased) v Western Australia (No. 2)*.[187] There, Barker J rejected an argument that the application was not properly authorised because the claim group description contained the following clause:

> provided that any person who is within the description contained in Section 190C(3) of the Native Title Act 1993 (As Amended) whether specifically named in this Schedule or a descendant of a person named in this Schedule is excluded from those persons on whose behalf the claim is brought.[188]

Justice Barker found that the applicants 'do not purport to be a subgroup of some larger group, and the material currently before the Court does not suggest they are'.[189] His Honour distinguished the case of *Dieri*, where the applicants had conceded the existence of people beyond the claim group description who belonged to the relevant native title holding group.[190] Perhaps if the people excluded by the proviso clause in *Martin* had been explicitly identified and the applicants were asked whether those people did in fact have rights in the claim area, the outcome may have been different.

'Trust-like' claims

Occasionally applicants will assert that there exists a small pool of true native title *holders* who have the necessary cultural knowledge and authority to be custodians of country on behalf of a larger pool of *beneficiaries*. This is more common in areas associated with the Western Desert Cultural Bloc, but is not limited to those areas nor universal among Western Desert claimants.[191]

---

184 ibid. [2432]–[2433].

185 ibid. [1000], [1439], [1933], [2475], [2505], [2608], [3397], [3790], [3817].

186 See also ibid. [1219], [2967]–[2968]. Also *Strickland v Western Australia* [2013] FCA 677.

187 *Martin (deceased) v Western Australia (No. 2)* [2009] FCA 635.

188 ibid. [8].

189 ibid. [99].

190 ibid. [100], citing *Dieri People v South Australia* [2003] FCA 187.

191 E.g. *Kite v South Australia* [2007] FCA 1662; *Reid v South Australia* [2007] FCA 1479; *Starkey v South Australia* [2011] FCA 456. Cf. *Risk v National Native Title Tribunal* [2000] FCA 1589; *Worimi v Minister for Lands (NSW)* [2006] FCA 1770.

These cases represent attempts by the applicants to translate their understandings of traditional law and custom into the language and structures of the *Native Title Act*. Those attempts have generally been unsuccessful. In *Kite* the applicant argued that the claim group was limited to five *nguraritja* (custodians) who were the true and only holders of native title but who held native title in a 'trust-like' relationship for a broader group of people.[192] Justice Finn described the relevant task as determining 'whether the designated claim group constitutes the entirety of the possible native title group suggested by the application and evidence'.[193] His Honour's initial view was that, in recognising that other people may have the 'benefit' of the native title rights, the applicant was effectively conceding that the application group did not cover the entire native title claim group.[194] Yet Finn J concluded that he was obliged to give the applicant the benefit of the doubt and assume for the purposes of determining authorisation (on a strike-out claim) that only the *nguraritja* were 'holders' of native title rights and interests.[195] (The claim was struck out for other reasons: people named as native title holders in the Form 1 were found on their own evidence not to fulfil the criteria for rights and interests that were set out in the Form 1.) Ironically, Finn J in *Kite* expressed discomfort about the applicant's description of traditional law and custom relating to *nguraritja*, saying:

> I have some concern that in this matter the claim may well owe more to concepts drawn from common law conceptions of property than from traditional laws and customs.[196]

Courts have tended to regard the purpose of a native title determination as setting out the entire class of people who have certain legal rights as against outsiders.[197] There has been a consistent reluctance to spell out in a determination the 'intramural' allocation of rights according to traditional law and custom.[198] In this sense a native title determination regulates the relationship between native title holders and other people, rather than the relationships amongst native title holders themselves. This objective would not be well served by a document that recorded only the 'custodians' of particular rights and not the people whose activities on the land are done in exercise of those rights. For example, an Aboriginal person fishing on their country might need to demonstrate to police that they are entitled to do so under their native title rights. That would require a means of matching their identity with the criteria for group membership listed in the native title determination — something that could not be done if the native title claim group were limited to the 'trustee' holders of the rights.

---

192 See also *Reid v South Australia* [2007] FCA 1479.

193 *Kite v South Australia* [2007] FCA 1662 [27].

194 ibid. [29]–[33].

195 ibid. [34].

196 ibid.

197 E.g. ibid. [25]–[28].

198 See cases collected above at fn. 173.

Social or cultural coherence not required

When the cases reject an application on the grounds that it is not authorised by, and made on behalf of, 'the true native title claim group' or 'the real native title claim group', they are not thereby asserting that a valid native title claim group needs to have some minimum degree of anthropological or political coherence or unity.[199] We need not assume for the purposes of authorisation that there exists a finite number of identifiable bounded groups whose territories tessellate across the map of Australia. Rather, there is a multitude of nested and overlapping levels on which people might join together for different purposes, depending on context.

For example, in the combined Mandingalbay Yidinji-Gunggandji claim, one of the applicants asserted that his authority came from the Gunggandji people alone and did not depend on the views of the Yidinji or Mandingalbay people.[200] Justice Spender rejected this view, at least insofar as it related to authorisation for the purposes of the *Native Title Act*. His Honour held that, because the claim was a joint claim of all three subgroups, the applicants must be authorised by the entire group regardless of whether that larger group might be considered 'artificial' from a cultural perspective.[201]

Similarly, where a claim group is defined partly by reference to descent from an apical ancestor, it is open to the applicant to argue that *not all* descendants of that ancestor are part of the claim group. There may be further criteria that a person must meet to possess rights and interests under traditional law and custom.[202] In *Wongatha*, once Lindgren J had found that rights and interests are held at an *individual level* under Western Desert law and custom, his Honour concluded that none of the alleged claim groups were in fact 'native title claim groups' — no matter how natural or appropriate those groupings appeared to the people who asserted them.[203] In *Hazelbane* Mansfield J found that the native title application should have been brought on behalf of the 'Finniss River Brinkin Group', constituted by a number of distinct

---

199 Cf. *Dieri People v South Australia* [2003] FCA 187 [55] where Mansfield J held that a native title claim cannot validly be made by a subgroup of 'the real native title claim group'. That was in the context of two applications that mutually recognised that they did not represent all of the people who, under Dieri law and custom, held native title in the claim area (see [53] and *Landers v South Australia* [2003] FCA 264 [32]). Similarly, Dowsett J in *Aplin on behalf of the Waanyi Peoples v Queensland* [2010] FCA 625 [17] described the native title claim group as 'those persons of Indigenous descent who claim a shared interest in land or waters pursuant to shared traditional laws and customs'.

200 *Combined Mandingalbay Yidinji-Gunggandji Claim v Queensland* [2004] FCA 1703.

201 ibid. [14]–[17]. See also *Que Noy v Northern Territory* [2007] FCA 1888 [23].

202 *Bodney v Bropho* [2004] FCAFC 226 [31] per Branson J, [90] per Stone J with whom Spender and Branson JJ agreed. Cited in *Hillig as Administrator of Worimi Local Aboriginal Land Council v Minister for Lands (NSW) (No. 2)* [2006] FCA 1115 [57].

203 *Harrington-Smith on behalf of the Wongatha People v Western Australia (No. 9)* [2007] FCA 31 [1142], [1933], [2506]–[2507], [2926], [3078]–[3080], [3505].

clans, and not merely by some of these clans.[204] There was no suggestion that the Finniss River Brinkin Group had any distinct existence or unifying characteristics. The sole relevant fact was that it allegedly comprised all of the rights-holders for the claim area.[205]

Further, the extent of the native title claim group will depend entirely on what the traditional law and custom says about the enjoyment of rights and interests in relation to land. If that law and custom provides for the inheritance of rights without any need to participate in any particular cultural activities, anyone who meets the relevant descent criteria will be part of the native title claim group. By contrast, if there is a traditional law requirement that rights are only held by people who observe and acknowledge the law, there may be descendants of an apical ancestor who do not form part of the native title claim group.[206] That is a question to be determined on the evidence about law and custom, on a case-by-case basis.

Nor is there any necessary relationship between the 'society' and the native title claim group for the purposes of the *Native Title Act*. For the purposes of establishing native title under s. 223, a society is a group of people united in and by their acknowledgement and observance of a common body of law and custom.[207] The native title claim group does not need to cover the entire society. It is perfectly acceptable for a subset of a society to be a native title claim group, so long as that subset covers all members of the society who hold rights and interests in the claim area.[208] In *Harrington-Smith (No. 5)*, Lindgren J confirmed that a native title claim group is only required to include those people who hold the rights and interests in the claim area *under* the society's laws and customs:

> It is conceivable that the traditional laws and customs under which the rights and interests claimed are held might, in whole or in part, be also traditional laws and customs of a wider population, without that wider population being a part of the claim group. I have rights

204 *Hazelbane v Northern Territory* [2008] FCA 291 [36].

205 Importantly, these observations relate to the issue of authorisation rather than the ultimate substantive question of who holds native title. Where it is asserted that native title is held by a particular group, courts may require evidence that this group is a 'traditional group' having a continued vitality and existence since sovereignty. If the group lacks that quality then the claim may fail. See *A.B. (deceased) (on behalf of the Ngarla People) v Western Australia (No. 4)* [2012] FCA 1268 [612]–[619]; *Dale v Moses* [15]–[19], [116]–[118].

206 *Bodney v Bropho* [2004] FCAFC 226 [31].

207 *Members of the Yorta Yorta Aboriginal Community v Victoria* [2002] HCA 58 [49]. See discussion in N Duff, *What's needed to prove native title? Finding flexibility within the law on connection*, AIATSIS Research Discussion Paper No. 35, AIATSIS Research Publications, Canberra, 2014.

208 *Kite v South Australia* [2007] FCA 1662 [22], citing *Hillig as Administrator of Worimi Local Aboriginal Land Council v Minister for Lands (NSW) (No. 2)* [2006] FCA 1115 [60]. See e.g. *De Rose v South Australia (No. 2)* [2005] FCAFC 110 [236]–[237]. In *Akiba on behalf of the Torres Strait Islanders of the Regional Seas Claim Group v Queensland (No. 2)* [2010] FCA 643 [471], [474], a single society was found to cover the entire Torres Strait and yet smaller, single-island claim groups had previously obtained determinations of native title.

> and interests in land under the laws of New South Wales and those laws are 'shared' with other persons, but it is not true that, as a result, my rights and interests in land are shared with them. The same laws apply so as to generate proprietorial rights in a person because of factual circumstances peculiar to that individual. Similarly, it is conceivable that traditional laws and customs shared by members of the Western Desert cultural bloc may apply so as to confer rights and interests on the Wongatha people in relation to the land and waters covered by the application which they do not confer on other members of the Western Desert cultural bloc. It is, of course, a different question what the evidence will prove.[209]

There is also no requirement that a claim group be limited to members of only one society.[210]

Representative structures in the authorisation process

The courts have been quite clear that authorisation must be given by the people who hold the native title rights and interests. Authorisation cannot be given by some other entity — unless, perhaps, that entity has itself been authorised by the claim group for this purpose.[211]

While there is nothing to prevent a corporation or association from recruiting and restricting its membership so that it overlaps perfectly with a native title claim group, the application cannot validly use membership of the corporation or association as the defining criterion for the native title claim group.[212] (For one thing, there would be no way of ensuring that the membership of the corporation continued in the future to reflect the native title holding group.) Neither may an applicant validly rely on the resolution of a corporation or association (without more) as the source of authorisation for the purposes of s. 61.[213]

If the traditional law and custom of a native title claim group empower a smaller 'representative' group or council to make decisions of the kind contemplated by s. 61, the decision of such a body will be sufficient to authorise an application. In such a case, however,

---

209 *Harrington-Smith on behalf of the Wongatha People v Western Australia (No. 5)* [2003] FCA 218 [52]–[53], cited in *Hillig as Administrator of Worimi Local Aboriginal Land Council v Minister for Lands (NSW) (No. 2)* [2006] FCA 1115 [62].

210 *Lardil Peoples v Queensland* [2004] FCA 298 [200], [207], [140]; *McNamara on behalf of the Gawler Ranges People v South Australia* [2011] FCA 1471. Interestingly, in *Daniel v Western Australia* [2003] FCA 666, R.D. Nicholson J appears to have been unconcerned about whether the claimant groups were part of the same or of different societies: his Honour found at [405] that the Aboriginal people who inhabited the claim area at the time when sovereignty was asserted 'did so as members of an "organised society" or "organised societies"'.

211 See generally J Southalan, 'Authorisation of native title claims: problems with a "claim group representative body"', *Australian Resources and Energy Law Journal*, vol. 29, no. 1, pp. 49–59, April 2010; cf. G O'Dell, 'Lodging a native title claim using a claim group representative body', *Australian Resources and Energy Law Journal*, vol. 28, no. 3, pp. 395–398, October 2009. Also *Dingaal Tribe v Queensland* [2003] FCA 999 [8]; *McKenzie v South Australia* [2005] FCA 22 [54]–[55].

212 *Kudjala People v Queensland* [2006] FCA 1564; *Reid v South Australia* [2007] FCA 1479.

213 *Booth v Queensland* [2003] FCA 418; *Reid v South Australia* [2007] FCA 1479.

the applicant may need to bring evidence establishing that the body does in fact have that authority under traditional law and custom.[214] Further, if there are conditions on the body's power to make decisions then evidence may be required establishing that those conditions have been met. For example, if traditional law and custom provides for decision-making by a group of elders after the elders have consulted with other members of the group, evidence of such broader consultation may be required.[215]

If there is no such traditional structure for decision-making, it is possible for a claim group to agree and adopt a process of decision-making that effectively delegates authority to a smaller group. But the evidence would need to disclose a process by which that delegation had taken place.[216] Ultimately, the applicants must be able to demonstrate how their authorisation can be traced to a decision of the native title claim group.[217]

Many claim groups around Australia delegate certain kinds of decisions to a 'working group': a committee smaller than the claim group but potentially larger than (or differently composed from) the applicant. The idea is for this committee to be in regular contact with each other and with their lawyers, formulating plans and relaying information. Working groups may be empowered to make certain low-level decisions (e.g. negotiating heritage agreements for exploration licences) while significant decisions are taken back to the claim group.[218]

An interesting example of the use of corporations in the claim process was demonstrated in a recent decision involving the Yindjibarndi people.[219] In that case, a claim group authorised applicants (by a contested majority vote) on certain conditions. (On this generally, see Section 4.1 below at 'Conditional appointment'.) One of those conditions was that the applicants would not take any decision that was not authorised by a particular Aboriginal corporation. This amounted to saying that the corporation's authorisation was necessary, but not sufficient, for the applicant to take steps in the claim. The corporation concerned happened to be associated with one of the two competing factions in the claim group. Justice McKerracher noted that this may be a contentious development but said that it was not for the court to judge the wisdom of the claim

---

214 Section 251B(a), NTA; *Moran v Minister for Land and Water Conservation (NSW)* [1999] FCA 1637 [34]; *Western Australia v Strickland* [2000] FCA 652 [77]–[78]; *Anderson v Western Australia* [2003] FCA 1423 [40]; *Van Hemmen on behalf of the Kabi Kabi People 3 v Queensland* [2007] FCA 1185 [24].

215 E.g. *Van Hemmen on behalf of the Kabi Kabi People 3 v Queensland* [2007] FCA 1185.

216 *Bolton on behalf of the Southern Noongar Families v Western Australia* [2004] FCA 760 [44]; Reid v South Australia [2007] FCA 1479 [46]. See J Southalan, 'Authorisation of native title claims: problems with a "claim group representative body"', *Australian Resources and Energy Law Journal*, vol. 29, no. 1, pp. 49–59, April 2010.

217 *Reid v South Australia* [2007] FCA 1479 [46], citing *Bolton on behalf of the Southern Noongar Families v Western Australia* [2004] FCA 760 [44].

218 D Ritter, 'Doing the business: a few observations on the working group model for the provision of native title legal services', *Indigenous Law Bulletin*, vol. 5, no. 28, pp. 12–13, October/November 2003; J Southalan, 'Authorisation of native title claims: problems with a "claim group representative body"', *Australian Resources and Energy Law Journal*, vol. 29, no. 1, pp. 49–59, April 2010.

219 *N.C. (deceased) v Western Australia (No. 2)* [2013] FCA 70.

group's decision, so long as that decision could be proven to be a properly made decision of the claim group as a whole.[220] The conditional authorisation was found to be valid.

Summary: native title claim group

Identifying, describing, defining and in many cases *negotiating* the outlines of the native title claim group is a complex process that requires close attention to both Australian law and traditional law and custom.

Where different applicants represent distinct groups who accept each others' separate existence, disagreements about the location of boundaries can be adjudicated by the court. Recognising that another group may hold shared rights in some areas will not require a jointly authorised claim. And where a clearly differentiated set of rights is claimed by a subgroup, the subgroup may succeed in pressing their claim separately from a larger group that subsumes them. But where overlapping applications are made on behalf of people who are in some sense part of the 'same mob', courts appear reluctant to become involved in potentially conflictual and ambiguous disputes about group identity. In such cases the political work must be done prior to lodging an application.

3.2 Authorisation by 'all the persons' in the native title claim group

Section 61(1) of the *Native Title Act* requires an applicant to be authorised by 'all the persons' who hold native title rights and interests in the claim area. This may at first suggest unanimity, or at least comprehensive participation. However, this ostensibly high threshold is relaxed by s. 251B, which states that the s. 61 requirement is met so long as 'the persons in the native title claim group' follow the decision-making procedures set out in s. 251B(a) and (b).[221] The word 'all' is omitted from s. 251B(a) and (b), and this has been interpreted as '[giving] the word "all" a more limited meaning than it might otherwise have'.[222] That is, s. 251B *stipulates* that authorisation by a smaller set of the native title claim group will constitute authorisation by 'all', provided certain conditions are met. There is no requirement for every single member of the claim group to participate actively in the authorisation process[223] and no requirement that the decision be

---

220 ibid. [56], [76], [99].

221 The question of whether authorisation under traditional law and custom must come from an active 'decision' as opposed to being the cultural entitlement of a particular person(s) is addressed below in Section 3.2 at 'Is a meeting actually required at all?'

222 *Lawson on behalf of the 'Pooncarie' Barkandji (Paakantyi) v Minster for Land and Water Conservation (NSW)* [2002] FCA 1517 [25] cited in *Harrington-Smith on behalf of the Wongatha People v Western Australia (No. 9)* [2007] FCA 31 [1265].

223 In *Quall v Risk* [2001] FCA 378 [33], O'Loughlin J said that 'all' could not be taken literally because a claim group may contain people whose youth or mental capacity prevents them from participating in decisions, and further because 'failure to obtain authorisation from members whose whereabouts are unknown could prevent an otherwise legitimate claim for native title from proceeding.' See also *De Rose v South Australia* [2002] FCA 1342 [928] ('"all" those who are

unanimous[224] (unless unanimity is dictated by traditional law and custom or by the process agreed and adopted by the claim group).[225]

The general test for whether authorisation has been given by the claim group was set out by Stone J in *Lawson*:

> It is sufficient if a decision [authorising an applicant] is made once the members of the claim group are given every reasonable opportunity to participate in the decision-making process…[226]

Even a meeting attended by a relatively small fraction of the claim group as a whole can validly authorise a claim. The fundamental principle is that everyone in the claim group must be given the *opportunity* to be involved.[227] And where decisions are to be made at a meeting the key question will be whether the group as a whole received sufficient notification of the meeting.[228] (Issues other than notification are discussed below at Section 3.3, 'Authorisation in practice'.)

What proportion of claim group members must be involved in authorisation?

Even though the 'reasonable opportunity' test articulated in *Lawson* has become the dominant measure of adequate authorisation, a slightly different test was introduced (perhaps implicitly) by French J in *Bolton*, requiring authorisation meetings to be 'fairly representative' of the native title claim group.[229] In considering whether a meeting is 'fairly representative' of the claim group, it is possible to distinguish two potential issues:

(i) **Numerical proportionality** — whether the number of people involved in authorising the application was large enough compared to the size of the broader claim group.

---

reasonably available and who are competent to express an opinion'); *Daniel v Western Australia* [2002] FCA 1147 [18]; *Anderson v Western Australia* [2003] FCA 1423 [40].

224 In *Lawson on behalf of the 'Pooncarie' Barkandji (Paakantyi) v Minster for Land and Water Conservation (NSW)* [2002] FCA 1517 [25], Stone J remarked that it would be technical and pedantic to regard s. 251B as allowing the non-involvement or non-agreement of a small number of individuals to cause an application to fail. The NTA creates no veto, though it may import one that exists within a traditional or agreed decision-making process.

225 *Starkey v South Australia* [2011] FCA 456 [55]; *Butchulla People v Queensland* [2006] FCA 1063 [34]; *N.C. (deceased) v Western Australia (No. 2)* [2013] FCA 70 [84], [96].

226 *Lawson on behalf of the 'Pooncarie' Barkandji (Paakantyi) People v Minister for Land and Water Conservation (NSW)* [2002] FCA 1517 [25].

227 The test as articulated in *Lawson* has been cited in a large number of cases, including *Weribone on behalf of the Mandandanji People v Queensland* [2013] FCA 255 [39]; *Kuruma and Marthudunera People v Western Australia* [2012] FCA 14 [31]–[32]; see also *Jurruru People v Western Australia* [2012] FCA 2 [31]–[32]; *Fesl v Delegate of the Native Title Registrar* [2008] FCA 1469 [68]; *P.C. (name withheld) on behalf of the Njamal People v Western Australia* [2007] FCA 1054 [22]; *Wharton on behalf of the Kooma People v Queensland* [2003] FCA 790 [34].

228 See e.g. *T.J. v Western Australia* [2015] FCA 818 [77]–[106].

229 *Bolton on behalf of the Southern Noongar Families v Western Australia* [2004] FCA 760 [46].

(ii) Representation of subgroups — whether all (or enough) of the various factions, 'families', clans, estate groups, descent groups or language groups participated.

For each of these issues, the lack of 'representativeness' might be due simply to a lack of sufficient participation or inadequate attendance at a meeting, or it might be because some claim group members expressly oppose the authorisation of the applicant or the application. As will be seen, simply avoiding a meeting will often be ineffective in preventing the meeting from validly authorising the claim; rather, it is incumbent on opponents to attend, air their opinion and bring others around to their view.

The case of *Moran* was decided shortly after the 1998 amendments that strengthened the authorisation requirements in the *Native Title Act*. There, Wilcox J set an extremely high standard for authorisation, requiring an applicant 'to identify by name all the people within the claimant group, or a collective body able to speak for the group as a whole'.[230] His Honour said that if there is no applicable traditional decision-making process, 'it must at least appear that the authorising individuals constitute a majority of the members of the group' which in turn would require an exhaustive identification of all the individuals in the claim group.[231] Subsequent cases, however, have not followed this stringent requirement — neither in relation to the identification of each claim group member by name, nor in relation to the need for an absolute majority.[232]

The later decision in *Bolton*, while not as stringent as *Moran*, was interpreted at the time as setting a similarly high bar for establishing valid authorisation.[233] In that case various claim groups had held meetings to authorise the amendment and combining of their respective applications. Justice French found that the relevant authorisation had not been established. One problem was the failure to specifically target the notification and advertising of the meeting to the full group of people as described in the application. The advertisements referred only to the name of the claim rather than to the apical ancestors listed in the Form 1 and the evidence was not sufficient to demonstrate that meeting notices had been sent to all descendants of those apical ancestors.[234] Another problem was the failure to establish that each person attending the meeting was in fact a member of the relevant claim group — attendees were not asked to provide details of their descent from relevant ancestors, rather their self-identification was treated as sufficient. Thirdly,

---

230 *Moran v Minister for Land and Water Conservation (NSW)* [1999] FCA 1637 [49].

231 ibid. [41].

232 See *Lawson on behalf of the 'Pooncarie' Barkandji (Paakantyi) People v Minister for Land and Water (NSW)* [2002] FCA 1517 [24]; *Risk v National Native Title Tribunal* [2000] FCA 1589 [43]–[49]; *Kuruma and Marthudunera People v Western Australia* [2012] FCA 14 [31]; also L Strelein, *Authorisation and replacement of applicants: Bolton v W.A. [2004] FCA 760,* Land, Rights, Laws: Issues of Native Title, vol. 3, no. 1, Native Title Research Unit, AIATSIS, Canberra, 2005. See also *Ngalakan People v Northern Territory* [2001] FCA 654 [53]: 'although it is not necessary for the court to name each individual member of the claimant group...it is necessary for the court, if the evidence permits, to identify the claimants as a group or as a community.' Also *Butchulla People v Queensland* [2006] FCA 1063 [27].

233 *Bolton on behalf of the Southern Noongar Families v Western Australia* [2004] FCA 760.

234 See also *T.J. v Western Australia* [2015] FCA 818.

and more ambiguously, French J found that there was 'no evidence that the meetings were, in any sense, fairly representative of the native title claim groups concerned'.[235] It is possible that on this third point his Honour was referring to the number of people who attended the meeting compared with the number of people in the wider claim group (the ratio appears to have been between 13 and 31 per cent).[236] That interpretation is supported by the following remark:

> It may be that there is a chronic difficulty that cannot be overcome despite [the NTRB's] most heroic efforts because of the apathy, lack of interest, or divided opinions held by members of the relevant native title claim groups. If that be so, that may be a reason for reconsidering whether the applications should proceed at all.[237]

In a commentary written shortly after the decision, Strelein interpreted French J as concluding that 'the numbers present at the meetings were insufficient to provide proper authorisation.'[238] Strelein was concerned that this would set an overly onerous benchmark for authorisation, with applicants unable to prosecute their claims merely because of the difficulty of getting enough people to a meeting:[239]

> *Bolton* also highlights the positive obligation on NTRBs and active claimants or applicants to identify the members of the claim group and solicit their involvement in the decisions that affect them…However, it should be acknowledged that NTRBs and active claimants cannot force the participation of potential native title holders in the management of the claim.[240]

Despite the understanding at the time that *Bolton* had laid down strict procedural rules for authorisation, the case has been cited in a great many subsequent cases *in tandem* with the 'reasonable opportunity' test in *Lawson*, with the result that meetings have generally been held to be 'fairly representative' when the whole claim group has been properly informed and given a reasonable opportunity to attend.[241] *Bolton* has been interpreted as relating primarily to the failure to prove that notification had occurred or that those who attended the meetings were in

---

235 *Bolton on behalf of the Southern Noongar Families v Western Australia* [2004] FCA 760 [46].

236 L Strelein, *Authorisation and replacement of applicants: Bolton v WA [2004] FCA 760*, Land, Rights, Laws: Issues of Native Title, vol. 3, no. 1, Native Title Research Unit, AIATSIS, Canberra, 2005, p. 4.

237 *Bolton on behalf of the Southern Noongar Families v Western Australia* [2004] FCA 760 [46].

238 L Strelein, *Authorisation and replacement of applicants: Bolton v WA [2004] FCA 760*, Land, Rights, Laws: Issues of Native Title, vol. 3, no. 1, Native Title Research Unit, AIATSIS, Canberra, 2005, p. 9.

239 Note in *Weribone on behalf of the Mandandanji People v Queensland* [2013] FCA 255 [48] Rares J indicated that in the circumstances of that case he would be unwilling to reject the validity of a meeting simply because of the difficulty in travel arrangements.

240 L Strelein, *Authorisation and replacement of applicants: Bolton v WA [2004] FCA 760*, Land, Rights, Laws: Issues of Native Title, vol. 3, no. 1, Native Title Research Unit, AIATSIS, Canberra, 2005, p. 11.

241 See *Kuruma and Marthudunera People v Western Australia* [2012] FCA 14 [32]; *Jurruru People v Western Australia* [2012] FCA 2 [31]; *Roe v Western Australia (No. 2)* [2011] FCA 102 [14]; *P.C. (name withheld) on behalf of the Njamal People v Western Australia* [2007] FCA 1054 [23]; *'Pooncari' Barkandji (Paakantyi) People v Minister for Land and Water Conservation (NSW)* [2006] FCA 25 [31]. In *Reid*

fact claim group members, and the failure to adequately describe the claim group in the meeting notices.[242] For example, Gilmour J adopted a fairly relaxed approach to the 'proportionality' issue (in full knowledge of the *Bolton* decision):[243]

> Although a meeting to replace an applicant should be attended by persons fairly representative of the claim group, authorisation can nonetheless be validly given by a small percentage of the whole claim group provided that the process leading to that authorisation has been appropriately notified and conducted. In *Coyne v Western Australia* [2009] FCA 533, for example, a meeting of 72 people (including 29 people opposed to its outcome) was able to authorise the change of applicant for a broader claim group of between 5,000 and 20,000. His Honour, Siopis J at [51] concluded that because the meeting had been widely notified, including that the meeting could consider changing the applicant, it could be inferred that:
>
>> Those who decided not to attend the meeting were content to abide by any decision made by those who did attend the meeting and...accordingly, the decisions made at the meeting were the legitimate binding expression of the view of the...claim group as a whole.

In *Coyne* Siopis J referred to French J's (post-*Bolton*) decision in *Anderson*[244] where French J focused on the number of people to whom meeting notices *had been given*, without any reference at all to the number of people who *actually attended the meeting*:[245]

> [I]n determining whether the Ballardong meeting was sufficiently representative of the claim group, French J did not have regard to the proportion of those attending the meeting compared to the number of the potential members of the claim group. What was significant to French J was the extent of the distribution of the notice of the meeting and its terms.[246]

---

v South Australia [2007] FCA 1479 [47] the meeting was found not to be fairly representative because of low turnout and defective notice.

242 *Dann v Western Australia* [2011] FCA 99 [42]; *Coyne v Western Australia* [2009] FCA 533 [42]. Note French J's earlier decision in *Anderson v Western Australia* [2003] FCA 1423 proceeded on similar lines as Bolton — his Honour (at [45]) pointed to inadequate attendance in conjunction with other problems such as inadequate notification and a failure to confirm and record the identity of those in attendance.

243 *Roe v Western Australia (No. 2)* [2011] FCA 102 [14], cited in *N.C. (deceased) v Western Australia (No. 2)* [2013] FCA 70 [81].

244 *Anderson v Western Australia* [2007] FCA 1733. At [36] French J said that he was satisfied that a 'sufficiently representative section of the native title claim group' was involved in the decision and went on to say 'In coming to that conclusion, I have regard to the wide ranging notification, both targeted and general, of the proposed meeting and what it was being asked to decide.'

245 *Coyne v Western Australia* [2009] FCA 533 [48].

246 ibid. See also *M.B. (deceased) v Western Australia* [2010] FCA 1110 [4]–[6]; *Sandy on behalf of the Yugara/Yugarapul People v Queensland* [2012] FCA 978 [38].

Certainly, a *combination* of inadequate notice and poor turnout can render a meeting ineffective[247] but I was unable to find any example of a case where mere low attendance, without other defects in the process, was held to be fatal to the validity of an authorisation decision.

In *Ward v Registrar of the National Native Title Tribunal*,[248] 11 individuals made affidavits deposing that they had not been consulted about the claim and had not authorised the applicant to 'do business' on their behalf. In applying the registration test, the registrar had said that '[i]f they are [members of the claim group] there is a real dispute about the application being properly authorised.' Reviewing the registrar's decision, Carr J found that the refusal to register the claim for defective authorisation was 'clearly open'. It is no doubt significant that this was not a case of people who had been invited to a meeting but had refused to give their consent. Rather, these people had not been involved in the process at all. (As is described in the paragraphs below, it would be unusual if the dissent of a mere 11 individuals out of a claim group numbering in the thousands was sufficient to justify a failure of the registration test, particularly without information about the seniority of those people, let alone in circumstances where their very membership of the claim group was not yet established.)

In *Bigambul (No. 2)*, two different factions within a claim group held competing meetings on the same day.[249] Justice Reeves found that the notices and advertisements for one of these meetings were deficient in that they did not give enough detail about the business to be conducted, which meant that claim group members were not given adequate opportunity to decide whether or not to attend. This was sufficient to render the meeting's outcomes legally ineffective.[250] Nevertheless, his Honour made the additional comment that because the numbers attending each meeting were approximately equivalent, neither group was 'a dissentient minority who are seeking to raise an intramural dispute' and, accordingly, neither faction could have prevailed in any case.[251] His Honour ordered representatives of each faction to attend mediation in order to agree on details of a future meeting of the *entire* claim group. There is therefore a suggestion in *Bigambul (No. 2)* that even a properly notified meeting might, in the exceptional circumstances of a rival meeting attracting an equivalent turnout, be incapable of providing adequate authorisation.

Finally, there are cases where the evidence establishes a process of traditional decision-making in which the bulk of the claim group does not need to be involved in the decision. In such cases, failure to consult or notify the group as a whole will not be fatal for authorisation. In *Que Noy* the applicant brought expert evidence of a decision-making process in which only the most senior people exclusively made decisions about country.[252] Justice Mansfield noted that there was no evidence of any broader consultation or notification beyond this small group of senior people but

247 *Reid v South Australia* [2007] FCA 1479 [47].

248 [1999] FCA 1732.

249 *Doctor on behalf of the Bigambul People v Queensland (No. 2)* [2013] FCA 746.

250 ibid. [48].

251 ibid. [69].

252 *Que Noy v Northern Territory* [2007] FCA 1888.

nevertheless held that the evidence was sufficient to support a finding that the group as a whole had made the authorisation decision according to its traditional decision-making process.[253]

Will opposition by a minority prevent authorisation?

In addition to the proportion of claim group members that must *attend* a meeting, we must consider the question of what proportion of claim group members must *agree* to a particular decision. The answer to this question is entirely dependent on the relevant decision-making process for the claim group — this may be a traditional process (which will need to be established by evidence) or it may be a process agreed or adopted (and the fact of agreement and adoption will need to be proven).[254]

If the applicable process required decisions to be unanimous then any dissent, even by a single person, could theoretically be enough to prevent a decision from being made. So it is *possible* for a traditional or adopted process to grant a 'veto' to every individual or to particular individuals such as senior law bosses or elders. However, in the absence of clear evidence courts have been reluctant to infer or assume that such a process does apply.[255] For example, in *Bidjara People #2* Ryan J said:

> [T]he applicants retain the authorisation, as I understand it, of the majority of the claimant group, but there are one or more dissentient members of the group. In that event, it can hardly be contended that the claim should lapse. However, it would also lead to injustice if the dissentient members were thereafter denied a voice in the determination of the claim… Accordingly, I consider…that such persons can be made parties pursuant to s 84(5).[256]

In both *Coyne*[257] and *N.C. (deceased) v Western Australia (No. 2)*[258] quite slim majorities were held to be sufficient to satisfy the authorisation requirements of the *Native Title Act*. In each case the process agreed and adopted by the claim group meeting allowed for majority decision-making. In *N.C.* McKerracher J considered that a 60 to 40 per cent division was capable of meeting the requirements of the legislation:

---

253 ibid. [35]. Appeal against this decision was dismissed: *Foster v Que Noy* [2008] FCAFC 56.

254 See *Combined Mandingalbay Yidinji-Gunggandji Claim v Queensland* [2004] FCA 1703 [41].

255 In addition to the following examples see *Lawson on behalf of the 'Pooncarie' Barkandji (Paakantyi) People v Minister for Land and Water Conservation (NSW)* [2002] FCA 1517 [25]; *T.R. (deceased) on behalf of the Kariyarra People v Western Australia* [2014] FCA 734 [46]–[48]; *Stock v Western Australia* [2014] FCA 179 [22]–[23]. Also, in the context of ILUA authorisation under s. 251A, *QGC Pty Ltd v Bygrave (No. 2)* [2010] FCA 1019 [95].

256 *Bidjara People #2 v Queensland* [2003] FCA 324 [7]. As explained below, the circumstances where dissentient members of the claim group will be allowed to join as respondents will be rare. See *Starkey v South Australia* [2011] FCA 456 [55]–[63]; *Rubibi v Western Australia* [2002] FCA 876 [19]–[24].

257 *Coyne v Western Australia* [2009] FCA 533.

258 *N.C. (deceased) v Western Australia (No. 2)* [2013] FCA 70.

> It is a recurring theme for the respondents to the application that the majority was too slim and not only had majority decision-making not been properly agreed, but that it required agreement by all people or almost all people. I do not consider this to be the case. In *Coyne v Western Australia* [2009] FCA 533, a meeting of 72 people was held to be able to authorise the replacement applicant where 29 people opposed the motion. Given the division present within the Yindjibarndi native title claim group, to suggest that unanimous or near unanimous approval of the decision-making process was required would 'make it extremely difficult if not impossible for a claimant group to progress a claim': see [*Lawson on behalf of the 'Pooncarie' Barkandji (Paakantyi) People v Minister for Land and Water Conservation (NSW)* [2002] FCAFC 1517 at [25]] per Stone J and [*P.C (name withheld for cultural reasons) on behalf of the Njamal People v Western Australia* [2007] FCA 1054 at [22]] per Bennett J.[259]

The judgments in *N.C.* and the earlier case of *Barnes*[260] suggest that the court will be more willing to accept that an authorisation decision has been made by the entire native title claim group, even in the face of concerted opposition, if everyone including the opposing voices has been notified about the meeting and had a reasonable opportunity to express their views there. The court in each of those decisions examined the way the meeting was conducted and found that in the circumstances a majority vote could be taken to represent the will of the group as a whole.[261]

In one of the *Butchulla* decisions Kiefel J stated that the *Native Title Act* does not require a meeting to be attended by all members of the claim group, nor the agreement of all in attendance.[262] Accordingly, her Honour looked to the evidence about the particular processes that were agreed and adopted at the meeting and found that those in attendance had agreed that no person had a veto. (The group had agreed on a consensus model but in the context of *that* meeting this did not mean 'unanimity'.)[263] In the later case of *Dann*, Barker J cited Kiefel J in support of the following proposition:

> It is the members of the claim group thus convened whose views are to be accepted. That there may be a few who do not share the majority view will not usually affect the validity of the group resolution…[264]

---

259 ibid. [96].

260 *Barnes on behalf of the Wangan and Jagalingou People v Queensland* [2010] FCA 533.

261 See also *T.J. v Western Australia* [2015] FCA 818.

262 *Butchulla People v Queensland* [2006] FCA 1063 [33], citing *Lawson on behalf of the 'Pooncarie' Barkandji (Paakantyi) People v Minister for Land and Water Conservation (NSW)* [2002] FCAFC 1517 [25] for the first proposition, and *Moran v Minister for Land and Water Conservation (NSW)* [1999] FCA 1637 [48] for the second.

263 On 'consensus' not meaning 'unanimity' see also *Kuruma and Marthudunera People v Western Australia* [2012] FCA 14; *Jurruru People v Western Australia* [2012] FCA 2; *Butterworth on behalf of the Wiri Core Country Claim v Queensland (No. 2)* [2014] FCA 590.

264 *Dann v Western Australia* [2011] FCA 99 [44].

The process for 'adopting and agreeing' a decision-making will be discussed in more detail below in Section 3.3 ('Authorisation in practice') but for now the relevant point is that the legislation itself does not impose a requirement of unanimity about the choice of decision-making process.

There have been some cases in which a faction's opposition to a particular claim or to the individuals constituting the applicant has led them to file their own overlapping claim or to seek joinder as a respondent party. This does not of itself mean that the principal claim is not authorised.[265] For example, the Ngadju people's application was overlapped by a number of claims made by (and on behalf of) people who were included within the Ngadju application group. It was clear that those 'dissentient' people wished to go their own way and explicitly did not authorise the Ngadju application.[266] Nevertheless, the matter proceeded to determination without any mention of authorisation problems or any need to use s. 84D(4)(a).[267]

Important consequences flow from the fact that a claim can be validly authorised even if some of the claim group oppose it or later withdraw their support. An individual or group may find that they are caught within the claim group description of a claim that they do not support. This may be because they do not consider themselves to be a member of the relevant group at all, or else they may consider that the principal claim is flawed in some way. (Perhaps it is controlled by the 'wrong people' or else wrongly includes or excludes certain people.) Being named on a claim will present difficulties for people who wish to register an overlapping claim: s. 190C(3) of the *Native Title Act* would prevent registration of the later-filed claim and therefore block any procedural rights under the future act regime. Assuming that the 'dissentients' have attempted unsuccessfully to convince the rest of the group to amend the claim group description to exclude them, their only remaining options are to seek joinder as a respondent and apply for the main claim to be struck out[268] or else apply for orders under s. 84D. Either way, if the only relevant objection is that the dissentients themselves do not support the principal claim, a strike-out application or s. 84D application is unlikely to succeed. The dissentients must be able to show that the claim is not authorised by the claim group as a whole. But so long as the relevant decision-making procedure was complied with, and all members of the claim group were given adequate notification and an opportunity to participate, the dissentients may find it difficult to establish a defect in authorisation. The only circumstance in which dissentients would be likely to succeed is where they represent an entire estate group or family group and the traditional or agreed process requires the consent of

---

265 See e.g. *Bidjara People #2 v Queensland* [2003] FCA 324 [7]; *Butterworth on behalf of the Wiri Core Country Claim v Queensland* [2010] FCA 325 [31]–[32].

266 E.g. *Champion v Western Australia (No. 2)* [2011] FCA 345; *Laing v South Australia (No. 2)* [2012] FCA 980; *Graham on behalf of the Ngadju People v Western Australia* [2012] FCA 1003.

267 *Graham on behalf of the Ngadju People v Western Australia* [2012] FCA 1455. As it happens, the overlaps had been dismissed or withdrawn by the time of the determination.

268 Although in *Central West Goldfields People v Western Australia* [2003] FCA 467 [12] Carr J indicates that the court has the power to 'remove' an individual and their descendants from the native title claim group, it is not clear what source of power the court would rely on in amending the application in this way. Ultimately Carr J declined because there was no evidence that the descendants of the person seeking 'removal' had authorised that course of action.

all such subgroups. Even then, there have been cases in which the majority of the claim group has successfully abandoned such a 'subgroup veto' in order to progress the claim.[269]

On the basis of the above analysis, future researchers may wish to investigate whether there is a subtle systemic 'majoritarian bias' in this area of law. Certainly the effect of the law is that, in some cases, individuals or subgroups may be included in a claim despite their disinclination to be members.[270] This will not be the case where traditional decision-making processes entrench the rights of subgroups to 'veto' such decisions. But in the absence of such a traditional process, the law's tendency is to avoid the derailment of claims by the objections of minorities.[271] This is partly due to the way strike-out applications work: courts will be very cautious in striking out a claim and set a high bar for opponents to meet. Perhaps it is also partly a matter of pragmatism in driving claims through to resolution, informed by a perception that the achievement of a native title determination is important as a matter of justice notwithstanding the quarrels of some of those involved. Or it may be an unavoidable consequence of a judicial process operating in a contested political space: in the face of conflicting accounts of how traditional decision-making should work, the version put forward by an isolated individual or minority might be less convincing. That is particularly so where it is contended that the group as a whole has chosen to depart from a traditional decision-making process.[272] These may be interesting questions for future research.

Must an authorisation meeting be representative of all subgroups?

Having dealt with the issue of raw proportionality, we turn now to a slightly different question: do all of the internal subgroups within a claim group need to be involved in the authorisation process? The answer given below is: no, or at least not necessarily. There is no strict requirement for the internal composition of a claim group to be reflected in the meeting that resolves to authorise a claim. Nevertheless, where important subgroups or factions are absent or under-represented, this may lead the court to doubt whether the meeting could properly be said to represent the claim group as a whole. As with the proportionality issue, the focus is on adequate notification and other circumstances related to the holding of the meeting.

In *Bolton* (the case in which the 'fairly representative' test was first articulated), French J made the following comment about the facts in that case:

---

269 See e.g. the comments about the ability for groups to decide to depart from traditional decision-making processes: in *Lawson on behalf of 'Pooncarie' Barkandji (Paakantyi) People v Minister for Land and Water Conservation (NSW)* [2002] FCA 1517 [21]; *Butchulla People v Queensland* [2006] FCA 1063 [31]–[32].

270 E.g. *T.R. (deceased) on behalf of the Kariyarra People v Western Australia* [2014] FCA 734 [11]. Note the similarity to the equivalent rule for generic 'representative proceedings' (also known as 'class actions') under the *Federal Court Act 1976*. Section 33E of that Act provides that the 'consent of a person to be a group member in a representative proceeding is not required' unless the person is a government, a minister, a public authority or a public officer.

271 It is instructive to note the comments of North J about the 'inherent improbability' of a traditional decision-making process that requires unanimity or consensus in all cases: *T.R. (deceased) on behalf of the Kariyarra People v Western Australia* [2014] FCA 734 [46]–[48].

272 E.g. *Lawson on behalf of 'Pooncarie' Barkandji (Paakantyi) People v Minister for Land and Water Conservation (NSW)* [2002] FCA 1517 [21]; also *Butchulla People v Queensland* [2006] FCA 1063 [31]–[32].

> [E]ven if it be accepted that each of the members who attended each of the meetings was a member of the relevant native title claim group, it is not established that they were in any sense representative of the various components of the native title claim group concerned.[273]

This reference to 'various components' suggests an implied requirement or preference for authorisation meetings to reflect the different subgroups that make up the broader native title claim group. But as noted above, *Bolton* has been interpreted in subsequent cases as being concerned primarily with the process leading up to the holding of the meeting than the turnout at the meeting itself.

Certainly, it is quite common for judges to observe in *support* of the adequacy of a particular meeting that the meeting was attended by a good cross-section of the various constituent subgroups,[274] and there have been cases where the under-representation of particular subgroups has been identified as a problem for authorisation by the claim group as a whole. But the cases in this latter category have tended to involve either situations where there was *no* evidence about the notification of the authorisation meeting[275] or where the evidence disclosed *problems* in the way the meeting was notified or held.[276] I was unable to find an example of a case in which a meeting that was properly notified to the full native title claim group was found to be ineffective in authorising an application solely on the basis that the people in attendance did not include representatives of all relevant subgroups.

The position is conveniently summarised by Collier J in the following passage:

> A recurrent concern expressed by the dissenting applicants was that there were not sufficient persons at the authorisation meeting [...] who were representative of all apical ancestors to make a decision to replace the applicant. Specifically, of the 146 persons in attendance at the authorisation meeting only descendants of four of six apical ancestors were present, and of them the majority were descendants of Nellie Yumbeina and 'Sally' mother of Mary Ann Beng...There is no substance to the dissenting applicants' complaint that those in attendance at the authorisation meeting were not representative of the claim group. There is no requirement that there be sufficient persons in attendance at an authorisation meeting who are representative of all apical ancestors in a claim.[277]

---

273 *Bolton on behalf of the Southern Noongar Families v Western Australia* [2004] FCA 760 [45].

274 E.g. *Dann v Western Australia* [2011] FCA 99 [24], [28], [42]; *Jurruru People v Western Australia* [2012] FCA 2 [35]; *Kuruma and Marthudunera People v Western Australia* [2012] FCA 14 [36]; *Weribone on behalf of the Mandandanji People v Queensland (No. 3)* [2013] FCA 662.

275 E.g. *Martin v Native Title Registrar* [2001] FCA 16 [14]–[18]; *Bodney v Western Australia* [2003] FCA 890 [41].

276 E.g. *Weribone on behalf of the Mandandanji People v Queensland* [2013] FCA 255; *Quandamooka People 1 v Queensland* [2002] FCA 259 [10], [46]; *Anderson v Western Australia* [2003] FCA 1423 [44]–[45].

277 *Doctor on behalf of the Bigambul People v Queensland* [2010] FCA 1406 [64]–[66]. See also *Dingaal Tribe v Queensland* [2003] FCA 999 [23], [25], [30], [34] — satisfactory notification and procedural protections meant that an under-representation of one clan at the meeting did not deprive the meeting of validity.

Even if the law does not strictly require an authorisation meeting to mirror the internal composition of the claim group, the absence or under-representation of particular subgroups might still play a part in the court's exercise of discretion (e.g. in deciding whether to make an order under s. 66B).[278] More generally, where a meeting exhibits this kind of imbalance it may lead to questions about whether the process of notification (and other aspects of its organisation, such as the choice of venue) was appropriate and adequate to meet the requirements of s. 251B.[279] Importantly, if there is evidence that traditional law and custom (or a process previously agreed and adopted by the broader claim group) imposes certain requirements about the representation of constituent subgroups, such traditional or agreed processes must be complied with to achieve effective authorisation.[280]

It has become common practice for authorisation meetings to pass resolutions stating that the people in attendance are 'sufficiently representative' of the claim group as a whole.[281] In uncontroversial situations this may be a useful confirmation of the meeting's adequacy. But in high-conflict situations where the representation of different groups or factions is likely to be politically significant, such a resolution may be given relatively little weight. The resolution might well show that the people *attending* the meeting consider it to be adequate but the court may be more interested in the opinion of those *absent* people who (for whatever reason) were *not* present to vote for or against such a resolution. Essentially, such a resolution is recursive 'bootstrapping' — if the meeting is not representative of the claim group as a whole, a resolution of that unrepresentative meeting will not validly bind the claim group.[282] Affidavit evidence by a person in attendance may be an additional or alternative avenue, particularly if it outlines the basis for the deponent's belief in the meeting's representativeness.[283] The opinion of an anthropologist is particularly apt in that regard. There is, however, certainly no *harm* in passing a resolution about representativeness.

May (or must) the application be authorised separately by the various constituent subgroups?

Distinct from the question of whether an authorisation meeting must be attended by a representative cross-section of the various subgroups in the claim group is the question of

---

278 See discussion in *N.C. (deceased) v Western Australia (No. 2)* [2013] FCA 70 [72]–[74], [99]–[106].

279 See discussion in *Weribone on behalf of the Mandandanji People v Queensland* [2013] FCA 255.

280 Where a group has previously decided that all subgroups must be involved, this will constrain later decisions. See also discussion in *Butterworth on behalf of the Wiri Core Country Claim v Queensland (No. 2)* [2014] FCA 590 on the ability to use an agreed process in the absence of all of the lineage groups.

281 E.g. *Tatow on behalf of the Iman People #2 v Queensland* [2011] FCA 802 [21].

282 In *Weribone on behalf of the Mandandanji People v Queensland* [2013] FCA 255 a resolution to this effect did not save a meeting because the holding of the meeting was based on a false premise (namely, that the claim group's composition had been altered). Given that the meeting notices invited the purportedly altered claim group to attend the meeting, it was a meeting of the purportedly altered claim group and not a meeting of the claim group.

283 See e.g. *Barnes on behalf of the Wangan and Jagalingou People v Queensland* [2010] FCA 533 [13].

whether an application must — or even whether it *may* — be authorised separately by each of the claim group's constituent subgroups. The answer, as with the other issues in this area of authorisation, depends on the evidence about traditional or agreed decision-making processes. If the relevant process requires or allows decisions to be made in this piecemeal way, courts will follow suit. If not, then courts will treat the claim group as an undifferentiated whole for the purposes of authorisation.

In *Que Noy*, for example, the applicants asserted that the 'decision of the claim group can be made by accumulating the separate decisions of the three peoples within it'.[284] When the expert anthropologist was asked how the three subgroups' separate decisions could be said to constitute a decision by the wider claim group, he said:

> In relation to those areas which belong to areas within that native title application, the claimants are of the view that they're able to discuss those particular parts of their country in separation from the others but in understanding of the decision made by the other groups about their common interest over the whole. This is, in part, because they want to make very clear their decision-making process and the basis on which they also cooperate.

Justice Mansfield accepted this explanation, finding that collectively the traditional decision-making process of the three subgroups 'involves each group undergoing its own traditional decision-making process, in light of decisions of the other groups, and a consensus being drawn from those group decisions'.[285]

Where a native title claim group is composed of a number of fairly distinct subgroups who have come together for the purpose of making a native title claim, there might not be a traditional decision-making process to draw on because decisions on this larger scale might not have arisen in pre-colonial times. In such cases, it may well be appropriate for decisions to be made separately at the smaller level and then aggregated to produce an all-of-claim-group authorisation decision — but a decision to agree and adopt such a process must be traceable to the entire claim group as a whole.[286]

For example, Finn J in *Akiba* doubted the validity of a purported authorisation process where each of four 'island clusters' in the Torres Strait had held its own separate authorisation meeting. His Honour was concerned that this 'cluster' approach was not clearly established in any traditional process (because there had been no reason for pan-Strait decision-making in pre-colonial times) and there had been no process for agreeing or adopting it (although there was a 'significant level of subsequent acquiescence').[287] Indeed, Finn J doubted that strict compliance with s. 251B was even

---

284 *Que Noy v Northern Territory* [2007] FCA 1888 [36].

285 ibid. Appeal against this decision was dismissed: *Foster v Que Noy* [2008] FCAFC 56.

286 An example of this working successfully is *Holborow v Western Australia* [2002] FCA 1428 [50].

287 *Akiba on behalf of the Torres Strait Islanders of the Regional Seas Claim Group v Queensland (No. 2)* [2010] FCA 643 [929]. Note that Finn J's treatment of 'subsequent acquiescence' as insufficient to constitute 'agreeing and adopting' within s. 251B(b) appears to be stricter than in other

possible in the circumstances of the case, due to 'logistical reasons' — presumably referring to the large number of Torres Strait Islanders who live elsewhere in Australia.[288] (Ultimately, his Honour applied s. 84D(4)(a) to proceed in spite of the defective authorisation.)

In one of the judgments relating to the *Combined Mandingalbay Yidinji-Gunggandji Claim*, a claim group member (Mr Noble) was dissatisfied with the combined group's decision to authorise particular applicants. He said that, because the group as a whole had purported to make an authorisation decision[289] rather than allowing the relevant subgroups to decide separately, the decision was legally ineffective. Justice Spender rejected this argument, holding that a decision of the subgroup was not necessary (nor sufficient) for a valid authorisation decision.[290] It appears that his Honour attributed this outcome to the legislation itself, rather than any evidence about the particular laws and customs of the relevant group(s):

> [Section 251B] speaks of all the persons in the native title claim group. 'All the persons in the native title claim group' are not simply all the Gunggandji People or all the Yidinji People or all the Mandingalbay People. Mr Noble misunderstands the provision of the Act when he claims, 'I was put on as an applicant by the elders of the Gunggandji People. Only the elders of the Gunggandji People can take me off.'[291]

On appeal the Full Court found no fault with Spender J's approach but the Full Court appears to have regarded the question as more a matter of *evidence* about decision-making processes than about a legally *predetermined* position.[292] Although the difference is not explicit, nor unambiguous, it would appear that, on the Full Court's approach, Mr Noble might have succeeded if he had been able to prove that an applicable traditional decision-making process required decisions to be made at the subgroup level, or else if the group as a whole had agreed and adopted such a rule.

Applicant need not reflect internal subgroup structure

The *Native Title Act* contains no requirement that the composition of the *applicant* reflect the constituent subgroups of the native title claim group, and no requirement that individual named applicants act 'on behalf' of their family, clan, estate group or faction.[293] (Indeed, as will be seen

---

cases. See *Noble v Mundraby* [2005] FCAFC 212 [18] and Section 3.3 below at 'Non-traditional decision-making process'.

288 *Akiba on behalf of the Torres Strait Islanders of the Regional Seas Claim Group v Queensland (No. 2)* [2010] FCA 643 [15], [929], [931].

289 In this case the decision was to withdraw authorisation and replace the applicant but the principle is the same for initial authorisation.

290 *Combined Mandingalbay Yidinji-Gunggandji Claim v Queensland* [2004] FCA 1703 [16]–[17], [43].

291 ibid. [16].

292 *Noble v Mundraby* [2005] FCAFC 212 [16]–[18].

293 *Coyne v Western Australia* [2009] FCA 533 [24]; *Doctor on behalf of the Bigambul People v Queensland* [2010] FCA 1406 [68]; *Roe on behalf of the Goolarabooloo and Jabirr Jabirr Peoples v Western Australia*

at Section 4.3, 'Obligations of the applicant', there may be limits to the extent to which applicants *may* act for subgroups as opposed to the group as a whole.)

In *N.C.* McKerracher J considered that the appointment of an applicant composed only of members of one faction was not only technically valid but also (on balance) a positive step that could lead to the resolution of the claim.[294] His Honour declined to exercise his discretion to refuse an order under s. 66B, saying that the order was necessary to avoid the continuance of a serious stalemate between the factions.[295]

Similarly in *Roe on behalf of the Goolarabooloo and Jabirr Jabirr Peoples v Western Australia*[296] there was a combined native title claim between the Goolarabooloo people and the Jabirr Jabirr people, with an applicant composed of one representative of each group. A serious disagreement developed. At a community meeting the claim group resolved to replace the two named applicants with a new applicant composed entirely of Jabirr Jabirr people. An order was made under s. 66B effecting that replacement, and leave to appeal against the s. 66B order was refused. The s. 66B order was held to be appropriate because the claim group meeting (which had included members of the Goolarabooloo people as well as Jabirr Jabirr people) had made its decision and there was no reason for the court not to give effect to the express wishes of the claim group.[297] The court also noted that if the s. 66B order were not made, the impasse between the two previous named applicants would continue.[298]

Will the participation of non–claim group members at a meeting void the authorisation given?

Occasionally it is implied that a meeting attended by some non–claim group members cannot validly authorise an application. For example, in one of the *Weribone* cases, Rares J held that a particular meeting had not been validly constituted because 'it called together persons who were not members of the claim group and entitled them to vote on the business that was conducted at that meeting.'[299] This was because the claim group description used in the meeting notice had referred to a particular apical ancestor whose 'addition' to the claim had not been previously authorised by the claim group.[300]

[2011] FCA 421.

294 *N.C. (deceased) v Western Australia (No. 2)* [2013] FCA 70 [103]–[106].

295 See also *Roe v Western Australia (No. 2)* [2011] FCA 102 [156] where Gilmour J's discretion under s. 66B was influenced by the fact that the proposed replacement applicants undertook not to continue to act as applicant on an overlapping claim (in order to avoid a conflict of interest).

296 *Roe on behalf of the Goolarabooloo and Jabirr Jabirr Peoples v Western Australia* [2011] FCA 421.

297 ibid. [24], [41].

298 ibid. [41].

299 *Weribone on behalf of the Mandandanji People v Queensland* [2013] FCA 255 [44].

300 It should be noted that there was an additional or alternative reason for Rares J's decision to reject the outcome of the meeting in *Weribone* — namely, that the meeting was conducted on the mistaken premise that the descendants of the 'new' ancestors were members of the native title claim group: ibid.

There are good reasons to hesitate before adopting a general rule stating that the presence and participation of non–claim group members will automatically invalidate the outcomes of a meeting. Sections 61 and 251B require that a decision be authorised by 'all the persons in a native title claim group' but says nothing of the effect of authorisation by a broader class of people. Certainly, if an authorisation meeting was contentious and had to be settled by a majority vote, the fact that non–claim group members had voted would be problematic. (Otherwise the applicants 'stack' the meeting with non-members.)[301] And if the relevant law and custom, or the agreed and adopted process, required that non-members not participate, that would be determinative. But there is no obvious reason why a unanimous or consensus decision would be ineffective simply because of the participation of people who are not members of the native title claim group.[302] That, indeed, was the approach adopted by Stone J in *Pooncarie*: her Honour said that if non–claim group members had voted at the meeting that would not affect the validity of the meeting's decisions because those decisions were made without dissent.[303]

In any case, the practice of NTRBs in recent years has been to ensure that meeting invitations are extended only to claim group members and that only claim group members take part in decisions. (The chair of a meeting may, however, invite the claim group members to decide whether non-members should be allowed to remain in the room.) This creates some complexity when groups wish to amend the claim group description. See below at Chapter 6.

Is a meeting actually required at all?

The preceding discussion has generally assumed that authorisation will be given at a meeting (or at a number of meetings, if the piecemeal approach such as in *Akiba* or *Que Noy* is adopted). But is a 'meeting' actually a necessary part of authorisation? Or can an applicant be authorised, for example, directly by their seniority and cultural status under traditional law and custom? What about a poll conducted at multiple sites without first holding a meeting to discuss the matter to be decided?

There is nothing in the *Native Title Act* that expressly requires authorisation to be given at a formal meeting of the claim group. Section 61 simply states than an application must be made by a 'person or persons authorised' by the native title claim group, and s. 251B is non-specific

---

301 In *Dodd on behalf of the Wulli Wulli People v Queensland (No. 2)* [2009] FCA 1180 [14] the court examined the voting record to determine whether an overly inclusive meeting could still give valid authorisation.

302 In a different context, Collier J engaged in a counter-factual analysis of voting at a meeting to determine whether an impugned aspect of the meeting (the selective provision of buses) could have had an effect on the meeting's outcomes: *Doctor on behalf of the Bigambul People v Queensland* [2010] FCA 1406 [39]. Her Honour concluded that even if all the people given access to buses had not attended, and assuming that all of those people voted for the resolutions that were made, the outcome would not have been any different. One can imagine an equivalent analysis being applied to a situation where people had voted who were later determined not to have been claim group members.

303 *Lawson on behalf of the 'Pooncarie' Barkandji (Paakantyi) People v Minister for Land and Water Conservation (NSW)* [2002] FCA 1517 [27].

about how this authorisation is to be given. All that is required is that authorisation be given via an applicable traditional process (s. 251B(a)) or, in the absence of a traditional process, a process agreed and adopted by the group (s. 251B(b)). On the face of it, it would seem possible for an applicant to be authorised under traditional law and custom simply because they possessed a high level of cultural knowledge and social status.

In practice, applicants who seek to rely on s. 251B(b) will need to bring evidence establishing that the claim group as a whole has agreed and adopted an authorisation process that does not require full claim group meetings. Such agreement and adoption must in turn require some input from the claim group as a whole — suggesting a need for at least one meeting, or perhaps some kind of distributed consultation process that can be proven to have included the entire claim group.[304] In *T.J.*[305] (discussed below) the organisers attempted to seek agreement on the decision-making process — a poll conducted at multiple sites without any formal meeting — by making the approval of such a process the subject of the first question on the poll. The effectiveness of this approach was doubted by Rares J, though his Honour did not specifically say that it would never be appropriate,[306] and applicants who assert that their authority derives directly from traditional law and custom without any need for a specific group 'decision' (s. 251B(a)) will have to bring evidence establishing the existence of that traditional law and custom. Courts are likely to need evidence from a number of claim group members to prove such a traditional process, and potentially anthropological evidence too, as the following cases demonstrate.

In *Johnson, in the matter of Lawson v Lawson*[307] there was uncontested evidence describing a process of traditional decision-making whereby each family group has a 'headperson' and the combined decisions of all of these headpersons together is sufficient for authorising things of the kind contemplated in s. 251B. In affidavit evidence, one of the named applicants said that there was no need for a vote about who was the headperson for each family, stating 'it was something we already knew; it's a combination of things that gives you that role.'[308] Justice Stone accepted that authorisation decisions could be (and indeed had to be) made by the small group of headpersons, without the need for a process for appointing those headpersons.[309] Her Honour said that '[i]f the Applicant wishes to make the case that the views of Elders who are not headpersons are to be taken into account, the Court needs some evidence to show why this

---

304 J Southalan, 'Authorisation of native title claims: problems with a "claim group representative body"', *Australian Resources and Energy Law Journal*, vol. 29, no. 1, pp. 49–59, April 2010. See also e.g. *Booth v Queensland* [2003] FCA 418 [8]–[11]. See e.g. *T.J. v Western Australia* [2015] FCA 818 [91] where Rares J appears to accept in principle the potential legitimacy of a decision-making process in which people come together to vote without actually convening a 'meeting' at which views are exchanged about the matters to be decided.

305 *T.J. v Western Australia* [2015] FCA 818.

306 ibid. [95]–[96].

307 *Johnson, in the matter of Lawson v Lawson* [2001] FCA 894.

308 ibid. [17].

309 ibid. [25]–[28].

is so.'[310] Importantly, though, the applicants did not assert that their authorisation flowed directly from their status as headpersons. (Indeed, they were seeking to prevent two other headpersons from replacing them under s. 66B.) Rather, their authorisation resulted from a *decision* made by the headpersons specifically in relation to the native title claim.[311] (In a later judgment, Stone J accepted evidence that the traditional process had 'broken down' and had been replaced by a different process agreed and adopted by the claim group at a large meeting.)[312]

In *Que Noy* Mansfield J expressed some concerns about the scarcity of evidence about the traditional decision-making process employed in that case.[313] His Honour noted that, beyond an assertion that the most senior people had been involved and that this was the proper way to make such decisions, there was no specific evidence about how such decisions would bind the broader group under traditional law. Nor was there any evidence that the rest of the group had been consulted or even notified. Nevertheless, the party opposing the authorisation decision brought no evidence to the contrary and so Mansfield J found that the authorisation had been sufficient for the purposes of the *Native Title Act*.[314]

In *Noonukul* the applicant asserted that his authorisation to make the application existed 'through Traditional Custom and Lore by the authority of the late Oodgeroo the late Kath Walker'. Justice Collier interpreted this as an assertion that Oodgeroo had authorised the applicant to make the application.[315] Considering that Oodgeroo passed away in 1993, it is perhaps more likely that the applicant was asserting a status-based authorisation derived from Oodgeroo's own cultural authority, or that Oodgeroo had bestowed on the applicant a cultural leadership role that included but was not limited to the bringing of a native title claim. In any case, Collier J found that there was no evidence to support the existence of any such traditional authorisation process, nor any evidence of how the traditional requirements had been satisfied.[316]

The idea that a person might be 'self-authorised' to bring a claim (that is, authorised directly under traditional law and custom by reference to their personal cultural status, independent of any decision by other claim group members) was entertained provisionally as a possibility in *Reid* but was rejected on the evidence.[317] Justice Finn found that there was no evidence that the rest of the claim group acknowledged the special status claimed by the applicant under traditional law and custom. Further, aspects of the applicant's evidence tended

---

310 ibid. [32].

311 See also *Kite v South Australia* [2007] FCA 1662. In that, even though the claim group was held to be 'self-identifying and self-authorising' (at [43]) the applicant claimed authorisation to bring the claim based on a meeting of the five members of the application group rather than based directly on his personal cultural status.

312 *Lawson on behalf of the 'Pooncarie' Barkandji (Paakantyi) People v Minister for Land and Water Conservation (NSW)* [2002] FCAFC 1517 [21].

313 *Que Noy v Northern Territory* [2007] FCA 1888 [35].

314 ibid. Appeal against that decision dismissed: *Foster v Que Noy* [2008] FCAFC 56.

315 *Walker on behalf of the Noonukul of Minjerrabah v Queensland* [2007] FCA 967 [35].

316 ibid. [35]–[38].

317 *Reid v South Australia* [2007] FCA 1479 [37]–[38].

to undermine his claim of authorisation-by-cultural-status: for example, he gave evidence that he had attempted to obtain the signatures of some of the claim group members — which would be unnecessary if he had the traditional cultural status he claimed.[318] While evidence showed that elders from *elsewhere* in the Western Desert region acknowledged the applicant's special status, this was not sufficient to show that he was authorised by the native title claim group for the area claimed.[319]

In one of the early *Strickland* decisions the registrar had rejected an application because of defective authorisation. Justice French (approved on appeal by the Full Court) found that this decision was wrong in the circumstances.[320] The applicant had asserted the following basis for their authorisation:

> …a traditional custom acknowledged by the members of the native title claim group of younger generations respecting elder generations and elder generations having authority to make decisions and deal with matters relating to traditional interests in land and waters on their own behalf and on behalf of younger generations…[321]

Justice French concluded that the registrar should have found this to be sufficient, saying:

> The brevity of the assertion may be criticised and it might be thought consistent with the two applicants merely arrogating authority to themselves without any or any meaningful consultation with the members of the native title claim group. On the other hand, neither the registrar nor this court is in a position to reject the contention that all relevant authority is vested in the elders of the relevant native title claim group and that the applicants fall into that category.[322]

Importantly, that assessment took place in the context of an application of the registration test (s.190C(3)) and therefore involved a mere initial assessment of the evidence. When the same claim was considered on its merits in the *Wongatha* judgment, Lindgren J rejected the applicants' account of their traditional authorisation-by-status:

> I do not accept Ms Strickland's evidence that she received the authorisation of other members of the Strickland/Nudding group. In my opinion, Ms Strickland, with the acquiescence of Ms Nudding, took decisions unilaterally in what they perceived to be the best interests of themselves and their children, and I do not accept that this was a traditional process of decision making of 'the Madawongga People' or otherwise provided for by laws and customs of the [Western Desert Cultural Bloc] within s 251B(a) of the NTA. No

318 ibid. [37].

319 ibid. [43].

320 *Strickland v Native Title Registrar* [1999] FCA 1530; *Western Australia v Strickland* [2000] FCA 652.

321 *Western Australia v Strickland* [2000] FCA 652 [27].

322 *Strickland v Native Title Registrar* [1999] FCA 1530 [57], cited with approval in *Western Australia v Strickland* [2000] FCA 652 [77]–[79].

> evidence was led from the biological descendants showing authorisation or, assuming it to be possible, ratification.[323]

Another example of the evidentiary difficulty in establishing 'self-authorisation' is the case of *Dingaal Tribe*. There, the applicant contended that:

> under the traditional law and customs of the Dingaal people, he is the only person entitled, and thereby authorised, to make the claim for native title on behalf of the claim group, and that no meeting, however constituted, can by any process remove that authority. It is inherent in his position that no meeting can make any decision authorising any other person to make a claim, or an application under s 66B, without his attendance at the meeting, and without his consenting to his own replacement in favour of a person or persons of whom he approves.

The evidence showed that a Dingaal claim group meeting had unanimously voted to make decisions about replacing the applicant, despite having been told of the applicant's views about his own cultural authority. Justice Cooper held that, in light of this evidence, he was unable to find that the traditional law and custom of the Dingaal people had the effect claimed by the applicant.[324]

A final case to consider is the recent decision of *T.J.*[325] In that case Rares J appeared to be open to the possibility that a native title claim group could validly make an authorisation decision by way of a secret ballot conducted at several locations simultaneously, without any actual 'meeting' at which views could be exchanged about the matters to be decided.[326] However, on the particular facts before him, Rares J considered that the process was fatally flawed because (amongst other reasons) the claim group members were not given a sufficient opportunity to understand, on proper information, the questions for decision.[327] Further, his Honour appears to have found fault with the process for 'agreeing and adopting' the decision-making process. A resolution approving the secret ballot process was set as the first question on the ballot and there was no provision for any alternative way of deciding the substantive issues if the first resolution was unsuccessful.[328] Finally, the notice sent to members had referred to an 'authorisation meeting' despite there being no intention to hold a 'meeting' — this was found to be misleading.[329]

The cases outlined above establish that the law does not specifically require a claim group meeting but that reliance on other mechanisms of authorisation carries certain risks and difficulties. Any alternative traditional process will have to be proven with anthropological evidence and any alternative 'agreed and adopted' process will need proof of how it was

323 *Harrington-Smith on behalf of the Wongatha People v Western Australia (No. 9)* [2007] FCA 31 [3432].

324 *Dingaal Tribe v Queensland* [2003] FCA 999 [21]–[22].

325 *T.J. v Western Australia* [2015] FCA 818.

326 ibid. [91].

327 ibid.

328 ibid. [95]–[96].

329 ibid. [92]–[100].

agreed and adopted, and how this agreement/adoption can be attributed to the native title claim group as a whole.

3.3 Authorisation in practice

Before the meeting – research and notification

The complex and strict legal standards for authorisation, and the important policy considerations underlying those standards, mean that considerable research, preparation and potentially negotiation will be required before a meeting is held. (Note that this section will deal with the usual situation where a meeting is necessary; traditional processes that do not require meetings will of course be run differently.)

As mentioned, the key legal test is whether 'the members of the claim group are given every reasonable opportunity to participate in the decision-making process.'[330] This means that giving proper notification of a meeting to the entire native title claim group is essential for legally effective authorisation.[331]

In *Brown v South Australia* Besanko J received evidence from several claim group members that they had not been notified of the purported authorisation meeting. His Honour said that 'the failure to give them notice of the meeting is fatal to the applicant's claim that she has been authorised to make the application and deal with matters arising in relation to it.'[332]

Despite the importance of proper notification, courts will adopt a pragmatic approach in preference to a technical or pedantic one.[333] In the 2010 *Bigambul* decision, Collier J considered that 'deficiencies in the notices of meeting or irregularities in relation to the conduct of the meeting' could be overcome where all of the evidence taken together showed that the native title claim group as a whole had had the opportunity to express its will.[334] It seems, for example, that a meeting notice could not be successfully challenged by people who were in fact aware of the meeting and its purpose but who chose not to attend.[335]

---

330 See Section 3.2 ('Authorisation by "all the persons" in the native title claim group') above.

331 Again, where the evidence establishes a traditional decision-making process that does not require the involvement of the bulk of the claim group, notification to the broader claim group may not be necessary: *Que Noy v Northern Territory* [2007] FCA 1888 [35]. Appeal against that decision dismissed: *Foster v Que Noy* [2008] FCAFC 56.

332 *Brown v South Australia* [2009] FCA 206 [40]. See also French J's conclusion in *Bolton on behalf of the Southern Noongar Families v Western Australia* [2004] FCA 760 [46] that 'each of the motions for amendment under s 66B suffers from the same fatal deficiency. The evidence is insufficient to demonstrate that there has been notification to members of the native title claim group as defined or that those who attended belonged to it.'

333 See e.g. *Lawson on behalf of the 'Pooncarie' Barkandji (Paakantyi) People v Minister for Land and Water Conservation (NSW)* [2002] FCAFC 1517; *Jurruru People v Western Australia* [2012] FCA 2 [31]–[32]; *Kuruma and Marthudunera People v Western Australia* [2012] FCA 14 [31]–[32]. See application of the 'practical approach' in *Sandy on behalf of the Yugara/Yugarapul People v Queensland* [2012] FCA 978 [42]–[44].

334 *Doctor on behalf of the Bigambul People v Queensland* [2010] FCA 1406 [71].

335 See *Wiradjuri Wellington v Minister for Land and Water Conservation (NSW)* [2004] FCA 1127 [9], [13]–[14].

The following discussion gathers together some elements of contemporary NTRB practice around authorisation meetings. It is based on informal interviews with a range of lawyers, anthropologists, field officers and native title claimants from around Australia, as well as the case law and my own experience. The discussion is not intended to be prescriptive or definitive or universally applicable — rather it is intended to provide a sketch outline of how the legal requirements are put into day-to-day practice.

Pre-meeting research

It is evident from the discussion in Section 3.2 above that a clear understanding and description of who is in the native title claim group is essential *before* an authorisation meeting is held. Of course, preparatory meetings might be held to discuss and determine that question ahead of the final authorisation meeting. A number of NTRBs have held 'land summits' for just this purpose.[336] When it comes to the operative authorisation meeting, the notification must be addressed to, and identify adequately, the people in the 'native title claim group' on which the applicant's case will be based. This means that any subsequent changes to the native title claim group will require new authorisation meetings. (See Chapter 6 below.) And, as mentioned earlier, multiple changes to the claim group description over time may raise questions in a judge's mind about whether the claim has a sound basis in anthropological reality.[337] All of this points to the importance of having a sound research foundation before the authorisation meeting is advertised.

Circulation of notices

Meetings should be notified sufficiently early to allow people to arrange their plans around attending. Efforts should be made to ensure that as many people are notified as is reasonably possible — failure to notify a significant proportion of the group may prevent valid authorisation.[338] The best way to get maximum coverage of a meeting notice will depend on the local context and is best informed by people with local knowledge and experience. The following methods commonly are used by NTRBs:

- **Newspaper:** Newspaper advertisements are placed at appropriate page-positions inside publications likely to be read by claim group members.[339] National papers such as the *Koori Mail*, *National Indigenous Times* or *The Australian* will be sure to reach those

336 See <http://aiatsis.gov.au/sites/default/files/products/monograph/mcavoy-cooms-2008-crow-flies-qld-south-native-title-services.pdf> and <http://ymac.org.au/wp-content/uploads/2013/05/Annual-Report-2006-15-Oct-2006.pdf>, pp. 6–15, viewed 12 August 2016.

337 E.g. *McKenzie v South Australia* [2005] FCA 22 [44]; *Velickovic v Western Australia* [2012] FCA 782 [40]; *Wyman on behalf of the Bidjara People v Queensland (No. 2)* [2013] FCA 1229 [566]–[567].

338 See e.g. *T.J. v Western Australia* [2015] FCA 818 [84]–[86], [113].

339 Justice French doubted that a meeting 'in fine print appearing among classified advertisements relating to creditors meetings of companies and the like, had any real prospect of coming to the notice of those who might need to know about the meeting': *Anderson v Western Australia* [2002] FCA 1558 [11]. Similarly, see *Ridgeway on behalf of the Worimi People, in the matter of*

claim group members who live away from the claim area. Local papers from all places where populations of claim group members are concentrated should be used.[340] The timing used by NTRBs varies according to context but often advertisements are placed 3–4 weeks before the meeting and again in subsequent weeks.

- **Mail-out:** Letters are mailed (and increasingly, emailed) directly to known claim group members listed on databases maintained by the NTRB. Some NTRBs send these out 6 weeks in advance and then again 3 weeks in advance, others prefer 4 weeks and 2 weeks. Repeated mail-outs are prudent both as a reminder and also to reduce the risk that some people have missed the notification completely. It is important to ensure the integrity of the contact database, both by ensuring that only claim group members are listed and by regularly updating for changes of address.
- **Phone:** In the final week or so before the meeting, phone calls might be made to claim group members who are known as key people. This ensures they are aware of the meeting and can also provide a chance to encourage them to attend. This method may not be practical for large groups and may not be necessary for groups whose addresses are well-known and who are comfortable with written communication.
- **Pin-ups:** Notices are physically pinned up around relevant communities — shopping centres, public noticeboards, schools, shire offices, women's and men's centres, sports clubs. For claim groups that are concentrated in a small number of geographically discrete communities, this will often be the most effective means of notification. For geographically dispersed groups it may be inefficient and ineffective. Where the membership of the target group overlaps with the membership of a PBC, sending the notice to the PBC office can be an effective way of getting the word out.
- **Radio:** Radio announcements are broadcast on local stations and can be broadcast in Aboriginal languages, Aboriginal English and English. Announcements are generally concentrated in the week (or perhaps two) immediately prior to the meeting.
- **Electronic technology:** Email, SMS, Facebook, Twitter and other forms of electronic communication can be useful, even indispensible, for proper notification; but this is highly dependent on the particular context and circumstances of the group in question. When documenting the use of these technologies, it may be necessary to bring evidence of the appropriateness of the particular technology. In contested matters it may be necessary to show that the relevant user account is active and is held by the intended recipient.
- **Word of mouth:** For purposes of evidence (see below at 'Proving the process and outcomes') it is useful to keep a record of which individuals or families have been informed by meeting organisers.

Russell v Bissett-Ridgeway [2001] FCA 848 [34]; *Sandy on behalf of the Yugara/Yugarapul People v Queensland* [2012] FCA 978 [39]–[42].

340 E.g. *Doctor on behalf of the Bigambul People v Queensland (No. 2)* [2013] FCA 746 [12].

Content of notices

At a minimum, the notice should include the name of the claim and the claim group (sometimes they are different, as in 'Yawuru' and '*Rubibi*' for the people and the claim respectively); the Federal Court number (particularly if there are numerous similar-sounding claims); the time, date and venue; a description of *who* is invited (see below) and of the *purpose* of the meeting (see below); and any other practical matters including contact details for the meeting's organisers.

The central purpose of a notice is to invite claim group members to attend the meeting. This requires that the notice describe the claim group in terms that allow people to know whether or not they are included in it.[341] It is worth remembering that the business of assigning names to groups is not as straightforward as might be imagined and that people may be unsure or may disagree about the name of the group that best describes them.[342]

In *Bolton* French J held that the notification was defective because it merely referred to the generic name of the native title claim and did not list the apical ancestors or set out any other means by which people could determine whether they were included.[343] By contrast, in *Butchulla* Kiefel J held that a meeting notice addressed to 'all persons on the Butchulla People native title claim' was sufficient in the circumstances. In that case, the apical ancestors for the claim were well-known among the claim group and a connection report had been completed. A previous meeting had been held and the NTRB had a database covering the attendees and other descendants of the apical ancestors. Nobody contended that any claim group members were unaware of the meeting, nor that non–claim group members had participated. Accordingly, the failure to describe the group in the meeting notice was not fatal to successful authorisation.[344]

A crucial function of a meeting notice is to identify the business that will be covered at the meeting. The question of how much information to include in a meeting notice involves some competing considerations. On the one hand, some decisions have held that an overly broad notice may not be sufficient to authorise particular decisions because it would not adequately alert potential attendees of the importance of attending.[345] On the other hand, there is a risk in being overly prescriptive about the business to be conducted at the meeting — if new issues come up at the meeting that fall outside the description in the meeting notice, any resolutions on those issues might be challenged later.

In the recent *Mandandanji* authorisation case[346] Rares J said that a notice 'must give fair notice of the business to be dealt with at the meeting to all members of the claim group' and 'must be sufficient to enable the persons to whom it is addressed…to judge for themselves whether

---

341 *Bolton on behalf of the Southern Noongar Families v Western Australia* [2004] FCA 760 [45]; *Brown v South Australia* [2009] FCA 206 [42].

342 See *T.J. v Western Australia* [2015] FCA 818 [78]–[83]; *Collins on behalf of the Wongkumara People v Harris on behalf of the Palpamudramudra Yandrawandra People* [2016] FCA 527 [32].

343 *Bolton on behalf of the Southern Noongar Families v Western Australia* [2004] FCA 760 [45]–[46].

344 *Butchulla People v Queensland* [2006] FCA 1063 [27]–[29].

345 *Weribone on behalf of the Mandandanji People v Queensland* [2013] FCA 255; *Ridgeway on behalf of the Worimi People, in the matter of Russell v Bissett-Ridgeway* [2001] FCA 848 [34].

346 *Weribone on behalf of the Mandandanji People v Queensland* [2013] FCA 255.

to attend the meeting and vote for or against a proposal or whether to leave the matter to be determined by the majority who do attend and vote at the meeting.'[347] The notice must allow the people entitled to attend to 'make an informed decision whether or not to be present'.[348]

On the facts in *Mandandanji*, the meeting notice was found to be defective because it did not define with sufficient precision the business that would be dealt with at the meeting. In that case, expert evidence produced after the filing of the initial application had indicated that an additional apical ancestor should be added to the claim group description. The meeting notice did not refer to the ancestor by name nor specify that any ancestor would be added, but stated merely that the meeting would authorise 'matters including…[a] claim group description that is consistent with the expert evidence, which may include amending the existing apical ancestors'.[349] Several specific circumstances led Rares J to conclude that this was insufficient: the sole purpose of the meeting was to add the ancestor to the claim group description — no other change to the claim group was ever anticipated. Further, the claim group members were dispersed across a large geographical area, meaning that individuals might not attend a meeting unless they thought it was very important. Those who lived in a particular town far from the meeting venue tended to belong to the faction who disagreed with the addition of the new ancestor and, in fact, those who might have voted against the addition gave evidence that they did not attend because they were unaware that the addition of the ancestor was to be decided at the meeting.[350]

The principles in *Mandandanji* were approved and applied by Reeves J in the subsequent decision in *Doctor on behalf of the Bigambul People v Queensland (No. 2)*.[351] Justice Reeves held that a notice stating that the meeting 'could include removing Apical Ancestors from the current claim group description' was inadequate (even misleading) because it was only ever intended to remove one particular ancestor.[352] His Honour said 'it is entirely conceivable that the descendants of [the ancestor] may have been so confident about their position as members of the [claim group] that they did not think it was possible that the…meeting notice was directed to their apical ancestor… out of the six named apical ancestors.'[353]

In the later case of *T.J.*[354] Rares J again found that a purported authorisation decision was flawed because, amongst other reasons, the notification did not adequately describe the matters to be decided. His Honour identified a number of flaws in the notice, one of which was that its description of the proposed decisions was complex and unlikely to be understood by its intended audience.[355] Another was that the proposed decision, which would result in the claim group revising its application so as to claim only non-exclusive rights, was couched in terms that did not

347 *Weribone on behalf of the Mandandanji People v Queensland* [2013] FCA 255 [40], [41], citing *Fraser v NRMA Holdings Limited* (1995) 55 FCR 452.

348 *Weribone on behalf of the Mandandanji People v Queensland* [2013] FCA 255 [41].

349 ibid. [8].

350 ibid. [35], [42]–[43].

351 *Doctor on behalf of the Bigambul People v Queensland (No. 2)* [2013] FCA 746.

352 ibid. [46].

353 ibid. [47].

354 *T.J. v Western Australia* [2015] FCA 818.

355 ibid. [99].

make this result apparent. There was evidence before the court that people were in fact misled by the notice such that they did not appreciate the consequences of this decision.[356]

Nevertheless, in the spirit of a pragmatic and non-pedantic approach to authorisation, courts are likely to allow deviations from the advertised agenda where such deviations would not disadvantage or prejudice anyone in the claim group. For example, in *Kuruma and Marthudunera People* an authorisation decision was shifted from the first to the second day of a two-day meeting because of inadequate attendance on the first day.[357] The meeting organisers were careful to ensure that no-one who had attended on the first day was unable to attend on the second day and efforts were made to recruit more attendees. The validity of the authorisation was not affected by the change in plans.

Similarly, in *Dann* the meeting notice indicated that the purpose of the meeting was to '[a]uthorise a working group, ensure the authorisation of the applicant (s.66B *Native Title Act*); and receive updates on Amangu claim business'.[358] This was held to constitute sufficient notice of the meeting in the circumstances. Justice Barker found that claim group members would have understood that agenda as referring to the need to reconsider the authorisation of the applicant in light of the death of one of the named applicants. His Honour said:

> The agenda then was intentionally open-ended. It was not necessarily limited to the replacement of only one person, namely the deceased CW. This is because it will often be difficult in advance of such a community meeting for a particular person or particular persons to be nominated. One may expect a claim group as large and widely dispersed as the Amangu claim group to wish to have the opportunity to canvas the authorisation of the applicant generally and to suggest a range of persons who might be authorised to act for the claim group in the future conduct of the proceeding…I do not consider that the resolution of the community meeting held on 11 March 2010 was defective by failing to describe more amply or in greater detail the names of a particular person or names of particular persons who might be nominated as a replacement applicant or replacement applicants. The question of authorisation of the claim group was fairly and squarely raised as an agenda item in the notices.[359]

There is also a dilemma in choosing the kind of language that will be used in an advertisement. The technical legal requirements applicable to notification may cause NTRBs to prefer technical language. However, the focus of the court's analysis will be on the notice's actual effectiveness in alerting the native title claim group to the meeting. That may mean that technical language needs to be simplified in some circumstances. Justice Rares in *Mandandanji* said on this point:

---

356 ibid. [96]–[106].

357 *Kuruma and Marthudunera People v Western Australia* [2012] FCA 14.

358 *Dann v Western Australia* [2011] FCA 99 [13].

359 ibid. [41].

> Notices of meeting of native title claim groups called to authorise the progress of claims under the Act need to be clearly, simply and directly expressed. The Court must be mindful that the class of persons to whom such notices will be addressed are not lawyers, but indigenous people from many varied walks of life who have greater and lesser degrees of sophistication and understanding. Ordinarily, it would not serve any purpose to require such notices to set out at great length and detail material of the nature that is sometimes sent to members of a corporation who are asked to consider amending or voting on resolutions put forward by directors.[360]

Some NTRBs include agenda items or even draft resolutions in their notices, though it is more common for this to be done in mail-outs than public advertisements. Issues of confidentiality or political/cultural sensitivity may weigh against that course of action in some cases.

Other matters

It will be necessary to choose the timing and location of a meeting to ensure maximum opportunity for attendance — or at least to ensure that particular sections of the claim group are not disadvantaged.[361] Also, different communities have different needs and preferences as regards the timing of meetings: weekdays versus weekends, school holidays versus term time, and even the need to avoid in advance those days on which funerals are likely to be held (e.g. Fridays). It may be necessary to accommodate these to maximise attendance.[362] When it comes to deciding on a time, place and other arrangements, NTRBs should be guided by the views of claimants themselves, in addition to field/liaison staff and general corporate knowledge. There appear to be varying views among NTRBs on whether such logistical details are strictly a matter of client-to-lawyer *instructions* or rather fall within NTRBs' own judgment in fulfilling their statutory functions. Certainly NTRB lawyers should think carefully about *whether* they should seek instructions (at least from the applicant).

The provision of buses or other forms of transport may be useful but could be contentious if there is a perception of 'stacking' a meeting.[363] Similarly, providing a travel allowance can enable a good turnout but must be handled carefully to avoid the perception that particular people are being 'paid to attend'.[364] Practice varies considerably across different NTRBs but it is common for the provision of transport or a travel allowance to be subject to clear written policies that set out the circumstances in which assistance will be available and the different amounts of assistance available in those circumstances. There may be complex formulae that determine these matters, depending on the location of the meeting, the location of the majority of traditional owners and the budget available. For the purposes of transparency (to counter the 'stacking'

---

360 *Weribone on behalf of the Mandandanji People v Queensland* [2013] FCA 255 [40].

361 See e.g. ibid. [48].

362 See *T.J. v Western Australia* [2015] FCA 818 [113].

363 See e.g. *Doctor on behalf of the Bigambul People v Queensland* [2010] FCA 1406; also the controversial '2011 meeting' in *N.C. (deceased) v Western Australia (No. 2)* [2013] FCA 70.

364 See *Dingaal Tribe v Queensland* [2003] FCA 999 [25] and *T.J. v Western Australia* [2015] FCA 818 [113]–[114].

perception) and for 'expectation management', NTRBs will generally seek to communicate these policies widely and then apply them consistently.

Another potentially important aspect of running a meeting is the establishment of a system for ensuring that everyone in attendance (or else everyone who votes) is a member of the native title claim group. In smaller, more cohesive groups this might simply involve claim group members voicing any concerns they have about the presence of particular people, passing a resolution stating that everyone in the room is a claim group member. In larger or more contentious meetings, organisers will take more stringent measures to establish the integrity of the meeting and to prove its integrity later. This may involve a 'sign-in' desk where each attendee can give their name; in some cases attendees may be asked to explain their connection to the group (e.g. by naming their family group or the ancestor from whom they derive their membership, or completing a form setting out their relevant family tree). Anthropologists may be on hand to observe or advise this process. Where a meeting contains a mixture of claim group members and non–claim group members, coloured cards or wrist-bands might be used to assist the counting of votes.

Attempts to prevent meetings

There have been a number of cases in which individuals have sought to restrain the holding of claim group meetings. The reasons for intervening have included disagreements about the claim group description or concerns about the anthropological basis for the claim in general.

In all but one of these cases the injunction sought has been refused.[365] The primary reason for these refusals is that the meeting cannot cause any harm to the parties seeking to restrain it — and certainly not the kind of irreparable harm that would justify an injunction. If the meeting is ultimately found not to have been properly called (e.g. because the meeting notice failed to invite certain people) then the decision purportedly made at the meeting will simply have no legal effect for the purposes of s. 61 or s. 66B of the *Native Title Act*. A further reason is that the kinds of questions raised by the objectors have tended to be substantive anthropological questions which are too complex to be decided on an urgent interlocutory basis and which will in any case be addressed at later hearings. Finally, where the convenors of the meeting have already incurred significant expense in advertising and organising the meeting, the balance of convenience has weighed against granting an injunction.[366]

---

365 *Gordon Charlie v Cape York Land Council* [2006] FCA 1418; *Gordon Charlie v Cape York Land Council (No. 2)* [2006] FCA 1683; *Wuthathi People No. 2 v Queensland* [2010] FCA 1103; *Bonner on behalf of the Jagera People #2 v Queensland (No. 3)* [2012] FCA 214; cf. *Taylor v Yamatji Marlpa Barna Baba Maaja Aboriginal Corporation* [2004] FCA 1010.

366 There is an additional argument against the granting of injunctions, though not one explicitly raised in the injunction decisions. That is that the members of a claim group, just like any other citizens, are free to hold a meeting in whatever manner they choose. Whether or not the meeting has any legal effect is a different matter. One should therefore be careful to distinguish between the right to hold a meeting (which belongs equally to everyone) and the ability to hold a meeting that will have a particular legal effect (which depends on a range of procedural factors as discussed above). See *Dodd on behalf of the Wulli Wulli People v Queensland* [2009] FCA 793 [4]; cf. *Weribone on behalf of the Mandandanji People v Queensland* [2013] FCA 255 [33].

However, in *Taylor v Yamatji Marlpa Barna Baba Maaja Aboriginal Corporation*[367] an NTRB was restrained from holding a claim group meeting for the purpose of considering a proposed mining agreement. Three members of the claim group (two of whom were named applicants on the native title claim) argued before Lee J that they possessed the sole right to speak for the relevant part of the claim area and so were the only individuals who were capable under traditional law and custom of giving consent to the proposed development. These three individuals contended that the representative body was failing to carry out its 'facilitation and assistance' functions under s. 203BC(1) by 'permitting' the claim group to use a decision-making process that was not consistent with traditional law and custom. Justice Lee granted the injunction. It is not clear from the face of the decision what aspects of this case distinguish it from other cases where injunctions were refused in similar circumstances.

At the meeting — decision-making processes

The decision-making process employed will be crucial in determining whether authorisation is legally effective for the purposes of s. 251B and s. 61.

Before proceeding to examine the two limbs of s. 251B, it is important to note a conceptual distinction between the decision-making process of a *meeting* and the decision-making process of a *native title claim group*. In the 2002 *Daniel* decision, French J assessed the evidence and found that the claim group in that case had routinely made decisions of the kind mentioned in s. 251B 'in accordance with a process of decision-making which has been adopted by the persons in the native title claim group and by inference agreed to by them over a period of time'.[368] That agreed/adopted process, in his Honour's view, involved 'the conduct of community meetings of the kind' that were convened in that case.[369] It is implicit in this formulation that his Honour saw the question of how to run any particular meeting as being distinct from the question of whether meetings of this sort are a legitimate way for group decisions to be made at all.[370] It is conceivable, for example, that according to some hypothetical traditional custom a public meeting is inappropriate and decisions should be made gradually over time in private. Or a different tradition may dictate that decisions cannot be made unless *all* affected people (or all of a particular class of respected authority figures) attend.

Although this conceptual distinction should be recognised and kept in mind, in practice judges have tended to focus on the meeting-level process rather than the meta-process into which meetings may (or may not) fit. For example, in the 2007 *Anderson* decision, French J relied on evidence about a meeting's notification process as establishing that the meeting represented a 'sufficiently representative section' of the claim group. The process adopted by that meeting was accordingly treated as sufficient to bind the claim group as a whole.[371] Similarly, Siopis J in *Coyne* held that because the meeting had been adequately notified, the court could safely infer that:

---

367 *Taylor v Yamatji Marlpa Barna Baba Maaja Aboriginal Corporation* [2004] FCA 1010.

368 *Daniel v Western Australia* [2002] FCA 1147 [51].

369 ibid.; also at [27].

370 See also *P.C. (name withheld) on behalf of the Njamal People v Western Australia* [2007] FCA 1054 [19]; *Ridgeway on behalf of the Worimi People, in the matter of Russell v Bissett-Ridgeway* [2001] FCA 848 [35].

371 *Anderson v Western Australia* [2007] FCA 1733 [36].

> Those who decided not to attend the meeting were content to abide by any decision made by those who did attend the meeting and...accordingly, the decisions made at the meeting were the legitimate binding expression of the view of the...claim group as a whole.[372]

Nevertheless, it is possible that in a given case it may be necessary to enquire about the extent to which decision-by-public-meeting is either a traditional decision-making process or a process agreed and adopted by the group. (See Section 3.2 above at 'Is a meeting actually required at all?')

Mutually exclusive hierarchy of processes in s. 251B

The two paragraphs of s. 251B set out two alternative methods for authorising an applicant to file a claim and to deal with related matters. Paragraph (a) speaks of a mandatory traditional decision-making process applicable to 'authorising things of that kind', and paragraph (b) speaks of a decision-making process 'agreed to and adopted by' the native title claim group.[373]

Two general features of the scheme set out by s. 251B can be noted:

- The two paragraphs have been interpreted by the courts as *mutually exclusive*: that is, an authorisation decision is made either by a mandatory traditional process, or an adopted and agreed process, but not both.[374]
- The two paragraphs are arranged hierarchically: paragraph (b) only applies if paragraph (a) does not — there is no 'choice' between the two.[375] Specifically, the evidence must establish as a matter of fact that there is no applicable traditional process before a paragraph (b) process can be relied on.[376]

---

372 *Coyne v Western Australia* [2009] FCA 533 [51].

373 Note that the term 'decision-making process' may refer to one or both of two separate concepts. The first is the *criterion for a valid decision*, i.e. the rule for determining whether a particular proposal has been approved or rejected. The criterion may require a majority of individuals, or a super-majority; or it may require the unanimous agreement of various constitutent subgroups; or it may require the assent of some veto-wielding individuals. By contrast, the process for reaching a decision may involve a number of different elements such as the opportunity for discussion, the attempt to reach consensus, the making of recommendations by respected elders, the conduct of a secret or open ballot, etc.

374 *Risk v Northern Territory* [2006] FCA 404 [77], citing *Dieri People v South Australia* [2003] FCA 187 [57].

375 Justice Lindgren said in *Harrington-Smith on behalf of the Wongatha People v Western Australia (No. 9)* [2007] FCA 31 [1230]: 'A native title claim group is not given a choice between traditional and non-traditional processes of decision-making. Consistently with the NTA's recognition of traditional laws and customs as the source of native title, s 251B recognises traditional laws and customs as the primary source of the decision-making process. It is only if there is no traditional process of decision-making in relation to authorising things of the "application for a determination of native title" kind, that para. (b) applies.'

376 See *Daniel v Western Australia* [2002] FCA 1147 [18]; *Duren v Kiama Council* [2001] FCA 1363 [5]; *Combined Mandingalbay Yidinji-Gunggandji Claim v Queensland* [2004] FCA 1703 [42].

These two propositions appear to be quite severe — and in a way that does not seem closely connected with any particular policy objective. The distinction between a traditional process and an agreed process will no doubt strike anthropologists as artificial.[377] And it seems like a strange reason for a claim to fail — that a claim group whose members have agreed and adopted a process of decision-making might nevertheless be faced with a judicial finding that a mandatory traditional decision-making process should have applied (despite the group's choice).[378]

In fact it is extremely rare for a claim to fail solely on this basis — usually there are other, more substantive problems that cause the court to find the authorisation to be defective.[379] In practice it should be possible for a claim group to avoid problems under the severe dichotomy of s. 251B by using one of the following strategies:

- clarifying that the process is indeed a traditional one, but that the group has merely (and superfluously) 'ratified' that process, confirming the requirements of the traditional process and undertaking to obey it;
- asserting that there is no traditional decision-making process that is directly applicable to decisions of this kind, so the claim group has agreed and adopted a process that is *consistent with* or *incorporates elements of* traditional decision-making principles or processes.

Each of these is addressed immediately below.

Traditional decision-making process

Before discussing the case law dealing with traditional decision-making processes, it is worth saying something about what these processes might actually look like. I cannot hope to capture the richness and complexity of such deeply contextual political systems and will make no attempt to do so here. But faced with the bare generic and abstract words of the *Native Title Act*, it may help to note some of the frequently recurring *elements* of traditional decision-making that can be observed in the native title case law. The following are some such elements, though they are certainly not exhaustive, universal or necessarily consistent with each other:

- Emphasis on views or decisions by elders or 'law bosses' — perhaps giving elders the 'final say' or else simply according greater weight to their views.[380]

---

377 See T Bauman & C Stacey, 'Agreement-making and free, prior and informed consent in the Australian native title landscape' in L Crowl, P Matbob & P D'Arcy (eds), *Pacific-Asian partnerships in resource development*, Divine Word University Press, Madang, 2014.

378 *Harrington-Smith on behalf of the Wongatha People v Western Australia (No. 9)* [2007] FCA 31 [2428]–[2430].

379 I was only able to identify one case in which the 'conflation' of traditional and agreed processes appeared to be the primary problem: *Evans v Native Title Registrar* [2004] FCA 1070. That case has not been cited in other decisions.

380 E.g. *Combined Gunggandji Claim v Queensland* [2005] FCA 575. This can go even to the extent of not requiring the consultation or notification of the rest of the claim group: *Que Noy v Northern Territory* [2007] FCA 1888 [35]. Appeal against this decision was dismissed: *Foster v Que Noy* [2008] FCAFC 56.

- Emphasis on subgroups (and even sub-subgroups) speaking as units on behalf of their members and their smaller areas of country. Again, this may amount to smaller groups having the 'final say' about their estates or about matters concerning their family-group, or else it may simply amount to 'bloc voting'.
- Emphasis on consensus, consultation, giving everyone a chance to speak and be heard, avoidance of outright open conflict. (This may involve the 'withdrawal' of people who disagree.)
- Certain individuals having particular responsibility or authority in particular areas because of their various associations with the area (descent, skin and associated dreamings, place of birth, place of being raised, relatives buried there, etc.) This may require their presence at any meeting that proposes to discuss business related to that area.[381]

(There have been a number of cases where particular individuals have asserted either that they are the only person authorised under traditional law and custom — with no need for any group decision — or else that they are the only person with the cultural authority to grant authorisation to any applicant.[382] While these assertions are certainly technically possible within the *Native Title Act*, they have rarely succeeded because the evidence has not been sufficient to support them.)

Native title barrister Susan Phillips has remarked that the *Native Title Act's* authorisation provisions amount to 'the unilateral imposition of a requirement that authority devolve upon an individual/s', and that this may in some cases be 'antithetical to the law and custom being relied upon'.[383] In defence of the *Native Title Act* it could be argued that this devolution of authority need not form a significant part of the legal relationships between the claim group, the applicant and the broader legal system. The actual legal authority of the applicant can be heavily limited by the terms of their authorisation, as described below in Section 4.1 at 'Conditional appointment'. In such cases the applicant can be seen as a mere agent or an interface between the claim group and the legal system. But following through with Phillips' critique, in many situations the group dynamics created by the appointment of an applicant with all the varied perceptions or assumptions about the importance and function of that role — may be in considerable tension with longstanding customary norms.[384] The

---

381 See D Ritter & M Garnett, *Building the perfect beast: native title lawyers and the practise of native title lawyering*, Land, Rights, Laws: Issues of Native Title, vol. 1, no. 30, Native Title Research Unit, AIATSIS, Canberra, 1999, p. 4.

382 *Dingaal Tribe v Queensland* [2003] FCA 999; *Starkey v South Australia* [2011] FCA 456.

383 S Phillips, 'The authorisation trail', *Indigenous Law Bulletin*, vol. 4, no. 28, pp. 13–15, March 2000.

384 For example, irrespective of its actual legal significance, claim groups and applicants alike may interpret the applicant role as a decision-making role, which may be in tension with norms of egalitarianism and self-help. Or the appointment of a younger person who is better capable of interacting with the English-language legal system may be in tension with norms around the status of elders.

native title claims process (and associated agreement-making) is a fairly novel kind of group activity that may not have any analogous precedent in pre-colonial or even pre-1993 life. As will be seen, the translation of traditional decision-making processes into this new sphere can be a fraught exercise.

Proving tradition and compliance with tradition

Traditional Aboriginal or Torres Strait Islander law and custom is treated in Australian courts as a matter of fact to be determined on evidence.[385] Accordingly, where applicants rely on a traditional decision-making process for their authorisation they must bring evidence to prove (a) what the traditional process requires, and (b) that the traditional requirements have been complied with.[386]

For example, if the applicant's authorisation is said to be given by a small group of elders from the claim group, the court will require some evidence establishing the elders' own authority to make that decision on behalf of the claim group.[387] Depending on the circumstances of the case, there may be extensive affidavit (or in-person) evidence from claim group members in addition to expert anthropological evidence[388] or, alternatively, the court may be satisfied on the basis of quite brief anthropological evidence.[389] In *Reid* Finn J did not consider that evidence from elders beyond the claim group was effective to support the applicant's contention that his authority was supported by traditional law and custom. The relevant evidence should be about the laws and customs observed and acknowledged by the actual members of the claim group.[390] A total lack of evidence about elders' authority has led to applications' authorisation being rejected.[391] This is but one example of the general proposition set out above in Section 3.2 at 'Is a meeting actually required at all?', that if authorisation is to be granted by a smaller 'representative' body within the claim group, the authority of that smaller body (whether under traditional law and custom or under a process agreed and adopted by the group) must be established by proof.[392]

It is important to recognise that claim group members might not share the same understanding of what tradition requires. Disagreement about traditional law and custom does not necessarily mean that tradition has been lost, although strong and sustained

385 This is basically the same as for proving Chinese or French law in Australian courts — it is a matter of expert evidence rather than legal submission.

386 See *Van Hemmen on behalf of The Kabi Kabi People 3 v Queensland* [2007] FCA 1185; *Ward v Northern Territory* [2002] FCA 1477 [27]–[41].

387 E.g. *Harrington-Smith on behalf of the Wongatha People v Western Australia (No. 9)* [2007] FCA 31 [3425], [3742]–[3750].

388 *Risk v Northern Territory* [2006] FCA 404; *Daniel v Western Australia* [2002] FCA 1147.

389 *Que Noy v Northern Territory* [2007] FCA 1888 [32]–[34]. Appeal against the decision was dismissed: *Foster v Que Noy* [2008] FCAFC 56.

390 *Reid v South Australia* [2007] FCA 1479 [43].

391 *Brown v South Australia* [2009] FCA 206.

392 *Moran v Minister for Land and Water Conservation (NSW)* [1999] FCA 1637 [34]; *Western Australia v Strickland* [2000] FCA 652 [77]–[78]; *Johnson, in the matter of Lawson v Lawson* [2001] FCA 894 [25]–[28]; *Anderson v Western Australia* [2003] FCA 1423 [40].

inconsistencies may make it difficult for the court to conclude that the claim group as a whole has an applicable traditional decision-making process.[393] Often Indigenous groups will not previously have had any reason to explicitly articulate the rules of decision-making, and the process of critically analysing, articulating, translating and applying these rules may result in different interpretations.[394]

In one of the *Combined Mandingalbay Yidinji-Gunggandji* decisions,[395] Spender J considered evidence about a meeting at which claim group members discussed the role of elders and subgroups in traditional decision-making. It was clear that some of the persons present did not consider the process followed by the meeting to be consistent with traditional law and custom; nevertheless, his Honour found that the authorisation decision was validly made.[396] It is not explicit in Spender J's reasons whether the decision was construed as a traditional one or an agreed one — though on appeal the Full Court interpreted his Honour as having approved the process under s. 251B(b).[397] (In another case, the court accepted that dissatisfaction with traditional decision-making had led the claim group to agree and adopt a new process under s. 251B(b).)[398] It is therefore possible at a meeting to deal with disagreements about traditional decision-making by agreeing and adopting a process.

Where a traditional process is used and only later challenged in court, things may be more difficult. The very fact of the challengers' disagreement weakens the applicants' version of tradition — though not necessarily fatally, as mentioned. If the only evidence about tradition is given by claim group members, the judge will have to weigh the competing accounts against each other. Expert anthropological evidence will therefore be important in providing an additional perspective and evidentiary foundation. From the perspective of applicants and their representatives, litigating tradition in this way can be unattractive: it can be unpredictable, costly and may damage relationships within the claim group. In light of that, it may be prudent to have an explicit discussion about decision-making processes at the meeting (whether to clarify what tradition entails or to agree and adopt a process in the face of disagreement about tradition).[399]

393 On disputes about tradition generally, see *Neowarra v Western Australia* [2003] FCA 1402 [177]; *Jango v Northern Territory* [2006] FCA 318 [396], [449].

394 *Harrington-Smith on behalf of the Wongatha People v Western Australia (No. 9)* [2007] FCA 31 [998]; S Phillips, 'The authorisation trail', *Indigenous Law Bulletin*, vol. 4, no. 28, pp. 13–15, March 2000.

395 *Combined Mandingalbay Yidinji-Gunggandji Claim v Queensland* [2004] FCA 1703.

396 ibid. [36]–[43].

397 *Noble v Mundraby* [2005] FCAFC 212 [18].

398 *Lawson on behalf of the 'Pooncarie' Barkandji (Paakantyi) People v Minister for Land and Water Conservation (NSW)* [2002] FCA 1517 [19]–[20].

399 See e.g. *Butchulla People v Queensland* [2006] FCA 1063 [6]–[13]. Also S Phillips, 'The authorisation trail', *Indigenous Law Bulletin*, vol. 4, no. 28, pp. 13–15, March 200, p. 15: 'The fact that the authorisation process will require groups to examine the proper flow of authority from the members to their representative and back will confer a benefit on the groups so that they confront issues which might destabilise them at the threshold of the claim process. Describing and committing to a process, whatever its source, should assist groups to deal with some of the

Proving the absence or inapplicability of tradition

The cases demonstrate a shift over the last 15 years or so from a strong emphasis on traditional decision-making as the default position to a more relaxed approach today. In some of the early post-1998 cases courts appear to have assumed that a claim group which has maintained traditional law and custom in relation to the substantive matter of rights and interests in land would also have maintained traditional ways of making decisions.[400] Soon after it was introduced into the *Native Title Act*, Phillips remarked that s. 251B(b):

> …is a troubling proposition. It requires an admission on behalf of the native title claimant group that it has either lost or does not have knowledge of any process of decision-making according to traditional law and custom 'for authorising…things of that kind'.[401]

In recent times there seems to have been a move away from this position, recognising that traditional processes may not be capable of dealing with the technical and contested reality of the *Native Title Act*.[402] Specifically, the cases have emphasised the words 'things of that kind' in s. 251B. A traditional decision-making process will not engage s. 251B(a) unless it 'must be complied with in relation to authorising things of that kind' — namely, authorising a person or persons to make a native title determination application and to deal with matters arising in relation to it.

For example, French J said in one of the *Anderson* decisions:

> [I]t may well be the case, in connection with the procedural aspects of native title litigation, that there is no relevantly applicable traditional decision-making method. Native title litigation is not exactly a traditional activity.[403]

Similarly, his Honour said in one of the *Daniel* judgments:

> [Section 251B(a)] seems to allow for the recognition of a process applicable by way of analogy to decision-making relating to the institution of native title proceedings under the Act. For that is hardly a matter likely to have been contemplated explicitly by traditional law and custom. It may be that it is sufficient…to identify traditional decision-making

fundamental issues and material which a native title claim requires in a way which does not cause the native title procedures to be divisive.'

400 See *Moran v Minister for Land and Water Conservation (NSW)* [1999] FCA 1637 [48]: 'In meritorious cases, [satisfying s. 251B(a)] is unlikely to be an onerous requirement. Traditional laws and customs are likely to exist in cases where the claimant group still maintains a vigorous communal life.'

401 S Phillips, 'The authorisation trail', *Indigenous Law Bulletin*, vol. 4, no. 28, pp. 13–15, March 2000, para. 14.

402 Note even though reliance on a non-traditional process will not necessarily be taken to imply that the claim group has 'lost its culture', it will still be necessary to ensure that the manner of authorisation and the evidence brought in support of authorisation is consistent with the rest of the case for connection: *De Rose v South Australia* [2002] FCA 1342 [924]–[933].

403 *Anderson v Western Australia* [2003] FCA 1423 [46].

> applicable to the exercise of responsibility for, or authority over the land or waters in question. Nevertheless it should not be surprising if there is some difficulty in applying traditional decision-making processes, albeit by closest analogy, to the conferring of the kind of authority contemplated by s 251B.[404]

In *Brown v South Australia* an applicant claimed to be authorised by a group of senior men and women. The evidence showed that these elders had 'stated that the applicant was responsible for the women's dreaming in the claim area and had to speak for her grandfather's country'.[405] Justice Besanko did not agree that this constituted authorisation for the purposes of the *Native Title Act*: He said:

> It is far from clear that the statement by the elder men and women constitutes an authorisation to make the native title determination application and deal with matters arising in relation to it.[406]

This last example shows that tradition's inapplicability to 'things of that kind' can pose a problem for applicants who seek to rely on s. 251B(a). But the ability to argue that traditional processes are inapplicable can be useful where applicants are seeking to rely on an agreed and adopted process under s. 251B(b). Indeed, as mentioned, applicants must in theory *disprove* the existence of an applicable traditional process as a precondition to being able to rely on s. 251B(b).[407]

An important decision on this point was *Lawson on behalf of 'Pooncarie' Barkandji (Paakantyi) People.*[408] In a previous decision Stone J had made findings about a particular traditional decision-making process whereby each family's 'headperson' would make decisions on behalf of the entire group. In the current case, several people wanted to replace the applicant via a different decision-making process involving individual voting at community meetings. In making the application under s. 66B, the replacement applicant did not directly challenge the traditional decision-making process but argued instead that that process did not apply to decisions of the kind *now* required in respect of the application. Justice Stone characterised their argument as follows:

---

404 *Daniel v Western Australia* [2002] FCA 1147 [14]. See also *Dann v Western Australia* [2011] FCA 99 [7]; *P.C. (name withheld) on behalf of the Njamal People v Western Australia* [2007] FCA 1054 [17].

405 *Brown v South Australia* [2009] FCA 206 [39].

406 ibid.

407 *Harrington-Smith on behalf of the Wongatha People v Western Australia (No. 9)* [2007] FCA 31 [2428]–[2430]; *Anderson v Western Australia* [2003] FCA 1423 [46]. In some decided cases the relevant decision-making process used by the group has been dealt with under s. 251B(b) rather than s. 251(a) because it was not a process dictated entirely by traditional law and custom, even though it utilised important elements or principles taken from tradition: e.g. *Dingaal Tribe v Queensland* [2003] FCA 999 [35]–[37]; *Dann v Western Australia* [2011] FCA 99 [7]; *Akiba on behalf of the Torres Strait Islanders of the Regional Seas Claim Group v Queensland (No. 2)* [2010] FCA 643 [929].

408 *Lawson on behalf of 'Pooncarie' Barkandji (Paakantyi) People v Minister for Land and Water Conservation (NSW)* [2002] FCA 1517.

> As I understand this submission it is that the traditional decision-making process has broken down and is *unable to cope* with the decisions required in respect of a native title application. As counsel for the Applicants expressed, experience since the claimant application was first made shows that the traditional decision-making process has been 'unable to sustain' the Claim Group which therefore has had resort to the more direct approach of having the members of the Claim Group directly vote on the issues relevant to this application.[409] (emphasis added)

Justice Stone agreed with the replacement applicant. Her Honour considered the evidence and concluded that:

> ...the history of difficulties in this matter supports the Applicants' claims that the Claim Group does not have a traditional decision-making process *capable of progressing the application*.[410] (emphasis added)

This is significant because it recognises the claim group's ability to move away from a traditional process that is not working well. An additional reason for Stone J's acceptance of the inapplicability of (or departure from) tradition was that the people at the meeting unanimously accepted a different decision-making process. Her Honour cited *Holborow* in support of that point, a case where French J said:

> The fact that the great bulk of members of the native title claim group were prepared to adopt the decision-making process used in this case contraindicates the existence of a mandatory traditional decision-making method.[411]

Note that a formal resolution is not required for a group to establish that it is not bound by any traditional process — the context or conduct of the meeting, or subsequent conduct, may provide the necessary evidence.[412] As mentioned above in Section 3.2 at 'Will opposition by a minority prevent authorisation?', applicants or opponents alike generally find it difficult to convince courts that there is an applicable traditional decision-making process that requires unanimity or allows vetos to particular individuals.[413] Whether this is evidence of a subtle 'majoritarian bias' in the law, or simply a consequence of the actual rarity of such decision-making processes, is beyond the scope of this book.

---

409 ibid. [20].

410 ibid. [22]. See also *Butchulla People v Queensland* [2006] FCA 1063 [32].

411 *Holborow v Western Australia* [2002] FCA 1428 [50]; *N.C. (deceased) v Western Australia (No. 2)* [2013] FCA 70 [79].

412 See e.g. *N.C. (deceased) v Western Australia (No. 2)* [2013] FCA 70 [79]–[80].

413 E.g. *T.R. (deceased) on behalf of the Kariyarra People v Western Australia* [2014] FCA 734 [46]–[48]; *Stock v Western Australia* [2014] FCA 179 [22]–[23]; *Lawson on behalf of the 'Pooncarie' Barkandji (Paakantyi) People v Minister for Land and Water (NSW)* [2002] FCA 1517 [25].

Scale of traditional decision-making

The discussion above dealt with situations where traditional decision-making processes existed but did not specifically apply to native title matters, or where the processes had fallen out of usefulness. Another situation in which existing traditional processes might not be required to be followed under s. 251B(a) is where the native title claim group is an aggregation of smaller groups who have their own traditional processes, but where there is no collective process that covers the entire claim group. This situation arises because there is no legal or anthropological requirement for the group holding the rights and interests to have any unified political organisation and authority. (See Section 3.1 above at 'Social or cultural coherence not required'.)

So where a claim covers a number of subgroups which do not share a common traditional process for making decisions, it will be necessary for members to agree and adopt a novel process.[414] That process might or might not share elements in common with the traditional processes of the smaller groups.

An interesting example is from the *Combined Gunggandji* proceedings,[415] where the claim group acted 'allegedly in accordance with traditional law and custom' by referring the question of authorisation to the elders. Justice Dowsett found that the aggregate claim group (consisting of subgroups with different traditional processes) did not have its own traditional decision-making process, despite the belief of claim group members. Instead, the claim group had agreed and adopted a process under s. 251B(b) whereby they undertook to abide by the elders' decision.[416]

Another example is provided by *Akiba*, in which Finn J found that the process by which the claim group had authorised the application was not traditional because there was no process by which all the Torres Strait Islanders as a single group had ever made decisions of this kind.[417] The process that had been adopted — meetings held for each of the four 'island clusters' — did draw on traditional practices but was 'no more than quite reasonable improvisation in the circumstances'.[418]

Non-traditional decision-making process

Assuming that there is no traditional process (whether because of the novelty of the task, the unfamiliar constituency for decision-making, the evolution of cultural patterns away from traditional models, or the inadequacy of tradition to cope with the extent of contestation involved in native title processes) the only way for a claim group to authorise an application is through a process they agree and adopt: s. 251B(b).

---

414 *Coyne v Western Australia* [2009] FCA 533; *Butchulla People v Queensland* [2006] FCA 1063 [30]; *Noble v Mundraby* [2005] FCAFC 212 (cited in *Roe v Western Australia (No. 2)* [2011] FCA 102 [15]); *Daniel v Western Australia* [2002] FCA 1147 [51]; *Holborow v Western Australia* [2002] FCA 1428 [42].

415 *Combined Gunggandji Claim v Queensland* [2005] FCA 575.

416 ibid. [2], referring to *Combined Mandingalbay Yidinji-Gunggandji Claim v Queensland* [2004] FCA 1703.

417 *Akiba on behalf of the Torres Strait Islanders of the Regional Seas Claim Group v Queensland (No. 2)* [2010] FCA 643 [928].

418 ibid. [929].

The most commonly used process under s. 251B(b) is the standard formal group meeting, often with decisions by simple majority voting through a show of hands. Other aspects may be built in, such as representation of subgroups in decision-making, a special role for elders, a process of consultation before and during meetings, and the like.

Circularity, resolutions versus proof by conduct

An immediately obvious puzzle in s. 251B(b) is that it seems necessary for a claim group to employ a method of decision-making in order to agree and adopt a method of decision-making. This suggests a circular recursion similar to the old question about the chicken and the egg.[419] This logical impasse can be sidestepped where there is no disagreement about the process to be adopted. The unanimous adoption of a decision-making process solves the problem conveniently.[420] Similarly, where there is no actual disagreement about the substantive decisions there will be no basis for challenging the adoption of the decision-making process even if people fervently disagree about it.[421] But where there is substantive disagreement at the meeting about both the decision-making process and the substantive result, the court will need to tackle the apparent circularity at some point. For example, if there are some people at a meeting who say that the decision-making process should be unanimous and others who say a majority vote is sufficient, surely the court can only resolve the anterior question of the decision-making process by preferring one process or the other?

In fact, courts generally approach this issue by treating the 'adoption' of a decision-making process as a matter of fact to be proven, rather than a decision to be made.[422] So a claim group can be found to have agreed and adopted a decision-making process even if they have not passed a resolution to this effect or dealt with the matter explicitly at all. The Full Court in *Noble v Mundraby* accepted that the adoption of a process could be proved solely by reference to the behaviour of the claim group members:

> Section 251B does not require proof of a system of decision-making beyond proof of the process used to arrive at the particular decision in question. The section accommodates a situation where a native title claim group agrees to follow a particular procedure for a particular decision even if other procedures are normally used for other decisions. Nor does s 251B require a formal agreement to the process adopted for the making of a particular decision.

---

419 The answer, of course, is that the egg came first because the dinosaurs that evolved into birds hatched from eggs, so that the very first animal we would be happy to call a 'bird' necessarily hatched from an egg too. Unfortunately no such neat solution exists in the world of native title authorisation.

420 See e.g. *N.C. (deceased) v Western Australia (No. 2)* [2013] FCA 70 [33].

421 See *P.C. (name withheld) on behalf of the Njamal People v Western Australia* [2007] FCA 1054; *Noble v Mundraby* [2005] FCAFC 212 [18]; *Daniel v Western Australia* [2002] FCA 1147 [34].

422 Justice French in *Bolton on behalf of the Southern Noongar Families v Western Australia* [2004] FCA 760 [44] said that a decision via s. 251B(b) was 'no light requirement' and that the authorisation process 'must be able to be traced to a decision of the native title claim group who adopt that process'. His Honour did not, however, say that there had to be a decision to adopt the process. See French J's decision in *Daniel v Western Australia* [2002] FCA 1147 [51].

> Agreement within the contemplation of s 251B may be proved by the conduct of the parties. There was evidence in this case that the claim group conducted itself at the meeting on the basis that it agreed to a vote by the members of the group to determine the question of authorisation. All persons present voted in favour of the motion. Nobody is recorded as leaving the meeting or refusing to vote or in any other way conducting to indicate dissent from the course adopted. There was thus evidence from the conduct of the claim group on which the primary judge could base his conclusion that the requirements of s 251B were satisfied.[423]

The Full Court said later in that judgment:

> We are unable to accept the submission that there must be a system of decision-making, separately agreed and adopted, before the members of the native title claim group can validly resolve to remove a person from the group that is 'the applicant' in a native title determination application.[424]

(Although some early cases reviewed substantial evidence about the claim group's habitual manner of making decisions over a considerable period of time,[425] there is nothing in the legislation to prevent claim groups from switching from one process to another even in a relatively short period.)[426]

Justice Stone in *Pooncarie* noted that s. 251B does not require a process to be agreed and adopted by *all* of the members of the claim group. Her Honour took this to mean that the *Native Title Act* will not impose a requirement for unanimity in relation to the anterior adoption of the decision-making process.[427] That was also the approach taken by Collier J in *Butterworth*, a case where nine family groups agreed with a proposed decision-making process, three disagreed

---

423 *Noble v Mundraby* [2005] FCAFC 212 [18], cited by cases including *N.C. (deceased) v Western Australia (No. 2)* [2013] FCA 70; *Jurruru People v Western Australia* [2012] FCA 2; *Fesl v Delegate of the Native Title Registrar* [2008] FCA 1469.

424 *Noble v Murgha* [2005] FCAFC 211. Cf. *Wharton on behalf of the Kooma People v Queensland* [2003] FCA 790 [42], cited in *Brown v South Australia* [2009] FCA 206 [23], suggesting two distinct steps: agreement to a particular process and then employment of that process to make the substantive authorisation decision. The apparent conflict may be resolved by treating the 'two distinct steps' idea as a conceptual framework rather than a literal requirement.

425 *Daniel v Western Australia* [2002] FCA 1147; *P.C. (name withheld) on behalf of the Njamal People v Western Australia* [2007] FCA 1054.

426 E.g. *Lawson on behalf of 'Pooncarie' Barkandji (Paakantyi) People v Minister for Land and Water Conservation (NSW)* [2002] FCA 1517; *Butchulla People v Queensland* [2006] FCA 1063 [32]; *N.C. (deceased) v Western Australia (No. 2)* [2013] FCA 70.

427 *Lawson on behalf of the 'Pooncarie' Barkandji (Paakantyi) People v Minister for Land and Water Conservation (NSW)* [2002] FCA 1517 [25]. Cited with approval in *Harrington-Smith on behalf of the Wongatha People v Western Australia (No. 9)* [2007] FCA 31 [1265]; *P.C. (name withheld) on behalf of the Njamal People v Western Australia* [2007] FCA 1054 [22]; *Fesl v Delegate of the Native Title Registrar* [2008] FCA 1469 [68]–[71].

and four were not represented at the meeting.[428] In that case the decision-making process was found to be adopted even though the relevant process required 'consensus'; consensus was held not to require unanimity. Perhaps significantly in that case, Collier J also examined the evidence about the proportion of individual attendees who supported or opposed the decision-making process; the fact that a clear majority of individuals agreed was taken to confirm the correctness of the decision.[429]

Justice McKerracher's judgment in *N.C. (deceased)*[430] is the most recent and comprehensive authority for a flexible, pragmatic approach to the 'agreement and adoption' issue. In that case the fact that the chair of the meeting allowed time for everyone to express a view, and nobody expressed any dissent as to the process adopted, overcame any later objections about the absence of a formal decision to adopt those processes.[431] In line with *Pooncarie* and *Butterworth*, McKerracher J explicitly rejected the proposition that a decision-making process needs to be adopted unanimously but did not articulate what the relevant criterion was. He said that '[o]n any view of the matter, the decision-making process was reasonable' and that the absence of any express dissent at the time was sufficient to support the inferred conclusion that the group had agreed and adopted the process that was in fact employed.[432]

In contrast to McKerracher J's approach to the question of adoption, Finn J's comments in *Akiba* tend to suggest that 'a significant level of subsequent acquiescence in the process adopted' is not sufficient to constitute agreement and adoption by the claim group as a whole.[433] Nevertheless, his Honour was willing to overlook any resultant flaw in authorisation, relying on s. 84D of the *Native Title Act*. In the recent decision in *T.J.*, Rares J found fault in a decision-making process where the first question on a secret ballot was whether voting by secret ballot would be 'agreed and adopted'.[434] Justice Rares noted that the subsequent questions on the ballot could not be decided if this first question was decided in the negative. His Honour noted that '[o]rdinarily, if a proposed process for voting is rejected, a meeting can agree to adopt a different voting or decision-making procedure and proceed with the other business notified'.[435] In this case, however, no alternative procedure was made available.

All in all, one would be forgiven for remaining somewhat unsatisfied by the case law's answer to the chicken-and-egg problem. There is no clearly articulated legal rule stating that the decision-making process can only be adopted by majority vote — and just as well, for such a rule would

---

428 *Butterworth on behalf of the Wiri Core Country Claim v Queensland (No. 2)* [2014] FCA 590 [14]–[20].

429 ibid. [14]–[28].

430 *N.C. (deceased) v Western Australia (No. 2)* [2013] FCA 70. See also *Butchulla People v Queensland* [2006] FCA 1063 [32]–[33].

431 See in particular *N.C. (deceased) v Western Australia (No. 2)* [2013] FCA 70 [91]–[94].

432 *N.C. (deceased) v Western Australia (No. 2)* [2013] FCA 70 [95], [97].

433 *Akiba on behalf of the Torres Strait Islanders of the Regional Seas Claim Group v Queensland (No. 2)* [2010] FCA 643 [928]–[929].

434 *T.J. v Western Australia* [2015] FCA 818 [95].

435 ibid.

be quite inappropriate in many cases.[436] Nor is there any particularly clear or intuitive answer for those claim group members whose preferred course of action is voted down by the operation of a decision-making process that they disagree with. In such situations the courts are in the unattractive position of having to decide either that the group is *incapable* of making a decision, or else that the decision ostensibly reached is valid despite the fact that people disagreed with the process. For lack of any other basis to make such a decision, it appears that courts may tend to favour the position of a clear majority (including, as in *Butterworth*, a majority of subgroups). This adds further support to the tentative 'majoritarian bias' hypothesis aired previously in Section 3.2 at 'Will opposition by a minority prevent authorisation?' The danger in that approach is that it may operate to the disadvantage of minority groups.

Although this book does not purport to provide any way out of the problem, there is certainly something to be said for an interpretation of s. 251B that leaves open the possibility that a group may simply be incapable of making a legally binding decision. That is, if the group lacks an applicable traditional decision-making process and cannot agree on any other kind of process, it is not inconceivable that, for the purposes of the *Native Title Act*, that is simply the end of the matter. On this view, no applicant can emerge from that situation validly claiming to be authorised via a decision-making process that was agreed and adopted by the group. This outcome may seem impractical or unfair from the perspective of the *Native Title Act's* statutory purposes, since it would act as a brake on the successful prosecution of claims. But if we are to take seriously the idea of Indigenous political groupings making their own decisions, it is difficult to see how the Australian legal system can resolve an apparent impasse at the most basic procedural level without simply resorting to 'picking winners'. That is, if a group of native title claimants are in evident disagreement about the fundamental procedural norms of how decisions are to be made, then for the Australian legal system to prefer one outcome over another would constitute the imposition of an external set of values. Perhaps such imposition is justifiable but the *Native Title Act* does not contain any justifying rationale nor provide any guidance about which procedural values should be imposed in the event of a deadlock. If the parliament does intend to create a majoritarian 'failsafe' — a default 'backstop' position if a group cannot come to its own decision internally — then this would be best articulated explicitly. But if, as seems evident in s. 251B, parliament intends to stay neutral in relation to intra-Indigenous decision-making, we should be prepared for the prospect of a group being simply unable to make any decision at all.

Proving the process and outcomes

The cases considered so far in this section (3.3, 'Authorisation in practice') make it clear that a court will require substantive evidence of the process of authorisation. In controversial cases, where people are likely to challenge an authorisation decision, this evidence will need to be comprehensive enough to withstand attack.[437] Nevertheless, Stone J's remarks in *Lawson* are relevant:

---

436 See Australian Law Reform Commission, *Connection to country: review of the Native Title Act 1993 (Cth)*, ALRC Report 126, at [10.56].

437 See e.g. *Bolton on behalf of the Southern Noongar Families v Western Australia* [2004] FCA 760; *Bodney v Western Australia* [2003] FCA 890.

> In an ideal situation one might wish for more precise identification of the Claim Group members and information on what proportion of the membership actually attended the meeting. I do not think, however, that the Act requires decisions of native title claim groups to be scrutinised in an overly technical or pedantic way. Unless a practical approach is adopted to such questions the ability of indigenous groups to pursue their entitlements under the Act will be severely compromised.[438]

Evidence about meetings is generally provided in affidavit form by the named applicants themselves,[439] by lawyers, anthropologists and by other people involved in the practical aspects of organising and running the meeting. Organisers' affidavits will typically attach copies of the newspaper advertisements (and depose to the dates they were published), copies of the mail-out and noticeboard notices (deposing to their respective dates and destinations), as well as attendance lists and minutes.[440]

The classic formulation of the matters to be proved in relation to an authorisation meeting is taken from one of the *Ward* decisions.[441] Justice O'Loughlin considered that the substance of the following questions should be addressed by the evidence, even though '[i]t may not be essential that these questions be answered on any formal basis such as in terms of the convening and conducting of a meeting in a commercial atmosphere':[442]

a) Who convened it and why was it convened?

b) To whom was notice given and how was it given?

c) What was the agenda for the meeting?

d) Who attended the meeting?

e) What was the authority of those who attended?

f) Who chaired the meeting or otherwise controlled the proceedings of the meeting?

g) By what right did that person have control of the meeting?

h) Was there a list of attendees compiled and, if so, by whom and when?

i) Was the list verified by a second person?

j) What resolutions were passed or decisions made?

---

438 *Lawson on behalf of the 'Pooncarie' Barkandji (Paakantyi) People v Minister for Land and Water (NSW)* [2002] FCA 1517 [28].

439 Note that a separate affidavit is required from each named applicant: *Doolan v Native Title Registrar* [2007] FCA 192 [66]–[67]; *Anderson on behalf of the Wulli Wulli People v Queensland* [2011] FCA 1158 [54].

440 Practitioners should be aware that minutes, depending on how detailed they are, may disclose the content of legal advice such that their full publication may waive legal professional privilege. Accordingly, a shorter 'outcomes' document may be more suitable for the purposes of proof.

441 *Ward v Northern Territory* [2002] FCA 171 [24]–[25]. It was used as a checklist in subsequent cases, e.g. *Tatow on behalf of the Iman People #2 v Queensland* [2011] FCA 802 [24]–[25].

442 *Ward v Northern Territory* [2002] FCA 171 [25].

k) Were they unanimous and, if not, what was the voting for and against a particular resolution?

l) Were there any apologies recorded?[443]

In relation to question (e), a process will be required to establish that the people attending and voting at the meeting are in fact members of the native title claim group.[444] In many cases this will be done by reference to descent from apical ancestors. But that will not be appropriate in every case, such as where there are 'multiple pathways' to the possession of rights and interests such that descent is neither necessary nor sufficient.[445] Commonly, a 'registration desk' is set up prior to a meeting, at which anthropologists or others will record names and take genealogical details or other information as necessary to determine which individuals are entitled to attend and participate.

Quality versus form in the decision-making process

The legal analysis above shows that the *formal* elements of authorisation processes loom large in judicial assessments. Who was invited, who attended, how were people notified? Was the decision-making process traditional or agreed? Was it followed?

One may well ask — what about the actual *quality* of decision-making? Not in the sense of 'reaching a good decision' (because the courts are explicitly not concerned with the merit or wisdom of the group's authorisation decision)[446] but rather the question of whether the decision-making process truly allowed the group as a whole to make a considered decision. If the decision was rushed, manipulated, dominated by only a few voices, based on false assumptions, afflicted by confusion or misunderstandings, can it still represent a valid decision for the purposes of the *Native Title Act*?

This question is raised partly in reference to the concept of 'free, prior and informed consent'. That concept is a crucial principle in the *United Nations Declaration on the Rights of Indigenous Peoples* and increasingly informs foreign and international law and practice in relation to indigenous peoples.[447] Although it is most relevant to actions taken by governments and third parties, it is

---

443 This checklist gives a good guide to the proper contents for minutes of the meeting: name of the claim group; meeting venue, date, start and finish times; attendance (including observers and organisers) and apologies; topics and summary of views expressed; resolutions passed (including proposers and seconders, numbers voting for, against, and abstaining).

444 *Bolton on behalf of the Southern Noongar Families v Western Australia* [2004] FCA 760; though note the flexible manner of addressing this in *Butchulla People v Queensland* [2006] FCA 1063.

445 J Grace, *Claimant group descriptions: beyond the strictures of the registration test*, Land, Rights, Laws: Issues of Native Title, vol. 2, no. 2, Native Title Research Unit, AIATSIS, Canberra, 1999, pp. 1–2, citing P Sutton, 'The system as it was straining to become: fluidity, stability, and Aboriginal country groups' in J Finalyson, B Rigsby & H Bek (eds), *Connection in native title: genealogies, kinship and groups*, CAEPR Research Monograph no. 13, ANU, Canberra, 1999.

446 *N.C. (deceased) v Western Australia (No. 2)* [2013] FCA 70 [76].

447 T Ward, 'The right to free, prior, and informed consent: indigenous people's participation rights within international law', *Northwestern Journal of International Human Rights*, vol. 10, no. 2, pp. 54–84, Winter 2011, p. 54.

also relevant to the way that intra-Indigenous decision-making is incorporated into the broader legal system. When governments decide to listen to a particular voice from an Indigenous group, in preference to other competing voices, that is unavoidably an exercise of power. When courts accept a particular outcome of a community meeting as binding on the group as a whole, this is similarly an exercise of power. The principle of free, prior and informed consent can only be satisfied via a group's representative if the appointment of the representative was also a free and informed decision of the group. In the context of native title claims the most pertinent and contentious scenario is where the authorisation or replacement of the applicant becomes a proxy for a decision to enter into an agreement with government or a mining company.[448]

In fact, there *is* scope in the current law for considerations about the quality of decision-making. It is possible that a validly called meeting in which the 'proper' process under s. 251B was followed may nevertheless be legally ineffective to authorise or de-authorise an applicant, if there are serious flaws in how the meeting was run. However, the cases do not set a particularly high bar and courts do appear more comfortable relying on the formal aspects of a meeting as indicators of its legal effectiveness.[449]

There are many considerations that may affect the substantive quality of decision-making at a meeting.[450] The selection of a chair for the meeting may be significant — a controversial choice or a chair who over- or under-intervenes may prevent a meeting from embodying a proper decision of the claim group.[451] Judges routinely emphasise the importance of giving differing views a sufficient opportunity to be heard. In *Barnes* a claim group meeting had resolved to replace two named applicants. Those two individuals complained that the claim group members had been

---

448 A variation on this theme occurred in *T.J. v Western Australia* [2015] FCA 818 where the authorisation meeting was fundamentally about whether the group would consent to a determination of native title that would be advantageous to a particular mining company.

449 There have been a number of cases in which bad information or false assumptions have been held to vitiate the outcome of a meeting. See e.g. *Weribone on behalf of the Mandandanji People v Queensland* [2013] FCA 255; *Carr on behalf of the Wellington Valley Wiradjuri People v Premier (NSW)* [2013] FCA 200. In *T.J. v Western Australia* [2015] FCA 818 a misleading notification and evidence that claim group members were in fact misled about the matters to be decided were among the reasons supporting Rares J's conclusion that the purported authorisation was invalid. By contrast, in *Butchulla People v Queensland* [2006] FCA 1063 [32] Kiefel J refused to find that a meeting was flawed simply because one family group (who did not attend the meeting) was mistaken in assuming that the meeting would be conducted according to a decision-making process that accorded them a veto over authorisation decisions.

450 For example, arguments about economic duress in an authorisation process were raised, albeit unsuccessfully, in *Johnson v Native Title Registrar* [2014] FCA 142.

451 See e.g. *Doctor on behalf of the Bigambul People v Queensland* [2010] FCA 1406 [42] where an allegation that a controversial person had co-chaired the meeting and direted people's voting was rejected. For a case where an indepednent chair was appointed and the court's positive view of the chair's conduct influenced the overall assessment of the decision-making process, see *N.C. (deceased) v Western Australia (No. 2)* [2013] FCA 70.

bullied and intimidated and that the meeting's outcomes were therefore legally ineffective.[452] Justice Collier examined all of the evidence (which involved some conflicting accounts of what happened at the meeting) and concluded that there was no bullying or 'railroading'. In particular her Honour found that the meeting was 'well-organised and well-facilitated', that all participants including the two outgoing applicants were 'given ample opportunity to advance their respective views'. Some of the facts that influenced this conclusion were:

- Before any resolutions were passed, the resolutions were displayed on a large screen in front of the participants at the meeting; they were moved and seconded; those in attendance were invited to speak for or against the resolution; and they were then voted on by a show of hands.
- Before [the resolution to de-authorise the current applicant] was passed, members of the existing applicant group were given the opportunity to address the meeting on the progress of the claim and what they had done for the claim during their time as applicant. Both [outgoing applicants] addressed the authorisation meeting at this time.
- Before [the resolution to authorise a new applicant] was passed, [NTRB] staff left the authorisation meeting for approximately 45 minutes to allow the respective family groups to decide on nominees for the proposed applicant group.[453]

Barnes demonstrates that courts will consider whether there have been 'effective processes' that give participants 'fair and reasonable opportunities to promote their views'. Some of the flaws that were alleged in that case, but ultimately found on the evidence not to have occurred, were that NTRB staff intervened in the group's deliberations and told the dissentient individuals to 'shut up'.[454] One may infer that, had these charges been substantiated, Collier J may have come to a different view about the adequacy of the decision-making process at the meeting.[455]

Similarly, in *N.C. (deceased)*[456] the court found that a contentious decision reached by only a slim majority was nevertheless an effective decision of the entire group. This was largely due to the integrity of the process achieved by the chair, an independent person who 'did an excellent job at keeping control and politely giving equal time to "for and against" arguments in relation to motions and amendments' and 'carefully explained the process and asked for an endorsement of the voting process' that had been used at a previous meeting.[457]

In *P.C. on behalf of the Njamal People* a meeting resolved to remove a named applicant because of his failure to sign a particular agreement with an outside party.[458] He had not attended the meeting. He later argued that the meeting's decision was invalid because the meeting had not

---

452 *Barnes on behalf of the Wangan and Jagalingou People v Queensland* [2010] FCA 533.

453 ibid. [22].

454 ibid.

455 For a similar set of allegations, which were similarly rejected, see *Doctor on behalf of the Bigambul People v Queensland* [2010] FCA 1406.

456 *N.C. (deceased) v Western Australia (No. 2)* [2013] FCA 70.

457 ibid. [35]–[36], [82], [87]–[92].

458 *P.C. (name withheld) on behalf of the Njamal People v Western Australia* [2007] FCA 1054.

been informed of the reasons for his refusal to sign. The court disagreed, saying that it was up to him to communicate his views to the rest of the group and that he had had ample opportunity to do so.[459] A similar outcome occurred in *Dann*.[460]

In *Daniel* the state government proposed to acquire land in the Ngarluma and Yindjibarndi claim area. An agreement was negotiated between the claimants and the state but one of the named applicants refused to sign. At a claim group meeting the group voted to replace the dissentient applicant with a person who was willing to enter into the agreement. The outgoing applicant opposed the replacement. In evidence he said that the claim group meetings in general were 'controlled by' the NTRB lawyers, that he and other claimants 'could not have a say' and that the lawyers would 'not listen or talk to them in a proper way'.[461] He did not attend the authorisation meeting in question but argued that it was flawed. Justice French accepted some of the arguments about problems in the way the meeting had been run but ultimately found that the meeting had validly resolved to remove the dissentient applicant:

> The process of decision-making undertaken on 12 August 2002 may be criticised as pressured by reason of the matters to which the decisions related, the magnitude of their impact on the lands of the claim group, the magnitude of the benefits that might flow under the State agreement, the limited time frame which persons there present were advised was available for finalising the State agreement, the input of the lawyers and the formal character of the resolutions which were eventually passed at the meeting. These factors have to be seen however in the context of the much longer period of negotiation which led up to the meeting of 10 July 2002 at which the claim group authorised execution of the State agreement. They received advice from their lawyers on 12 August. That advice may have been emphatic. However, it is not to be supposed that members of the claim group which had been for so long engaged in processes associated with their native title determination application and with the negotiation of the State agreement were not capable of making an informed decision reflected in the resolutions which were eventually passed. In my opinion, the applicant, Mr David Walker, is as a result of the decisions taken at the meeting of 12 August 2002, no longer authorised by the claim group to make the application or to deal with matters arising in relation to it.[462]

---

459 ibid. [35], [39]. Justice Bennett also rejected (at [37]) an argument that claim group meetings are analogous to voluntary associations, in which members are required to act reasonably in respect of each other and may complain to the court if improperly treated.

460 *Dann v Western Australia* [2011] FCA 99, especially [44].

461 *Daniel v Western Australia* [2002] FCA 1147 [46].

462 ibid. [52].

Although this *outcome* suggests that courts will not be quick to overturn or ignore the outcomes of meetings on the basis of the quality of decision-making, the *reasoning* suggests that it could happen. If, for example, the relevant decision had been forced into a single meeting rather than stretched over several months, the result may have been different.

Another, more recent case regarding the Yindjibarndi people gives even more support to the idea that confusion, manipulation or lack of proper understanding may render an apparently valid decision ineffective. In *T.J.*[463] Rares J found a number of procedural flaws in a purported decision that would have authorised a replacement applicant and the amendment of the application so as to give up any claim to exclusive possession native title. Among the problems Rares J identified was the fact that several members of the erstwhile replacement applicant gave evidence of their understanding of the proposed resolutions which was directly contradictory to the actual legal effect of those resolutions. They were unaware of the consequences of the decisions they were effectively asking the rest of the group to make.[464] The reason for this, as Rares J found, was that a mining company had 'orchestrated' the voting procedure 'to a considerable degree' and was actively seeking the outcome that would have transpired had the authorisation decision been successful.[465] Justice Rares stated that, even if the process had satisfied the requirements of s. 66B of the *Native Title Act* in formal terms, he would nevertheless have exercised his discretion not to grant the orders sought. Among the reasons for that conclusion were: (a) the mining company's role in the process; (b) the fact that valuable shopping vouchers were provided to some of those who voted, to the exclusion of those who might have voted against the proposed measures; and (c) the high likelihood and, indeed, the established fact that people would be misled by the circulated notice about the nature and consequences of the decisions proposed.[466] This case demonstrates that substantive aspects of decision-making may be relevant to its legal effectiveness, such that mere formal compliance may not be enough.

Overall, the cases indicate a pragmatic approach by the courts. The decisions that native title groups must make are often difficult and contentious and there may not be sufficient time or resources for longer or more thorough processes of imparting information, consultation and consensus-building. Interestingly, I was unable to find any cases in which the very format of decision-making — the 'big meeting' — was criticised for being an inappropriate mechanism for good quality decision-making.[467] Given the difficulty in transmitting complex legal information across cultural divides, and given the potential constraints that the meeting format may impose on effective communication, it is worth thinking about whether the 'big meeting' is always the best forum. In many cases, multiple informal,

---

463 *T.J. v Western Australia* [2015] FCA 818.

464 ibid. [101]–[106].

465 ibid. [115].

466 *T.J. v Western Australia* [2015] FCA 818 [114]–[117].

467 Although in *T.J. v Western Australia* [2015] FCA 818 [91] there was a suggestion that a complete lack of opportunity to discuss the issues at hand could render a decision invalid, in circumstances where the written material circulated beforehand was inappropriate to the audience and indeed objectively misleading. See also T Bauman, '"You mob all agree?" The chronic emergency of culturally competent engaged Indigenous problem solving', *Indigenous Law Bulletin*, vol. 6, no. 29, August 2007 (<http://www.austlii.edu.au/au/journals/ILB/2007/44.html>, viewed 9 August 2016).

small-group discussions may be more effective in reaching a truly considered group decision, which can then be finally expressed or recorded in a 'big meeting'. Future researchers may wish to consider how well the current law reflects the principle of free, prior and informed consent, and whether it is open to courts to draw on the international case law to inform their decisions in this regard.

4. Actions by the applicant

The previous two chapters dealt with the general concepts of authorisation, native title claim group and applicant, and covered the processes by which a claim group can authorise an applicant. This chapter focuses on what comes afterwards — the exercise by applicants of their functions as applicant. How far does the applicant's autonomy extend and what rules constrain how it can act?

Under s. 251B the claim group authorises an applicant both to make an application and to 'deal with matters arising in relation to' the application. There is a broad range of matters that could conceivably be included in this second limb:

- engaging, retaining and terminating the services of lawyers;
- making amendments to the Form 1, including changing the claim group description, claim area description, combining or splitting the claim;
- making or responding to interlocutory applications (e.g. seeking or resisting orders for strike-out; seeking to join another claim as respondent or resisting another party becoming respondent on the principal claim; seeking costs from another party; applications about evidentiary issues or scheduling; or appealing from a court's decision);
- discontinuing the native title determination application;
- negotiating and agreeing to a consent determination, or proceeding with contested litigation;
- negotiating and making future acts agreement (see Chapter 7 below).

However, the law does not necessarily or in all circumstances allow applicants to take such actions without specific authorisation or direction by the native title claim group. The next section explains the circumstances in which applicants do and do not enjoy this sort of autonomy, and the following section (4.2, 'Disagreement, disability or death within the applicant') goes further to examine the consequences of active opposition from within the claim group.

4.1 Extent of applicant autonomy

Is an applicant, once authorised, given delegated powers to make decisions in respect of a claim? Or is an applicant a mere name on the paperwork, a mere formality made necessary by the unincorporated nature of the claim group? In fact, native title determination applications have been described as 'representative proceedings', akin to 'class actions'.[468] As Reeves J pointed out in *Levinge*, this means that:

---

468 *Tigan v Western Australia* [2010] FCA 993 [10]; *Butchulla People v Queensland* [2006] FCA 1063 [39]; *Ankamuthi People v Queensland* [2002] FCA 897 [7]; *Bullen v Western Australia* [2010] FCA 900 [50] (not disturbed on appeal); *Augustine v Western Australia* [2013] FCA 338 [10]; *Doolan v Native Title Registrar* [2007] FCA 192 [62]; *Close on behalf of the Githabul People #2 v Queensland* [2010] FCA 828 [2], [25]; *Levinge on behalf of the Gold Coast Native Title Group v Queensland* [2012] FCA 1321

> the authorised Applicant has commenced the proceedings on behalf of the persons who 'according to their traditional laws and customs hold the common or group rights and interests comprising the particular native title' over this claim area: see s 61(1) of the NTA. Thus, while the authorised Applicant had the authority to commence the proceedings and has the exclusive authority to continue to deal with them, the proceedings remain throughout those of the [native title claim group]. It is its native title claim.[469]

A claim group does not need to give applicants specific directions covering all of the eventualities that may arise during the course of the claim proceedings. Section 62A of the *Native Title Act* confirms that the applicant 'may deal with all matters arising under this Act in relation to the application'. As will be seen in the cases below, in the absence of any indication to the contrary a properly authorised applicant has the power to take any step in the proceedings. Section 62A also has the effect that the claim group cannot take steps in the proceedings *except* via the actions of the applicant (though the position is somewhat different in the case of ILUAs, see Section 7.1 below).[470]

But the authorisation given by the claim group to the applicant is not necessarily 'all or nothing' or 'once and for all'. The initial act of authorisation can place specific limitations on what an applicant can do (see below in this section at 'Conditional appointment'). Further, under s. 84D(1) of the *Native Title Act* the court can order the applicant to demonstrate that they are authorised to be 'dealing with a matter…arising in relation to' the application. An order under s. 84D(1) can be made on the court's own motion or on the application of a party to the proceedings or of a member of the native title claim group.[471] If authorisation is lacking then the court may make such other orders as appropriate: s. 84D(4)(b).

A quite separate way in which the applicant's authority may be qualified arises from the fact that many steps in the proceedings require an exercise of the court's discretion. When considering how to exercise that discretion, the court may wish to be satisfied that applicants have consulted with the claim group. Examples of this are provided in the cases below.

Of course, when we speak of applicants 'taking steps' in the proceedings, we are generally referring to *their lawyers* taking the relevant steps. Except in the case of self-represented litigants, in practice it is the lawyers who will file documents, make submissions and do the many other things that we normally think of the applicant 'doing'. In the discussion that follows, therefore, when a reference is made to an applicant doing something this may well be a reference to the applicant's lawyers doing the thing on the instructions of the applicant. But in some of the cases, individual members of the applicant have purported to act directly in the proceedings. In other

---

[47]; *Weribone on behalf of the Mandandanji People v Queensland* [2011] FCA 1169; *Roe on behalf of the Goolarabooloo and Jabirr Jabirr Peoples v Western Australia* [2011] FCA 421 [36].

469 *Levinge on behalf of the Gold Coast Native Title Group v Queensland* [2012] FCA 1321 [47].

470 See *Anderson on behalf of the Wulli Wulli People v Queensland* [2011] FCA 1158 [49]; *Close on behalf of the Githabul People #2 v Queensland* [2010] FCA 828 [32]–[33]; *Tigan v Western Australia* [2010] FCA 993; *Ankamuthi People v Queensland* [2002] FCA 897 [7]. See also this section below at 'Disagreement between applicant and some members of the claim group'.

471 Section 84D(2), NTA.

cases, a disagreement among the members of the applicant, or between the applicant and the claim group, has led lawyers to be uncertain about the instructions on which they should act. The legal–ethical aspects of such a situation are important but a detailed discussion of them is beyond the scope of this book.[472] At the end of this chapter I will state some of the legal–ethical operating assumptions that reflect standard practice among most NTRBs.

Amendments and errors

Authorisation is given to an applicant to make and prosecute a particular application. (This is implicit in the language of s. 251B.) This means that even if a particular *applicant* has been given authority by the claim group, there may still be a question as to whether the particular *application* has been authorised by the group.

In *Carr*[473] Jagot J found that an application was not authorised (or that the applicant was not authorised to make the application) because there was confusion about which version of the claim group description had been approved at the authorisation meeting. The meeting notice and the resolutions read out at the meeting defined the proposed claim group by reference to some 38 apical ancestors (including E.W.), whereas the Form 1, as filed, listed only 37 (and did not include E.W.). Justice Jagot said she was unable to be satisfied either that the meeting had authorised the application as it was filed, or that the meeting had genuinely intended to authorise an application that would include E.W. as an apical ancestor.[474] So even though all of the people who were listed in the Form 1 had in fact voted to authorise *the applicant*, the evidence did not establish that they had authorised *the application*. Her Honour dismissed the application, declining to hear it under s. 84D(4)(a).[475]

Taken at face value, this application-specific view of authorisation would tend to suggest that any *amendment* to the application would need to be specifically authorised by the claim group. An amended application would not be the same application that had been authorised by the

---

472 See Tim Wishart's very useful discussion of those issues: T Wishart, 'The multifaceted statutory responsibilities faced by representative body lawyers', address to the 4th Annual Native Title Summit, convened by Lexus Nexus, 11–12 July 2012, Brisbane, available at <http://www.qsnts.com.au/publications/TheMultifacetedStatutoryResponsibilitesFacedByRepresentativeBodyLawyersandWhatThisCouldMeanForYou.pdf>, viewed 15 August 2016.

473 *Carr on behalf of the Wellington Valley Wiradjuri People v Premier (NSW)* [2013] FCA 200.

474 ibid. [48].

475 See also *Harrington-Smith v Western Australia (No. 9)* [2007] FCA 31 [2735]. Another case involving a similar error was *Wyman on behalf of the Bidjara People v Queensland* [2012] FCA 921. In that case an application had been filed that mistakenly omitted an important area of country. Because the legislation does not allow for the expansion of claim areas, a fresh application over the omitted part had to be filed. As a trial was set to begin soon there was no time for fresh authorisation meetings. The applicants sought to rely on their previous authorisation to file the claim that was always intended to be filed. It is not clear from Reeves J's judgment whether his Honour accepted that the initial authorisation could extend to the fresh application but in the circumstances he ordered the applicant, under s. 84D(1), to bring evidence of authorisation.

claim group. And, sure enough, in cases where significant amendments to the application have been proposed (such as changes to the claim group description or the claim area), courts have generally sought specific reassurance that the claim group has at least been consulted about it.[476] But this should be seen as a matter of the court's discretion rather than the applicant's power. In *P.C. (name withheld)*, Bennett J allowed certain technical amendments to the Form 1 without any additional authorisation from the claim group, saying:

> Section 62A of the Act relevantly provides that the applicant in a claimant application may deal with all matters arising under the Act in relation to the application. That includes the amendment of the application from time to time.[477]

Similarly, French J in one of the *Anderson* decisions said:

> There is no procedural requirement for any particular form of decision-making process by members of a native title claim group to authorise amendments to a claim outside the kind of amendment covered by s 66B. No doubt, properly authorised applicants have the authority to apply to the Court to amend an application from time to time.[478]

His Honour went on to emphasise the importance of the court's discretion in deciding whether to allow the amendment and concluded that in the face of substantial dissent (in this case dissent from named applicants) the amendment should be refused on discretionary grounds.[479]

So applicants do have the power to *seek* amendments to the Form 1 without the need to obtain specific prior authorisation from the native title claim group. However, the court has discretion in deciding whether to *grant leave* to amend and may require evidence about the extent to which the claim group has been consulted. Further, the court has the power under s. 84D to require evidence about whether the applicant remains authorised to take a particular step in the proceedings. Finally, different considerations will apply where the applicant is authorised on the basis of explicit limiting conditions. (See below in this section at 'Conditional appointment'.)

Interlocutory steps, discontinuance, consent determination

Native title claims can be lengthy and procedurally complex. Many varied interlocutory issues might arise between the initial filing of the Form 1 and the final disposal of proceedings. In

476 E.g. in *Doctor on behalf of the Bigambul People v Queensland (No. 2)* [2013] FCA 746 and *Weribone on behalf of the Mandandanji People v Queensland* [2013] FCA 255, amendments to the claim group description were seen as requiring the authorisation of the pre-amendment claim group. See also *Lovett on behalf of the Gunditjmara People v Victoria (No. 3)* [2011] FCA 867.

477 *Drury v Western Australia* [2000] FCA 132 [12]; *P.C. (name withheld) on behalf of the Njamal People v Western Australia* [2007] FCA 1054 [40]. See also *Grant v Minister for Land and Water Conservation (NSW)* [2003] FCA 621 [32].

478 *Anderson v Western Australia* [2003] FCA 1423 [37].

479 ibid. [48]–[49].

most of the cases dealing with such interlocutory matters there is no mention of the applicant's authorisation (except, obviously, where an alleged lack of authorisation is the very subject of the interlocutory application). As mentioned, s. 62A confirms that an applicant has the power to deal with 'matters arising under this Act in relation to the application'. That means that s. 62A is the source of the applicant's power to do those things, subject to s. 84D(1).

As with the cases about amendment (discussed above) though, the question of the *applicant's power* is distinct from the question of the court's *discretion*. In deciding whether or not to grant leave or make orders sought, the court may seek reassurance that the applicant is acting in accordance with the wishes of the claim group. As will be discussed below (at 'Conditional appointment') that may involve an assessment of any conditions qualifying the applicant's original authorisation.

One area in which these propositions are clearly demonstrated in the case law is where applicants seek to discontinue their application. In *Close on behalf of the Githabul People #2*, Collier J held that s. 62A is unambiguous and should not be read narrowly.[480] The applicant (and only the applicant) has authority to take steps in the proceedings, including discontinuing the proceeding, and is not obliged to seek the approval of the claim group to do so.[481] Her Honour recognised that evidence of dissent may be relevant to the court's discretion but in the circumstances the alleged lack of authority arose merely from the fact that the authorisation meeting occurred several days after the filing of the notice of motion to discontinue. Leave to discontinue was granted (on conditions not presently relevant).

In *Levinge on behalf of the Gold Coast Native Title Group*, Reeves J adopted Collier J's view of the law but faced a different factual situation.[482] In *Levinge* there was 'no evidence that the members of the [claim group] have been informed about this application to discontinue these proceedings, or consulted in any way to obtain their views about it'.[483] Because Reeves J had 'no means of knowing whether the [claim group] agrees with, or opposes, this application to discontinue its native title claim', his Honour exercised his discretion to refuse leave to discontinue.[484] The cases of *Levinge* and *Close* were applied in *Augustine*.[485] There, Gilmour J confirmed that the applicant does not need to obtain the approval of the claim group before seeking leave to discontinue but the fact that the applicant had done so in that case was relevant to the exercise of the court's discretion.

Another area in which the claim group may have strong views is the filing of a notice of change of solicitor. There have been a number of cases dealing with disagreement *within* the applicant in relation to the engagement of new solicitors (see Section 4.2 below, 'Disagreement, disability or death within the applicant') but there is also a question as to whether the applicant

480 *Close on behalf of the Githabul People #2 v Queensland* [2010] FCA 828 [32].

481 ibid. [32]–[33].

482 *Levinge on behalf of the Gold Coast Native Title Group v Queensland* [2012] FCA 1321 [39]–[42].

483 ibid. [46].

484 ibid. [46], [50].

485 *Augustine v Western Australia* [2013] FCA 338 [14]–[16]. See also *K.K. (deceased) v Western Australia* [2013] FCA 1234 [33]–[38].

must obtain specific authority from the claim group before directing new solicitors to file a change of solicitor. I was only able to identify two cases on this topic. In one of the recent *Bigambul* decisions,[486] the applicant had directed new lawyers to file a notice of change of solicitors. A significant number of claim group members then signed a petition stating that they were unaware of the applicant's intention to change solicitors, that they had not authorised the change and that they still actively disagreed with it. The matter came to court when an application was made under s. 66B to replace the applicant. Justice Reeves refused the s. 66B order on the grounds that the proposed replacement applicant was not properly authorised. Importantly, his Honour did not state that the change of solicitors was ineffective for want of authorisation. (The new solicitors appeared for the existing applicant at the s. 66B hearing.) The specific authorisation of the claim group was evidently not considered necessary for that step to be validly taken. No doubt that is because the filing of a notice of change of solicitor does not require the court's leave and so does not involve the exercise of the court's discretion.[487] This was confirmed in the more recent *Gomeroi People* decision,[488] where an applicant was allowed to change solicitors notwithstanding that the applicant's original authorisation was subject to an explicit 'expectation' that there be no change in legal representation without a claim group decision. In that case there was no positive evidence of any disagreement between the applicant and the claim group and the court found that the previous resolution containing the 'expectation' did not amount to a condition on the applicant's authority.

The final kind of step in the proceedings that will be addressed here is the decision whether to agree to a consent determination or else to proceed to trial. Judgments accompanying consent determinations frequently stress the need for the court to be satisfied that the parties have come to a free agreement on the basis of adequate information and legal advice.[489] Generally there is no occasion for the court to 'look behind' the applicant's agreement to the consent determination, and so questions of authorisation are rarely mentioned.[490] In uncontentious cases where there is an apparent defect in authorisation, the court may well rely on s. 84D(4)(a) to proceed in spite of that defect.[491]

---

486 *Doctor on behalf of the Bigambul People v Queensland (No. 2)* [2013] FCA 746.

487 Note in *Tigan v Western Australia* [2010] FCA 993 the applicant was held not to have validly filed the notice of change of solicitor because there was disagreement among the named applicants. In that case a meeting of claim group members had authorised the change of solicitor but this was not considered relevant to the question. So that case shows that authorisation by the claim group is not sufficient for a change of solicitors but tells us little about whether it is necessary. See also *Anderson on behalf of the Wulli Wulli People v Queensland* [2011] FCA 1158 [49]; *A.D. (deceased) on behalf of the Mirning People v Western Australia* [2013] FCA 565.

488 *Gomeroi People v Attorney General (NSW)* [2016] FCAFC 75.

489 E.g. *Nelson v Northern Territory* [2010] 190 FCR 344 [10]; *Lovett on behalf of the Gunditjmara People v Victoria* [2007] FCA 474 [37]–[39].

490 A brief mention of a pre-determination authorisation meeting was made in *Wik and Wik Way Native Title Claim Group v Queensland* [2009] FCA 789 [37]. Many consent determination cases make no mention of such matters.

491 E.g. *Goonack v Western Australia* [2011] FCA 516 [17]; *Barunga v Western Australia* [2011] FCA 518 [19].

In any case it is common practice, though not universal, for NTRBs to organise a claim group meeting to authorise or ratify the entry into the consent determination. Such a meeting is likely to be useful and prudent regardless of the legal requirements. Further, there may be ILUAs associated with the consent determination that do require specific authorisation (see Section 7.1 below, 'Entering and authorising ILUAs') and there will be a need to nominate the RNTBC for after the determination (see Section 8.1 below, 'Nominating a PBC for determination') and, more generally, to talk about the management of native title post-determination.

Conditional appointment

When a claim group authorises an applicant it can place express conditions on the authorisation.[492] The effect of these is to define the terms on which the applicant is authorised; to delimit the circumstances in which the applicant can continue to claim to be authorised. In this way the claim group can set out clearly what it wants the applicant to do and not do.[493] (It is important that such conditions be expressed as such and not merely as 'expectations': see *Gomeroi People v Attorney-General (NSW)* [2016] FCAFC 75.)

Some common conditions include:

- prohibition on negotiating or entering future act agreements without specific authorisation by the claim group;
- prohibition on changing solicitors without specific authorisation by the claim group;[494]
- prohibition on agreeing to a consent determination without specific authorisation by the claim group;
- prohibition on discontinuing or amending the application without specific authorisation by the claim group;
- making continuing authorisation dependent on a minimum level of communication between applicant and claim group, or a particular method of consultation or decision-making, or the future execution of an agreement between subgroups of the native title claim group.[495]

---

492 Note that these limitations can also be imposed by the claim group subsequent to the initial authorisation of the applicant: *Ward v Northern Territory* [2002] FCA 1477 [15], citing *Daniel v Western Australia* [2002] FCA 1147.

493 *Daniel v Western Australia* [2002] FCA 1147; *Anderson on behalf of the Wulli Wulli People v Queensland* [2011] 197 FCR 404 [60]; *Far West Coast Native Title Claim v South Australia* [2012] FCA 733 [50]–[59].

494 See e.g. *Ward v Northern Territory* [2002] FCA 1477 [41]; also *N.C. (deceased) v Western Australia (No. 2)* [2013] FCA 70 in which the applicant was authorised on the condition that it would only take legal advice from the in-house lawyer of a particular Aboriginal corporation.

495 In *Far West Coast Native Title Claim v South Australia* [2012] FCA 733 a member of a subgroup of the native title claim group argued that the authorisation of the applicants (which was linked to the merging of two previously overlapping claims) had been conditional on certain protections for his subgroup. He alleged that the conditions had not been met and so the applicants' authorisation had been lost. Justice Mansfield was willing to entertain this argument but required

(Two other common conditions, relating to majority decision-making and the arrangements upon the death or retirement of applicants, will be discussed below in sections 4.1 ('Extent of applicant autonomy') and 5.1 ('How can the composition of the applicant be changed?') respectively — these conditions are *enabling* rather than restrictive.)

It would be risky for a claim group to restrict the applicant from taking literally *any* step in the proceedings without specific authorisation, since the litigation may demand quick action with no time for holding a claim group meeting to provide legal representatives with instructions directly.

It is important to be clear about what consequences flow from the breach of a condition such as those listed above. The lack of authorisation to take a specific step in the proceedings will be relevant in three ways:

- It will be relevant to the court's exercise of discretion.
- It may be the subject of an order under s. 84D(1) or (4).
- If the applicant attempts to act in breach of the condition this may provide a ground for replacing the applicant under s. 66B.

So, for example, a condition might prohibit the applicant from agreeing to a consent determination without submitting the decision to a full claim group meeting. If an applicant purported to do so, when the matter came to court the judge may well decide that it would not be appropriate to make the determination under those circumstances. Even for actions that do not require the court's leave the court has the power to maintain the status quo until authorisation has been sorted out. For example, if an applicant filed a notice of change of solicitor in breach of a condition to the contrary, the solicitor on the record would indeed be changed,[496] but the court could make orders (probably under s. 84D) requiring an authorisation meeting to be held before any further step in the litigation could be taken.[497] In effect the 'unauthorised' act would be neutralised and could be reversed by the court's intervention under s. 84D. Justice Mansfield made the following comment about s. 84D in this context in the *Far West Coast Claim*:

> [I]n my view, s 84D (in addition to the facilitative power in s 84D(4) considered by Gilmour J in *Roe*) also encompasses that concept of the claim group, by the terms of its authorisation, maintaining its ultimate authority. It does so in a way which facilitates the enforcement of that status, as it does not require any specific authorisation under s 251B for a claim group member

---

further evidence about the original authorisation process in order to determine whether those conditions had in fact been imposed at the time.

496 Note that this is the opposite case from that in *Ankamuthi People v Queensland* [2002] FCA 897, *Ward v Northern Territory* [2002] FCA 171, or *Tigan v Western Australia* [2010] FCA 993. In those cases it was members of the claim group who attempted to change solicitors without acting through the applicant or attempting first to replace the applicant.

497 Similar orders in respect of a fresh authorisation meeting were made in *Doctor on behalf of the Bigambul People v Queensland (No. 2)* [2013] FCA 746 and *Weribone on behalf of the Mandandanji People v Queensland* [2013] FCA 255.

> to apply to secure adherence to the terms of the authorisation. Instead, the Court is given the power and the discretion to decide in all the circumstances what action is appropriate where there is a departure by the applicant from the terms of the authorisation.[498]

The consequences of an applicant's breach of condition may extend beyond the immediate action in question. Depending on the wording and intention of the specific condition, the breach of condition could also lead to the lasting *loss* of the applicant's (or the individual named applicant's) authority to deal with the claim at all.[499] This would then have implications for replacing the applicant under s. 66B. As French J pointed out in *Daniel*, the loss of authorisation in such circumstances is an automatic consequence of the breach: 'It does not require a separate decision-making process in order to establish it.'[500] It does not follow, however, that the applicant or individual named applicants *cease to be applicant* upon their breach of a condition. As discussed previously in Section 2.1 at 'Eligibility to be named applicant', a loss of authorisation does not automatically bring about a change in the composition of the applicant.[501] Certainly, s. 66B application can be brought on the basis of the loss or excess of the applicant's authority,[502] but the persons comprising the proposed replacement applicant must show they have been authorised by the claim group.[503]

One innovative way of giving more immediate 'bite' to appointment conditions is to specify that a named applicant who breaches a condition is no longer authorised *but the other remaining named applicants continue to be authorised.* The effect of this is that the remaining named applicants can approach the court for an order under s. 66B and can demonstrate *both* that the 'outgoing' named applicant is no longer authorised, *and* that the remaining named applicants are authorised to remove the 'outgoing' person. This way, the removal of a named applicant can be done quickly without an expensive meeting.

---

498 *Far West Coast Native Title Claim v South Australia* [2012] FCA 733 [59]. See also *Roe v Kimberley Land Council Aboriginal Corporation* [2010] FCA 809 [49]–[55].

499 E.g. *N.C. (deceased) v Western Australia (No. 2)* [2013] FCA 70. In *Chapman on behalf of the Wakka Wakka People 2 v Queensland* [2007] FCA 597 [9] Kiefel J said that '[t]he continuance of authorisation must depend upon the terms of the authorisation, a matter upon which the NTA did not speak.' Although her Honour was speaking in a slightly different context, it adverts to the idea that the ongoing authorisation of the applicant may be something that depends on the specific conditions under which they were appointed.

500 *Daniel v Western Australia* [2002] FCA 1147 [16].

501 The question of whether there are alternative ways of removing a named applicant other than 66B is addressed below in Section 5.1 at 'Non-66B method'. Assuming provisionally that such alternatives exist, it remains the case that the no-longer-authorised named applicants will retain their status as applicant until they are removed: *P.C. (name withheld) on behalf of the Njamal People v Western Australia* [2007] FCA 1054 [48].

502 Section 66B(1)(a)(iii) and (iv).

503 Section 66B(1)(b).

Such a condition was used in the recent case *N.C. (deceased)*,[504] along with some other very tight conditions. In that case there were two factions within the claim group who had strong disagreements about the best way to proceed with the claim and with mining agreements. One faction was associated with a particular Aboriginal corporation — Yindjibarndi Aboriginal Corporation (YAC). By majority vote at a large meeting a new set of named applicants was authorised subject to four conditions:

a) the applicant appoints YAC as agent and receives legal advice from YAC's in-house lawyers, and no named applicant receives any separate legal advice or representation without YAC's consent;

b) the applicant does not make any decision affecting the claim area without first receiving written consent from YAC;

c) the named applicants do not hold any further s. 66B meetings without YAC's prior written consent;

d) if a named applicant dies, becomes unwilling to act or breaches any of the previous conditions, that named applicant is no longer authorised and the remaining members remain authorised.

These conditions effectively entrench the current applicant against replacement and, just as significantly, entrench the control of YAC. (It should be noted, however, that any member of the claim group could request the NTRB to hold a meeting and, if that meeting validly resolved to replace the applicant, nothing in these conditions would prevent the proposed replacement applicant from approaching the court for an order under s. 66B.) Justice McKerracher considered that authorisation on these conditions would 'effectively place one of the two factions of the native title claim group in control of all decisions concerning the native title application'.[505] However, his Honour considered that the court's role was not to question the wisdom or merit of the claim group's decision, only to determine whether that was in fact the decision of the claim group as a whole.[506] His Honour agreed to grant the order under s. 66B.

Disagreement between applicant and some members of the claim group

The claim group has no power to take any step in the proceedings other than through its authorised representative(s), the applicant. Courts have consistently rejected attempts by claim group members, regardless of how numerous or representative they are, to take independent steps in the proceedings. Changing solicitors (or preventing change of solicitor) is an issue that has arisen a number times in this context — in each such case, the court held that the claim group (even by overwhelming majority) cannot direct new legal representatives to file a notice of change of

504 *N.C. (deceased) v Western Australia (No. 2)* [2013] FCA 70.

505 ibid. [73].

506 ibid. [56], [99].

solicitor; only the applicant can.[507] In another example, non-applicant members of the claim group purported to instruct their NTRB to challenge in court the boundaries of a neighbouring claim.[508] The court considered that the representative body's refusal to act as 'instructed' was appropriate.[509]

The legislative basis for this exclusive role of the applicant is the same as that underpinning the applicant's power to act without specific authority: s. 62A of the *Native Title Act*. In one of the *Roe* decisions, it was argued that s. 62A is merely 'permissive' — *empowering* the applicant to take steps in the proceedings but not necessarily *restricting* the equivalent power of other members of the claim group.[510] Justice Gilmour rejected this argument, holding that s. 62A should be read as saying '*it is* the applicant *who* may deal' with all matters arising in relation to the claim, meaning that no-one else is so empowered.[511]

Where there is disagreement between claim group members and the applicant about the best way to handle a particular aspect of the claim, the only appropriate remedy is to hold a meeting to authorise a replacement of the applicant under s. 66B.[512] In special circumstances the court may allow the joinder of dissentient individuals as respondents.[513] Those circumstances, however, are rare and exceptional. And in any case these respondents cannot control the conduct of the claim.[514]

---

507 *Ankamuthi People v Queensland* [2002] FCA 897; *Tigan v Western Australia* [2010] FCA 993; *Anderson on behalf of the Wulli Wulli People v Queensland* [2011] FCA 1158 [49].

508 *Barunga v Western Australia (No. 2)* [2011] FCA 755 [145], [209].

509 ibid. [160].

510 *Roe v Kimberley Land Council Aboriginal Corporation* [2010] FCA 809 [37]–[42].

511 ibid. [39]. Cited in *Anderson on behalf of the Wulli Wulli People v Queensland* [2011] FCA 1158 [41], [49].

512 *Ankamuthi People v Queensland* [2002] FCA 897 [6]; *Starkey v South Australia* [2011] FCA 456 [56]; *Far West Coast Native Title Claim v South Australia* [2012] FCA 733 [31]; *Barunga v Western Australia (No. 2)* [2011] FCA 755 [201]. See also cases collected in Section 5.1 at 'Withdrawal or loss of authorisation'.

513 *Far West Coast Native Title Claim v South Australia* [2012] FCA 733 [35]–[41]; *Starkey v South Australia* [2011] FCA 456 [46]–[48]; *Button v Chapman on behalf of the Wakka Wakka People* [2003] FCA 861 [9]. Note that both *Combined Dulabed & Malanbarra/Yidinji Peoples v Queensland* [2004] FCA 1097 [44]–[45] and *Bidjara People #2 v Queensland* [2003] FCA 324 [5]–[7] rejected the earlier view in *Kulkalgal People v Queensland* [2003] FCA 163 that the court has no power to join claim group members as respondents in any circumstances.

514 *Starkey v South Australia* [2011] FCA 456 [55]–[63]; *Far West Coast Native Title Claim v South Australia* [2012] FCA 733 [38]. Note in *Rubibi v Western Australia* [2002] FCA 876 [19]–[24] Merkel J considered whether the court should exercise its discretion to grant joinder and distinguished between claim group members who were 'merely disputing the manner in which a claim is being contested or some incidental aspect of it' and those who opposed the claim on substantive grounds or asserted competing rights and interests inconsistent with those claimed by the main application. His Honour said that only the latter should succeed in their joinder application. Although that case's position on the necessity of the dissentient respondents filing their own s. 61 application is at odds with later cases (see Section 2.2 above at 'Joinder'), Merkel J's view about the discretionary grounds for joinder are consistent with the other cases.

Justice French (as his Honour then was) has characterised s. 66B as 'a facultative provision directed to maintaining the ultimate authority of the native title claim group'.[515] So the claim group is ultimately in control but, in the immediate instance of taking steps in the proceeding, only the applicant can act. The *Native Title Act* gives the applicant the formal status in proceedings as the sole conduit for action by the claim group but does not give the applicant any independent source of authority over the claim group. One may regard the applicant's formal monopoly as providing for order, stability and consistency in the conduct of the litigation: native title claimants are expected to sort out their disagreements through the authorisation process rather than bringing them to court. This allows the court to know who speaks for the group as a whole, and gives the court a basis for deciding how to deal with dissident and minority voices. In *Butterworth*, Logan J said that the *Native Title Act* contemplates that:

> there will be occasions when it will be necessary for an applicant to consult with a native title claim group. Consult does not equate with 'be dictated to by a member of'. A member of a native title claim group, where a need for consultation arises, is entitled to be given an opportunity to be heard, nothing more and nothing less than that.[516]

And elsewhere in the same judgment:

> To consult with a native title claim group means to extend an opportunity to that group to be heard on appropriate occasions. It does not mean that a single member or group of members in a native title claim group can presume to dictate the decisions which a native title claim group might have from time to time to make as a way of giving guidance to an applicant in respect of the carriage of a native title application.[517]

Two judgments of Mansfield J have indicated that ordinary claim group members can (without any particular authorisation of their own) use s. 84D of the *Native Title Act* to exercise supervisory control over applicants without the need to resort to s. 66B.[518] The claim group can enforce its status as the 'ultimate authority' by applying for an order under s. 84D requiring the applicant to demonstrate that they are authorised to take a particular step. If the applicant is found not to be so authorised, the court may make orders as appropriate under s. 84D(4)(b). This may possibly extend to directing the claim group to hold an authorisation meeting to establish authorisation one way or another.[519] But it seems that s. 84D(4)(b) does no more than provide a mechanism for bringing

---

515 *Daniel v Western Australia* [2002] FCA 1147 [16], [54].

516 *Butterworth on behalf of the Wiri Core Country Claim v Queensland* [2010] FCA 325 [39].

517 ibid. [31].

518 *Starkey v South Australia* [2011] FCA 456 [64], [71]; *Far West Coast Native Title Claim v South Australia* [2012] FCA 733 [59].

519 See *Sandy on behalf of the Yugara/Yugarapul People v Queensland* [2012] FCA 978 [48]. See also *Doctor on behalf of the Bigambul People v Queensland (No. 2)* [2013] FCA 746 [65], [67].

issues back to the claim group; I was unable to find any case where s. 84D(4)(b) was used to give direct effect to the wishes of the claim group despite the disagreement of the applicant.[520]

So the legal position on the autonomy of the applicant can be summarised as follows. The applicant is the only element within the claim group that is capable of taking steps in the proceedings. Ordinary members of the claim group can neither dictate to the applicant in the performance of their role nor take steps in the proceedings in their own right. The claim group as a whole can of course prescribe limits as to which actions are authorised and which are not; the group can also decide later in time that the applicant is no longer authorised (either at all or in relation to a particular proposed action). But these limits on authority cannot directly determine the steps taken in the proceedings on behalf of the group — the applicant can either do as they are told or be replaced, but until a 'renegade' applicant is replaced, the group's wishes will remain unfulfilled. The important exception to this is where the applicant seeks to take a step that is opposed by the group, and this step requires the exercise of the court's discretion. In those cases, the court may decline to exercise its discretion on the basis that the claim group disagrees or has not been consulted.

4.2 Disagreement, disability or death within the applicant

The discussion of applicant autonomy above assumed a unified applicant. Special complications arise when the members of the applicant do not all agree on the same course of action or when some of the named applicants are unavailable to participate in a decision, whether because of death, incapacity or mere communication problems.

Can an applicant act by majority if the terms of appointment say so?

Although the case law on this topic is quite scant, the position is reasonably clear. If the claim group has specifically authorised its applicant on the express condition that it may act by majority, courts will respect that procedure.

'Acting by majority' refers to a situation where an applicant purports to take a particular step in the proceedings but a minority of named applicants either disagree with the taking of the step or are unable to participate due to unavailability, disability or death. So a claim group will, at the same time as authorising the applicant, specify that the applicant may act on the basis of a majority position. The possibility of such an arrangement was considered in one of the *Anderson* decisions concerning the Ballardong claim group in Western Australia.[521] Justice French considered that, where an applicant could not decide on a single course of action, it would be appropriate for the claim group to replace the applicant with a new set of named applicants who *would* be able to agree. His Honour went on:

---

520 Cf. *Far West Coast Native Title Claim Group v South Australia (No. 4)* [2012] FCA 1468 where something like this was rejected by Mansfield J.

521 *Anderson v Western Australia* [2003] FCA 1423.

> Alternatively, it may be that the authority conferred upon the applicants is conferred in terms that enable it to be exercised according to a majority vote. That would, however, depend upon the terms of the authority. I express no concluded view on the efficacy of such a procedure.[522]

In a different case called *Anderson* (this time relating to Queensland's Wulli Wulli people),[523] Collier J held that 12 out of 15 named applicants could validly choose new lawyers for the claim group even in the face of explicit opposition from the remaining three named applicants. This was because the claim group had expressly authorised the applicant on conditions including the following: 'Decisions of the Applicant shall be on the basis of a majority vote and all Applicants shall abide by a majority decision.'[524] Her Honour said that she did not consider that s. 61(2)(c) should be interpreted so as to 'remove the autonomy of the native title claim group itself to place a condition on the manner in which the applicant can make effective decisions'.[525] Her Honour referred to French J's remark quoted above, and concluded that:

> It is entirely reasonable, and consistent with the terms and purpose of the Act to promote progress of a claim, that the claim group should be able to so qualify the decision-making role of the applicant. In my view, the Act supports an approach whereby the claim group sanctions decisions of the applicant by majority, and further supports effect being given to majority decisions of the applicant in such circumstances.[526]

Justice Collier's judgment was cited favourably by Mansfield J in *Far West Coast*,[527] although it was not directly applicable to the facts in that case. Some of the decisions discussed in the next section ('Can an applicant act by majority without an explicit provision?') are expressed in broad terms that might suggest unanimity is *always* required in applicant decision-making. However, they are distinguishable on their facts: they are cases where there was no express term allowing majority decision-making. I was unable to find a case other than *Anderson on behalf of the Wulli Wulli People* that directly concerned a claim group's explicit authorisation of decisions by majority.

Can an applicant act by majority without an explicit provision?

Where there is no express term of appointment allowing action by majority, the outright disagreement by even one named applicant will be sufficient to render the applicant's purported

522 ibid. [48].

523 *Anderson on behalf of the Wulli Wulli People v Queensland* [2011] FCA 1158.

524 ibid. [7].

525 ibid. [60].

526 ibid. [61].

527 *Far West Coast Native Title Claim v South Australia* [2012] FCA 733 [50]–[54].

actions legally ineffective.[528] However, the mere non-participation of an individual named applicant (including by reason of disability or death) will not necessarily prevent the applicant from taking steps in the proceeding.

In *Tigan*[529] Gilmour J analysed the relevant legislative language and underlying policy considerations and considered that applicants cannot make decisions by majority. Section 61(2)(c) states that, where a claim group has authorised one or more persons to make a native title claim, 'the person is, or the persons are jointly, the applicant.' His Honour referred to the dictionary definition of 'jointly' as 'in conjunction, in combination, unitedly, not severally or separately'.[530] The consequence of their joint appointment, in his Honour's view, was that the named applicants must act 'in concert' and cannot 'cause the applicant to deal with a matter arising under the Act in relation to the application by majority decision'.[531] On the specific facts of that case, this result meant that the instructions purportedly given to a law firm to act for the claim group and to file a notice of change of solicitor 'were not actions by, or authorised by, the applicant'.[532] Justice Gilmour ordered the registrar to remove the notice of change of solicitor from the court file and return it to the purported replacement law firm.[533]

In the 2011 *Weribone* decision, Logan J adopted Gilmour J's 'compelling analysis' from *Tigan*.[534] Justice Logan similarly focused on the word 'jointly', noting that although the word appeared in the *definition* of the applicant:

> that definition has a role to play in terms of indicating the way in which the persons who comprise the applicant must act. They must act 'jointly' and 'jointly' does not mean by majority.[535]

Both Logan J and Gilmour J had drawn support from passages from Kiefel J's decision in *Butchulla People*.[536] Her Honour said in that case:

---

528 Note that a slightly different position applies to 'future act' agreements, considered below in Chapter 7.

529 *Tigan v Western Australia* [2010] FCA 993.

530 ibid. [19].

531 ibid. [28].

532 ibid. [29].

533 In a later decision concerning the same proceedings, Gilmour J remarked in passing that the claim group's lawyer 'necessarily takes its instructions…from the…applicant which consists of five persons who are required to act unanimously': *Barunga v Western Australia (No. 2)* [2011] FCA 755 [145]. It is not clear whether his Honour would have come to a different view had there been a term allowing majority decision-making but in any event the remark had no bearing on the case's outcome since none of the named applicants had given the lawyer any instructions.

534 *Weribone on behalf of the Mandandanji People v Queensland* [2011] FCA 1169 [20].

535 ibid. [22].

536 *Butchulla People v Queensland* [2006] FCA 1063.

> The evident purposes of s 61 are to provide for representation of the claim group, to limit the number of persons who may act as 'the applicant' in the proceedings and, when more than one person is authorised, to require them to act in concert with each other.[537]

Her Honour considered that s. 61(2)(c) 'obliges those authorised as representatives to cooperate with each other'[538] and noted that this requirement is not a 'term or condition of appointment' but rather 'a statutory requirement having as its purpose the efficient prosecution of claims'.[539]

Tigan was again approved in *Far West Coast Native Title Claim*.[540] Justice Mansfield in that case considered that *Tigan* and *Anderson on behalf of the Wulli Wulli People* were consistent with each other: his Honour said that *unless* there is an express condition to the contrary the law requires the agreement of all named applicants who are able and willing to act.[541]

An interesting situation involving a divided applicant arose in the recent case of *A.D. (deceased)*.[542] One member of an eight-person applicant applied for a declaration stating that a new firm of solicitors had been appointed to represent the claim group. The remaining members of the applicant submitted that decisions could only be made by consensus. The dissentient individual eventually agreed that his application for a declaration should be dismissed by consent. The novel factor: the applicant (excluding the dissentient individual) sought a costs order against the dissentient individual. The individual argued that the costs application was invalid since the applicant could only seek costs via a unanimous decision, and he was withholding his consent to such a course of action. Justice McKerracher disagreed. He held that standing instructions to seek costs where appropriate are part of the 'usual retainer of a legal representative'.[543]

Importantly, Mansfield J in *Far West Coast* specified that agreement is required among those applicants 'who are able and willing to act'.[544] This implies that the withdrawal, death or illness of one named applicant will not prevent the remaining active applicants from making

---

537 ibid. [38].

538 ibid. [39].

539 ibid. [42].

540 *Far West Coast Native Title Claim v South Australia* [2012] FCA 733 [54].

541 ibid. In *Roe v Kimberley Land Council*, Gilmour J considered that only the applicant had standing to sue the NTRB on behalf of the claim group, meaning both members of the applicant 'acting jointly': *Roe v Kimberley Land Council Aboriginal Corporation* [2010] FCA 809 [42]. This decision does not shed much light on the 'majority' question since the case involved a 50–50 split between the two named applicants. Similarly, in *Ward v Northern Territory* [2002] FCA 171 four out of 16 living named applicants purported to instruct new solicitors to file a notice of change of solicitor. Justice O'Loughlin found that this minority decision did not amount to a valid instruction by the applicant and ordered that the notice be marked '[r]ejected pursuant to the order of the court': *Ward v Northern Territory* [2002] FCA 171 [9], [29].

542 *A.D. (deceased) on behalf of the Mirning People v Western Australia* [2013] FCA 565.

543 ibid. [20]. Note the slightly different context in *Roe v Kimberley Land Council Aboriginal Corporation* [2010] FCA 809 [57]–[58] — in that case the dissentient member of the applicant formally had separate representation.

544 *Far West Coast Native Title Claim v South Australia* [2012] FCA 733 [54].

decisions. Similarly, Rares J in *Smallwood* considered that 'the Act empowers all the living and competent members of a duly authorised applicant to act jointly notwithstanding that one or more of their original number may have died or become incapable after the commencement of proceedings.'[545] Arguably this would also cover a case where all reasonable attempts have been made to seek instructions from an individual but where contact cannot be made. Note that the Commonwealth, in its capacity as a respondent party in a number of cases, has argued that the death of a named applicant deprives the applicant of authority and that the applicant cannot act jointly if some of its members are deceased.[546] I was unable to find any case where this argument has been accepted by a court. Indeed, there are a number of cases in which important steps in the proceedings have been taken by applicants whose members include deceased persons; if the Commonwealth's view prevailed then an order under s. 66B would have been required first to remove the deceased persons.[547]

What are the consequences of disagreement within the applicant?

If there is no express term allowing action by majority, it seems that the applicant will be paralysed by a disagreement between its members. The applicant will not necessarily cease to be authorised (unless some of the named applicants are in breach of the terms of their authorisation) but the applicant will be unable to take any further step in the proceedings.[548] That failure to prosecute the claim may in turn leave the way open for the application to be dismissed or struck out.[549]

Courts have consistently demonstrated their determination not to let stalemates within the applicant delay the resolution of proceedings. In general, the favoured option is to force a change to the composition of the applicant so as to produce an applicant capable of agreeing. Most of

---

545 *Smallwood on behalf of the Juru People v Queensland* [2014] FCA 331 [35].

546 In *A.D. (deceased) on behalf of the Mirning People v Western Australia* [2013] FCA 565 the Commonwealth submitted that 'where named individuals cannot agree to act in concert (due to death or incapacity), or will not (due to disagreement), the claim group must replace the named applicants' under s. 66B. The court did not need to decide the matter, because there was no agreement between the living applicants in any case.

547 E.g. *W.F. (deceased) on behalf of the Wiluna People v Western Australia* [2013] FCA 755; *B.P. (deceased) v Western Australia* [2013] FCA 760 where the applicant consented to a determination of native title despite some of its members being deceased. See also *Wurrunmurra v Western Australia* [2012] FCA 1399. *FQM Australia Nickel Pty Ltd v Bullen* [2011] FCAFC 30 concerned whether a mining company was bound by the 'right to negotiate' provisions even at a time when all named applicants were deceased. Note, however, that a new (living) applicant had been authorised by the time the legal representatives were instructed to pursue the litigation concerning the mining company.

548 *Anderson on behalf of the Ballardong People v Western Australia* [2003] FCA 1423 [50].

549 Note this is not an automatic consequence. For example in *Weribone on behalf of the Mandandanji People v Queensland* [2011] FCA 1169, Logan J was content simply to state that the purported majority decision was of no effect and made no further orders about the conduct of the application other than to extend time for the filing of connection material.

the cases assume that this will be done by a replacement of the applicant under s. 66B after a claim group meeting.[550] Some judges consider that the court has the power to break the deadlock by removing certain named applicants as parties under r. 9.08 of the Federal Court Rules 2011 (previously O. 6 r. 9 of the old Federal Court Rules).[551] The debate around this latter mechanism is discussed in Section 5.1 below at 'Non-66B method'. Clearly, if such a mechanism were used, the court ought to be very confident that it could identify the faction within the applicant that held the confidence of the claim group as a whole.[552]

Although an applicant's inability to agree on the next steps in a proceeding will not make the application an abuse of process,[553] the court may nevertheless consider that the most appropriate response to an intractable deadlock is to dismiss the proceedings. One option is for the court to make a 'springing order' stating that the proceedings will stand dismissed unless a unanimous applicant applies for further programming directions. This sets up a choice for the current named applicants: either come to an agreement, resolve the deadlock through a s. 66B replacement, or let the application be dismissed.[554] The Explanatory Memorandum to the *Native Title Amendment (Technical Amendments) Bill 2007* specifically mentioned such springing orders as the kind of orders that might be made under s. 84D(4)(b).[555] Alternatively, the court may be more specific in referring the named applicants to mediation towards arrangements for the holding of a s. 66B meeting.[556]

Separate legal representation

Occasionally individual named applicants (or ordinary claim group members) will express a desire for separate legal representation. Certainly, there is no legal impediment to a private individual

550 *Anderson on behalf of the Ballardong People v Western Australia* [2003] FCA 1423 [50]–[51]; *Tigan v Western Australia* [2010] FCA 993 [28]; *Weribone on behalf of the Mandandanji People v Queensland* [2011] FCA 1169 [22]; *Far West Coast Native Title Claim v South Australia* [2012] FCA 733 [54].

551 Justice Kiefel has been the main proponent of this view in the context of disagreement within the applicant as opposed to the death or incapacity of a named applicant: *Chapman v Queensland* [2007] FCA 597 [13]–[14]; *Button v Chapman on behalf of the Wakka Wakka People* [2003] FCA 861 [9]. Her Honour did apply the same logic to situations where named applicants are unwilling or unable to act in the role: *Butchulla People v Queensland* [2006] FCA 1063. See also e.g. *Central West Goldfields People v Western Australia* [2003] FCA 467 [10]; *Doolan v Native Title Registrar* [2007] FCA 192 [69].

552 See Gilmour J's comments in *Roe v Kimberley Land Council Aboriginal Corporation* [2010] FCA 809 [49]–[52] on the use of s. 84D to allow one of two applicants to proceed with the application.

553 See *Button v Chapman on behalf of the Wakka Wakka People* [2003] FCA 861.

554 *Anderson on behalf of the Ballardong People v Western Australia* [2003] FCA 1423 [50]–[52], where French J relied on the general power under s. 23, *Federal Court Act 1976* to issue the springing order.

555 *Roe v Kimberley Land Council Aboriginal Corporation* [2010] FCA 809 [44], [52].

556 That was the approach, in different circumstances, in *Weribone on behalf of the Mandandanji People v Queensland* [2013] FCA 255 and *Doctor on behalf of the Bigambul People v Queensland (No. 2)* [2013] FCA 746. See also *Holborow v Western Australia* [2002] FCA 1428 [9]. Justice O'Loughlin ordered mediation in *Ward v Northern Territory* [2002] FCA 171 in circumstances where there was confusion over who were the named applicants.

engaging the services of a legal practitioner to give advice about their rights and obligations as a named applicant.[557] But the native title claim group has only one legal representative in the proceedings, namely the solicitor on the record.[558] The applicant (acting jointly) provides instructions to the solicitor on behalf of the claim group. A lawyer engaged by an individual named applicant cannot be heard and cannot file documents unless an application is made to join the individual as a party to the proceedings. Such an application is highly unlikely to be granted.

In *Johnson on behalf of the Barkandji (Paakantyi) People*[559] Stone J criticised attempts by the two opposing factions within the applicant to obtain separate legal representation. Her Honour said:

> These attempts reveal a fundamental misunderstanding of the role of applicants in native title determination applications. Such applicants are representatives of the claimant group; they have no personal interest other than as members of the claimant group and for this reason their interests do not differ from each other or from the claimant group and separate representation is inappropriate and unacceptable.[560]

Dissentient members of the applicant may find it difficult to obtain funding for separate legal representation, since the funding attaches to the claim rather than the individual.[561]

4.3 Obligations of the applicant

A number of cases emphasise the applicant's role as representative of the entire claim group rather than just one subset of it. For example, Kiefel J said in *Butchulla People*:

> The claim group has permitted each family to nominate a person to be authorised by the wider group. From the [current named applicants'] perspective the composition of the '*applicant*' reflects the various family interests. Such an approach is not however consistent with the nature of claims for native title determination nor the interests of the members of the claim group in it. The interest of each member is identical. The NTA does not recognise

557 E.g. *P.C. (name withheld) on behalf of the Njamal People v Western Australia* [2007] FCA 1054; *Roe v Kimberley Land Council Aboriginal Corporation* [2010] FCA 809; *Placer (Granny Smith) Pty Ltd and Granny Smith Mines Limited/Western Australia/Ron Harrington-Smith & Ors on behalf of the Wongatha People* [2000] NNTTA 75. This statement is subject to any exclusivity terms in any retainer that the named applicant may have signed — or a condition of authorisation that prohibits separate lawyers (*N.C. (deceased) v Western Australia (No. 2)* [2013] FCA 70).

558 E.g. *Stock v Western Australia* [2014] FCA 179 [14].

559 *Johnson on behalf of the Barkandji (Paakantyi) People v Minister for Land and Water Conservation (NSW)* [2003] FCA 981.

560 ibid. [8]. Cited with approval by French J in *Sampi v Western Australia (No. 2)* [2005] FCA 1567 [24], [27].

561 See comments in *Barunga v Western Australia (No. 2)* [2011] FCA 755 [144] made by the Kimberley Land Council's then Chief Executive Officer. These do not represent the view of the court but rather the administrative practices of the NTRB.

> any sub-groups within the wider group having a different interest, as cases concerning the issue of authorisation consistently point out. It follows that, so far as the NTA is concerned, each person authorised is a representative of the entire claim group.[562]

Her Honour made that observation in the context of deciding whether individual named applicants could be removed as parties by the court without the need for an application to replace the applicant under s. 66B. (See Section 5.1 below at 'Non-66B method'.) Her Honour's observation should not be understood as saying that the *Native Title Act* does not allow group-based models of representation in the applicant, insofar as the group's expectations or motivations are concerned. Indeed, given the emphasis in s. 251B on traditional decision-making, it would be natural for the law to support claim groups that wish to ensure equal representation of subgroups through the composition of the applicant. For example, if the broader claim group set clear expectations that the named applicants would act as representatives for subgroups, and if the named applicants failed to meet this expectation, the claim group could replace the applicant under s. 66B. The effect of Kiefel J's remarks above is that the courts will not enforce these intramural roles on the group's behalf; if the group wants each subgroup represented then it needs to achieve this through an authorisation process.

In both *Que Noy*[563] and *Far West Coast Native Title Claim*,[564] Mansfield J highlighted the fact that applicants are authorised by the claim group as a whole rather than by subgroups, while simultaneously recognising that individual named applicants may well serve the actual political function of representing subgroups. His Honour made no suggestion that this was improper. (Of course, the claim group may want each named applicant to represent the group as a whole rather than their respective subgroup. In that case they could make this an express condition of appointment, or simply remain silent on the matter.)[565]

Perhaps more pertinent than the question of whether applicants are permitted to represent or promote the interests of their particular subgroup is the question of the named applicants' *personal* interest. Numerous cases have stated that the applicant's role is representative in nature and not a personal right. Accordingly, applicants have the same interest in the proceedings as any other member of the claim group and do not have any special personal stake in the proceedings.[566] Building from this, several cases have characterised the applicant's position as being analogous

562 *Butchulla People v Queensland* [2006] FCA 1063 [41].

563 *Que Noy v Northern Territory* [2007] FCA 1888 [21]–[25].

564 *Far West Coast Native Title Claim v South Australia* [2012] FCA 733 [39]–[40], [60].

565 E.g. *Anderson on behalf of the Wulli Wulli People v Queensland* [2011] FCA 1158 [7].

566 *Johnson on behalf of the Barkandji (Paakantyi) People v Minister for Land and Water Conservation (NSW)* [2003] FCA 981 [8]; *Roe v Kimberley Land Council Aboriginal Corporation* [2010] FCA 809 [36]; cited in *FQM Australia Nickel Pty Ltd v Bullen* [2011] FCAFC 30 [15]. Also *Button v Chapman on behalf of the Wakka Wakka People* [2003] FCA 861 [9].

to a fiduciary.[567] A case from outside the native title context, *Bulun Bulun*,[568] established that a fiduciary relationship and fiduciary obligations could arise as a consequence of traditional law and custom and of the expectations that an Indigenous group has of its senior members.

More recently, Rares J considered this issue in the Mandandanji proceedings. In *Weribone* it became clear that the existing applicant lacked the authorisation of the claim group, but the proposed replacement applicant had also failed to demonstrate its authorisation. In the circumstances, Rares J considered it necessary to make orders protecting the assets held on behalf of the group. His Honour held that the relationship between the applicant and the claim group 'has hallmarks of a fiduciary relationship'.[569] Such a relationship carries obligations not to derive any unauthorised benefit and not to allow a conflict of interest between the fiduciary and the claim group.[570] The powers of a fiduciary are not to be used for any ulterior purpose.[571] Justice Rares did not find it necessary to delve too deeply into the details and scope of the applicant's fiduciary obligations but considered that they were sufficient to support the asset control orders made in that case. The current-but-no-longer-authorised applicant was required to account for all money paid or payable under future act agreements, ILUAs and cultural heritage agreements, whether held by the named applicants, associated corporations or other persons. Such moneys were to be paid to the registrar of the court to hold on trust for the claim group until the authorisation situation could be worked out.

Note that Rares J acknowledged that the fiduciary obligation not to derive an unauthorised benefit from the relationship would not necessarily prevent the named applicants from receiving 'reasonable and appropriate remuneration, reimbursement or reward for necessary work, expenses and activity to be undertaken by or on behalf of an applicant in giving effect to reasonable, necessary or appropriate actions relevant to the particular agreement'.[572] Beyond these allowances, however, the applicant's position 'could not be used to enrich the applicant or its members or others at the expense or to the detriment of the native title claim group as a whole'.[573]

The comments just made relate to the named applicants' personal obligations to the broader constituency they represent — the application group (remembering that this book uses that term to refer to the group described in the Form 1, whether or not they also turn out to be the same as the native title holding group). Justice Rares' decision contains a second strand of reasoning, this time relating to the relationship between the applicant (acting on behalf of the application

567 See *Charlie Moore & Ors (Yandruwandha/Yawarrawarrka) and David Mungeranie & Ors (Dieri)/Eagle Bay Resources NI/South Australia* [2005] NNTTA 53 [44]; *Placer (Granny Smith) Pty Ltd and Granny Smith Mines Limited/Western Australia/Ron Harrington-Smith & Ors on behalf of the Wongatha People* [2000] NNTTA 75; *Bradley Foster & Ors (Waanyi Peoples)/Copper Strike Ltd/Queensland* [2006] NNTTA 169; [2006] NNTTA 61 [39].

568 *Bulun Bulun v R & T Textiles Pty Ltd* [1998] FCA 1082.

569 *Weribone on behalf of the Mandandanji People v Queensland* [2013] FCA 255 [61].

570 ibid. [62].

571 *Weribone on behalf of the Mandandanji People v Queensland (No. 2)* [2013] FCA 485 [50].

572 *Weribone on behalf of the Mandandanji People v Queensland* [2013] FCA 255 [64].

573 ibid. [65].

group) and whichever group of people is ultimately determined to be the true native title holders. Justice Rares noted that the future act provisions in the *Native Title Act* are intended to secure benefits for the actual common law holders of native title.[574] The applicant's power to negotiate agreements with future act proponents is an 'interim status' accorded to a 'mere procedural intervener' who may be subsequently displaced when a determination of native title is made.[575] The role of applicant 'involves the duty to act on behalf of not only the claim group which that party represents but also all the persons who hold native title'.[576] In light of this:

> Claimants for native title have rights and powers under Div 3 of Pt 2 of the Act to negotiate some reasonable and proportionate benefit for themselves as a stopgap until the identity of the actual holders of native title is determined by the Court. Those rights and powers must not be used by those claimants in a way that ignores or defeats the rights and interests of the true native title holders.[577]

His Honour characterised this relationship between the applicant and the 'true native title holders' as being fiduciary in nature.[578]

4.4 Legal professional obligations

Partly as a recap of the main points covered in this chapter, and partly as a practical guide to the legal–ethical issues raised by the applicant/claim group relationship, it is worth laying down some working assumptions about the duties owed by lawyers working in native title. I call these 'assumptions' because it is beyond the scope of this book to provide a fully reasoned justification for them. They reflect what I understand to be fairly widespread and representative practice amongst NTRB lawyers, balancing the various risks, uncertainties and practical imperatives. Other practitioners may well come to different conclusions than those set out below — above

---

574 *Weribone on behalf of the Mandandanji People v Queensland (No. 2)* [2013] FCA 485 [45]: 'It can hardly have been the intention of the Parliament that persons who were simply claimants be able to use their mere and contestable status to enrich themselves to a substantive and permanent extent at the expense of the true native title holders.'

575 *Weribone on behalf of the Mandandanji People v Queensland* [2013] FCA 255 [66].

576 *Weribone on behalf of the Mandandanji People v Queensland (No. 2)* [2013] FCA 485 [46].

577 ibid. [47]. Also, at [46]: '[S]ubject to observing the fiduciary duties the party owes to the true native title holders, [the applicant] is entitled to bargain for and obtain an appropriate and reasonable benefit in all the circumstances which can be enjoyed pending the result of the final hearing.'

578 *Weribone on behalf of the Mandandanji People v Queensland* [2013] FCA 255 [58].

all, it is incumbent on all native title lawyers to give these issues their careful and independent consideration and to make their own judgments. The assumptions are as follows:

- Lawyers owe fiduciary obligations to the applicant (jointly) *as well as* the native title claim group (jointly).[579] I will not proffer a view at this point as to whether it is possible to identify either one of these definitively as 'the client' — as appears below, different obligations are owed to each.
- Most NTRBs tend, at a very general level, to speak of the native title claim group as the 'real client' and the effective decision-making entity, although in particular scenarios things may not be so clear-cut. NTRB lawyers will often seek to defer to the claim group on significant decisions rather than assume that the applicant has the cultural or political authority to make such decisions autonomously. NTRBs will often be cautious in following the applicant's instructions on significant issues without being satisfied that the claim group either *has* endorsed or *probably would* endorse that course of action.
- However, for the reasons explained in Section 4.1 above ('Extent of applicant autonomy'), lawyers may only take instructions from the applicant (jointly), not from the claim group directly; and if there has been no explicit authorisation allowing majority decision-making, this means instructions must be given unanimously by all of those able and willing to act.
- Instructions should be sought before taking any step in the proceeding. However, instructions may be given at high or low levels of generality: for example, an applicant may instruct the lawyers to resolve all outstanding extinguishment/tenure issues in a claim, conceding or pursuing legal or factual points wherever the lawyers think it proper to do so. A broad instruction such as this would then give lawyers latitude to use their own judgment in dealing with the respondents without being forced to seek instructions on each technical point. Before such an instruction is given, however, the lawyer should discuss the scope of their instructions first, using examples if necessary, to ensure that everyone shares the same understanding. If there is any doubt about a particular point that the lawyers propose to concede, they should approach the applicant to confirm their instructions.
- Where the claim group has directed the applicant to take a certain step and the applicant refuses[580] to instruct the lawyers in line with the group's direction, the lawyer cannot treat the group's direction as an 'instruction'. The only way for the group's wishes to be vindicated is to replace the 'recalcitrant' applicant and have the new applicant give the instruction. The replacement can be done by way of a fresh authorisation meeting

579 See for comparison the situation of lawyers acting for representative plaintiffs in class actions: S Degeling & M Legg, 'Fiduciary obligations of lawyers in Australian class actions: conflicts between duties', *University of New South Wales Law Journal*, vol. 37, no. 3, pp. 914–938, December 2014.

580 This includes a refusal by one or more individual named applicants in circumstances where a unanimous instruction is required, or a refusal by a majority of named applicants in circumstances where a majority instruction is sufficient.

or (if the situation was anticipated at a previous authorisation meeting) by a 'springing' condition that automatically authorises the conforming members of the applicant to remove any non-conforming individuals. (See Section 5.1 below at 'Section 66B method'.)

- Where the claim group has directed the applicant *not* to take a particular step and the applicant instructs the lawyers to take the step anyway, the lawyers may consider ceasing to act rather than follow the applicant's unauthorised instructions. The NTRB can then convene a claim group meeting in the exercise of its functions under s. 203BB of the *Native Title Act*, at which the claim group can authorise a replacement applicant. In the recent *Gomeroi* decision, the current lawyers did not have the opportunity to cease to act because the very decision the applicant was making was to change lawyers.[581] In that case, the new lawyers would have had to consider the appropriateness of accepting the retainer in circumstances where the claim group had expressed an expectation that the applicant not change lawyers without specific group authorisation. Nothing said here should be taken as a criticism of that decision or a comment on its appropriateness.
- A lawyer's response to unauthorised instructions or the absence of instructions cannot be resolved by s. 84D(4) of the *Native Title Act*; it is a matter of legal professional obligations rather than native title authorisation.
- Where there is a proposed change to the composition of the applicant, as described in the next chapter, it would appear that the 'outgoing' applicant is still the only valid source of instructions until the court has actually ordered the change of applicant; thereafter, the replacement applicant is the only valid source of instructions. The question of how lawyers should handle potential conflicts of professional duties as between the outgoing and replacement applicant will be addressed briefly below at the beginning of Chapter 5.
- Where there is a proposed change to the composition of the native title claim group itself, as described below in Chapter 6, it seems necessary that there will also be a change to the character or identity of 'the client' for legal–ethical purposes. The point in time when this change actually occurs is a matter of some complexity and uncertainty. It is discussed further in Section 6.2 ('Authorisation by proposed amended claim group') below.

---

581 *Gomeroi People v Attorney General (NSW)* [2013] FCA 81.

5. Changing the composition of the applicant

There are several different circumstances which may lead a claim group to consider changing the composition of the applicant:

- the death of a named applicant;
- the voluntary retirement of a named applicant;
- an active decision by the claim group to withdraw authorisation from one or more of the named applicants, including a decision to replace them wholesale;
- the discovery that a named applicant was never a member of the claim group, or an amendment to the claim group description in the Form 1 resulting in a named applicant no longer being a member of the claim group;
- the automatic loss of authority following from a breach of a condition of appointment;
- a deadlock situation where internal disagreement within the applicant is making further progress unworkable.

In none of these situations is a change in the applicant's composition strictly mandatory or automatic. If a named applicant dies, their name will remain on the court file and the Register of Native Title Claims until it is removed; nothing in the *Native Title Act* directly requires such removal.[582] (See Section 5.1 below at 'Death or incapacity' for more on this point.) And even where a claim group has resolved to replace the applicant, if the nominated replacement applicant for whatever reason decides not to approach the court for orders reflecting that change, they will not be contravening any law, nor will they become the applicant.

But in certain circumstances a change of applicant may become practically necessary. Because of the requirements discussed above in Chapter 4, circumstances may arise where the existing applicant is unable to take any steps in the proceedings and the court may threaten to strike out the application unless something is done. For example, where applicants are required to act unanimously but some of them disagree, or where the evidence clearly demonstrates that the existing applicant is no longer authorised, a change in the composition of the applicant may be necessary to save the application from dismissal.[583]

582 *FQM Australia Nickel Pty Ltd v Bullen* [2011] FCAFC 30 [33]. Deceased individuals are routinely allowed to remain as named applicants, particularly (for whatever reason) in Western Australia: e.g. *W.F. (deceased) on behalf of the Wiluna People v Western Australia* [2013] FCA 755; *A.D. (deceased) on behalf of the Mirning People v Western Australia (No. 2)* [2013] FCA 1000; *B.P. (deceased) v Western Australia* [2013] FCA 760.

583 *Anderson on behalf of the Ballardong People v Western Australia* [2003] FCA 1423 [50]–[51]; *Tigan v Western Australia* [2010] FCA 993 [28]; *Far West Coast Native Title Claim v South Australia* [2012] FCA 733 [53]–[54]; *Weribone on behalf of the Mandandanji People v Queensland* [2013] FCA 255 [55]; *Doctor on behalf of the Bigambul People v Queensland (No. 2)* [2013] FCA 746.

Before examining the mechanics of changing the applicant, a point of legal ethics should be briefly raised for consideration. At the end of the last chapter there is a short list of working assumptions about legal professional obligations as they relate to the specific context of native title. Among these is the proposition that lawyers owe fiduciary duties to both the applicant and the native title claim group but must take instructions only from the applicant. This leads to some ambiguity about the identity of 'the client' for the purposes of legal professional obligations. Often this will not pose any problem because the interests of the applicant and the claim group are aligned. But where there is any controversy about a proposed change to the composition of the applicant, practitioners will need to consider carefully how to handle the potential for conflict between their duties to the current applicant and their duties to the claim group.

As will be seen below, a common first step in replacing the applicant is the convening of a claim group meeting. Although there may appear to be a potential conflict here, particularly if the applicant expressly objects to the holding of a meeting, such conflict is essentially illusory. Any person is free to call a meeting at any time and if an NTRB chooses to assist with organising the meeting, that may be regarded as an exercise of its functions under s. 203BB of the *Native Title Act*. The holding of a meeting is not a step in the proceedings and need not be an act attributable to the legal practitioner. If the claim group decides at such a meeting to withdraw the authorisation of the current applicant and authorise a replacement, that is a matter for the group.

A more substantial potential for conflict arises when the court is first approached about replacing the applicant. Focusing for now on s. 66B of the *Native Title Act* (as will be seen below, this is the only method used for changing the applicant in controversial situations), the process begins with an interlocutory application being made *by the members of the proposed replacement applicant.* The immediate question is whether it is permissible or appropriate for the lawyers, who currently take their instructions from the 'outgoing' applicant, to help the proposed replacement applicant make this interlocutory application. Similarly, is it permissible for the current applicant's lawyers to file (or even depose) affidavits in support of the s. 66B application?

Generally, NTRB practice has been to answer these questions in the affirmative. Perhaps proceeding from the general standpoint that the 'true client' is the claim group rather than the applicant, NTRB lawyers have generally been comfortable with acting for proposed replacement applicants in circumstances where the lawyers are satisfied that the claim group has authorised the replacement. In a strictly technical sense, this involves acting simultaneously for more than one party to the proceedings — or more accurately, one party and one or more non-parties who are entitled to make an interlocutory application in the proceedings. In itself, this does not necessarily involve any conflict of duties. The relevant instructions to file the s. 66B application and accompanying affidavits are given by the proposed replacement applicant rather than the current applicant and so there is no conflict with the duty to act only on instructions. The key question is whether the duties still owed to the current applicant, including the duty of fidelity in particular, make it improper to act for the proposed replacement applicant.

One way of thinking about this problem may be to divide the various legal–ethical obligations into three categories: those owed to the claim group, those owed to the applicant, and those owed to both. For example, the duty to act on instructions pertains only to the applicant whereas the duties to avoid conflicts of personal interest and not to use or disclose confidential information are owed to both. Within this schema it may be that the duty of fidelity can be construed as applying to the claim group only, or at least applying to the claim group *in priority to* the applicant.

Whether this is accepted or not, there will certainly be situations where it is inappropriate for a practitioner to continue to act for both the current applicant and the proposed replacement applicant. If the practitioner is satisfied that the latter is authorised by the claim group while the former is not, the practitioner may decide to 'cease to act' for the current applicant. If the current applicant wishes to put evidence or submissions against the s. 66B application, they can do so with separate legal representation. (NTRB funding processes may be relevant to this.) Indeed, this appears to be the generally accepted practice among NTRBs, although the decision to 'cease to act' is rarely formalised by filing a notice under r. 4.05 of the Federal Court Rules 2011. That way, while there is a de facto separation between the 'claim lawyers' and the current applicant, the 'claim lawyers' remain on the record after the order under s. 66B is granted. And, if the order is refused (e.g. on the grounds that there was a defect in the claim group's authorisation of the replacement applicant) the 'claim lawyers' continue to act for the current applicant until such time as a successful s. 66B application is made (or the applicant terminates the retainer).

Although this book gives no definitive answer, the above discussion provides at least a starting point for conceptualising the issues. Prudence requires practitioners to keep these issues in mind and to develop their own conclusions and strategies. The ethical conduct rules that govern the legal profession were no doubt drafted without specific regard to the special circumstances of native title, and situations may well arise where compliance either seems impossible or else would require time and resources that are simply not available. Perhaps the time has come for sui generis rules or exceptions to be written into the legal conduct rules so that native title lawyers can operate on a surer footing.

5.1 How can the composition of the applicant be changed?

In order to set out the legal requirements for changing the composition of the applicant it is necessary to identify the statutory basis for such a change. The obvious starting point is s. 66B of the *Native Title Act*, which provides that '[o]ne or more members of the native title claim group… may apply to the Federal Court for an order that the member, or the members jointly, replace the current applicant for the application…' However, there is divergent case law about whether s. 66B is the *only* means by which the composition of the applicant can be changed.[584]

584 The currently unsettled state of the law was noted in *Dodd on behalf of the Gudjala People Core Country Claim #1 v Queensland* [2011] FCA 690 [9]; *Weribone on behalf of the Mandandanji People* v *Queensland* [2011] FCA 1169 [18]. The key cases were mentioned by North, McKerracher and Jagot JJ in *FQM Australia Nickel Pty Ltd v Bullen* [2011] FCAFC 30 [30] but the Full Court distinguished those cases and did not express a view on the controversy. I was unable to identify any other Full Court decision dealing with the issue.

One line of cases holds that any change to the make-up of the applicant must be made through the procedure set out in s. 66B.[585] The opposing line of cases takes the view that changes can also be made by amending the application under r. 8.21 of the Federal Court Rules 2011 (O. 13 r. 2 of the old Federal Court Rules)[586] or alternatively by a court order removing a named applicant as a party under r. 9.08 (previously O. 6 r. 9).[587]

An amendment to the *Native Title Act* in 2007 looked as though it might have resolved this difference of judicial opinion but appears not to have done so. Prior to the *Native Title Amendment (Technical Amendments) Act 2007*, s. 66B only applied to situations where authorisation had been either withdrawn or exceeded. Accordingly, courts were required to find other means of altering the composition of the applicant in cases of death, disability or voluntary withdrawal. With the passage of this amendment, however, death, incapacity and willingness to step down were added as grounds for replacement under s. 66B. Justice Siopis in *Sambo*[588] held that s. 66B now 'covers the field' in relation to changing the composition of the applicant. Certainly that was the intention expressed in the Explanatory Memorandum accompanying the amendment[589] and the position consistently taken by the Commonwealth in litigation on the subject.[590] Nevertheless, there are post-2007 cases which specifically address this position and reject it, maintaining that s. 66B does not have the monopoly.[591] At the time of writing, no Full Court case has resolved the issue.

It should be noted that the judicial disagreement is really only relevant to cases where one or more named applicants have died, become incapacitated or proposed to voluntarily step down.

---

585 *Sambo v Western Australia* [2008] FCA 1575; *J.E.D. (deceased) v Western Australia* [2008] FCA 1684 [2]; *Murgha on behalf of the Combined Gungandji Claim v Queensland* [2011] FCA 1317 [3]–[4]. See also French J's decision in *Anderson v Western Australia* [2003] FCA 1423 [3], [30]–[36]; *P.C. (name withheld) on behalf of the Njamal People v Western Australia* [2007] FCA 1054 [4]; *A.D. (deceased) on behalf of the Mirning People v Western Australia* [2013] FCA 565 [18].

586 Note in *Anderson v Western Australia* [2003] FCA 1423 [30]–[36], [41] and *P.C. (name withheld) on behalf of the Njamal People v Western Australia* [2007] FCA 1054 [4], amendment under O. 13 r. 2 was considered to be an available mechanism but subject to the requirements of s. 66B.

587 *Central West Goldfields People v Western Australia* [2003] FCA 467; *Butchulla People v Queensland* [2006] FCA 1063; *Chapman on behalf of Wakka Wakka People (No. 2) v Queensland* [2007] FCA 597; *Lennon v South Australia* [2010] FCA 743; *Dodd on behalf of the Gudjala People Core Country Claim #1 v Queensland* [2011] FCA 690 [26]; *Roberts v Northern Territory* [2011] FCA 242.

588 *Sambo v Western Australia* [2008] FCA 1575 [25]–[30]; approved in *Murgha on behalf of the Combined Gunggandji Claim v Queensland* [2011] FCA 1317. This view was also apparently endorsed by Gilmour J in *Roe v Western Australia (No. 2)* [2011] FCA 102 [153]. It is slightly unclear whether Gilmour J was giving his own endorsement to the view in Sambo or merely reciting the Commonwealth's submissions.

589 *Sambo v Western Australia* [2008] FCA 1575 [27]–[28].

590 E.g. *Roe v Western Australia (No. 2)* [2011] FCA 102.

591 *Lennon v South Australia* [2010] FCA 743; *Dodd on behalf of the Gudjala People Core Country Claim #1 v Queensland* [2011] FCA 690 [13]–[17].

In any other situation, such as the addition of a new named applicant or the contested removal of a living individual who still wishes to retain their position, the cases generally agree that s. 66B is the only appropriate mechanism.[592] I was only able to identify one case where an alternative method was used in controversial circumstances, and even in that case it was clear that the applicants did not wish to be part of the claim.[593]

This book will not attempt to reach a conclusion about which of the two judicial views about the exclusivity of s. 66B is correct. Instead, the 'non-66B' approach will be briefly explained before a more detailed examination of the process under s. 66B. There is value in understanding the way in which each approach characterises 'the applicant' as corporate or several.

Non-66B method

The proposition that a named applicant can be removed without resort to s. 66B depends on a characterisation of each named applicant as a party in their own right. Rule 9.08 of the Federal Court Rules 2011 states:

> A party may apply to the Court for an order that a party that has been improperly or unnecessarily joined as a party, or has ceased to be a proper or necessary party, cease to be a party.[594]

In those cases where this has been regarded as an appropriate basis for removing a named applicant, the court has interpreted each named applicant as being a distinct party with their own personal authorisation

592 See how the two types of situation are treated differently in *Far West Coast Native Title Claim v South Australia* [2012] FCA 733 [31], [54] and *Anderson on behalf of the Wulli Wulli People v Queensland* [2011] FCA 1158 [58]. For discussion, see *Sambo v Western Australia* [2008] FCA 1575 [21].

593 In *Chapman* Kiefel J used O. 6 r. 9 to remove two named applicants as parties to the claim on the basis that they had 'refused to cooperate' with the other named applicants and had 'evinced an intention to no longer act in a representative capacity': *Chapman on behalf of the Wakka Wakka People #2 v Queensland* [2007] FCA 597 [1]. There was no meeting held to revoke their authorisation and no evidence that they consented to their removal; instead, the evidence showed that they had refused to participate in applicant meetings and future act negotiations and had even supported a strike-out motion against the claim. Justice Kiefel considered that their removal was appropriate because they were not 'proper or necessary' parties to the litigation (at [7]). In a related decision in the same proceedings, Kiefel J said that the removal of those individuals would not leave the claim group without adequate representation and that such removal was justified because their 'role as applicants has become untenable': *Button v Chapman on behalf of the Wakka Wakka People* [2003] FCA 861 [9].

594 The old rule, O. 6 r. 9, did not require a party to apply; rather, the power could be exercised on the court's own motion.

from the claim group.[595] On this view, so long as the criteria in r. 9.08 are satisfied and it is in the interests of justice to do so,[596] it is open to the court to order the removal of such a party.

There are two related assumptions underlying this approach:

- that the claim group's original authorisation continues in respect of the remaining named applicants (that is, it is implicit in the claim group's original authorisation that they do not intend authorisation to be withdrawn in the event that one or more of the named applicants is unable or unwilling to continue in the role);[597]
- that the applicant does not represent a delicate balance of sectional interests, so that the court need not be concerned that the loss of one subgroup's representative would undermine the overall legitimacy of the applicant.[598]

Against this, the Commonwealth has pressed the view in litigation that claim groups often appoint named applicants to represent subgroups, reflecting the culturally specific mode of decision-making particular to the claim group. In those circumstances, claim groups appoint the applicant as a single integrated unit, with the expectation that there will be an opportunity to replace any named applicant who dies or steps down.[599] By analogy to electoral politics, this would be akin to an expectation that a by-election will be triggered by a retirement or death. On this view, resort to s. 66B is necessary for rebalancing an applicant to prevent the (unintentional) 'stacking' of the applicant in favour of one subgroup or another.

Lawyers for native title claim groups can avoid some of the ambiguity on these issues by asking claim groups to be explicit in their authorisation resolutions. Just as claim groups can specify whether the applicant should make decisions unanimously or by majority, they can also specify whether each named applicant will retain their authorisation as an individual even after one of their number has died or stepped down. If the terms of authorisation specify this, the remaining members of the applicant can apply under s. 66B to remove the outgoing individual without holding a new meeting.[600] Conversely, if the terms of authorisation explicitly state that the entire applicant will lose authorisation if any of them dies or withdraws, then arguably a new meeting would be necessary before taking further steps in the litigation. If the terms of authorisation are silent on this matter, it seems that courts may apply those assumptions outlined above and use r. 9.08 of the Federal Court Rules 2011.

595 E.g. *Central West Goldfields People v Western Australia* [2003] FCA 467 [10]. Note in *Doolan v Native Title Registrar* [2007] FCA 192 [69]–[79], Spender J points out that in some parts of the NTA the term 'applicant' is used to refer to an individual member of the joint applicant.

596 *Dodd on behalf of the Gudjala People Core Country Claim #1 v Queensland* [2011] FCA 690 [6].

597 *Butchulla People v Queensland* [2006] FCA 1063 [42]; *Chapman on behalf of the Wakka Wakka People #2 v Queensland* [2007] FCA 597 [10]; *Lennon v South Australia* [2010] FCA 743 [26]. Note that in *Chapman* Kiefel J indicates that the assumption may be displaced by evidence to the contrary.

598 *Butchulla People v Queensland* [2006] FCA 1063 [41].

599 *Dodd on behalf of the Gudjala People Core Country Claim #1 v Queensland* [2011] FCA 690 [21].

600 *Coyne v Western Australia* [2009] FCA 533 [53]–[56].

Change to composition of the proposed replacement applicant between authorisation and application

The same logic that underpins the 'non-66B' approach to *changing* the applicant also applies to situations where one or more of the individuals authorised to be the applicant dies or withdraws *before* the application[601] is first made.

This was the situation in both *Butchulla* and *Doolan* (by coincidence, two cases concerning the same native title claim).[602] In each case, some of the individuals who were authorised at a claim group meeting decided after the meeting that they did not wish to act as applicant. Justice Kiefel in *Butchulla* and Spender J in *Doolan* respectively held that the remaining individuals were still properly authorised even though the composition of the ultimate applicant was different from that authorised at the claim group meeting.

These two cases were decided on slightly different bases. Justice Kiefel's decision in *Butchulla* was based on the understanding that 'authorisation' under the *Native Title Act* is granted personally rather than collectively, such that the continued participation of the other authorised individuals is *irrelevant* to the authorisation of any named applicant.[603] By contrast, Spender J expressly rejected this 'several' view of authorisation and accepted that s. 61(2) 'contemplates an authorisation of persons to act collectively, rather than each of them personally'.[604] Even so, Spender J found that this joint authorisation was granted subject to an implied condition — namely that the application would be made by the named persons 'or so many of them as remain willing and able to act'.[605] His Honour said:

> There is, in my opinion, an implication in an authorisation of a group to act collectively in a representative capacity that that authorisation has to be understood as recognising the vicissitudes that accompany joint action, particularly where (as is frequently the case) the persons authorised to make an application for a native title determination are elderly, and subject to the possible incidents of old age.

In Spender J's view, this implied term of authorisation applied whether the relevant individual was unable or unwilling to act as applicant.[606] Note that this implied condition corresponds to the first assumption outlined above.

Justice Spender's approach was adopted in *Smallwood*, where Rares J held that the authorisation of a joint applicant is implicitly subject to life's 'vicissitudes, expected and unexpected events'.[607] This meant that the joint authorisation of the applicant would not necessarily be vitiated if one

---

601 Note that this applies equally whether the 'application' in question is a Form 1 filed under s. 61 or an application to replace the applicant under s. 66B.

602 *Butchulla People v Queensland* [2006] FCA 1063; *Doolan v Native Title Registrar* [2007] FCA 192.

603 *Butchulla People v Queensland* [2006] FCA 1063 [35]–[45].

604 *Doolan v Native Title Registrar* [2007] FCA 192 [56].

605 ibid. [57].

606 ibid. [58]. See also *Anderson v Western Australia* [2003] FCA 1423 [42].

607 *Smallwood on behalf of the Juru People v Queensland* [2014] FCA 331 [37].

of its members declined to accept the role at some time between the date of authorisation and the date of lodging an application under s. 66B. Justice Rares went on:

> Of course, if a claim group resolved in clear terms that its intention were that particular persons be appointed personally as representing particular families or factions within the claim group, so that the membership of the applicant as authorised could be seen to reflect a deliberate and intentional choice of individuals who were regarded as essential members to comprise the applicant, it may be that the result would be different...[608]

In the circumstances, his Honour examined the evidence and the context of the application, noting there was no indication that the claim group was 'factionalised'. Note that this would correspond to a rebuttal of the second assumption outlined above. Justice Rares accordingly made orders under s. 66B notwithstanding that some of the authorised persons had chosen not to accept their appointment.

Section 66B method

Section 66B of the *Native Title Act* allows one or more persons to apply to replace the existing applicant. In this context 'replace' covers any change to the composition of the applicant: for example, if it is proposed to simply add a new named applicant or remove an existing one, the previous applicant is said to be 'replaced' by a new joint applicant consisting of the previous named applicants plus or minus the relevant individual.[609]

In order to obtain an order under s. 66B, the prospective replacement applicant must satisfy the court of four statutory criteria as well as convincing the court to exercise its discretion in favour of replacement (discussed below at 'Discretion'). The four criteria are:[610]

a) There is a claimant application (or a compensation application).

b) Each person applying for the order is a member of the native title claim group.

c) The persons applying for the order are authorised by the claim group to make the native title application[611] and to deal with matters arising in relation to it.

d) A member of the current applicant has died or become incapacitated; or consents to their removal; or has exceeded their authority; or is no longer authorised by the claim group.[612]

---

608 ibid. [38].

609 *Que Noy v Northern Territory* [2007] FCA 1888 [8] (not challenged on appeal).

610 *Daniel v Western Australia* [2002] FCA 1147 [17]; cited in *Ward v Northern Territory* [2002] FCA 1477 [15]; *Lawson on behalf of 'Pooncarie' Barkandji (Paakantyi) People v Minister for Land and Water Conservation (NSW)* [2002] FCA 1517 [16].

611 Note that s. 66B requires only that the replacement applicant be authorised to make and deal with the underlying native title application. Authorisation to make the s. 66B application is inferred from that principal authorisation: *Que Noy v Northern Territory* [2007] FCA 1888 [11] (not challenged on appeal). Nevertheless, there is no reason not to include an explicit resolution authorising the s. 66B application.

612 Note that prior to the 2007 amendment, the grounds for removal were limited to the third and fourth items listed, namely loss or excess of authority.

The first two criteria are fairly self-explanatory. The last two will now be dealt with in turn.

Authorisation of the replacement applicant

Just as s. 61(1) requires that the applicant be authorised by the claim group, so too does s. 66B(1)(b) require that any subsequent replacement be similarly authorised. A note accompanying s. 66B(1)(b) confirms that s. 251B contains the requirements for such authorisation. That means that the discussion above in Chapter 3 is equally applicable to this context. (Indeed, many of the cases cited in that discussion are cases concerning s. 66B.)

In most circumstances, satisfying s. 66B(1)(b) will require a fresh claim group meeting to be held. The only exceptions to this are:

(i) where the group's decision-making process does not require meetings (see Section 3.2 above at 'Is a meeting actually required at all?');

(ii) where no *new* authorisation decision is required because the original terms of authorisation explicitly confirmed the continuing authorisation of individual named applicants.

This second situation effectively mirrors the situation described above at 'Non-66B method'. The remaining named applicants retain their original authorisation and can simply approach the court for orders removing the name(s) of the outgoing individual(s).[613] The difference from the 'non-66B' approach is that under s. 66B a court will require evidence that the original terms of authorisation explicitly provided for this kind of contingency.[614] Two cases in which this principle has been applied, albeit in a slightly different context, are *Coyne* and *Anderson*.[615] In each of those cases, a claim group meeting was held for s. 66B purposes but one of the newly authorised named applicants died before the s. 66B application was heard. At each meeting, a resolution was passed authorising all of the incoming applicants 'or such of them as are eligible to act as an applicant and who remain willing and able to act in respect of the application in the future'. Accordingly, the surviving individuals were still sufficiently authorised even though their co-appointees were deceased.

For claim groups that are vulnerable to conflict or controversy, practitioners may wish to go further than those in *Coyne* and *Anderson* by setting conditional authorisations that explicitly confirm the ongoing authorisation of any named applicant who acts in accordance with those conditions (more on conditional authorisation below). This creates the equivalent of a 'springing order' because it allows a non-conforming named applicant to be removed by the other named applicants without any need for a claim group meeting. The conforming named applicants simply

---

613 The remaining named applicants may need to file an affidavit deposing to the terms and circumstances of their original authorisation and the circumstances justifying the removal of the outgoing named applicant(s).

614 That appears to be the basis for Siopis J's decision in *Sambo v Western Australia* [2008] FCA 1575 [32]; it is more clearly accepted by Dowsett J in *Murgha on behalf of the Combined Gunggandji Claim v Queensland* [2011] FCA 1317 [4].

615 *Coyne v Western Australia* [2009] FCA 533 [53]–[56]; *Anderson v Western Australia* [2007] FCA 1733 [37]–[38].

apply under s. 66B, point to the breach of the condition as the basis for removal, and point to the terms of their original authorisation as evidence for their ongoing authorisation.

In the absence of a specific resolution, the claim group's endorsement of the surviving named applicants may be inferred from its conduct, though this is not a common occurrence. In the 2011 case of *Murgha*[616] there were two named applicants and one of them died. Between his death and the s. 66B application to remove his name, the claim group met for an unrelated purpose (the authorisation of an ILUA) and made no attempt to replace the remaining applicant or appoint any additional individuals. In the circumstances Dowsett J inferred that the claim group intended for the surviving named applicants to continue as the sole applicant.[617] His Honour therefore removed the deceased applicant without an explicit decision of the claim group.

Consistency between original and subsequent decision-making process

In the past there has been some suggestion that a claim group's decision to replace the applicant must be made using the same decision-making process as was used to authorise the original applicant.[618] For example, in *Lawson v Lawson* Stone J dismissed a motion under s. 66B on the basis that the decision to replace the applicant had not been made according to the same decision-making process initially used to authorise the applicant.[619] Conversely, in *Daniel* French J found that the claim group's authorisation meeting had been validly held, and this finding was supported by the fact that the claim group had employed the same decision-making process in previous authorisation decisions.[620]

There is, however, no firm rule requiring '66B decisions' to be made according to the same decision-making process as was originally used to authorise the claim. The core requirement, as with any authorisation decision, is that the process used by the claim group must meet the criteria in s. 251B. A claim group may validly decide to replace an applicant using a different process to the one used to authorise the applicant, so long as the process employed can be said to be either traditional or agreed and adopted.[621] There is no requirement to give prior notice that a different decision-making procedure will be employed, nor to make an explicit decision about the decision-making process.[622] In *N.C. (deceased)* McKerracher J held that a claim group may make decisions by a series of different processes so long as the group as

---

616 *Murgha (Combined Gunggandji Claim) v Queensland* [2011] FCA 1317.

617 ibid. [4]–[5]. See also *Wurrunmurra v Western Australia* [2012] FCA 1399 [15]–[17], where Gilmour J found that a claim group had implicitly decided that the six deceased members of the applicant would remain as named applicants and that the surviving two would be continued to deal with all matters relating to the claim.

618 See L Strelein, *Authorisation and replacement of applicants: Bolton v WA [2004] FCA 760*, Land, Rights, Laws: Issues of Native Title, vol. 3, no. 1, Native Title Research Unit, AIATSIS, Canberra, 2005, p. 8.

619 *Johnson, in the matter of Lawson v Lawson* [2001] FCA 894 [25]–[32].

620 *Daniel v Western Australia* [2002] FCA 1147 [51].

621 *Butchulla People v Queensland* [2006] FCA 1063 [31].

622 ibid. [32]; *Noble v Mundraby* [2005] FCAFC 212 [18].

a whole may be said to have agreed and adopted each respective process.[623] Even where the original decision-making process was characterised as 'traditional', the claim group may still validly make authorisation decisions by a different process if the traditional process can be shown to have broken down and the new process was agreed and adopted by the group.[624]

Grounds for removal or replacement

Withdrawal or loss of authorisation

The most pertinent ground to consider for replacement is the loss or withdrawal of authority: s. 66B(1)(a)(iii). That is because in most cases where there has been a specific claim group meeting to authorise a *replacement* applicant, that meeting will have explicitly or implicitly withdrawn the authorisation of the *existing* applicant. In practical terms that means that in most cases where the authorisation requirement in s. 66B(1)(b) is satisfied, the 'no longer authorised' requirement in s. 66B(1)(a)(iii) is also satisfied.[625]

Regardless, there are two ways of demonstrating that the current applicant is no longer authorised by the claim group:

a) a positive decision of the claim group (whether by explicit resolution or implied from the authorisation of a replacement);

b) by operation of a condition on the original authorisation.

The first is the most direct. Although s. 251B does not in its terms apply to the withdrawal of authorisation, that section has been held to define the relevant decision-making process for such withdrawal.[626] Accordingly, the same notification and process requirements apply to a decision to remove an applicant as to appoint one in the first place.[627] Note that there is no requirement that the 'outgoing' applicant attend the meeting at which their authority is withdrawn.[628] As mentioned, a decision to authorise a replacement applicant may implicitly

---

623 *N.C. (deceased) v Western Australia (No. 2)* [2013] FCA 70 [86]–[97].

624 *Lawson on behalf of 'Pooncarie' Barkandji (Paakantyi) People v Minister for Land and Water Conservation (NSW)* [2002] FCA 1517.

625 See e.g. *Lungunan v Western Australia* [2012] FCA 78 [5], where a claim group resolved that the current applicant was no longer authorised in circumstances where some named applicants had died and others were unwilling to continue to act. The court made the s. 66B order based on the satisfaction of s. 66B(1)(b)(iii).

626 *Daniel v Western Australia* [2002] FCA 1147 [14]; *Ward v Northern Territory* [2002] FCA 1477 [15]; *Lawson on behalf of the 'Pooncarie' Barkandji (Paakantyi) People v Minister for Land and Water Conservation* [2002] FCA 1517 [14].

627 Note comments in *Wharton on behalf of the Kooma People v Queensland* [2003] FCA 790 [33].

628 *Combined Mandingalbay Yidinji-Gunggandji Claim v Queensland* [2004] FCA 1703 [41]; *Que Noy v Northern Territory* [2007] FCA 1888 [29]. See also *Holborow v Western Australia* [2002] FCA 1428 [19]; *Wiradjuri Wellington v Minister for Land and Water Conservation (NSW)* [2004] FCA 1127.

de-authorise the existing applicant.[629] Nevertheless, it would be prudent for NTRB lawyers assisting with a claim group meeting to suggest that a specific 'de-authorisation' resolution be made to avoid any ambiguity.

The second method of demonstrating loss or withdrawal of authorisation is to make the original authorisation contingent on certain conditions. This way, when a particular pre-determined event occurs the authorisation will cease automatically without the need for an additional decision by the claim group.[630] As mentioned earlier, conditional authorisation in this way could be used to 'cancel' the applicant's authorisation in the case where any of the named applicants dies or steps down. Conditional authorisation can also be used to ensure that applicants make decisions within boundaries set by the claim group as a whole. (Loss of authorisation in these circumstances would also fall within s. 66B(1)(b)(iv), described below.)

In some circumstances it may be possible for claim group members to show that the applicant has simply lost authorisation as a consequence of the previous consensus having broken down. Evidence of such a loss of authorisation, however, would not be sufficient by itself to sustain an order under s. 66B because there would be nothing to demonstrate that a proposed replacement applicant had the necessary authorisation. For example, in *Weribone* two factions within a claim group each held their own separate meeting to authorise a new applicant.[631] Justice Rares found that neither meeting was validly notified and so neither could properly sustain an order under s. 66B. However, in light of the clear disagreement within the claim group his Honour also found that 'there is no longer an applicant authorised by the claim group to make or prosecute the existing application and deal with matters arising in relation to it.'[632] Accordingly, Rares J ordered the competing factions to mediate towards the holding of a new meeting to break the impasse. *Weribone* differs from the approach taken in *Lawson v Lawson*, where Stone J held that the applicant's 'loss of confidence' amongst the broader claim group *did not* equate to a loss of authorisation.[633] In that case, her Honour considered that a specific decision of the claim group was required to 'strip' the applicant of its authority.[634] Despite this divergence, it remains clear in any case that an order under s. 66B will require a demonstration of the replacement applicant's authorisation, something that will not be established by evidence showing the current applicant's *lack* of authorisation.

As mentioned earlier in the discussion of s. 66B, it is possible to set up a sort of 'springing order'. When the claim group authorises the applicant and places conditions on their authority, the group can also specify that each individual named applicant will *continue* to be authorised so long as they do not breach those conditions. The group can make it even clearer and specifically

629 The inference in such a case would be analogous to that drawn in *Murgha (Combined Gunggandji Claim) v Queensland* [2011] FCA 1317.

630 *Daniel v Western Australia* [2002] FCA 1147 [15].

631 *Weribone on behalf of the Mandandanji People v Queensland* [2013] FCA 255.

632 ibid. [55].

633 *Johnson, in the matter of Lawson v Lawson* [2001] FCA 894 [27].

634 See also *Anderson v Western Australia* [2003] FCA 1423 [41]; *Ward v Northern Territory* [2002] FCA 1477 [15]; both citing *Daniel v Western Australia* [2002] FCA 1147 [15].

authorise each of the named applicants to apply under s. 66B to replace any who do not stay within the boundaries of their authority. This means that, if the need arises, the conforming members of the applicant can point to the terms of their original authorisation as evidence of both the outgoing individuals' *lack* of authority and the remaining individuals' *ongoing* authority for the purposes of s. 66B.

Judges making orders based on the loss of authorisation often emphasise that they are making no judgment about whether the withdrawal of authority is fair, wise or justified.[635] In *P.C.* an outgoing named applicant complained that the claim group would not have replaced him if they had been informed of his reasons for refusing to sign certain documents.[636] Justice Bennett rejected this complaint, saying that so long as the withdrawal of authority could be shown to flow from the claim group, it was not for the court to judge whether the group's decision was well-founded.[637] In a different case dealing with similar facts, the claim group withdrew their authorisation from a named applicant who refused to sign a particular ILUA and the fact that he later *signed* the ILUA was irrelevant to the question of his removal under s. 66B.[638]

Death or incapacity

The death or incapacity of a named applicant is one of the grounds for replacement under s. 66B(1)(a)(ii). This ground is straightforward to establish and where a claim group holds a meeting to authorise the remaining applicants to continue (or alternatively to authorise an entirely new set of named applicants) it is a simple matter to obtain an order under s. 66B.

For clarity on this topic, it is worth considering four different questions that arise specifically in relation to the death of a named applicant (note the discussion is also relevant to cases of mere incapacitation):

i) Is the person still a member of the applicant even though they are deceased?

ii) Does the law require deceased individuals to be removed as applicants?

iii) Are the remaining named applicants still authorised?

iv) Will the death of an individual prevent the applicant from acting?

The answer to the first question is 'yes'. The authority for this is the Full Court decision in *FQM*.[639] In that case a mining company argued that, upon the death of the last surviving named applicant, there was no longer any 'registered native title claimant' and therefore no 'native title party' with whom the company was obliged to negotiate.[640] The Full Court agreed with the trial judge that deceased named applicants remain registered native title claimants until their names

635 E.g. *Lawson on behalf of the 'Pooncarie' Barkandji (Paakantyi) People v Minister for Land and Water Conservation (NSW)* [2002] FCA 1517 [29].

636 *P.C. (name withheld) on behalf of the Njamal People v Western Australia* [2007] FCA 1054 [26]–[35].

637 ibid. [39]; *Roe v Western Australia (No. 2)* [2011] FCA 102 [12], [16].

638 *Doctor on behalf of the Bigambul People v Queensland* [2010] FCA 1406 [23], [70]–[71].

639 *FQM Australia Nickel Pty Ltd v Bullen* [2011] FCAFC 30.

640 The mining company was relying on the definition of 'native title party' in s. 30(1)(a), NTA.

are removed from the Register of Native Title Claims. In coming to this decision the Full Court relied on the fact that s. 66B provides for the replacement of an applicant who has died.

On the second question: as indicated earlier there is no legal duty or requirement to remove the name of a deceased named applicant.[641] Although in Queensland cases it has become common practice to do so,[642] the accepted practice in Western Australia appears to be to allow claim groups to retain the names if they wish. For example, in a 2012 Western Australia consent determination Gilmour J had to decide whether there was any defect in authorisation for a claim whose applicant included six deceased individuals.[643] Two successive claim group meetings had resolved to leave the applicant unchanged despite the passing of the six individuals. His Honour found this to be evidence of an intention for the six deceased individuals to remain named on the application, with the surviving two members authorised to deal with matters arising under the claim.[644] Justice Gilmour said that he did not consider that the death of the six created any defect in authorisation that would prevent the consent determination, but if it did he would have allowed the matter to proceed under s. 84D(4).[645]

The third question asks whether a consequence of an individual's death is that the surviving applicants lose their authorisation. This question was addressed above in sections 4.2 and 5.1 at 'Non-66B method'. It forms the basis for the judicial disagreement regarding s. 66B 'covering the field'. Ultimately, the question is about the intention of the claim group, which is to be settled by a combination of evidence and assumptions. If the evidence establishes that the claim group intended for individual applicants to retain their authorisation even if others pass away, the survivors should be able to obtain an order under s. 66B to remove the deceased individuals.[646] Such an intention may be an explicit term of authorisation but may also be inferred from other evidence.[647] The evidence may, however, show that the claim group sees the applicant as representing sectional interests such that the death of one individual requires a new appointment from the same subgroup in order to maintain appropriate balance. In such cases, an order under s. 66B would not be appropriate until a replacement representative had been appointed. In the absence of evidence either

---

641 There are examples from both consent determinations and litigated determinations: e.g. *Hunter v Western Australia* [2012] FCA 690; *Dodd v South Australia* [2012] FCA 519; *A.B. (deceased) (on behalf of the Ngarla People) v Western Australia* [2012] FCA 1268.

642 E.g. in *Murgha on behalf of the Combined Gunggandji Claim v Queensland* [2011] FCA 1317 [3], Dowsett J said 'I am now asked by [the surviving member of the applicant] to remove [the deceased member of the applicant] as an applicant so that the application can proceed to a consent determination.'

643 *Wurrunmurra v Western Australia* [2012] FCA 1399.

644 ibid. [16].

645 ibid. [17]. See also *Barunga v Western Australia* [2011] FCA 518.

646 *Coyne v Western Australia* [2010] FCA 1052.

647 See *Murgha on behalf of the Combined Gunggandji Claim v Queensland* [2011] FCA 1317; *Wurrunmurra v Western Australia* [2012] FCA 1399 [16]; *Barunga v Western Australia* [2011] FCA 518 [12]–[19]; *Sharpe v Western Australia* [2013] FCA 599 [20]–[21]. Also *W.F. (deceased) on behalf of the Wiluna People v Western Australia* [2013] FCA 755.

way, judges will need to rely on assumptions, and it is those differing assumptions that underlie the judicial disagreement mentioned before.

The fourth question relates to the rules governing actions by the applicant, covered in Chapter 4 above. That chapter referred to the view of Mansfield J in one of the *Far West Coast* decisions that the law requires agreement among 'all the authorised persons *who are able and willing to act*' (emphasis added).[648] Accordingly, the fact that deceased individuals are unable to participate in decision-making does not prevent the applicant from making valid and binding decisions. This result is confirmed by those instances where the court made a consent determination of native title even though some of the named applicants were deceased.[649]

Consent

One of the grounds for an order under s. 66B is that at least one of the named applicants 'consents to his or her replacement or removal': s. 66B(1)(a)(i). This consent must be established by evidence, though such evidence need not specifically include an affidavit from the outgoing individual.[650]

Before the 2007 amendments to s. 66B, there was no explicit basis in the legislation for removing a named applicant on the basis of their consent. However, in *Anderson* French J found that a person who no longer wished to continue acting as applicant could be removed under (the then equivalent of) s. 66B(1)(a)(iii) on the basis that they were 'no longer authorised by the claim group'.[651] This was because:

> ...authorisation, of its very nature, is only able to be conferred upon a willing party. A party unwilling to continue as an applicant may therefore be replaced on the basis of an implied lack of authority.[652]

As with the other grounds under s. 66B, it is necessary for the replacement applicant to demonstrate that they are properly authorised to act as applicant: s. 66B(1)(b). This requires either a fresh authorisation from the claim group or else (if the replacement applicant is the same as the existing applicant minus the outgoing member) a finding that the remaining named applicants retain their original authorisation.[653]

648 *Far West Coast Native Title Claim v South Australia* [2012] FCA 733 [54]. See also *Smallwood on behalf of the Juru People v Queensland* [2014] FCA 331 [35].

649 E.g. *W.F. (deceased) on behalf of the Wiluna People v Western Australia* [2013] FCA 755; *B.P. (deceased) v Western Australia* [2013] FCA 760. The fact that these were consent determinations is relevant because they necessarily involved the applicant taking an active step in the proceedings.

650 *Kuruma and Marthudunera People v Western Australia* [2012] FCA 14 [9]–[11].

651 *Anderson v Western Australia* [2003] FCA 1423.

652 ibid. [42].

653 See e.g. *Roe v Western Australia (No. 2)* [2011] FCA 102.

Excess of authority

An applicant may be removed or replaced if one or more of its members 'has exceeded the authority given to him or her by the claim group to make the application and to deal with matters arising in relation to it': s. 66B(1)(a)(iv).

To make out this ground for replacement, the incoming applicant (who may be an entirely new set of named applicants or may simply comprise the existing named applicants minus the individual who is to be removed) must do two things:

i) demonstrate the extent of the authority given by the claim group to the current applicant;

ii) point to some conduct on the part of the current applicant (or any of its members) that is said to exceed that authority.[654]

In *Ward v Northern Territory*, Mansfield J set out a fairly strict test for establishing an excess of authority under s. 66B(1)(a)(iv).[655] His Honour stated that the claim group's authority will be exceeded only if one of the following applies:

a) the authority so conferred was subject to some expressed limitation or restriction which has been exceeded;

b) the authority so conferred was subject to the continuing supervision and direction of the native title claim group *and* there is some resolution or direction of the native title claim group which has not been complied with;

c) the authority so conferred has, by some further decision of the native title claim group, been made subject to some expressed limitation or restriction which has been exceeded, or has been made subject to the continuing supervision and direction of the native title claim group *and* there is some resolution or direction of the native title claim group which has not been complied with.[656]

Despite the apparently exhaustive nature of this test, Mansfield J took a more flexible approach in *Que Noy*.[657] In that case Mansfield J concluded that the scope of the original authority does not have to be 'precisely delineated' by the evidence and it does not need to have been 'clearly and explicitly expressed' at the time it was given.[658] Rather, the question of whether the claim group's authority has been exceeded is a factual matter to be determined on the whole of the available evidence.[659] The evidence in *Que Noy* showed that the claim group's authority had been exceeded by a named applicant who had purported to negotiate unilaterally about a proposed future act without including the other named applicants. The individual had

---

654 *Que Noy v Northern Territory* [2007] FCA 1888 [15].

655 *Ward v Northern Territory* [2002] FCA 1477. Note at that time it was labelled paragraph (ii).

656 ibid. [15].

657 *Que Noy v Northern Territory* [2007] FCA 1888.

658 ibid. [21].

659 ibid.

also purported to refuse the claim group's solicitors access to the area affected by the proposed future act. Even if the individual had been acting with the authority of her subset of the claim group, she had certainly not been acting within the authority of the claim group as a whole.[660] If it were necessary to fit *Que Noy* into Mansfield J's three-limb test in *Ward*, it could be said that the original authority was subject to a limitation whereby the named applicants would act as a group rather than unilaterally.

It is not necessary for the claim group to hold a meeting and actively decide that their authority has been exceeded; rather it is sufficient for the proposed replacement applicant to show how the conduct of the current named applicant(s) went beyond the authority originally given.[661] However, despite this 'automatic' aspect of s. 66B(1)(a)(iv), the proposed replacement applicant must still be able to demonstrate that they are authorised to replace the existing applicant.[662] As mentioned previously, this requires either a fresh claim group meeting *or* a finding that the remaining named applicants have retained their original authorisation. Unlike the case for death, incapacity or unwillingness, where an excess of authority is alleged courts may be less inclined to infer that a claim group *implicitly* intended to authorise the original applicant on terms that would dispense with the need for a fresh meeting.[663] Given the potentially contentious nature of such situations, courts may require evidence that the claim group made this an explicit term of authorisation.[664] So in the absence of this kind of special term, there will need to be a fresh meeting before s. 66B(1)(a)(iv) can be successfully deployed.

Note that a named applicant need not take any positive step in order to exceed their authority; a *refusal* to act may constitute an excess of authority for the purposes of s. 66B(1)(a)(iv).[665]

What if the applicant was never authorised at all?

There have been cases in which claim group members who are dissatisfied with the current applicant have sought to demonstrate that the applicant was never validly authorised to bring the application at all. Although that may be a good basis on which to seek to have the claim struck out, it is not a ground for seeking replacement under s. 66B.

An early case dealing with this issue was *Moran*.[666] In that case a member of the claim group sought to replace the current applicant under s. 66B. Justice Wilcox found not only that the proposed replacement applicant was not properly authorised but also that the original

660 ibid. [22].

661 *Daniel v Western Australia* [2002] FCA 1147 [15]–[16].

662 See *Sambo v Western Australia* [2008] FCA 1575 [32].

663 Section 66B has repeatedly been characterised as a provision directed to maintaining the claim group's 'ultimate authority': *Daniel v Western Australia* [2002] FCA 1147 [16]. Cf. *Doolan v Native Title Registrar* [2007] FCA 192 [58].

664 Such a term was employed by the Yindjibarndi people as described in *N.C. (deceased) v Western Australia (No. 2)* [2013] FCA 70.

665 E.g. the refusal to sign an agreement when the claim group wished for it to be signed: *Daniel v Western Australia* [2002] FCA 1147.

666 *Moran v Minister for Land and Water Conservation (NSW)* [1999] FCA 1637.

authorisation of the existing applicant was defective *at the time it was purportedly conducted.* His Honour found that the native title claim was therefore foredoomed to fail. (At this time the *Native Title Act* did not yet contain the power under s. 84D(4)(a) to hear a claim despite a defect in authorisation.)[667] Accordingly the native title application was dismissed as an abuse of process.

There was a similar result in *Fesl*, where Spender J allowed the existing applicant to discontinue the claim rather than allow the proposed replacement applicant to obtain an order under s. 66B.[668] His Honour held that there can be no order under s. 66B unless there is a validly authorised native title application in the first place: 'Authorisation as a fact is a threshold requirement for the operation of s 66B of the Act.'[669] On the hearing of the application for leave to appeal from Spender J's decision, the Full Court expressed some doubt about Spender J's approach but refused leave to appeal on the grounds that the proposed replacement applicant may not have been properly authorised either.[670]

In *Turrbal People*[671] and *Williams v Grant*[672] the court held that a s. 66B hearing is not the occasion for exploring whether the original authorisation of the claim was valid. The court held in both cases that a person wishing to attack the initial authorisation of the claim should bring a strike-out application under s. 84C. It may be added that s. 84D is potentially relevant to such situations also.

Discretion

Under s. 66B(2) the court *may* make the order if satisfied that the grounds are established. The court has a residual discretion not to make an order under s. 66B.[673] It is very rare for judges to refuse orders under s. 66B on discretionary grounds.[674] In the vast majority of cases where the conditions in s. 66B(1) are satisfied, courts have made the order as sought.[675] In some cases the discretion is not mentioned at all and in others the court simply states that there is no reason not to make the orders.[676] It would be impractical to give an exhaustive catalogue of all of the factors which have influenced courts' exercise of their discretion under s. 66B(2). The following examples are merely illustrative:

---

667 ibid. [47]–[48].

668 *Fesl v Queensland* [2005] FCA 120.

669 ibid. [5].

670 *Davidson v Fesl* [2005] FCAFC 183 [22]–[28].

671 *Turrbal People v Queensland* [2008] FCA 316 [26].

672 *Williams v Grant* [2004] FCAFC 178.

673 *Ward v Northern Territory* [2002] FCA 171 [16]; *Daniel v Western Australia* [2002] FCA 1147 [18], [54].

674 For an example of discretionary grounds militating against making orders under s. 66B, see *T.J. v Western Australia* [2015] FCA 818 [107]–[117]. These factors included evidence of manipulation of the process by an outside party and the influence of benefits provided to some voters.

675 Indeed, I was unable to find an instance of a court declining to make an order in circumstances where the requirements of s. 66B(1) were otherwise satisfied. While there is some mention of the 'interests of justice' in *Weribone on behalf of the Mandandanji People v Queensland* [2013] FCA 255 [52], the substantive decision at [50]–[54] related to problems in the authorisation of the replacement applicant.

676 E.g. *Ward v Northern Territory* [2002] FCA 1477 [42].

- Where a claim group meeting was held pursuant to a court order, and the meeting resolved unanimously and overwhelmingly to replace the applicant, this is a strong reason in favour of making an order under s. 66B.[677]
- Where an individual has avoided signing an important agreement that is supported by the group as a whole, to refuse an order under s. 66B would be to undermine the authority of the claim group.[678]
- Where the NTRB and the state have devoted extensive resources and a high priority to the claim, a named applicant's lack of cooperation in negotiating towards a consent determination has been treated as a factor in favour of removing that individual.[679]
- The fact that a claim group is divided, even bitterly so, does not constitute a sufficient reason for declining to make an order under s. 66B.[680] Nevertheless, the division between factions and their respective representation within the applicant may be a factor relevant to the exercise of discretion.[681]
- By contrast, longstanding division between the named applicant on the one hand and the rest of the claim group on the other, will support an order under s. 66B.[682] Similarly, where the removal of one named applicant will allow the remaining applicant to act jointly without dispute.[683]
- A potential conflict of interest on the part of the proposed replacement applicant could be relevant to the exercise of discretion, such as where the proposed replacement applicant is also a member of the applicant for a neighbouring or overlapping claim.[684]

---

677 *Tatow on behalf of the Iman People #2 v Queensland* [2011] FCA 802 [27].

678 *Daniel v Western Australia* [2002] FCA 1147 [54]. Also *Simpson on behalf of the Wajarri Elders v Western Australia* [2004] FCA 1752 [4]; *Doctor on behalf of the Bigambul People v Queensland* [2010] FCA 1406 [71]; *P.C. (name withheld) on behalf of the Njamal People v Western Australia* [2007] FCA 1054.

679 *Combined Mandingalbay Yidinji-Gunggandji Claim v Queensland* [2004] FCA 1703 [43]–[45].

680 *Roe v Western Australia (No. 2)* [2011] FCA 102 [134]; *Doctor on behalf of the Bigambul People v Queensland* [2010] FCA 1406; *'Pooncarie' Barkandji (Paakantyi) People v Minister for Land and Water Conservation (NSW)* [2006] FCA 25 [36]; *Que Noy v Northern Territory* [2007] FCA 1888 [41].

681 *N.C. (deceased) v Western Australia (No. 2)* [2013] FCA 70 [99]–[106].

682 *P.C. (name withheld) on behalf of the Njamal People v Western Australia* [2007] FCA 1054; *Holborow v Western Australia* [2002] FCA 1428 [51].

683 *Wiradjuri Wellington v Minister for Land and Water Conservation (NSW)* [2004] FCA 1127 [17].

684 In *Roe v Western Australia (No. 2)* [2011] FCA 102 Gilmour J found that the alleged conflict would be extremely unlikely to materialise in the circumstances of that case and accordingly concluded that it would be an insufficient basis for refusing orders under s. 66B. His Honour did, however, consider that the mere semblance of conflict might be relevant to the exercise of discretion and so accepted undertakings from the relevant individuals to step down from their applicant role in one or other of the two claims.

Notwithstanding the matters just mentioned, the court's discretion under s. 66B(2) does not invite the court to exercise its own judgment about the substantive merits of the proposed replacement of the applicant. In *P.C.* Bennett J explained the position as follows:

> The withdrawal and conferring of authority for the purposes of a s 66B application must be shown to flow from the claim group [...] Once this is established, the actions of the claim group and the means by which it makes decisions is a matter for it. It is not for the Court to interfere with decisions reached in accordance with the Act. It is not for the Court to consider the wisdom of those decisions or whether, in this case, there is merit in [the outgoing applicant's] concerns. It is for him to communicate those concerns, if he wishes to do so, to the other claimants and for the applicant, on receipt of instructions from the claim group, to act as authorised.[685]

In that case, the outgoing named applicant had argued that the claim group had not properly appreciated the reasons why he had refused to sign certain agreements and so their decision to remove him on that basis was not fully informed. For this reason he asked the court not to make the order under s. 66B. Justice Bennett refused this request and made the order.

The decision in *P.C.* has been cited in subsequent decisions.[686] Note that in *Weribone* Rares J seems to have favoured a different approach, whereby the decision of a claim group might not be given effect if it was demonstrably misled or misinformed about the facts.[687] Similarly, in *T.J.*[688] Rares J also indicated that a range of factors would influence his exercise of discretion against granting an order under s. 66B (one of which was that the claim group had been misled). *P.C.* and the two decisions of Rares J could potentially be distinguished on the basis that the lack of information in *P.C.* could have been remedied if the outgoing applicant had attended the claim group meeting and put his case to the group. In any case, Rares J's decision in *Weribone* and *T.J.* was ultimately based on a failure to meet the requirements of s. 66B(1) rather than on discretionary grounds.

Documents required

If an order is made under s. 66B to replace the applicant it appears that a separate interlocutory application must be made for leave to amend the Form 1 to reflect the change.

---

685 *P.C. (name withheld) on behalf of the Njamal People v Western Australia* [2007] FCA 1054 [39].

686 See e.g. *Roe v Western Australia (No. 2)* [2011] FCA 102 [12]; *N.C. (deceased) v Western Australia (No. 2)* [2013] FCA 70 [76].

687 *Weribone on behalf of the Mandandanji People v Queensland* [2013] FCA 255 [49], [51]–[54].

688 *T.J. v Western Australia* [2015] FCA 818.

There are several parts of the Form 1 that could conceivably require amendment following a s. 66B order. Most obviously the 'NAME OF APPLICANT(S)' section on the first page would need to be changed. Depending on how much detail had been provided in the original, Item 2 of Part A may also require amendment — this is the statement of the capacity in which the applicant is entitled to make the application. Schedule R, which sets out the more detailed account of the applicant's authorisation, will need to be updated unless the replacement applicant is relying on an existing 'springing' conditional authorisation of the kind discussed earlier in this section. Finally, the details of any amendments to the Form 1 would need to be separately recorded at Schedule S.

Under r. 8.21 of the Federal Court Rules 2011 the applicant may apply for leave to amend an originating application. Assuming the s. 66B application is successful, the replacement applicant would be the relevant party to seek leave. Although the grant of leave for amending the Form 1 is a discretionary matter for the court, it will generally not be difficult to obtain leave where the court has already made an order under s. 66B.[689] For example, in one case Gilmour J allowed the amendment of a claim to reflect the replacement of the applicant and waived the requirement for an amended application to be filed and served.[690]

Note that previously the *Native Title Act* explicitly required each of the members of the replacement applicant to swear an affidavit attesting to the matters in s. 62(1)(a)(iv) and (v).[691] That requirement was repealed in 2007,[692] apparently as part of several changes intended to clarify that there is no need to reapply the registration test after a s. 66B order.[693] Nevertheless, the court will still require an evidentiary basis for orders under s. 66B and in some cases this may involve the provision of affidavit evidence by one or more members of the replacement applicants. In particular it will be necessary to satisfy the court that each member of the incoming named applicant is a member of the native title claim group, has been authorised as applicant, and is ready, willing and able to act in that capacity.[694]

5.2 Consequences of a failed s. 66B application

Bringing an application under s. 66B carries certain risks. If a proposed replacement applicant establishes that the current applicant lacks authority but then fails to obtain an order under s. 66B, the claim will be left without a currently authorised applicant.

---

689 E.g. *Tatow on behalf of the Iman People #2 v Queensland* [2011] FCA 802 [28].

690 *Lungunan v Western Australia* [2012] FCA 78 [9].

691 Section 64(5), NTA. See e.g. *P.C. (name withheld) on behalf of the Njamal People v Western Australia* [2007] FCA 1054 [25].

692 *Native Title Amendment (Technical Amendments) Act 2007* (Cth).

693 Items 1.245–1.249, Explanatory Memorandum to the Native Title Amendment (Technical Amendments) Bill 2007.

694 E.g. *Smallwood on behalf of the Juru People v Queensland* [2014] FCA 331.

The most serious risk is that the court may consider striking out the application under s. 84C for failure to satisfy the requirements of s. 61.[695] Although the court will be cautious in using this power, such an outcome is possible where the claim group is hopelessly deadlocked and the application is unlikely to proceed.[696]

Arguably the risk of strike-out has diminished since the introduction of s. 84D(4) in 2007. That subsection gives the court the discretion to hear and determine a claim despite a defect in authorisation. Accordingly, authorisation difficulties no longer necessarily mean that an application is 'foredoomed to failure'.[697]

A less dramatic alternative to strike-out is for the court to order the claim group to hold a fresh authorisation meeting. The power to make such an order can be found in s. 84D(4)(b) and has been exercised in two recent cases in Queensland.[698]

695 E.g. *Moran v Minister for Land and Water Conservation (NSW)* [1999] FCA 1637. Of course, if the challengers fail to establish that the existing applicants have lost their authorisation then there will be no problem in the application continuing as before: *Johnson, in the matter of Lawson v Lawson* [2001] FCA 894.

696 *Ward v Northern Territory* [2002] FCA 171 [26]–[27].

697 See ibid. [27].

698 *Weribone on behalf of the Mandandanji People v Queensland* [2013] FCA 255 and *Doctor on behalf of the Bigambul People v Queensland (No. 2)* [2013] FCA 746.

6. Changing the claim group description

During the course of a native title claim it may become necessary to amend the claim group description in the Form 1, whether to remedy an error or omission, to incorporate the results of new anthropological research, to combine neighbouring or overlapping claims, or to allow a single claim to be split up.

This chapter will set out the process by which this should ideally be done. This involves a 'two step' process whereby members of the pre-amendment claim group meet first to give their approval of the change, and then members of the proposed claim group meet either to confirm the authorisation of the existing applicant or else to authorise a new applicant.[699] The chapter will raise in passing some of the legal–ethical implications of changing the composition of the native title claim group but will not attempt to draw out all of the implications or give any conclusive answers. In this regard the reader should also see Section 4.4 ('Legal progessional obligations') and the introduction to Chapter 5.

6.1 Authorisation by pre-amendment group

The Form 1 for a native title claim, like the originating application in any Federal Court proceedings, may be amended under r. 8.21 of the Federal Court Rules 2011.[700] Amendments under r. 8.21 can only be made with the court's leave, which must be sought by way of an interlocutory application. The grant of leave is discretionary and courts will consider a range of factors in the exercise of their discretion.[701] One important factor is whether the applicant consulted with the claim group and obtained their approval to seek the amendment.[702] Note that specific authorisation is not technically a requirement for amendment; s. 62A is clear in its confirmation of the applicant's legal competence to take such a step in the proceedings.[703] Strictly speaking, their authority to seek an amendment

699 *Kudjala People v Queensland* [2006] FCA 1564 [13]–[15]; *Dodd on behalf of the Wulli Wulli People v Queensland (No. 2)* [2009] FCA 1180 [3], [14].

700 Note that while s. 64, NTA imposes certain constraints on the kinds of amendments that can be made, it would be misleading to refer to an amendment 'under s. 64': *Strickland v Western Australia* [2013] FCA 677 [11]; *Anderson v Western Australia* [2003] FCA 1423 [37]; *P.C. (name withheld) on behalf of the Njamal People v Western Australia* [2007] FCA 1054 [4]; see also *Holborow v Western Australia (No. 2)* [2013] FCA 1040 [4]. The note to s. 64(1) states that '[t]he Federal Court Rules provide for the amendment of applications.'

701 E.g. *Strickland v Western Australia* [2013] FCA 677 [14]; *Eora People – Brown v Minister for Land and Water Conservation (NSW)* [2000] FCA 1238 [22]–[23].

702 E.g. *Hatfield on behalf of the Darumbal People v Queensland* [2012] FCA 796 [6].

703 *P.C. (name withheld) on behalf of the Njamal People v Western Australia* [2007] FCA 1054 [40], citing *Drury v Western Australia* [2000] FCA 132; (2000) 97 FCR 169 [12]. See also *Anderson v Western Australia* [2003] FCA 1423 [37]; *Grant v Minister for Land and Water Conservation (NSW)* [2003] FCA 621 [32].

is derived simply from their original authorisation as applicant.[704] Nevertheless, because the *Native Title Act* places such importance on the 'ultimate authority of the native title claim group'[705] and because an amendment to the claim group literally *changes who the claim group is*, courts have tended to treat specific approval[706] by the claim group as a de facto procedural requirement.[707] It may be that actual authorisation would be necessary (still as a matter of discretion) if the original terms of authorisation specified that the applicant did not have the authority to amend the claim group description unilaterally.

Accordingly, if an applicant seeks to change the claim group description they will generally need to show that the *pre-amendment* claim group (from whom the applicant derives its authority) has endorsed the change. This will generally mean the same kind of process that would satisfy s. 251B.[708] All of the procedural and logistical considerations discussed above in Section 3.3 ('Authorisation in practice') would potentially apply here.[709]

In cases where the proposed amendment would remove parts of the claim group, courts may be concerned to know whether the affected people have been involved in the decision to amend or at least consulted. That is not a determinative factor but will certainly be given considerable weight.[710] Leave will also be more likely to be granted where the decision to amend the claim group description is based on anthropological advice and group discussion.[711]

---

704 *Drury v Western Australia* [2000] FCA 132 [12]; *Anderson v Western Australia* [2003] FCA 1423 [37], [48]. See also *Harrington-Smith on behalf of the Wongatha People v Western Australia (No. 9)* [2007] FCA 31 [3388]; *Champion v Western Australia* [2009] FCA 1141 [4]–[13]; *Walker on behalf of the Yaegl, Bundjalung and Gumbaynggirr People v Minister for Land and Water Conservation (NSW)* [2003] FCA 947 [16]; *McKenzie v South Australia* [2005] FCA 22 [56].

705 *Daniel v Western Australia* [2002] FCA 1147 [16].

706 The term 'approval' is used here to distinguish it from the technical requirement of authorisation under ss 61 and 66B.

707 In a number of cases the court has acted as if compliance with s. 251B is a necessary step for the valid amendment of a claim group description, without specifically identifying the source of that requirement: *Doctor on behalf of the Bigambul People v Queensland (No. 2)* [2013] FCA 746 [48], [57]; *Weribone on behalf of the Mandandanji People v Queensland* [2013] FCA 255 [43]; *Holborow v Western Australia (No. 2)* [2013] FCA 1040 [5], citing *Lovett on behalf of the Gunditjmara People v Victoria (No. 3)* [2011] FCA 867 [9]; *Kudjala People v Queensland* [2006] FCA 1564 [13]–[15]; *Hillig as Administrator of Worimi Local Aboriginal Land Council v Minister for Lands (NSW) (No. 2)* [2006] FCA 1115 [51].

708 Although s. 251B is not specifically directed to amendment, it serves as a guide: *Atkins v Western Australia* [2013] FCA 773 [14], citing *Lovett on behalf of the Gunditjmara People v Victoria (No. 3)* [2011] FCA 867 [9].

709 That is plain from *Doctor on behalf of the Bigambul People v Queensland (No. 2)* [2013] FCA 746 and *Weribone on behalf of the Mandandanji People v Queensland* [2013] FCA 255, two cases where deficiencies in the notification and conduct of meetings were sufficient reason for the refusal of the proposed amendment.

710 *Hatfield on behalf of the Darumbal People v Queensland* [2012] FCA 796 [13].

711 ibid.

Recent case law indicates that the wording of meeting notices can be critical to the validity of the relevant meeting. In both *Doctor* and *Weribone*, attempts to alter the claim group description were unsuccessful because the meeting notice was held to be insufficiently specific about the nature of the decision to be made at the meeting.[712] In *Weribone* the meeting notice stated that '[t]he authorisation meeting will authorise matters including…A claim group description that is consistent with the expert evidence, which may include amending the existing apical ancestors.'[713] Justice Rares observed that the notice made no mention of the person proposed to be added as an apical ancestor and did not mention that the meeting was being called specifically for the purpose of adding her as an apical ancestor. Given that existing claim group members would have to travel considerable distances to attend (and without a travel allowance) Rares J considered that potential attendees needed this specific information in order to make an informed decision about whether or not to attend. Accordingly, there was no proper notice of the meeting and the meeting's decisions were incapable of constituting a decision of the claim group.[714] In reaching this decision Rares J considered it significant that the people calling the meeting had specific information about the proposed apical ancestor and a specific intention in calling the meeting but did not reflect that information or intention in the meeting notice.[715]

There was a similar result in *Doctor on behalf of the Bigambul People*.[716] The meeting notice stated one of its purposes was to authorise 'an amendment to the application which could include removing Apical Ancestors from the current claim group description'.[717] Justice Reeves held that 'the word "could" did not fairly reflect the background to the proposal which was to be considered at the meeting' because an anthropologist had already given an opinion that a particular apical ancestor (Sally) should be excluded from the claim group description and the claim group members who had requested the meeting had done so with the intention that Sally be removed.[718] In this sense, Reeves J held, the meeting notice was not frank in stating that the proposal was to remove Sally and only Sally. Similarly, his Honour considered the use of the plural 'ancestors' was misleading in this context.[719] Justice Reeves also rejected the proposition that *Weribone* could be distinguished on the grounds that that case dealt with the *addition* rather than the *removal* of an apical ancestor. If anything, his Honour held, the latter case deserved a *greater* specificity in the meeting notice.[720]

Of course, the adequacy of any given meeting notice will be assessed in light of all of the circumstances. Nevertheless, these two cases raise issues that ought to be considered explicitly by lawyers assisting claimants to advertise meetings ahead of a proposed change.

---

712 *Doctor on behalf of the Bigambul People v Queensland (No. 2)* [2013] FCA 746; *Weribone on behalf of the Mandandanji People v Queensland* [2013] FCA 255.

713 *Weribone on behalf of the Mandandanji People v Queensland* [2013] FCA 255 [8].

714 ibid. [9], [35], [42]–[43].

715 ibid. [34], [41].

716 *Doctor on behalf of the Bigambul People v Queensland (No. 2)* [2013] FCA 746.

717 ibid. [8], [11].

718 ibid. [46].

719 ibid.

720 ibid. [47].

Participation in decision-making by non-members of pre-amendment claim group

There have been cases in which members of the proposed amended claim group have participated in the decision to approve of the amendment. This is clearly not satisfactory from the point of view of the policy considerations mentioned earlier because it is the pre-amendment claim group whose 'ultimate authority' is relevant to the proposed change to the Form 1. But is the inclusion of not-yet-members of the claim group enough to deprive the claim group's decision of any legal relevance or effect? Not necessarily, according to Dowsett J's decision in *Wulli Wulli*.[721] In that case a meeting was held that included both claim group members and people who would be members of the claim group if the Form 1 were amended. Justice Dowsett considered that the validity of the meeting's decision to amend the claim group depended on a detailed examination of the voting and attendance records:

> It may be that the numbers are such that the resolution would have been passed in any event, in which case it would seem to me that the resolution is valid. On the other hand, if there is any reason to believe that the outcome was affected by the inclusion of votes by people who were not, themselves, members of the claim group, then the position may be otherwise.[722]

After considering the evidence Dowsett J considered that the worst case scenario would be that in which all of the non-members voted for the resolution and all of the 'against' votes came from claim group members. Proceeding on that assumption his Honour calculated that the resolution to change the claim group description would still have passed by a comfortable margin even if all non-members had been excluded from voting. Accordingly his Honour was willing to grant leave to amend.[723]

This 'practical approach' was held not to be applicable in two similar cases, *Doctor* and *Weribone*.[724] In those cases Reeves and Rares JJ respectively held that a meeting of the proposed amended claim group was incapable of giving the necessary approval of the amendment. In *Doctor* the *Wulli Wulli* approach could not be followed because the effect of the proposed amendment was to remove an apical ancestor as well as add further ancestors. Under those circumstances it would be impossible to determine how the descendants of the 'removed' ancestor would have voted and it could not be said that the meeting was a meeting of 'all the persons' who hold native title in the claim area.[725] In *Weribone* it does not appear that any party specifically argued that the *Wulli Wulli* approach should be used but, in any case, Rares J considered that the results of the

---

721 *Dodd on behalf of the Wulli Wulli People v Queensland* [2009] FCA 793; *Dodd on behalf of the Wulli Wulli People v Queensland (No. 2)* [2009] FCA 1180.

722 *Dodd on behalf of the Wulli Wulli People v Queensland* [2009] FCA 793 [7].

723 *Dodd on behalf of the Wulli Wulli People v Queensland (No. 2)* [2009] FCA 1180 [14].

724 *Doctor on behalf of the Bigambul People v Queensland (No. 2)* [2013] FCA 746; *Weribone on behalf of the Mandandanji People v Queensland* [2013] FCA 255 [44].

725 *Doctor on behalf of the Bigambul People v Queensland (No. 2)* [2013] FCA 746 [61].

meeting could not be relied upon because it was conducted on a mistaken premise (namely that the previous meeting had successfully expanded the claim group).

Despite not being followed in those two cases, *Wulli Wulli* provides a logical basis for dealing with the admittedly imperfect circumstance of a meeting that includes proposed members as well as current members of the claim group. If the view of the current claim group can be discerned from the results of the meeting, that will be sufficient for the purposes of an application to amend the Form 1.[726]

6.2 Authorisation by proposed amended claim group

Because s. 61 requires the applicant to be authorised by the native title claim group, a change to the composition of the native title claim group raises the question of the applicant's continued authorisation. This question will affect both the court's exercise of discretion in allowing the amendment in the first place as well as the substantive issue of the application's ongoing authorisation (for the purposes of s. 84D(1), s. 84C(1), etc.). The question of precisely *when* the relevant change to the claim group's composition occurs will be dealt with below.

In the case of an *expanded* claim group there is clearly a need for the new members to join with the existing members to give a fresh authorisation to the applicant. Section 61 requires applicants to be authorised by the entire claim group. Where an amendment results in the inclusion of new people within this definition, there will necessarily be some people who have never had the opportunity to be involved in authorising the claim or the applicant.[727] Accordingly, the applicant's initial authorisation by the pre-amendment group is no longer enough because that smaller group no longer constitutes 'all the persons' who hold native title. Therefore, before the applicant is able to take any further step in the proceedings they will be required to demonstrate that the newly constituted claim group has made a fresh decision to authorise the applicant.[728]

In the case of an amendment to *remove* some claim group members, the situation is not so clear-cut. Admittedly, the post-amendment claim group is in some abstract sense a 'different' group of people to the pre-amendment group. But it still seems true to say that 'all the persons' in the amended claim group have authorised the current applicant, since everyone who is now a claim group member already had the opportunity to participate in the original authorisation decision. To be sure, the current claim group members gave their original authorisation *in the company of*

---

726 Another example is in *P.C. (name withheld) on behalf of the Njamal People v Western Australia* [2007] FCA 1054, where the claim group as described in the Form 1 was identical to the list of named applicants, even though all parties accepted that the actual claim group was a larger group of people. The larger group resolved to amend the Form 1 and Bennett J granted leave to amend without requiring evidence that the pre-amendment group (i.e. the named applicants only) had met separately to authorise the change.

727 See *Hatfield on behalf of the Darumbal People v Queensland* [2012] FCA 796 [9].

728 See *Smallwood on behalf of the Juru People v Queensland* [2014] FCA 331 [9]; *Holborow v Western Australia (No. 2)* [2013] FCA 1040 [23]; *Dodd on behalf of the Wulli Wulli People v Queensland (No. 2)* [2009] FCA 1180 [3].

other people who are not now part of the claim group. But it is not clear why the departure of those people from the claim group should affect the continuing effect of the authorisation previously given. Perhaps in some cases there may be policy reasons similar to the 'balance of sectional interests' argument discussed previously in Section 5.1 ('How can the composition of the applicant be changed?') that make a new authorisation decision politically necessary. There may be named applicants who draw their support from people who are now no longer in the claim group and whose removal is sought by those who remain. But that simply explains why a group may *wish* to hold a new authorisation meeting (as they are free to do at any time). What is at issue here is whether the law *requires* such re-authorisation. I was unable to identify a case addressing this point directly.[729] There are indications, however, that courts will generally treat a reduced claim group in the same way as an expanded group; that is, by requiring evidence that the post-amendment group has separately authorised the applicants.[730] In *Wongatha* there had been a purported amendment to reduce the claim group but there was no evidence that either the pre- or post-amendment group had authorised the amendment.[731] Accordingly Lindgren J did not need to decide whether authorisation of the pre-amendment group would have been sufficient. Still, his Honour accepted the following submission by the state, which would seem to cover amendments to reduce claim groups as much as amendments to expand them:

> ...where there has been a re-definition of the claimant group, as is the present case, fresh evidence or further evidence of authorisation is appropriate before it can be said, in relation to the newly defined claimant group, that the applicants have been authorised...[732]

In *Augustine* a proposed amendment would have removed the ancestors of the Goolarabooloo people from the claim group description, leaving only Jabirr Jabirr people.[733] Ultimately the

---

729 In *Martin (deceased) v Western Australia (No. 2)* [2009] FCA 635 the proposed amendment introduced a proviso into the claim group description that would exclude people currently included in the claim group. Justice Barker allowed the amendment without evidence of a separate authorisation by the remaining post-amendment claim group, although his Honour did not consider the question of authorisation specifically. In *Brown v South Australia* [2009] FCA 206 there were several flaws in the authorisation process such that the question of whether the post-authorisation group's separate authorisation was required did not arise. In *Walker on behalf of the Yaegl, Bundjalung and Gumbaynggirr People v Minister for Land and Water Conservation (NSW)* [2003] FCA 947 there was no issue about whether the post-amendment group had authorised the claim; the only controversy was about whether the authorisation of the pre-amendment group was necessary (at [12]).

730 In *McKenzie* the claim was amended to reduce the number of families in the claim group; this was held to require a fresh authorisation but in the context of the original claim having been filed in 1995, before the more stringent authorisation requirements were introduced. Thus the amended claim was treated as a 'fresh claim' triggering the authorisation requirements of the post-1998 NTA: *McKenzie v South Australia* [2005] FCA 22 [53], [56].

731 In fact, this situation arose in three separate instances in the case: *Harrington Smith on behalf of the Wongatha People v Western Australia (No. 9)* [2007] FCA 31 [1224], [2732], [2735].

732 ibid. [2734].

733 *Augustine v Western Australia* [2013] FCA 338 [55].

amendment was not pursued but there are indications that Gilmour J had some sympathy for the view that a 'Jabirr Jabirr-only' authorisation would have been required.[734] Certainly, it would be prudent for a claim group's lawyers to convene separate authorisation meetings of the pre- and post-amendment groups even if it is technically arguable that the latter is unnecessary in the case of a reduction in the claim group description.

Whether the amendment expands or reduces the claim group, the references above to authorisation by the 'post-amendment' group means authorisation by the larger or smaller group of people who *will* become the native title claim group if the amendment application is successful. There is no need to wait until the amendment application is granted before holding a meeting of the post-amendment group. Indeed it will usually be most efficient to hold the meetings of the pre- and post-amendment groups back-to-back, on the same day or on successive days, to reduce travel costs and delays. This way the court can consider the application to amend at the same time as the issue of the applicant's authorisation, rather than at two separate hearings held months apart.

Where amended claim group authorises replacement applicant

The previous discussion dealt with the minimum procedural requirements for amending the claim group description. However, a change to the claim group description may also be accompanied by a change to the composition of the applicant, particularly where the amendment means that one or more members of the existing applicant must be removed because they are no longer a member of the claim group[735] or where an expansion of the claim group means that new named applicants are politically or culturally necessary to represent the incoming claim group members.

A replacement of the applicant in these circumstances will be handled in the same manner as discussed previously in Section 5.1 ('How can the composition of the applicant be changed?'), that is, by application under s. 66B (or r. 9.08 for those judges who consider that alternative method open).[736] Importantly, where a s. 66B application coincides with a proposed change to

---

734 ibid. [57]–[58].

735 Section 61(1), NTA states that a person must be a member of the claim group in order to file an application. But, as discussed in Section 2.1 above at 'Eligibility to be named applicant', once the application is filed a change in a person's eligibility to be a named applicant does not necessarily entail an immediate and automatic change in their status as applicant. Section 61(2) states that where an application is made by 'a person or persons authorised to make the application' then 'the person is, or the persons are jointly, the applicant'. The Act does not specifically state the consequences of an amendment to the claim group description that excludes one of the named applicants. It seems likely that a court may decline to allow the amendment unless satisfied that the post-amendment claim group has already authorised a replacement applicant whose members were all included in the post-amendment claim group description. Otherwise the amended application would be vulnerable to strike out under s. 84C for its failure to comply with s. 61(1).

736 *Holborow v Western Australia (No. 2)* [2013] FCA 1040 [6].

the claim group description, it is the *post*-amendment group whose authorisation is required for the purposes of s. 66B(1)(b).[737]

In the simplest case, where all members of the current (i.e. pre-66B) applicant are willing to cooperate with the amendment of the claim, the sequence of events is as follows:

1. Two meetings are notified — a meeting of the pre-amendment group followed by a meeting of the post-amendment group.[738]
2. Pre-amendment group gives the existing applicant approval to apply for leave to amend claim group description.
3. Post-amendment group decides that existing applicant is no longer authorised and proceeds to authorise replacement applicant.
4. Existing applicant applies for leave to amend the claim group description.
5. Proposed replacement applicant applies under s. 66B.
6. Court considers application for leave to amend claim group description.
7. If leave to amend is granted, court considers s. 66B application.

In this scenario the court deals first with the application for leave to amend the claim group description (brought by the original applicant) and subsequently deals with any s. 66B application (brought by the proposed replacement applicant).[739] If the former application fails and the court refuses leave to amend, the s. 66B application is likely to fall away since the authorisation decision of the purported 'post-amendment' group will be legally ineffective (subject to what is said above

---

737 *P.C. (name withheld) on behalf of the Njamal People v Western Australia* [2007] FCA 1054 [40]–[49]. Note in *Martin (deceased) v Western Australia (No. 2)* [2009] FCA 635 the s. 66B application preceded the amendment application because the sole applicant had died and had to be replaced before the amendment application could proceed. Respondents had argued that the authorisation given by the pre-amendment group would be necessarily defective, since by proposing an amendment to the claim group description the new applicants were necessarily saying that the existing pre-amendment application group was not the correct native title holding group. Justice Barker rejected this argument, concluding that authorisation by the pre-amendment claim group was sufficient.

738 Obviously, the notice for the first meeting will need to be addressed to the current claim group and the notice for the second meeting will need to be addressed to all of those people who *might* be included in the claim group if the first meeting decides to amend. Admittedly, this may cause hurt or embarrassment if people come to the second meeting only to be told that the first meeting did not decide to add them to the group. If that outcome is a real possibility and would cause real problems, meeting organisers might consider spacing the two meetings a month or so apart if the resources to do so are available.

739 Note that the reverse occurred in *Martin (deceased) v Western Australia (No. 2)* [2009] FCA 635 but only because the sole applicant had died, meaning no living applicant was capable of moving the court to consider the amendment to the claim group. Accordingly, the s. 66B application was dealt with first in order to appoint a new applicant who then applied for leave to amend the claim group description. Another scenario in which a s. 66B application would be handled first is where the current applicant refuses to apply for leave to amend, discussed below.

in Section 6.1 at 'Participation in decision-making by non-members of pre-amendment claim group').[740] If, however, the court grants leave to amend the claim group description then the newly amended claim group can substitute a new applicant via s. 66B.

At first glance, the transition from Step 3 to Step 4 appears to generate a dilemma. The existing applicant appears to have already been de-authorised by the time they bring the amendment application, which casts doubt on their authority to bring the application for leave to amend. In *P.C.* Bennett J dealt with this apparent puzzle by reiterating the existing applicant's continuing status as applicant notwithstanding any change to their authorisation.[741] Her Honour considered that until a s. 66B order is made the existing applicant has the power to take steps in the proceedings, and in the circumstances the withdrawal of authorisation at the second meeting should not preclude the existing applicant from applying for amendment.[742] This indicates that judicial flexibility can prevent the amendment/66B process from being derailed by legal technicalities, particularly now that s. 84D(4) allows the court to proceed with a claim despite a defect in authorisation (a provision that was not available to Bennett J). Certainly there was no mention of such a dilemma in *Smallwood*, a case that followed the seven-step process set out above.[743]

In any case, any latent ambiguity can be removed if the post-amendment group makes a resolution along the following lines:

> The current applicant remains authorised until such time as the native title application is amended to reflect the decisions made at the meeting of the pre-amendment native title claim group. When that amendment takes place, the current applicant will no longer be authorised and the replacement applicant will be authorised to make the native title application and to deal with matters arising in relation to it.

Such a resolution would make matters abundantly clear to the court in considering both the amendment application and the s. 66B application.

Where outgoing applicant refuses to make the application for amendment

In some cases the proposed change to the claim group description may be controversial. Where a claim group has resolved to amend the Form 1 but one or more of the current named applicants refuses to carry out the claim group's instructions, what can be done? (Or, better yet, what should be done beforehand to prepare for this eventuality?)

If the original authorisation of the current applicant was subject to conditions allowing for majority decision-making (see Chapter 4 above), the opposition of a minority of named applicants will not be fatal. In that case the remaining majority can instruct the solicitors to apply to the court for leave to amend the Form 1 notwithstanding the division within the applicant.

---

740 See *Doctor on behalf of the Bigambul People v Queensland (No. 2)* [2013] FCA 746 [48].

741 *P.C. (name withheld) on behalf of the Njamal People v Western Australia* [2007] FCA 1054 [48].

742 ibid. [40]–[49].

743 *Smallwood on behalf of the Juru People v Queensland* [2014] FCA 331.

But if majority decision-making was not specifically authorised,[744] or if there is no majority of current named applicants willing to do the claim group's bidding, then there is no choice but to replace the applicant under s. 66B before proceeding to the amendment application.

Before explaining the mechanics of running a s. 66B application in tandem with an application for leave to amend the Form 1, it is necessary first to deal with an ambiguity in the interpretation of s. 66B(1). Section 66B(1) specifies that only 'members of the native title claim group' can apply to replace the current applicant. But in the context of an application to amend the Form 1, does 'native title claim group' refer to the pre-amendment group or the group described in the proposed amended Form 1? (For current purposes I will call this latter group the 'post-amendment' group, irrespective of whether an amended Form 1 has been filed.)

A 'formalist' approach to this question would treat the contents of the Form 1 as entirely determinative of the composition of the native title claim group. On this view, until an amended Form 1 is filed, only individuals who fall within the claim group description in the pre-amendment Form 1 may validly apply under s. 66B. Equally, any proposed replacement applicant would need to demonstrate that they had been authorised by the pre-amendment claim group.

By contrast, what might be called a 'factualist' approach allows the s. 66B applicants to argue that, by the time their s. 66B application comes before the court, the 'post-amendment' claim group *has already become* the 'native title claim group' as a matter of *fact*. This approach de-links the question of who constitutes the claim group from the current state of the Form 1.

The legal argument in support of the factualist approach essentially repeats what is said earlier in this book in Section 3.1 ('The "native title claim group": conceptualising the authorising constituency'). The term 'native title claim group' in s. 66B is defined in s. 61(1), and the definition in s. 253 refers back to s. 61. The definition in s. 61(1) does not refer to the group of people who *claim* to hold native title but rather to those who *really do* hold native title.[745] But, as the identity of the native title holders is one of the ultimate issues to be determined in the proceedings, the determination of composition of the 'native title claim group' for procedural purposes is treated as a *hypothetical exercise*.[746] The court asks whether the applicant's authorisation *would be* valid *assuming the applicant's own version of the facts*.[747]

Importantly, this is not the same as simply asking whether the applicant is authorised by the persons described in the Form 1. Indeed, in a great many cases applicants have been found to

---

744 See Section 4.2 ('Authorisation by "all the persons" in the native title claim group') above.

745 *Harrington-Smith on behalf of the Wongatha People v Western Australia (No. 9)* [2007] FCA 31 [72], [1189], [1216]. See also *Risk v National Native Title Tribunal* [2000] FCA 1589 [60], cited in *Worimi Local Aboriginal Land Council v Minister for Lands (NSW)* [2007] FCA 1357 [20].

746 *Harrington-Smith on behalf of the Wongatha People v Western Australia (No. 9)* [2007] FCA 31 [1192]–[1193], [1253], [2433], [2747], [3387]; *Kite v South Australia* [2007] FCA 1662 [21].

747 It was in this sense that Mansfield J used the term 'native title claim group' to mean 'the persons on whose behalf a grant of native title should be made if the native title determination application is successful': *Dieri People v South Australia* [2003] FCA 187 [56]. Other judges have used the phrase 'alleged claim group' — one could even use the term 'claimed claim group'.

be inadequately authorised precisely *because* the claim group description in the Form 1 does not cover all of the people in the 'native title claim group':

- *Hillig as Administrator of Worimi Local Aboriginal Land Council v Minister for Lands (NSW) (No. 2)* [2006] FCA 1115 — the claim was dismissed for uncertainty of claim group because of contradictions in the Form 1 between Schedule A (the claim group description), Schedule F (factual basis) and Schedule R (basis for authorisation), and also between those and various statements in affidavit evidence filed in support of the application.
- *McKenzie v South Australia* [2005] FCA 22 [40]–[44] — the claim was struck out for reasons including that the claim group description in the Form 1 did not properly describe the 'native title claim group'. The description consisted of a mere list of people, membership of which had fluctuated over time, and for which the court could divine no descriptive criteria. Further, the list was said to be over-inclusive and under-inclusive by the applicant's own evidence.
- *Hazelbane v Northern Territory* [2008] FCA 291 [35]–[36] — the applicant's own evidence suggested that the native title claim group extended beyond those clans that were described in the application. For this and other reasons the claim was struck out.
- *Risk v National Native Title Tribunal* [2000] FCA 1589 [62]–[67] — the Form 1 listed only eight people, even though affidavit evidence filed in support of the claim indicated that native title was held by a broader group of people.
- *Tucker on behalf of the Narnoobinya Family Group v Western Australia* [2011] FCA 1232 [41] — the applicant conceded under cross-examination that members of a broader group did in fact hold some rights in the area. Accordingly an assertion to the contrary could not be maintained in good faith and the application was struck out for want of authorisation.

The cases establish that the 'native title claim group' is defined by the totality of *all* material brought forward by the applicant in support of their claim, including:[748] the Form 1 and any supplementary pleadings; any proposed amended pleadings;[749] any written or oral submissions made on behalf of the applicant; and any evidence brought on behalf of the applicant.[750] (One ethical issue for practitioners to consider is whether affidavit evidence should be filed on behalf of the applicant notwithstanding that some members of the current applicant are actively resisting the course of action in support of which those affidavits are being filed. This may

748 In *Moran v Minister for Land and Water Conservation (NSW)* [1999] FCA 1637 [32], Wilcox J said 'In order to decide whether that requirement is satisfied, it is first necessary for the Court to determine who constitutes the "claim group". This must be done by reference to the document or documents making the claim.'

749 *Velickovic v Western Australia* [2012] FCA 782 [16], [20], [39]–[40].

750 See *Hillig as Administrator of Worimi Local Aboriginal Land Council v Minister for Lands (NSW) (No. 2)* [2006] FCA 1115 [55]; *Tucker on behalf of the Narnoobinya Family Group v Western Australia* [2011] FCA 1232 [16], [42].

come down to a question of how far the applicant's implicit instructions go, particularly where the claim group itself appears to intend for the evidence to be filed. To avoid any uncertainty, one option is for the relevant affidavits to be filed on behalf of the 's. 66B applicants', that is the individuals who are seeking orders under s. 66B to replace the current applicant.)

Further, at least two cases have treated the decisions made at authorisation meetings as being potentially determinative of the composition of the native title claim group. In *Weribone* a meeting was held to authorise an amendment to the claim group description and a second meeting was held to allow the amended claim group to authorise a replacement applicant.[751] The first meeting was found to have been ineffective because its notification was defective. As a consequence, the second meeting was said not to have been a meeting of the native title claim group because the first meeting had failed in its attempt to change the composition of the claim group.[752] Similarly, in *Doctor on behalf of the Bigambul People* the notification for a meeting was held to be defective such that the meeting 'was not competent to make any changes to the constitution of the [native title claim group]'.[753] The implication from these cases is that a properly constituted meeting could have the direct effect of altering the composition of the native title claim group, even before any amendment is made to the Form 1.

It is worth noting in passing that the distinction between the formalist and factualist approaches may have important implications for the practical application of legal ethics. Depending on which view one takes, the identity of a lawyer's client may change either at the point where an amended Form 1 is filed or at the point where the pre-amendment claim group authorises the amendment and this amended application is authorised by the 'post-amendment' claim group. If the transition is at all contentious, lawyers will need to take a principled stance on this issue one way or another and be ready to defend that stance if need be. Again, it is beyond the scope of this book to deal with this question in depth; at this point it is simply raised for consideration. (Further below in Section 6.2, 'Authorisation by proposed amended claim group', a similar issue is discussed in relation to replacing the applicant in the midst of an amendment process.)

The legal arguments in favour of the factualist approach are fairly orthodox, even though they have not been applied directly to s. 66B before. As will be seen in the remainder of this chapter, the factualist approach appears to provide a more straightforward means of dealing with contentious amendment applications than the formalist approach. Nevertheless, because there is no explicit judicial guidance on the issue, I will consider how each of the approaches might work in practice. The inclusion of the formalist approach in my analysis will make it necessary to consider two scenarios separately: firstly, where the proposed replacement applicant is composed entirely of individuals who are existing members of the pre-amendment claim group; and secondly, where one or more members of the proposed replacement applicant are members of the 'post-amendment' claim group only. As will become apparent, on the factualist approach there is no need to make this distinction.

---

751 *Weribone on behalf of the Mandandanji People v Queensland* [2013] FCA 255.

752 ibid. [43]–[44].

753 *Doctor on behalf of the Bigambul People v Queensland (No. 2)* [2013] FCA 746 [55].

Replacement applicant composed entirely of pre-amendment claim group members

As mentioned, if the existing applicant refuses to give instructions to amend the Form 1, the only way for the amendment to proceed is to replace the applicant first, so that the replacement applicant can seek leave to amend. On the formalist view described just above, this process will be simpler if all members of the proposed replacement applicant are part of the pre-amendment claim group. In this situation there is nothing preventing the proposed replacement applicant from pressing their s. 66B application *before* the hearing of the application for leave to amend. The members of the proposed replacement applicant will have no difficulty in demonstrating that they are all 'members of the native title claim group' as required by s. 66B(1). If their s. 66B application is successful then the new applicant can then apply for leave to amend the Form 1.[754]

The one potential complication in this process is that s. 66B(1)(b) requires the replacement applicant to be *authorised* by the 'native title claim group'. On the formalist approach, this refers to the authorisation of the *pre-amendment* claim group. If that is so, the proposed replacement applicant will need to show that they have been authorised by the pre-amendment group as well as the post-amendment group: the former in order to become applicant before the Form 1 is amended and the latter in order to remain authorised afterwards. This is most easily done if the pre-amendment group specifically authorised the replacement applicant at the first of the two meetings. Therefore, if any controversy is anticipated, it would be advisable to ask both the pre- and post-amendment groups to authorise the replacement applicant. This would remove any doubt. However, in many cases this will not be possible, for example because it would not be politically or culturally appropriate for the pre-amendment group to have any say in the choice of the replacement applicant. One way around this would be for the pre-amendment group to pass a resolution pre-authorising *whichever* individuals are chosen by the post-amendment group to replace the current applicant — this could be thought of as a 'blank-cheque' authorisation.

If none of this has occurred and the pre-amendment group has simply not addressed the issue of s. 66B, one might attempt to 'constructively' attribute the post-amendment group's authorisation decision to the pre-amendment group. Using the same logic as described earlier in Section 6.1 (at 'Participation in decision-making by non-members of pre-amendment claim group') it may be possible to argue that the people who voted in the second meeting (i.e. the post-amendment group) were also speaking on behalf of the pre-amendment group. This is not necessarily a strong line of argument and it will depend on the particular facts (especially on whether the change to the claim group's composition involved an expansion only or the removal of some claim group members).[755]

---

754 Practitioners' duties will need to be considered very carefully in this situation. If the current applicant will not instruct the solicitors to file the application for leave to amend, there is an argument that the solicitors cannot *file* the amendment application until the order under s. 66B is actually made. One way of handling this situation efficiently, while still complying with the duty to act only on instruction, is to circulate a draft amendment application on behalf of the prospective replacement applicant. This way, once the s. 66B order is granted, an oral application for leave to amend can be made in court on behalf of the replacement applicant.

755 Clearly it will be difficult to argue that the authorisation decision of the post-determination group can also be attributed to the pre-determination group if the post-determination group does not contain all of the members of the pre-determination group.

If none of the above arguments can be established, the only remaining option is to resort to the factualist approach. It would be necessary to argue that, by the time the s. 66B application is considered by the court, the 'post-amendment claim group' has already in fact become the 'native title claim group' and so the authorisation of the 'post-amendment' group is sufficient to satisfy s. 66B(1)(b).

Replacement applicant contains some individuals not part of pre-amendment claim group

If the proposed replacement applicant contains one or more individuals who are not members of the pre-amendment claim group, there is an additional layer of complexity. On the formalist approach, the composition of the 'native title claim group' does not change until the Form 1 is actually amended with the court's leave. Until that happens, some members of the proposed replacement applicant are 'not yet' members of the native title claim group and therefore cannot validly make an application under s. 66B. Section 84D(4) cannot help in this situation: the problem is not lack of authorisation, it is ineligibility to apply under s. 66B at all.

Formalist approach, interim applicant

So long as we are operating within the formalist approach, the only way to progress the amendment application in such circumstances is to file two s. 66B applications. The first would be heard before the filing of the amendment application and would appoint an 'interim applicant' composed only of individuals who are already part of the pre-amendment group. Assuming the interim applicant succeeds in getting an order under s. 66B, it can then instruct the solicitors to file an application for leave to amend.[756] The second s. 66B application would be heard after leave to amend is granted[757] and would replace the interim applicant with a final replacement applicant comprising all individuals who were authorised by the post-amendment claim group.

The chronology for this manoeuvre would be as follows (noting that steps 7–9 could be dealt with together at the same hearing):

1. At first meeting, pre-amendment group authorises existing applicant to apply for leave to amend claim group description.
2. At second meeting, post-amendment group decides that existing applicant is no longer authorised and authorises replacement applicant.
3. Existing applicant refuses to apply for leave to amend claim group description.
4. Proposed interim applicant applies under s. 66B to replace current applicant.

---

756 As mentioned previously, the interim applicant may seek leave to file the application in court and have it heard immediately. Leave is more likely to be granted if the draft application has been circulated well before the hearing.

757 Strictly speaking, given we are working here on the provisional assumption that the state of the Form 1 determines the composition of the 'native title claim group' for the purposes of s. 66B, properly the second s. 66B application should wait until the actual filing of the amended Form 1. However, courts are likely to be flexible in this regard.

5. Proposed interim applicant circulates draft application for leave to amend claim group description.
6. Proposed ultimate replacement applicant applies under s. 66B to replace interim applicant.
7. Court considers first s. 66B application.
8. If court grants s. 66B order, court then considers application for leave to amend claim group description.
9. If leave to amend is granted, court considers second s. 66B application.

There is one crucial question that must be addressed if this procedure is to be used: is the interim applicant authorised by the pre-amendment native title claim group? As discussed earlier in this section (at 'Replacement applicant composed entirely of pre-amendment claim group members') the best case scenario is where this issue was considered explicitly at the first meeting (i.e. the meeting of the pre-amendment claim group). If the meeting organisers suspect in advance that the current applicant is likely to resist the group's will in relation to filing the amendment application, it would be prudent to ask the first meeting to expressly authorise an interim applicant.

As mentioned before, it may be improper or difficult for the pre-amendment group to predict which individuals will be part of the post-amendment applicant and so they may simply choose to appoint one or a handful of *new* individuals solely for the task of filing the amendment application. Alternatively they could resolve to make each member of the current applicant's authority conditional on their willingness to file the amendment application, which would then allow all of the 'non-recalcitrant' members of the current applicant to simply apply under s. 66B to be the interim applicant. Of course, if these troubles could be foreseen in advance of the meetings, the best option would simply be to pass a resolution at the first meeting authorising the current applicant to make decisions by majority (assuming, of course, that the 'recalcitrant' members of the applicant are in the minority).

However, the unwillingness of one or more members of the current applicant to file the amendment application may have come as a surprise to the legal advisers. In this case, the best that can be done within the formalist approach is either to hold a fresh meeting to authorise an interim applicant or else to argue that the pre-amendment group should be understood as having *implicitly* intended to authorise the interim applicant. A court might be willing to entertain such an inference in these circumstances in order to avoid the perversity, delay and cost of a fresh meeting. It would be difficult to justify from a policy perspective an outcome where the group must convene a new meeting to authorise an interim applicant in circumstances where both the pre- and post-amendment groups have already clearly expressed their wishes for the future conduct of the claim.[758]

[758] Note that s. 84D could possibly apply to assist the interim applicant here. Certainly s. 84D cannot absolve the legal representatives of their duty to act only on instructions and so the circuitous route of installing an interim applicant cannot be escaped. But, when it comes to the question of

Factualist approach, redefine 'native title claim group'

In light of the difficulty just described of proving the authorisation of an interim applicant, it may be desirable or even unavoidable to jettison the formalist approach and embrace the factualist view. To summarise: this alternative approach involves arguing that the 'post-amendment' claim group *has already become* the 'native title claim group' mentioned in s. 66B(1), regardless of the fact that no amendment to the Form 1 has yet been made. If that argument is accepted there is no need for an interim applicant; the replacement applicant simply applies for an order under s. 66B and, if it is granted, applies for leave to amend the Form 1 to reflect the new state of affairs. This alternative approach is thus much simpler in terms of procedure and evidence, although it requires slightly more in the way of legal argument. While I was unable to identify any cases to date in which the factualist approach has been applied in the specific context being discussed here, it may be considered as the mere logical extension of the well-established body of law discussed previously in Chapter 3.

Where original authorisation was defective

In some cases where an applicant has sought to amend the claim group description it has transpired that their original authorisation by the pre-amendment claim group was defective on its own terms. That is, the applicant was never properly authorised by the people on behalf of whom the claim was ostensibly brought.

In *Velickovic* McKerracher J dealt with such a situation in the context of a strike-out motion.[759] The NTRB argued that the claim should be struck out because (amongst other reasons) (a) the claim group description contained internal inconsistencies; and (b) there was no evidence that the claim had ever been authorised. The applicant conceded these flaws, but sought an adjournment of the strike-out application so that it could hold a 're-authorisation' meeting and also file an amended Form 1 addressing the problems in the claim group description. Justice McKerracher held that such an adjournment would be futile because it would constitute an attempt by 'a different set of people or a different claim group…to reauthorise the claim made on behalf of an earlier set of people'.[760] For this and a number of other reasons, his Honour struck out the claim.

Justice McKerracher's decision suggests that, at least in the context of that case, an initially flawed authorisation could not be cured at the same time as seeking an amendment

---

the interim applicant's authorisation, s. 84D(4) might grant the court some latitude in allowing a s. 66B application without actual proof of authorisation. This would involve convincing the court that the current applicant was dealing with the matter of the proposed amendment without authorisation (for the purposes of para. (3)(b)) and then arguing that an appropriate order in the circumstances would be to make an order appointing the interim applicant (or alternatively removing the recalcitrant members of the current applicant).

759 *Velickovic v Western Australia* [2012] FCA 782.

760 ibid [37].

to the claim group description. His Honour's reasoning still leaves open the possibility of doing one of these things at a time.[761] It does not appear that counsel for the applicant had specifically proposed embarking on the standard two-step process outlined earlier in this book, namely giving the existing claim group the opportunity to authorise the amendment and then asking the (proposed) post-amendment group to re-authorise the claim as amended. If that course of action had been proposed, perhaps McKerracher J would have come to a different view, although there were a number of other factors in that case weighing against an adjournment.[762]

Indeed, where the initial authorisation is defective and the claim group description needs changing, it would be open for the court under s. 84D to allow the amendment application despite the current flaw in authorisation. Once amended, the post-amendment group could then authorise or replace the applicant. That view is supported by the decisions in *Sharpe*[763] and *Barunga*.[764] It is also analogous to the situation in *Walker*, where the judge allowed an amendment application without evidence of authorisation by the pre-amendment claim group.[765] In that case, however, the court relied not on s. 84D (which was not available at the time) but rather on the fact that the application was filed before the authorisation requirements were introduced in 1998.[766] Hence the outcome was the same as under s. 84D: the absence of a strict legal requirement for authorisation meant that the court was free to allow the current applicant to amend the application, shifting the focus onto authorisation by the post-amendment group.

6.3 Summary on changing claim group description

Perhaps more than any other part of native title practice, changing the composition of the claim group description requires practioners to pay close and critical attention to questions around the identity of the client, the taking of instructions, and the flow of authorisation from claim group to applicant.

---

761 op. cit. Note that in *Strickland v Western Australia* [2013] FCA 677 [12], Jagot J interpreted *Velickovic* as presenting a 'logical conundrum' on the grounds that whenever an applicant approaches the court to amend the claim group description, the applicant is implicitly or explicitly conceding that the current claim group description does not cover 'all the persons' who hold native title in the claim area. As soon as that concession is made, Jagot J continued, the court must conclude that the original claim was never validly authorised. This seems to be precisely the kind of technical difficulty that s. 84D is intended to address.

762 It seems, for example, that even the proposed amended claim group description was inherently flawed: *Velickovic v Western Australia* [2012] FCA 782 [38]–[40].

763 *Sharpe v Western Australia* [2013] FCA 599 [17]–[21].

764 *Barunga v Western Australia* [2011] FCA 518 [12]–[21].

765 *Walker on behalf of the Yaegl, Bundjalung and Gumbaynggirr People v Minister for Land and Water Conservation (NSW)* [2003] FCA 947.

766 ibid. [16].

The process of amending the claim group description brings into play two important elements of the law on authorisation: the requirement that the applicant and the claim have the support of all of the people on whose behalf the claim is brought; and the imperative to ensure that the claim group endorses any major steps taken by the applicant in the proceedings. The latter imperative governs the process for amending the Form 1 and the former requires that the post-amendment claim (and its applicant) be endorsed by the post-amendment claim group.

There are numerous conceptual, practical and ethical puzzles that must be confronted and the clear lesson from the foregoing discussion is that careful planning and risk assessment are crucial. Each of the steps, from advertising the relevant meetings, to the possible decisions that might be at each meeting, to the getting of instructions, right through to the sequence of court hearings should be mapped out and tested for potential pitfalls. Given the time, cost and effort involved in convening legally effective meetings, it is generally preferable to deal with potentially difficult situations ahead of time rather than trying to fix things retrospectively.

This transition from the old claim group to the new requires careful planning in relation to the sequencing and content of meetings and court applications. The accepted practice is the so-called 'two-step process'. In summary, the optimal order of events appears to be as follows:

1. The meeting organisers issue two meeting notices: one addressed to the current pre-amendment, group inviting them to attend a meeting to authorise the amendment and one addressed to the proposed post-amendment group. The meeting notice should specify the substance of the proposed change in sufficient detail to allow people to decide whether to attend or not.

2. The first meeting is held and the pre-amendment group authorises the change.

3. The second meeting is held soon after, at which the post-amendment group re-authorises the applicant or authorises a new applicant.

4. The existing applicant files an application for leave to amend. The proposed replacement applicant, if any, files a s. 66B application.

5. The court decides the amendment application on the basis of the first meeting. If that is successful the court goes on to determine whether the second meeting establishes the continued authorisation of the applicant — or in the case of a new applicant, the court goes on to decide the s. 66B application on the basis of the second meeting.

If the lawyers for the claim group are unable to obtain instructions from the current applicant to apply for leave to amend, the only way to give effect to the pre- and post-amendment groups' decisions is to bring forward the s. 66B application so that it is determined before the amendment application. This will be most straightforward if courts adopt what I have described as the 'factualist approach' whereby the 'native title claim group' is defined by reference to the totality of the applicant's pleadings, evidence and submissions, and potentially also the pre-amendment claim group's decision at the first meeting to alter the composition of the claim group. That approach appears to be the most consistent with other aspects of the law on authorisation and avoids some of the perverse outcomes that might otherwise emerge. Nevertheless, in the absence of direct authority on the issue, courts may well prefer the 'formalist approach' with the consequence that the 'native title claim group' cannot change until the Form 1 is officially amended. In that case, it will still be possible in some situations to proceed with the amendment without the need for a fresh authorisation meeting but this will require additional procedural steps and evidentiary complexity, and will simply not be possible in all cases.

7. Authorisation and decision-making in agreement-making

Both during a native title claim and after the determination, native title claimants and holders may find themselves engaged in agreement-making with a range of stakeholders including government agencies, infrastructure providers and resource companies.[767] At a policy level, the involvement of the broader claim group in the negotiation and approval of these agreements is crucial both because of the potential impacts of development and because of the often contentious questions around financial benefits. Accordingly, authorisation is as important to the agreement-making process as to the claims process.

The *Native Title Act* provides for two kinds of agreements: ILUAs and so-called 's. 31 agreements'. ILUAs are special agreements that are registered by the Native Title Registrar. Registration has several legal effects: it places all native title holders for the area in the position of being parties to the agreement even though only the named applicants are signatories;[768] it allows the agreement to validate prospective future acts that would otherwise be invalid under the *Native Title Act*;[769] and it allows the retrospective validation of future acts that have already been invalidly done.[770] Section 31 agreements are somewhat simpler: they just record the consent of the native title claimants/holders to the doing of a particular future act or class of future act. Section 31 agreements are not registered but they do have a special status under the legislation, described below in Section 7.2 ('Entering and authorising s. 31 agreements').

The authorisation requirements for ILUAs and s. 31 agreements are different and will be discussed separately.

7.1 Entering and authorising ILUAs

An ILUA is made in relation to a particular geographical area. There are three different 'types' of ILUA that may be used, depending on whether there are registered claims and/or RNTBCs in that area:

---

767 Specifically, agreement-making is likely because, at its strongest, the NTA grants only a 'right to negotiate', not a right to control activities on native title land (ss 25–44). Tribunal decisions about whether particular future acts will be allowed to proceed are overwhelmingly decided in favour of proponents. Thus there is a strong pressure on native title parties to negotiate.

768 Section 24EA, NTA. Note s. 41 has a similar effect in relation to s. 31 agreements but only to the actual 'state deed', not the ancillary agreement. For more on this, see Section 7.2 below at 'The legal mechanics of s.31 agreements'.

769 Section 24EB, NTA.

770 Section 24EBA, NTA. Note this section also allows the parties to agree to vary the legal effect of intermediate period acts.

- **Area agreements** — *must* be used if there are no RNTBCs in the area covered by the agreement; *may* be used if there is one or more RNTBC for the area but only if there are also some parts of the area that have no RNTBC.[771] So for areas where there has been no determination of native title at all, an area agreement must always be used.
- **Body corporate agreements** — *must* be used if there is an RNTBC for every part of the agreement area (even if different parts of the agreement area are covered by different RNTBCs). *Must not* be used in any other situation.
- **Alternative procedure agreements** — *may only* be used if there is an RNTBC for part of the agreement area and no RNTBC for another part of the area; *must not* be used if there are no RNTBCs or if RNTBCs cover the entire agreement area. There is no situation in which this form of ILUA *must* be used; it is simply an optional alternative to the area agreement in situations where there is an RNTBC for part of the area.

Table 1: Situations where different types of ILUA can or must be used

	Area ILUA	Body Coorporate ILUA	Alternative Procedure ILUA
RNTBCs cover entire agreement area	Unavaliable	Mandatory	Unavaliable
No RNTBCs in agreement area	Mandatory	Unavailable	Unavaliable
Part of agreement area has RNTBC, part does not	Optional	Unavaliable	Optional

Despite being described as different 'types' of ILUA, the only significant distinction lies in the different processes by which the ILUA is registered.[772] Briefly put:

- An Area ILUA must be authorised by all of the people who hold or may hold native title in relation to the agreement area.
- A Body Corporate ILUA merely needs to be executed by the RNTBC (or all of the RNTBCs) for the agreement area, subject to informing at least one of the NTRBs for the area of its intention to enter into the agreement.
- An Alternative Procedure ILUA needs to be executed by the RNTBC (or all of the RNTBCs) for the agreement area *and* by the NTRB (or all of the NTRBs) for the area and, if anyone objects on the basis that it would not be fair and reasonable to register the agreement, the registrar must determine that objection.

771 Section 24CC–CD, NTA.

772 There are other minor differences not relevant for present purposes, including the subject matter that can be covered by each type of agreement and the form of the application and accompanying material.

Area ILUA

As mentioned, if a native title claim group wants to use the ILUA method of agreement-making before they have an RNTBC, they must use an Area ILUA. Because of the length of time required to resolve native title claims, the majority of agreements to date have been made in the pre-RNTBC phase, and so Area ILUAs are the most common type of ILUA today.[773] As more and more claims are determined and more RNTBCs are established, we should expect to see increasing numbers of Body Corporate and Alternative Procedure ILUAs.

Area ILUAs are governed by s. 24CA–CL of the *Native Title Act* and the authorisation requirement is in s. 24CG(3).[774] Compliance can either be proved directly (see s. 24CG(3)(b)) or else certified by the NTRB under s. 203BE(5). (See s. 24CG(3)(a).) The requirement is as follows:

i) that all reasonable efforts have been made (including by consulting all representative Aboriginal/Torres Strait Islander bodies for the area) to ensure that all persons who hold or may hold native title in relation to land or waters in the area covered by the agreement have been identified;

ii) that all of the persons so identified have authorised the making of the agreement.

A note to s. 24CG(3) clarifies that the meaning of 'authorised' is found in s. 251A. Section 251A contains the same two-limb test familiar to us from authorisation of native title claims under s. 251B: if there is an applicable process under traditional law and custom, that process must be followed; if not, then an agreed/adopted process must be followed. Subject to what is said below in this section at 'Who must authorise an Area ILUA?' about the scope of the authorising constituency, most of the case law about s. 251B can be applied to the interpretation of s. 251A and vice versa. This means that the commentary above in chapters 3 and 5 can be applied to Area ILUAs. As Logan J said in *Fesl*:

> Section 251A plays an identical role in relation to native title group 'authorisation' decisions as referred to in s 24CG(3)(b)(ii) to that which s 251B plays in relation to native title claim group 'authorisation' decisions under s 61 of the Native Title Act. The language employed in s 251A compared to that in s 251B is very similar and each gives content to the word 'authorise' in a provision in which the word 'all' appears in relation to the making of 'authorisation' decisions. The analogy of application between the two sections is indeed a close one. In my opinion therefore, each of the propositions which I have distilled from cases concerning s 251B has like application, mutatis mutandis, to the meaning and effect of s 251A and in relation to the impact of that section on 'authorisation' for the purposes of s 24CG(3)(b)(ii) of the Native Title Act...The facts of this case make it unnecessary to decide whether and to what

---

773 See ILUA summaries produced by AIATSIS Native Title Research Unit at <http://aiatsis.gov.au/sites/default/files/docs/research-and-guides/native-title-research/IluaSummary.pdf> and <http://aiatsis.gov.au/publications/products/whats-new-native-title-june-2016>, viewed 9 August 2016.

774 In fact, the only requirement in s. 24CG(3) is for an ILUA registration application form to contain a certain *statement about* authorisation. The true operative requirements are in s. 24CK and CL, which refer back to the contents of the statement in s. 24CG(3). Nevertheless, the cases generally refer to s. 24CG(3) and, for simplicity, that tendency will be adopted in this book.

> extent principles to be distilled from cases concerning s 251B are congruent with all of the observations made by Branson J in Kemp's case in relation to s 251A.775

If the authorisation requirements are not complied with then the ILUA cannot be registered. (See s. 24CK and CL.) This in turn means the agreement cannot validate any future acts and will not bind the broader native title holding group. (See s. 24AA(3) and EA–EBA.) Whether or not the agreements would retain any contractual effect at all will depend on issues of contractual law and agency beyond the scope of this book.

Who must be party to an Area ILUA?

Before considering the authorisation requirements for an Area ILUA it is necessary to identify who must, and may, be a party to it. Section 24CD of the *Native Title Act* states that the parties to an Area ILUA must include *all* members of a category called 'the native title group'.[776] This should not be confused with the 'native title *claim* group'. The native title group is made up of the following:

- all 'registered native title claimants' for the area covered by the agreement (s. 24CD(2)(a));[777]
- all RNTBCs for the area (s. 24CD(2)(b));[778]
- for any part of the agreement area that does not have a registered native title claimant or RNTBC, at least one person who claims to hold native title in the area or at least one NTRB for the area (s. 24CD(2)(c) and (3)).[779]

---

775 *Fesl v Delegate of the Native Title Registrar* [2008] FCA 1469 [72]–[73].

776 Section 24CD(1).

777 Whether or not this refers to every member of the applicant for every registered claim is considered below.

778 The decision-making process of an RNTBC entering an ILUA is considered below in Section 7.1 at 'Body Corporate ILUA' and in more detail in Section 8.2 ('Decision-making within RNTBCs').

779 Section 24CD(3) specifies that where the ILUA area does not include any registered claims or determinations, the native title group is limited to one or more of: 'any person who claims to hold native title' and any NTRB for the area. It is unclear why this obvious result, which would follow automatically from the drafting of s. 24CD(2), needed to be spelled out separately. Note also that for any area covered by a registered native title claim, non-members of the registered native title claim group are not mandatory parties. *Corunna v South West Aboriginal Land and Sea Council* [2015] FCA 491 [37]–[38].

Importantly, the third dotpoint does not require *every* individual who claims to hold native title in the relevant area to be a party. That is so despite the potential ambiguity in the use of the word 'any' in s. 24CD(2)(c)(i) and s. 24CD(3)(a). It would be possible to read those provisions as saying that *any* person who claims to hold native title in the relevant area is a necessary party to the ILUA. But in *Murray*[780] Marshall J held that s. 24CD(1) will be satisfied in respect of areas lacking an RNTBC or registered native title claimant if *just one* of the many people who claim native title in the relevant area is a party to the ILUA.[781] His Honour held that the function of s. 24CD was different to the authorisation function of s. 24CG(3)[782] and concluded that the latter sufficiently protected the interests of people who claimed to hold native title.[783] Based on this we can say that s. 24CD(2)(i) and (3)(a) have a purely formal function, namely to ensure that there is at least one party in respect of areas where there is no registered native title claim and no RNTBC.[784] The actual identity of that party does not much matter, since after the ILUA is registered it will bind *all* persons who hold native title in the relevant area whether they were party to the agreement or not: s. 24EA(1)(b).[785] By contrast, s. 24CG(3) has the more substantive function of protecting the interests of all native title holders in circumstances where no determination of native title has yet been made. So for groups or individuals who feel that they have been left out of an ILUA negotiation process or who oppose the making of an ILUA, the relevant complaint is that they have not authorised the IULA, rather than that they have not been made a party.[786]

A second 'mandatory party' requirement is that the state, territory or Commonwealth (as relevant) must be party to any Area ILUA that provides for the surrender of native title rights and interests to them.[787] Finally, any other person not listed above *may* be a party (if the other parties agree) but their being a party is not necessary for the ILUA to be valid and registrable.[788]

The constrained role of the named applicants: QGC Pty Ltd v Bygrave (No. 2)

Before moving on it is necessary to consider in more detail what s. 24CD means when it says that certain entities *must* be parties. Certainly the term 'must' does not appear to create a positive obligation on anyone to do any particular thing (unlike, for example, s. 174 of the *Native Title Act*, which provides that a person 'must not refuse or fail to produce a document' required by a summons). That is, no-one will be committing a civil or criminal wrong by not becoming a party.

780 *Murray v Registrar of the National Native Title Tribunal* [2002] FCA 1598 [38]–[49]. An appeal against the decision was dismissed: *Murray v Registrar of the National Native Title Tribunal* [2003] FCAFC 220.

781 Note Marshall J was dealing with a situation where there were no registered native title claimants or RNTBCs in the entire agreement area and was therefore interpreting s. 24CD(3). There is no reason to doubt, however, that his Honour's reasoning would apply equally to s. 24CD(2)(c).

782 *Murray v Registrar of the National Native Title Tribunal* [2002] FCA 1598 [43]–[45].

783 ibid. [49].

784 See *QGC Pty Limited v Bygrave (No. 2)* [2010] FCA 1019 [69].

785 ibid. [88].

786 *Murray v Registrar of the National Native Title Tribunal* [2002] FCA 1598 [47].

787 Section 24CD(5).

788 Section 24CD(4) and (6).

In *QGC Pty Limited v Bygrave (No. 2)* Reeves J gave some implicit support to the proposition that s. 24CD(1) works as a 'deeming provision' such that a registered native title claimant *becomes* a party by operation of s. 24CD(1).[789] With respect, this is not the most natural available reading of that section and (as argued below) is not necessary to achieve the same ultimate result. In my view the best way to think of s. 24CD(1) is as part of the definition of *what an Area ILUA is*. Section 24CA provides that '[a]n agreement meeting the requirements of sections 24CB–24CE is an indigenous land use agreement';[790] conversely, an agreement not meeting those requirements is *not* an indigenous land use agreement. In this sense, s. 24CB–CE contains threshold criteria that must be satisfied before an agreement can even be *considered* for registration. This is not the same as saying that s. 24CD(1) stipulates a condition for the registration of an ILUA; s. 24CK and CL explicitly and exhaustively set out the conditions for registration and these conditions are slightly different from those in s. 24CD.[791] Rather, if the persons specified in s. 24CD are not parties to the agreement, then by the combined operation of s. 24CA and CD(1), the agreement is simply not an ILUA. Accordingly, it cannot even be considered for registration as an ILUA — it will never get to the point where s. 24CK or CL apply.

This leads to another important question: what does it mean to *be a party* to the agreement? In the ordinary contractual meaning of the word, a party is a person who has agreed to the terms of the agreement. On this view, actual agreement is both necessary and sufficient to a person's status as a party. But in *QGC Pty Limited v Bygrave (No. 2)* Reeves J did not consider it necessary for a registered native title claimant to sign, assent to or even *consent to* the agreement in order to be a party to it.[792] His Honour considered that s. 251A operates to position the native title claim group as the 'true' contracting entity, with the registered native title claimant occupying a role analogous to an agent.[793] Accordingly, in his Honour's view, where the native

789 Counsel for the applicant in *QGC Pty Limited v Bygrave (No. 2)* [2010] FCA 1019 made this suggestion among other submissions summarised at [53], and Reeves J said at [69] that he 'essentially agree[d] with' counsel's submissions at [53].

790 Section 253 states that '"indigenous land use agreement" has the meaning given by sections 24BA, 24CA and 24DA.'

791 Section 24CK applies to ILUAs certified by an NTRB (discussed below) and sets out two conditions: the first essentially requires any objections to registration to have been adequately resolved; the second requires all RNTBCs within the agreement area to be parties to the agreement. Similarly, s. 24CL sets out two conditions for ILUAs that are not certified by an NTRB: one is that the authorisation requirement in s. 24CG(3) has been satisfied; the other is that the parties to the contract include any person who is a registered native title claimant or RNTBC for any part of the agreement area by the end of the ILUA notification period, and any person who becomes a registered native title claimant after the end of the ILUA notification period provided that their native title application was filed before the end of that period. Note that neither s. 24CL nor s. 24CK mentions the 'third dotpoint' parties, i.e. those referred to in s. 24CD(2)(c) and (3).

792 *QGC Pty Limited v Bygrave (No. 2)* [2010] FCA 1019 [96]–[109].

793 ibid. [97]–[100]. Indeed, his Honour said that 'no privity of contract is created between the person or persons who wish to carry out future acts on the land concerned and the members of the registered native title claimants who are acting as representative parties under s 24CD'. This may be taken to say

title claim group has authorised the making of the agreement there is no additional step that must occur before the claim group's representative (i.e. the registered native title claimant) will be considered to be a party to the agreement.

With respect, this is a difficult position to understand. If one follows through Reeves J's agency analogy, one can imagine a situation where a principal has instructed an agent to sign (or otherwise communicate acceptance of) a contract but where the agent refuses to do so. It is not clear that under those circumstances a contract actually exists between the principal and another contracting party.[794] It is even less clear that the *agent* itself could be considered to be a party to the agreement in those circumstances, which after all is what s. 24CD requires. Further, what purpose would be served by s. 24CD(1), CK(3) and CL(2) (which requires certain persons to be parties) if mere authorisation by the unincorporated group of native title holders or claimants is sufficient? Under what circumstances could an agreement satisfying s. 203BE(5) or s. 24CL(3) *fail* to satisfy s. 24CD(1), CK(3) or CL(2), if valid authorisation is all that is required for a registered native title claimant to be treated as a party? With respect, it seems to unduly stretch the meaning of 'party' and 'agreement' to describe as a party somebody who manifestly does not agree to proposed terms.

This analysis is reinforced when one considers that the parties to an Area ILUA may include RNTBCs as well as registered native title claimants. It is true that an RNTBC's power to enter an ILUA is *constrained* by the 'consultation and consent' provisions of the Native Title (Prescribed Bodies Corporate) Regulations 1999 (PBC Regulations) (as described below in Section 8.2, 'Decision-making within RNTBCs') and also that an agent RNTBC 'must' manage the native title rights and interests 'as authorised by the common law holders',[795] but the *Corporations (Aboriginal and Torres Strait Islander) Act 2006* (CATSI Act) specifically provides for the means by which an Aboriginal corporation may become a party to a contract. In the absence of such means being employed, there is no obvious legal mechanism by which the RNTBC could become a party merely because the common law native title holders had authorised it to do so. And it would

---

that no *special* or *greater* privity exists between the proponents and the registered native title claimant than exists between the proponents and the group at large. Section 24EA effectively puts *all* native title holders in the position of contracting parties, and s. 61(1) stipulates that the applicant (and therefore the registered native title claimant) must be a member of the native title claim group. So even if only in their capacity as generic members of the native title claim group, the registered native title claimant appears to be bound as if they were a party.

794 It is interesting to compare the case of *Tigan*, where a claim group meeting authorised a change of solicitor but where not all of the applicants agreed to instruct the new solicitor. Because of the lack of unanimity, the applicant was found not to have given any legally effective instructions to the new solicitor. The court accordingly ordered the notice of change of solicitor to be removed from the court file. The fact that the claim group had authorised the change of solicitor was irrelevant to the question of whether a change had in fact taken place: *Tigan v Western Australia* [2010] FCA 993 [10]–[12], [30].

795 Section 57(1), NTA; reg. 7(1)(b), PBC Regulations. See also *Walmbaar Aboriginal Corporation v Queensland* [2009] FCA 579.

certainly be a strange interpretation of s. 24CD to say that a corporation could be a party to an agreement even though its board had positively resolved not to accept the agreement's terms and had clearly communicated such non-acceptance.

Finally, Reeves J's interpretation of s. 24CD is at odds with reg. 7(2)(b) of the Native Title (Indigenous Land Use Agreement) Regulations 1999 (ILUA Regulations). That provision requires every Area ILUA registration application to be accompanied by 'a statement by each party to the agreement, signed by or for the party, that the party agrees to the application being made'. In the case of an RNTBC or an applicant who refused to sign or otherwise agree to such a statement,[796] the application for registration would not comply with reg. 7(2)(b) or s. 24CG(2) of the *Native Title Act*. Accordingly the ILUA would be rejected for registration. This outcome tends to support an interpretation of s. 24CD that *does* require the actual assent of each party to the ILUA.

Importantly, Reeves J's interpretation of s. 24CD was explicitly directed at avoiding a situation whereby an individual member of the applicant could unilaterally 'veto' an agreement that was supported by the claim group at large.[797] But Reeves J's judgment contained a number of *other* interpretive arguments which were sufficient by themselves to achieve the parliamentary intention that his Honour had identified, without any need to resort to the kind of 'constructive contract' just discussed.

Firstly, Reeves J interpreted the term 'registered native title claimant' in a way that did not align exactly with the definition of 'applicant' under s. 61(2). Section 253 defines the term 'registered native title claimant' as 'a person or persons whose name or names appear in an entry on the Register of Native Title Claims as the applicant in relation to a claim'. Justice Reeves held that s. 253 'is to be construed to mean that one or more (but not necessarily all) of the persons who are named in the entry on the Register may comprise the registered native title claimant'.[798] This means that the registered native title claimant may be a mere *subset* of the applicant and that one or more individual named applicants can be left out of the native title claimant.[799] Those members of the applicant that *are* named as the registered native title claimant in respect of the ILUA then 'act as representative parties for the native title contracting group to allow that group to enter into the ILUA'.[800]

796 It is unlikely that a statement signed 'for' a person who disagreed with the statement would satisfy the requirements of reg. 7(2)(b).

797 *QGC Pty Limited v Bygrave (No. 2)* [2010] FCA 1019 [90]–[95], [106].

798 ibid. [83].

799 See generally ibid. [71]–[86].

800 ibid. [84]. Note that Reeves J appears to adopt a slightly different position elsewhere in the judgment, namely that the registered native title claimant has an identical composition to the applicant and that a subset of the registered native title claimant is then named as the 'representative parties' to an ILUA: see e.g. [2], [87]. This slightly divergent position does not appear to be consistent with his Honour's view (at [84]) that 'the whole of, or any, registered native title claimants in relation to the land or waters in the area covered by an ILUA, have to be parties to that ILUA.'

Secondly, Reeves J did not consider that there is any legislative requirement that the registered native title claimant act jointly or unanimously.[801] In his Honour's view the provisions of s. 61(2), which require the applicant to act jointly, do not apply to the role of registered native title claimants in the ILUA process. Further, even if joint or collective action were required, Reeves J did not consider that this would require unanimity.[802]

These two arguments seem to be strong enough to avoid a situation where dissentient members of the applicant could prevent the registration of an ILUA that had been authorised by the claim group as a whole. They also cover situations where members of the applicant are unable to assent to the agreement because of death or incapacity. Additionally, the removal of such dissentient individuals through s. 66B or the non–s. 66B mechanisms discussed above in Section 5.1 ('How can the composition of the applicant be changed?') provides another means by which the claim group could ensure that the named applicants complied with the group's wishes[803] (particularly where the named applicants' entry into ILUAs authorised by the claim group was made an express condition of their continued authorisation). Indeed, Reeves J endorsed the prospect of doing just that, in the event that s. 24CD really did require all members of the registered native title claimant to consent to being a party to the ILUA. His Honour considered that in that case:

> s 24CD should be construed so that it requires that so many of the persons who comprise the '*registered native title claimant*' as are willing and able to do so, are named as the representative parties to an ILUA. Thus, if a person is named as a representative party and he or she does not consent to being a party, that party's name can then be either removed or disregarded, without affecting the status of the agreement as an ILUA under the ILUA provisions of the Act.[804]

---

801 *QGC Pty Limited v Bygrave (No. 2)* [2010] FCA 1019 [87]–[89].

802 In this connection his Honour referred (ibid. [89]) to *Lawson v Minister for Land and Water Conservation (NSW)* [2002] FCA 1517 [25] and *Fesl* at [26], [71]. These cases discuss the idea of unanimity in *claim group* decisions rather than in applicant decisions. Nevertheless, there are cases that do support his Honour's position, as summarised above in Section 4.2 ('Disagreement, disability or death within the applicant'), particularly if the initial authorisation of the applicant under s. 61 or s. 66B stipulated that majority decisions would be sufficient to bind the whole.

803 Justice Reeves rejected the argument that s. 66B offered the only appropriate solution where one or more named applicants refused to sign an ILUA: *QGC Pty Limited v Bygrave (No. 2)* [2010] FCA 1019 [118]–[119]. This was on the basis that it was unnecessary to resort to s. 66B in light of his other conclusions about s. 24CD, and also because the 's. 66B solution' would imply that a failure to replace the applicant in case of death or incapacity would deprive the agreement of its status as an ILUA.

804 ibid [123].

In *Prior on behalf of the Juru (Cape Upstart) People v Queensland (No. 2)*, Rares J faced a similar situation to that in *QGC (No. 2)* and reached an equivalent result but without relying on Reeves J's 'constructive contract' concept.[805] In that case a consent determination had been negotiated concurrently with two ILUAs over the claim area. One of the named applicants had not signed or otherwise communicated assent to the ILUAs. The individual was ordered to file an affidavit explaining the failure but no affidavit was forthcoming and the failure remained unexplained. Justice Rares noted that the situation was similar to that in *QGC (No. 2)* and that no party before him had argued that Reeves J's construction of s. 24CD was wrong. Justice Rares accordingly found that the ILUAs could be validly entered into (and, presumably, registered) without the individual's signature or other expression of consent.[806] Importantly, in following Reeves J's decision in *QGC (No. 2)* Rares J referred only to those passages relating to the two arguments outlined above, namely that not all of the named applicants need to be named as representative parties, and even if they did their decision need not be unanimous.[807] Justice Rares summarised Reeves J's decision as follows:

> His Honour decided that it was not necessary for all persons who comprised the applicant in proceedings in this Court to be unanimous in deciding to enter into an indigenous land use agreement. Reeves J held that the requirement in s 24CD(1) of the Act that all persons in the native title group (as defined in s 24CD(2)(a)) had to be parties to an indigenous land use agreement was capable of being satisfied by making a party to it any one or more of those persons whose names appeared in the Register of Native Title Claims as an applicant or member of an applicant in relation to a claim to hold native title. His Honour held that s 24CD(1) and (2) had the effect that if one such person were made a party to an indigenous land use agreement, he or she would, as a representative, bind the others and make them parties to the agreement (*QGC* 189 FCR at 437 [84]).[808]

The example of *Prior* demonstrates that the result in *QGC (No. 2)* can be reached and justified without any reliance on the idea that a person can be a party to an agreement despite actively opposing its terms.

---

805 *Prior on behalf of the Juru (Cape Upstart) People v Queensland (No. 2)* [2011] FCA 819.

806 ibid. [34]–[36]. This finding was merely subsidiary to a conclusion that the consent determination ought to be made under s. 87. It was not an express finding about the registrability of the two ILUAs.

807 Justice Rares (ibid. [35]) referred to paragraphs [84]–[95] of *QGC (No. 2)*. Those paragraphs deal with the two arguments just summarised. The further position, that the consent of the registered native title claimant is not necessary to be a party, appears at paragraphs [96]–[119] of Reeves J's judgment and is not referred to by Rares J.

808 *Prior on behalf of the Juru (Cape Upstart) People v Queensland (No. 2)* [2011] FCA 819 [35].

Conclusion on applicant role in ILUAs

If the more constrained reading of *QGC (No. 2)* above is accepted then the role of named applicants in relation to the ILUA process can be summarised as follows:

- It is necessary for at least one member of the applicant to formally assent to the agreement embodied in the ILUA. Ordinarily that assent would be expressed in the form of a signature on the document, but not necessarily.
- If one or more member of the applicant refuses or is unable to agree with the terms of the ILUA, their non-assent will not prevent the registration of the ILUA; either because they can be excluded from that subset of the applicant called the 'registered native title claimant', or because the registered native title claimant can become a party to the agreement without the unanimous support of all of its constituent members.

If all of the named applicants refused to assent to the ILUA, then arguably there would be a need to replace the applicant under s. 66B before the ILUA could be registered.

Some have suggested that the outcome in *QGC (No. 2)* ought to be written explicitly into the *Native Title Act*, rather than relying on an interpretation of the current provisions. For example, the legislation could specify that authorisation by the native title claim group (or native title holders) is sufficient for registration and that no further step is required. Alternatively, the amendments could stipulate that where the authorisation is certified by the NTRB, the NTRB can be empowered to execute the agreement on behalf of the group.

Who must authorise an Area ILUA?

Having dealt with the question of who must be a party to an Area ILUA, it is now possible to proceed to ask whose authorisation is required before the ILUA can be registered. This question is not easily answered, at least not on the current state of the case law. The main area of controversy concerns whether, and in what circumstances, the authorising constituency must include people who have an unregistered claim or who have not lodged a native title claim at all. Put another way, the issue is whether registered claim groups have a special status such that they are the only people whose authorisation is necessary. And if so, what does this mean for situations where there are no registered native title claimants? The most succinct way of expressing the current state of the law (which will be explained afterwards) is by way of the following table:

Table 2: An attempt to capture the difficult state of the current law

The agreement area covers: ↓ And also: →	A competing person asserting native title with no application at all	Competing unregistered application	Competing registered claim
No claims at all	Unclear — most likely all asserters with a prima facie case must be involved		
One unregistered claim	Unclear — most likely all asserters with a prima facie case must be involved		
Multiple unregistered claims	Unclear — most likely all asserters with a prima facie case must be involved	Members of all unregistered claim groups with a prima facie case	
One registered claim	Generally only members of the registered claim group, but in some circumstances also mere asserters with a prima facie case	Generally only the members of the registered claim group, but in some circumstances also members of an unregistered claim group if it has a prima facie case	
More than one registered claim	Probably only members of the registered claim groups, but in some circumstances also mere asserters with a prima facie case	Generally only the members of the registered claim groups, but in some circumstances also members of an unregistered claim group if it has a prima facie case	Members of each registered claim group

The spirit of the ILUA authorisation requirements is basically the same as for the claims authorisation requirements. The underlying policy objectives include:

- ensuring that the substantive rights of the actual native title holders (whoever they may turn out to be) are protected pending the final determination of those rights;
- ensuring that procedural benefits are only available to those who meet a minimum threshold, so that plainly unmeritorious claims cannot be used to access procedural rights or to interfere with others' enjoyment of those rights;
- ensuring efficiency and certainty for third parties.[809]

The main difference between authorising native title applications and authorising Area ILUAs is the scope of the authorising constituency. In Chapter 3 we saw that the central concept for authorising native title applications is the 'native title claim group', defined as 'all the persons…who, according to their traditional laws and customs, hold the common or group rights and interests comprising the particular native title claimed'.[810] As we learned, for the purposes of s. 61 of the *Native Title Act*, that group is defined solely by reference to the case put forward by the applicants, as contained in their Form 1, their other pleadings, their submissions and their evidence. For the purpose of authorising Area ILUAs, the legislation contains three relevant formulations of the necessary authorising constituency:

- 'all persons who hold or may hold native title': s. 24CG(3)(b) or s. 203BE(1)(b);
- 'persons holding native title': s. 251A, chapeau;
- 'the persons who hold or may hold the common or group rights comprising the native title': s. 251A(a) and (b).

On its face, the differences in the wording may appear to be unintentional and without significance. Indeed, at least two judges have concluded that the words 'persons holding native title' in the chapeau to s. 251A mistakenly omit 'or may hold', so that s. 251A *should* read 'persons holding *or who may hold* native title in relation to land or waters in the area covered by an indigenous land use agreement authorise the making of the agreement if…'[811] Apart from that drafting slip, however, the remaining differences have been interpreted by courts as holding legally significant distinctions, as explained below.

The chief difficulty in articulating a coherent account of the rules for authorising ILUAs is the apparent inconsistency between previous case law and the more recent case of *QGC v Bygrave* (a case subsequent to *QGC (No. 2)*, discussed earlier). Below is an outline of what the *Bygrave* case says, followed by an analysis of its relationship to previous cases and some guidance about how the law might be applied in practice.

---

809 See e.g. *Fesl v Delegate of the Native Title Registrar* [2008] FCA 1469 [21]; *QGC Pty Limited v Bygrave (No. 2)* [2010] FCA 1019 [59]; *QGC Pty Limited v Bygrave* [2011] FCA 1457 [111]–[112].

810 Section 61, NTA.

811 *QGC Pty Limited v Bygrave (No. 2)* [2010] FCA 1019 [42]; citing *Fesl v Delegate of the Native Title Registrar* [2008] FCA 1469 [60].

The decision in QGC v Bygrave

The chapeau to s. 251A stipulates that if either paragraph (a) or (b) is satisfied, this will constitute authorisation by 'persons holding native title in relation to land or waters in the area covered' by the agreement. As mentioned, judges have concluded that this should be read as 'persons holding *or who may hold* native title' — thus bringing the words in the chapeau into line with those in ss 24CG(3)(b) and 203BE(5).[812] Taken together, then, this means that compliance with either paragraph (a) or (b) will satisfy the requirements of s. 24CG(3)(b) or s. 203BE.

Each of s. 251A(a) and (b) require an authorisation decision to be made by the persons who hold or may hold 'the common or group rights comprising the native title'. In *QGC v Bygrave*,[813] Reeves J noted that this particular form of words appears just three times in the *Native Title Act*: in s. 251A, in s. 225 (setting out the compulsory contents of a native title determination), and in s. 61 (stipulating the persons who must authorise an applicant bringing a native title claim). From this fact Reeves J inferred that s. 251A is connected to s. 61 such that parliament intended that a group of people cannot 'insist on being involved in the authorisation process under s 251A, without following the process prescribed by Div 1 of Pt 3 of the Act' [814] (which relevantly contains s. 61, s. 62A and s. 66B — the sections dealing with the identity, authorisation and powers of the applicant). Taken by itself, this suggests that the existence of a native title application under s. 61 is what determines who must be involved in authorising an ILUA. On that logic, the definition of the native title claim group as set out in the Form 1 and other applicant materials determines the necessary authorising constituency for an ILUA.

But Reeves J went further to say that the words in s. 251A(a) and (b) refer only to the members of a *registered* native title application — that is, an application that has passed the registration test in s. 190B and C. His Honour pointed to a number of considerations in support of the view that only the members of a registered claim were necessary for proper ILUA authorisation:

- **Credibility threshold:** One of the rationales for the 1998 amendments to the registration test provisions was 'to limit the number of people and groups with whom non-indigenous parties were required to negotiate'.[815] Similarly, the second reading speech stated that the 1998 amendments were designed 'to put in place a registration test for claims which ensures that those negotiating with developers have a credible claim' on the basis that 'an effective registration test as the gateway to the statutory benefits which the act [sic] provides is essential'. And again, it was 'essential to the

812 In line with the correction to the apparent drafting error mentioned earlier: *QGC Pty Limited v Bygrave (No. 2)* [2010] FCA 1019 [42], citing *Fesl v Delegate of the Native Title Registrar* [2008] FCA 1469 [60].

813 *QGC Pty Limited v Bygrave* [2011] FCA 1457 [105].

814 ibid. [115]. See also the passages from *Commonwealth v Clifton* [2007] FCAFC 190 referred to in *QGC Pty Limited v Bygrave* [2011] FCA 1457 [113], [114].

815 *QGC Pty Limited v Bygrave* [2011] FCA 1457 [111], quoting *Commonwealth v Clifton* [2007] FCAFC 190 [49]. It is worth noting that nothing in the ILUA provisions of the NTA actually requires proponents to negotiate with native title holders, i.e. the role of the 'right to negotiate' provisions in Subdivision P. Thus the comment in *Clifton* could be taken to be referring only to the right to negotiate rather than the ILUA regime.

continuing acceptance of the right to negotiate process that only those with a credible native title claim should participate'.[816]

- **Party requirements:** Section 24CL(2) provides that an ILUA cannot be registered unless every registered native title claimant for the area (including those whose claims were made in response to the ILUA notice) is a party. The focus in s. 24CL(2) on *registered* claims was taken by Reeves J to suggest that the mere making of a native title application is not enough to entitle a group to participate in the authorisation process.[817]
- **Lodging claims in response to ILUA notice:** Similarly, s. 24CH(2)(d) states that an ILUA notice must set out certain procedural options for any person who claims to hold native title in the agreement area and who disputes the authorisation of the ILUA. For ILUAs that are certified by the NTRB, such a person can lodge a written objection with the registrar disputing the ILUA's compliance with s. 203BE(5). For ILUAs that are not NTRB-certified, the dissatisfied person can make a native title determination application 'in response to the notice': s. 24CH(2)(d)(ii). Justice Reeves saw this as implying that people who are not part of an existing claim group cannot insist on being included in the authorisation process unless they file a new claim and get it registered.[818]
- **Workability:** At a policy level, Reeves J noted several reasons why the legislature would not have intended to allow people who did not have a registered claim to prevent the registration of an ILUA. Firstly, without a duly authorised applicant, proponents would not know who to negotiate with or whether a person who claimed to represent an unregistered group really spoke with their authority.[819] Secondly, requiring a claim to be submitted to the discipline of the registration test ensured that proponents only had to deal people with credible claims and also ensured that the rights and interests that would potentially be affected by the ILUA were properly identified and described.[820]

Informed by all of these considerations, Reeves J concluded that the persons referred to in s. 251A(a) and (b) are 'that group, or those groups of Aboriginal persons, that have demonstrated they may hold the group rights comprising the specific set of native title rights concerned, by

816 *QGC Pty Limited v Bygrave* [2011] FCA 1457 [112], quoting *Commonwealth v Clifton* [2007] FCAFC 190 [50].

817 ibid.

818 *QGC Pty Limited v Bygrave* [2011] FCA 1457 [116]; and at [117], quoting *Murray v National Native Title Tribunal* [2003] FCAFC 220 [23]. See also *Kemp v Native Title Registrar* [2006] FCA 939 [53]. It is not clear how this affects the position of objectors under the s. 24CK process for NTRB-certified ILUAs. There is no equivalent invitation to them to lodge a claim and yet they may object on the basis that the ILUA has not been authorised according to the requirements of s. 203BE(5), which are not relevantly distinguishable from those in s. 24CG(3). In Reeves J's view, a person who is not part of any registered claim would have no right to insist on participating in the ILUA's authorisation. It is therefore not clear on what other basis they could make an objection under s. 24CK.

819 *QGC Pty Limited v Bygrave* [2011] FCA 1457 [111], [118].

820 ibid.

filing a native title determination application under Pt 3 of the Act and having that application duly registered under Pt 7 of the Act'.[821] That is, according to *QGC v Bygrave*, an ILUA *must be authorised by the members of a native title claim group whose application has been registered* and *need not be authorised by anyone else.*

Note that Reeves J in *QGC* was careful not to give any opinion on how the law would operate in the case of multiple registered claim groups within the agreement area.[822] That situation could arise either because the claim area covered parts of multiple *neighbouring* claims or because there are multiple *overlapping* claims that are capable of registration because they do not share any common membership.[823] Despite the judgment's reticence on the subject, it seems reasonably clear from his Honour's reasoning that two or more registered claim groups would have an equal right to decide on the authorisation of an ILUA. The 'discipline' and merits-assessment involved in the registration test would vouch equally for any claim that was registered. The requirement for registered native title claimants to be parties would apply equally to all. The predictability and workability arguments would similarly favour the equal standing of all registered claims in the ILUA area. For the result to be any different would require some kind of merits test to determine which of the multiple registered claim groups really are the people who 'may hold' the native title rights and interests. That would effectively require an immediate resolution of the very question to which the claim proceedings are directed and would not give any certainty to third parties wanting to get deals done. For all of these reasons, everything said by Reeves J in *QGC* suggests that multiple registered claim groups would all need to authorise an ILUA for it to be registrable.

Understanding the law in light of QGC v Bygrave

On the facts of *QGC v Bygrave*, there was one group with a registered claim (the Bigambul people) and another group who had not filed an application at all (Kamilaroi/Gomeroi). Justice Reeves held that an authorisation process in which the latter group had not participated was still valid and sufficient for the registration of the ILUA. A group without a registered claim, in Reeves J's view, is irrelevant and unnecessary to meet the requirements of s. 251A (or at least where it is competing with a registered claim).

To get to this point, Reeves J had to distinguish an existing authority — *Kemp v Native Title Registrar*.[824] In *Kemp*, a registered native title claim group authorised an Area ILUA. A single person (Mr Kemp) who was not a member of that group challenged the registration of the ILUA on the basis that he was a native title holder for the ILUA area but had not participated in the authorisation decision. Justice Branson in that case held that the ILUA should not have been registered because it had not been authorised by Mr Kemp, even though Mr Kemp was not a member of any native title claim group, let alone a registered one.[825] The test applied by Branson J to determine whether Mr Kemp was a person who 'may hold' native title was to ask

821 ibid. [121].

822 ibid. [123].

823 Section 190C(3), NTA.

824 [2006] FCA 939.

825 ibid. [51]–[59].

whether his claim to hold native title was 'merely colourable' and 'without substance'.[826] Having found Mr Kemp's case to be stronger than that standard, Branson J considered that he ought to be treated as a person whose authorisation was necessary under s. 24CG.

In *QGC v Bygrave*, Reeves J explicitly did not hold that *Kemp* was wrongly decided, but instead distinguished the case. His Honour cited three reasons why *Kemp* was not applicable to the facts at hand. Firstly, Mr Kemp had been a respondent to the registered native title claim, which meant he had established to the court's satisfaction that he had at least a sufficient interest in the proceeding to warrant his joinder as a party. By contrast, the Kamilaroi/Gomeroi people had not become a respondent party to the registered Bigambul claim. This meant the Kamilaroi/Gomeroi had not had to outline the nature of their claimed rights and interests nor the area where they claimed to hold them. All the registrar had been given was an affidavit by an anthropologist, with no opportunity for cross-examination.[827] Secondly, Mr Kemp's failure to make a claim was explained by his inability to obtain sufficient funding, whereas the Kamilaroi/Gomeroi had not given any reason for not filing a claim.[828] Finally, Reeves J considered that the ILUA considered in *Kemp* had an 'overwhelmingly destructive effect' on the native title rights and interests, which made it appropriate to cast a wider net in determining whose authorisation was required. The ILUA between the Bigambul people and QGC, on the other hand, was of a different and less serious nature.[829]

With respect, it is difficult to see how parties and their lawyers should apply these distinguishing factors to future scenarios so as to predictably and consistently determine when an authorisation process needs to include people who are not part of a registered claim group. The first factor does not seem to address Reeves J's reasons for concluding that a group's authorisation was only necessary if they had a *registered* claim. His Honour had focused on the role of registration as a gateway to the procedural benefits under the legislation, ensuring a minimum threshold of merit as well as a proper authorisation process. Yet Mr Kemp had not made a native title claim at all, let alone a registered one. Further, as we have seen (Section 2.2 above at 'Joinder') joinder by an individual does not require any evidence of authorisation and in Mr Kemp's case the evidentiary basis for his joinder does not appear to be any greater than that put forward by the Kamilaroi/Gomeroi.[830] It is therefore hard to see why the mere fact of joinder would have exempted Mr Kemp from Reeves J's requirement for a registered claim. Similarly, it is not clear how the second distinguishing factor bears on any of the reasons cited by Reeves J in support of his Honour's interpretation of s. 251A. Merely having a good reason for not filing a claim does not say anything about the probable merit of the claim one *would* have filed, nor about one's authority to represent the putative claim group. Certainly, no-one is able to take advantage of the right to negotiate under Subdivision P (which is reserved for registered native title claimants)

826 ibid. [59].

827 *QGC Pty Limited v Bygrave* [2011] FCA 1457 [81].

828 ibid. [82].

829 ibid. [85].

830 *Davis-Hurst on behalf of the Traditional Owners of Saltwater v Minister for Land and Water Conservation (NSW)* [2003] FCA 541 [10], [23]–[29].

based solely on having a valid excuse for not filing a claim. The third distinguishing factor, relating to the effect of the ILUA under consideration, does not emerge naturally from the facts of the two cases. The ILUA in *Kemp* does not appear to have explicitly provided for the surrender or extinguishment of native title, nor for the validation of any future acts. Instead, it recognised that the registered native title claim group 'hold[s] native title in the land and waters concerned'; regulated the exercise of the native title rights; provided a role for a local Aboriginal council in the management of the conservation areas in the agreement area; and obliged the registered native title claim group to discontinue their claim.[831] By contrast, the Bigambul-QGC provided for the construction of a liquefied natural gas facility in the agreement area — with potentially significant and long-lasting physical impacts. Although Reeves J distinguished the *Kemp* ILUA on the basis that it involved the 'loss of native title rights', a close examination of the effect of the two agreements does not disclose such a substantial difference.

The factual differences between *Kemp* and *QGC* do not appear to be so significant as to intuitively lead to such different outcomes, and in *Kemp* Branson J considered that *textual* considerations were the 'strongest argument in favour' of interpreting s. 24CG as covering people outside the registered native title claim group.[832] In Branson J's view the drafters of s. 24CG could have easily limited its application to registered native title claim groups but did not do so. Her Honour considered that there was no compelling reason to import such a limitation into the meaning of s. 24CG.[833] These interpretive considerations were not dependent on the facts of the case and it is not apparent that Branson J's decision would have differed had her Honour been faced with the facts in *QGC*.

Kemp is not the only pre-*QGC* case that seems to run against the interpretation of s. 24CG adopted by Reeves J in *QGC v Bygrave*. In *Fesl*[834] Logan J rejected a challenge against the registration of an ILUA that had been authorised at a meeting attended by members of three groups.[835] None of the groups had a registered claim at the time: two had failed the registration test and the third group had discontinued its registered claim two years earlier. Justice Logan held that the requirements of s. 24CG had been satisfied on the facts, even where members of the discontinued claim group did not agree with the authorisation decision. The basis for Logan J's decision was that, in anthropological terms and in spite of the legal formalities, all three groups really constituted a single native title holding group.[836] (And, applying the case law from s. 251B, his Honour found that a mere subset of the claim group could not exercise a veto, in the absence of some traditional decision-making rule to that effect.) On Reeves J's reasoning, none of these

---

831 *Kemp v Native Title Registrar* [2006] FCA 939 [7].

832 ibid. [55].

833 ibid [58].

834 *Fesl v Delegate of the Native Title Registrar* [2008] FCA 1469.

835 In the final result, the court held that all three together constituted the same group for the purposes of determining whether one or more authorisation meetings were required. See further below in Section 7.1 at 'Process for authorisation'.

836 *Fesl v Delegate of the Native Title Registrar* [2008] FCA 1469 [54], [63].

groups would meet the definition in s. 251A of 'persons who hold or may hold the common or group rights comprising the native title' since none of them had a registered claim in place. Accordingly, none ought to have been relevant to the authorisation of the ILUA. The fact that Logan J found that s. 251A applied to these unregistered groups suggests that his Honour was relying on an interpretation of that section that diverges from that of Reeves J. Justice Logan's willingness to look behind the particular claims filed by the respective groups, focusing instead on the substance of their claims, further detracts from the emphasis in *Bygrave* on the making and registration of applications.

In *Murray*[837] an ILUA was registered over an area where there had never been a native title claim (not even an unregistered one). A representative of the Boonerwrung people, a group who asserted native title rights over the relevant area, became a party to the agreement for the purposes of s. 24CD. There was a second group who claimed to be part of the Boonerwrung people, but whose membership (and claim to hold native title) was not accepted by the main group. This second group had not been informed about the content of the ILUA, let alone been invited to authorise it. Nevertheless the registrar registered the ILUA on the basis that the second group could not establish a prima facie claim to hold native title in the relevant area and so were not people whose authorisation was required by s. 24CG(3). The second group challenged the registrar's decision in the Federal Court. This challenge was rejected by Marshall J on the grounds that (a) s. 24CD does not require *everyone* who asserts native title to be a party; and (b) the registrar's findings about the weakness of the second group's case were open on the facts. Justice Marshall's decision was found to be correct on appeal.[838] So *Murray* represents a superior court's endorsement of an application of the 'prima facie case' test for the purposes of s. 24CG(3). In this case, as in *Fesl*, there was no registered native title claim group to compete with the 'mere asserters'. This may provide some slight basis on which the two cases can be distinguished from *Kemp* and *QGC*. Still, in terms of legal principle they do tend to weaken the force of the arguments put forward in *QGC* for the primacy of the registered claim in the application of s. 24CG. Examining how s. 24CG operates in the absence of a registered claim tells us something about the meaning and intention of that section, which do not seem to support the logic underlying the *QGC* decision.

Where does this leave us? The most recent case on the subject sets out a general rule that only the members of a registered native title claim group need to authorise an ILUA. In one previous case an ILUA's registration was successfully challenged on the grounds that an individual with no claim at all had not participated in the authorisation.[839] In two further cases an ILUA was

---

837 *Murray v Registrar of the National Native Title Tribunal* [2002] FCA 1598.

838 *Murray v Registrar of the National Native Title Tribunal* [2003] FCAFC 220.

839 In the recent case of *Corunna v South West Aboriginal Land and Sea Council* [2015] FCA 491, a named applicant whose claim was not registered applied for a declaration stating that his claim group's separate authorisation was required for the registration of an ILUA that had been authorised by the relevant registered claim groups. Justice Barker at [67] said that he did not need to decide whether *Kemp* or *QGC* applied to the situation. Because the application for a declaration was

found to be properly authorised despite the absence of any registered claim, with the Full Court of the Federal Court applying a test based on 'prima facie' merit rather than the formal fact of registration. *QGC* can ostensibly be distinguished on the basis of a few factual differences from these other cases. But those distinguishing factors do not readily help us determine when the registered claim group will be sufficient or when a wide net must be cast.[840] It seems that the law will remain in this unsatisfactory state either until a test case is taken to the Full Court to resolve the confusion or until the legislation itself is amended.[841]

In the meantime, NTRBs are likely to adopt a pragmatic approach: where there is one or more groups competing with a registered claim group, or where there are no registered claim groups, prudence suggests a more inclusive process should be followed. (Just what this inclusive process might look like will be described below.) Where things are more clear-cut and the NTRB can be confident that the registered claim group represents all of the people with any native title rights and interests in the area, they may limit their authorisation process to the registered group and take comfort in the *QGC v Bygrave* decision. This latter approach would be most suited to situations where litigation or negotiations towards a determination are already well-advanced, such that the relevant evidence has already been assembled and the 'field' of potential native title holders already identified.

Process for authorisation

The discussion above has addressed the question of whose authorisation is necessary. It is now necessary to describe how that authorisation is to be obtained. Briefly summarised, this involves the following steps:

a) the identification stage;

b) forming a judgment about whether there is one or multiple 'true' groups;

c) notification of the meeting (assuming one is necessary);

d) holding the meeting;

e) recording the results.

As discussed earlier, steps (c) to (e) are governed by the same basic principles as for the authorisation of native title claims. Those persons whose authorisation is necessary must be given a reasonable opportunity to learn of the process and participate in the decision-making,

---

premature (the ILUA had not yet been lodged for registration) there was no need to decide whether the applicant's claim group could insist on participating in the authorisation decision.

840 See <http://www.claytonutz.com/publications/news/201205/01/bigambul_bygrave_uncertainty_in_the_law_of_authorisation_of_indigenous_land_use_agreements.page#13>, viewed 24 August 2016.

841 Note that recent attempts to amend the NTA in this regard were unsuccessful: N Duff, 'Reforming the native title act: baby steps or dancing the running man?', *Australian Indigenous Law Review*, vol. 17, no. 1, pp. 56–70, 2013. Although the Australian Law Reform Commission's review of the Act extended to issues of authorisation, it did not consider this question in any detail and did not recommend any changes to the Act: Australian Law Reform Commission, *Connection to country: review of the NTA 1993 (Cth)*, ALRC Report 126, 2015, para. 10.25.

and decisions are to be made by a traditional or an agreed process.[842] Steps (a) and (b) are explained sequentially below.

The identification stage

Step (a), the 'identification stage', arises because s. 24CG(3)(b) and s. 203BE(5) each sets out a two-stage process[843] for authorising Area ILUAs, requiring that:

(i) all reasonable efforts have been made to ensure that all persons who hold or may hold native title in relation to land or waters in the area covered by the agreement have been identified;

(ii) all the persons so identified have authorised the making of the agreement.

In *QGC* Reeves J analysed the language used here and elsewhere in the *Native Title Act* and concluded that paragraphs (i) and (ii) refer to two separate categories of people.[844] His Honour interpreted paragraph (i), the identification stage, as pertaining to:

> every individual, group of persons, or community, of Aboriginal or Torres Strait Islander descent, who holds native title, or by any means makes a claim to hold native title, or otherwise has a characteristic from which it is reasonable to conclude that person, group, or community holds native title, in any part of the area covered by the agreement.[845]

Justice Reeves characterised s. 24CG(3)(b)(i) as referring to an 'expansive and inclusive' group.[846] His Honour also considered that the words in s. 24CG(3)(b)(ii) 'all the persons so identified' referred to this same expansive group. So his Honour concluded that s. 24CG(3)(b)(ii) required evidence that any person asserting native title in the agreement area had authorised the ILUA.[847] But his Honour did not consider that this was the same authorising constituency as was mentioned in s. 251A(a) and (b). Justice Reeves held that s. 251A(a) and (b) concerned a narrower group than that described in s. 24CG(3)(b)(ii).[848] So in his Honour's view an ILUA must be authorised by all the people who claim to hold native title in the area, but the definition

---

842 *Fesl v Delegate of the Native Title Registrar* [2008] FCA 1469 [68]–[74].

843 The separate consideration of these two 'steps' was endorsed in *Fesl* (ibid. [48]–[52]).

844 *QGC Pty Limited v Bygrave* [2011] FCA 1457 [92].

845 ibid. [101].

846 ibid. [96], [101]. Although Reeves J refers to *Kemp v Native Title Registrar* [2006] FCA 939 [56] in support of this proposition, it is perhaps important that Branson J did not construe the words in s. 24CG(3)(b)(i) quite so expansively. Her Honour treated s. 24CG(3)(b) as defining the necessary constituency for authorisation and concluded that a person's assertion of native title must meet a minimum threshold of credibility for them to be considered as someone who 'may hold' native title. Her Honour's interpretation of s. 24CG(3)(b)(i) is therefore more constrained than that of Reeves J.

847 *QGC Pty Limited v Bygrave* [2011] FCA 1457 [102].

848 ibid. [103].

of what *constitutes* authorisation excludes anyone who is not part of a registered claim. This is the point of divergence between *QGC* and *Kemp*.

It has been pointed out that the 'identification' stage in paragraph (i) is effectively redundant on this narrow reading of s. 251A.[849] If the only people whose authorisation is necessary are the narrow category mentioned in s. 251A(a) and (b), why bother identifying an entirely different set of people as a preliminary exercise? However, in those cases (like *Kemp*, *Fesl* and *Murray*) that are distinguishable from *QGC*, the 'identification step' has a clear and useful function: to work out who needs to be involved in the authorisation step.[850] In *Murray* Marshall J agreed with a submission that 'a person should not necessarily be regarded as someone who may hold native title simply because they say they do so hold native title.'[851] And Branson J in *Kemp* held that there would be no need to obtain the authorisation of a person whose assertion was 'merely colourable'.[852]

So in those non-*QGC* cases, taking 'reasonable steps' to identify the necessary authorising constituency requires the applicants and their legal advisers to apprise themselves of the relevant facts and reach an informed conclusion. Where sufficient anthropological research has not yet been conducted, or where the identity of the native title holding group is in contention, reasonable steps may involve one or more 'identification' meetings prior to the ultimate authorisation meeting.[853] In other cases, the 'identification stage' takes place through the prior process of research, negotiation or even litigation, such that only the 'authorisation' stage need be addressed through a formal meeting. Or perhaps there *is* open contestation about who are the 'right people for country' but those advising the native title party conclude that the most prudent course is *not* to call a meeting but rather to rely on their anthropological material in support of 'reasonable efforts'. That approach was effective in *Murray*.[854]

Where a meeting is considered necessary to satisfy the 'identification step', the standard considerations of sufficient notice will arise. This means advertising the meeting sufficiently widely, intensively and early.[855] It also requires appropriate wording to describe those to whom the notice is addressed. If there is uncertainty or controversy about the definition of the native title holding group (e.g. the particular ancestors from whom the native title holders are descended or else the particular criteria that give rise to rights) the most prudent notice would be a generic one addressed to anyone who claims to (or believes that they) hold native title in the agreement

---

849 See <http://www.claytonutz.com/publications/news/201205/01/bigambul_bygrave_uncertainty_in_the_law_of_authorisation_of_indigenous_land_use_agreements.page>, viewed 24 August 2016.

850 Note that Branson J in *Kemp v Native Title Registrar* [2006] FCA 939 [45]–[46] explicitly did not decide whether a person's authorisation would be necessary if they had not been identified through 'reasonable efforts' but nevertheless had a prima facie claim.

851 *Murray v Registrar of the National Native Title Tribunal* [2002] FCA 1598 [75].

852 *Kemp v Native Title Registrar* [2006] FCA [59].

853 E.g. *Fesl v Delegate of the Native Title Registrar* [2008] FCA 1469 [48]–[51].

854 *Murray v Registrar of the National Native Title Tribunal* [2002] FCA 1598.

855 *Fesl v Delegate of the Native Title Registrar* [2008] FCA 1469 [48]–[51].

area. That way the 'identification' stage can begin from a sufficiently broad base to minimise the chance of overlooking or excluding a native title holder.[856]

Note it is very rare, and rarely advisable, to treat the 'identification' step as an opportunity to disentangle the intramural distribution of rights within a claim group so as to determine whether there is a particular subgroup who has a special relationship with the area covered by the ILUA. One would need to be sure that *none* of the other members of the broader claim group had *any* rights or interests in the agreement area before one could confidently proceed with seeking the authorisation of the estate or clan group alone. If not, the entire claim group should be involved (at least in the sense of being invited to any ultimate authorisation meeting) and if there are people within the group who under law and custom have a greater say about a particular area, this needs to play out intramurally. That is, everyone should be invited to participate in the decision, but those people who do not 'speak for' the particular area would be expected to defer to those who do.

The decision-making stage

Once the identification stage is complete (whether by a meeting or by research or negotiation), those seeking to get an ILUA registered must move onto the substantive authorisation step.

The authorisation step is reasonably simple for a single claim group (whether registered or not) with no-one from outside the group asserting rights. In that situation the process for authorising ILUAs is effectively the same as for authorising applicants.[857] That means the central requirement is for all persons in the group to be given the opportunity to participate in the decision-making, which will generally involve a minimum standard of notification as detailed above in sections 3.2 ('Authorisation by "all the persons" in the native title claim group') and 3.3 ('Authorisation in practice'). The process will be either traditional or adopted and, unless either of those processes provides for a 'veto', the dissent of an individual or subgroup will not be fatal to the decision.[858] The group is a single constituency that makes a single decision by whatever process is applicable.

But the legal principles above — whether in *QGC* or the other cases — leave open the possibility that more than one group may be entitled to participate in the authorisation process. If so, the question is whether these multiple groups should make separate decisions or a combined decision. As explained below, the answer will depend on whether the multiple

---

856 Interestingly, this approach was the subject of some recent judicial criticism, albeit in the context of authorising a claim rather than an ILUA. In *Collins on behalf of the Wongkumara People v Harris on behalf of the Palpamudramudra Yandrawandra People* [2016] FCA 527, it was noted at [32] that the meeting notice in that case 'assumes that any recipient of the notice, without any information beyond the description of the area of land to be claimed, will know if they hold or may hold native title in relation to the area'. Her Honour considered that this assumption 'is neither justified nor proven by any evidence'.

857 *Fesl v Delegate of the Native Title Registrar* [2008] FCA 1469 [72]–[73].

858 *QGC Pty Limited v Bygrave* [2011] FCA 1457 [122]; *Fesl v Delegate of the Native Title Registrar* [2008] FCA 1469 [26], [68]–[74].

groups can be characterised merely as different versions of substantially the same native title-holding group. So before an ILUA authorisation meeting is held, a judgment must be made about whether there is 'in reality' one native title holding group or multiple groups for the purpose of the authorisation decision.

Separate decisions

The default position is that, where multiple claim groups (whether registered or unregistered) are entitled to participate in the authorisation decision, the authorisation decision of each of those groups is to be made separately according to whatever traditional or adopted process applies to each.

In *Kemp* Branson J explicitly rejected the idea that all potential native title holders should be lumped into a single authorising constituency and left to make a single decision.[859] Her Honour said:

> Section 251A is not intended to provide, and does not provide, a means whereby a single authorising decision can be obtained which is binding on two or more groups where their respective claims to hold native title in an area are in conflict. This can be seen from the reference in paragraph (a) to a process of decision-making that, under the traditional laws and customs of the persons who hold or may hold the common or group rights comprising the native title, must be complied with in relation to authorising things of that kind. It is hard to imagine any such process of decision-making where the respective claims of two groups to hold the native title are in conflict; it would require traditional laws and customs in relation to jointly authorising things binding on the members of both groups.[860]

A consequence of this is that (subject to what is said in the next section, 'Combined decision') each of the groups entitled to participate in the authorisation decision wields an effective veto capable of preventing the registration of an ILUA. This outcome is consonant with the outcomes of the authorisation regime, as described earlier. One can imagine a scenario in which two neighbouring groups have each lodged applications, neither of which makes any claim to the land of the other. If a proponent wants an ILUA that covers part of the land of each group, the proponent will have to negotiate with each group. If one of the groups does not wish to enter into the agreement then there does not seem to be any policy basis for denying it that choice. Indeed, the position would be equivalent if the proponent decided to make a separate ILUA with each of the neighbouring groups over their respective claim areas.

Combined decision

A complication arises where the multiple application groups are judged, as a matter of anthropological fact, to be effectively the same single group. In such cases it is this larger, super-group that is treated as the relevant authorising constituency for an ILUA.

In *Fesl* members of three claim groups attended a meeting about a prospective ILUA. Each group received sufficient notification and opportunity to participate. One of the groups (Gubbi Gubbi #2)

---

859 *Kemp v Native Title Registrar* [2006] FCA 939 [40]–[41].

860 ibid. [41], quoted in *Fesl v Delegate of the Native Title Registrar* [2008] FCA 1469 [62].

did not agree with the decision of the others (Kabi Kabi #2 and Kabi Kabi #3) to enter into the ILUA. The registrar's delegate found that the authorisation was valid for the purposes of s. 24CG despite the Gubbi Gubbi's lack of agreement. Reviewing that decision, Logan J did not consider that the registrar had erred:

> There was evidence…before the Delegate, to which she referred in her reasons, to the effect that, in spite of the different names and spellings used for the Kabi Kabi and Gubbi Gubbi, each referred to the same group of people. The Delegate's consequential conclusion, which was also open on the evidence, was that Kabi Kabi, Gubbi Gubbi and other variant spellings were ways of naming one broader group of related persons who, together, assert native title interests in relation to the project area.[861]

His Honour contrasted this with that in *Kemp*, where there were 'conflicting claim groups, not one group in which there happened to be differing views'.[862] Accordingly, Logan J found that:

> The non-participation or, as the case may be, dissent of the [Gubbi Gubbi group members] did not affect the validity of the authorisation decision…There was evidence before the Delegate by reference to which she was entitled to conclude that the authorisation decision had been duly made and that each of the [Gubbi Gubbi persons] had been given a reasonable opportunity to participate in the adoption of a decision-making process and in the decision-making process itself.[863]

Importantly, the delegate had found that the Kabi Kabi/Gubbi Gubbi people had no applicable traditional decision-making process, and Logan J found that this conclusion was open on the evidence.[864] This meant that, for instance, there was no traditional rule requiring the assent of various subgroups within the Kabi Kabi People. Further, no such decision-making rule was agreed and adopted by the group. Accordingly the members of the Gubbi Gubbi claim group, even if they had been found to constitute a distinct subgroup, could not complain that their separate assent was required for a valid decision.

The reported decision does not disclose whether the various claim groups had partially overlapping memberships or not. But in any case that issue did not form part of Logan J's reasoning. The factual judgment about the singular nature of the various claim groups was based on general anthropological evidence (including, in this case, the fact that the same group-name was used by all three, albeit with different spellings).

The process of determining the bounds of the 'true' group, regardless of the content of the respective Form1s, seems analogous to the question of whether a native title application has been authorised only by a subset of the 'true' native title claim group, discussed above in Section 3.1

---

861 *Fesl v Delegate of the Native Title Registrar* [2008] FCA 1469 [54].

862 ibid. [63].

863 ibid. [74].

864 ibid. [55].

('The "native title claim group": conceptualising the authorising constituency'). The difference, perhaps, is that in the case of ILUAs the registrar can consider a range of material and is not limited to the applicant(s)'s evidence, pleadings and submissions. Indeed, there may not be an applicant.

There is nothing in *Fesl* to suggest that Logan J's reasoning applies only to unregistered claim groups. It is plausible, for example, that three *neighbouring* (rather than overlapping) applications might be filed by substantially the same group of people and subsequently registered. If an ILUA were proposed that covered land within each of the three claim areas, then the members of all three claim groups would participate in an authorisation decision according to whatever traditional or agreed process was applicable. A different scenario might involve a registered claim overlapped by an unregistered native title application. This is a fairly common situation because of s. 190C(3), which prevents the registration of an overlapping claim that shares some members in common with an already registered claim. On a strict application of *QGC*, only the registered native title claim group would be relevant to the ILUA authorisation process; the unregistered native title claim group would be effectively excluded. If the *Kemp* approach applied in the circumstances of a particular case, proper authorisation would require the involvement of the members of the unregistered claim group (assuming their claim had sufficient prima facie merit). Applying *Fesl*, if the unregistered group and the registered group could be considered in reality to be different iterations of the same underlying group, then a single authorisation decision encompassing both groups would be sufficient to register the ILUA.

A final type of scenario to consider is where there are simply no claims lodged with the court at all. There would be no Form 1s to consult to determine the respective memberships of the various competing groups, so the task of determining how a decision should be made and by whom would demand a cautious approach. Anthropological research and/or a broadly notified meeting may be required to identify the people who 'may hold' native title in the agreement area and the question of whether one decision or multiple decisions are required would need to be addressed by the *Fesl* test.

When an RNTBC is involved

As mentioned earlier, if the area covered by an Area ILUA includes an area for which there is an RNTBC, the parties to the agreement will include the RNTBC as well as the native title claimants.[865] In such cases it is necessary to be clear about whose authorisation is necessary and how it is to be obtained.

The key provisions are s. 24CG(3) and either s. 24CL or s. 24CK. The former requires the ILUA registration application to *attest to the fact* that the ILUA is properly authorised, and the latter two respectively require that the fact of authorisation either be proven or be certified by the NTRB.[866] The words of s. 24CG(3) do not distinguish between native title claimants and RNTBCs — the requirement simply relates to the 'persons who hold or may hold native title'. This raises the

---

865 See s. 24CD(2)(b), CK(3) and CL(2)(a). Of course, if the agreement area is covered entirely by RNTBCs then an Area ILUA cannot be used and either a Body Corporate or Alternative Procedure ILUA must be used.

866 On certification by the NTRB see s. 203BE(5), which reproduces the provisions of s. 24CG(3).

prospect of an ambiguity in the legislative scheme because, for some purposes, a trustee RNTBC is the legal holder of native title rather than the individual common law holders.[867] Does this mean that the ILUA authorisation requirements for trustee RNTBCs are different from those for agent RNTBCs? Or should the words 'common law' be read into s. 24CG(3)?

Ultimately it makes no difference. Because of the 'consultation and consent' provisions in the PBC Regulations, an RNTBC cannot enter into an ILUA without first consulting with and gaining the consent of the common law holders. The prescribed process for consultation and consent is basically identical to the process set out in s. 251A (and RNTBCs cannot use alternative consultation processes for ILUAs). This means that where an Area ILUA includes an RNTBC, the common law holders' consent needs to be obtained in exactly the same way as their authorisation would be given in the pre-determination situation.

Where the common law holders in the determined area are a different group from those in the undetermined area, there will need to be separate authorisation processes. Where the common law holders are the same group in the determined and undetermined area (which may result from a claim being split into Part A and Part B, with Part B being determined later in time) a single authorisation process can be conducted in which the common law holders/native title claim group authorise both the applicant's and the RNTBC's entry into the ILUA.

Documentation

When an Area ILUA is lodged with the Native Title Registrar for registration, it must be accompanied by a range of documentation specified in the ILUA Regulations and *Native Title Act*, including:[868]

- a written application for registration: s. 24CG(1), *Native Title Act*;
- a copy of the agreement: s. 24CG(2), *Native Title Act*;
- a statement by each party to the agreement, signed by or for the party, that the party agrees to the application being made: reg. 7(2)(b), ILUA Regulations;
- either:
  - a statement that the authorisation requirements have been met together with a 'further statement briefly setting out the grounds on which the Registrar should be satisfied that the requirements are met'; or
  - a certificate under s. 203BE(1)(b), *Native Title Act* from *all* NTRBs in the agreement area;[869]

[867] See e.g. *Santo v David* [2010] FCA 42.

[868] The required information and documentation goes beyond those listed but only the most relevant are mentioned here. See s. 24CG, NTA and reg. 7, ILUA Regulations.

[869] Section 24CG(3), NTA and reg. 7(2)(f), ILUA Regulations.

- in cases where an RNTBC is a party to the ILUA but not all of the NTRBs for the agreement area are parties — a document mentioned in sub-regulation 9(2) of the PBC Regulations: reg. 7(2)(g), ILUA Regulations;[870]
- in cases where none of the NTRBs for the agreement area are parties — a statement by one of the parties about whether at least one NTRB has been informed of the intention to enter into the agreement: reg. 7(4), ILUA Regulations.[871]

The s. 203BE(1)(b) certificate is a short document, usually two to three pages long. It should state: that it is a certificate issued for the purposes of that provision; the opinion that the requirements of s. 203(5)(a) and (b) have been met; and the reasons for that opinion.[872] The statement of reasons does not need to be supported by additional evidence or records.

The material provided in support of an uncertified ILUA is more extensive. In general it would include the details about the authorisation meeting (if there was one) including how it was notified, how well attended it was, what processes were used to ensure that those attending were people who hold or may hold native title, what decision-making process was used, and what decision was reached. It may include an anthropological opinion as to how representative the meeting was of the broader group and about whether the decision-making process was traditional or, if not, how it was agreed and adopted. Copies of the relevant notification advertisements or letters could be included, along with attendance lists, extracts of minutes,[873] and the like.

Objections and registration

The choice between certification or reliance on a statement supported by material is more than a mere matter of documentation. The procedural steps leading to registration differ according to which option is taken.

Upon receiving an application for the registration of an Area ILUA, the Native Title Registrar must issue notifications to certain specified parties and the public at large: s. 24CH, *Native Title Act*. Amongst other information, this notification must include a statement about the actions that can be taken by people who claim to hold native title in the agreement area.

For certified ILUAs the statement provides that within three months of the notification date, 'any person claiming to hold native title in relation to any of the land or waters in the area covered by the agreement may object, in writing to the registrar, against registration of the

---

870 The reference to sub-reg. 9(2) appears to be a mistake, an inadvertent failure to update the ILUA Regulations following amendments in 2011 to the PBC Regulations. The intended reference is most likely to reg. 9(1) of the PBC Regulations, discussed in Section 8.2 ('Decision-making within RNTBCs') below.

871 In this case the intention is not simply to state *whether* the NTRB has been informed but in fact to state *that* the NTRB has been informed.

872 Section 203BE(6)(b), NTA.

873 Note that minutes, depending on how detailed they are, may risk disclosing the content of legal advice and thereby waive privilege. Hence a shorter 'outcomes' document may be more appropriate for proof purposes.

agreement on the ground that the requirements of paragraphs 203BE(5)(a) and (b) were not satisfied in relation to the certification': s. 24CH(2)(d)(i), *Native Title Act.*

For ILUAs not certified by the NTRB, within three months of the notification date 'any person claiming to hold native title in relation to land or waters in the area covered by the agreement may wish, in response to the notice, to make a native title determination application or equivalent application under a law of a State or Territory': s. 24CH(2)(d)(ii), *Native Title Act.*

Certified ILUAs

According to s. 203BE(5) of the *Native Title Act* an NTRB 'must not' certify an ILUA unless it is of the opinion that the authorisation requirements have been met.[874] Nevertheless, the *Native Title Act* provides for an objections process for ILUAs that are certified by an NTRB. This represents the only specific legislative oversight of an NTRB's certification decision, although there could conceivably be practical repercussions for NTRBs or their directors if they are wrong in their assessment or negligent in their performance of the certification function.[875] Importantly, if there are no objections or all objections are withdrawn, then the registrar *must* register the ILUA regardless of the registrar's own view about the adequacy of the authorisation process.[876]

If the ILUA is certified by the relevant NTRB(s) for the agreement area, then the conditions for registration are contained in s. 24CK of the *Native Title Act.* Section 24CK(2) stipulates that the Native Title Registrar may not register the ILUA unless one of the following is true:[877]

(a) No objection under s. 24CI against registration of the agreement was made within the notice period.

(b) One or more objections under s. 24CI against registration of the agreement were made within the notice period, but they have all been withdrawn.

(c) One or more objections under s. 24CI against registration of the agreement were made within the notice period, all of them have not been withdrawn, but none of the persons making them has satisfied the registrar that the requirements of paragraphs 203BE(5)(a) and (b) were not satisfied in relation to the certification of the application by any of the representative Aboriginal/Torres Strait Islander bodies concerned.[878]

---

874 These requirements are identical to those in s. 24CG(3): *QGC Pty Limited v Bygrave* [2011] FCA 1457 [34]; *Weribone on behalf of the Mandandanji People v Queensland (No. 2)* [2013] FCA 485 [44].

875 Such repercussions could, theoretically, include the withdrawal or non-renewal of recognition as an NTRB: see s. 203AH(2). See D Roe & E McCartney, 'Certification of ILUAs – Benefits, risks and mitigation factors', paper presented at the National Native Title Conference, convened by the Australian Institute of Aboriginal and Torres Strait Islander Studies, Townsville, 4–6 June 2012.

876 Section 24CK(1), NTA.

877 In addition, s. 24CK(3), NTA requires that all RNTBCs within the agreement area be parties to the ILUA at the date of the registration decision. There seems to be no important difference between this and the requirement in s. 24CD(2)(b).

878 Section 24CK(2), NTA.

Although there is no formal burden of proof, s. 24CK(2)(c) is framed to suggest that the onus is on the objector to convince the registrar that the authorisation requirements have not been met, rather than on the NTRB to show that the requirements *have* been met. In deciding whether an objection should be upheld, the registrar must take into account any information provided by the objector or by the NTRB. The registrar has discretion to consider other information but is under no obligation to do so.[879]

Uncertified ILUAs

Area ILUAs that are not certified by the relevant NTRB(s) are governed by s. 24CL of the *Native Title Act*. Section24CL provides no formal process of objection equivalent to s. 24CK. Instead, s. 24CL(3) simply requires the registrar to 'consider' whether the requirements in s. 24CG(3)(b) have been met.[880] That is a straightforward process in which the registrar takes into account certain information and makes an administrative decision about whether the authorisation requirements are satisfied. The registrar must consider the statements contained in the application including the 'further statement briefly setting out the grounds on which the registrar should be satisfied that the requirements are met', described in s. 24CG(3)(b). The registrar must also take into account any other information provided by any other person or body (including any NTRB).[881] As with s. 24CK(4), the registrar may, but need not, consider other matters.

Section 24CL is slightly more stipulative than s. 24CK in regard to the persons who must be party to the ILUA. Whereas s. 24CK(3) requires only that the parties include all RNTBCs in the agreement area as at the date when the registrar proposes to register the agreement, s. 24CL(2) goes further. It requires the parties to include any RNTBC and any registered native title claimant in the agreement area at the end of the three-month notice period, as well as any registered native title claimant whose claim was lodged before that time and accepted for registration afterwards.[882] This requirement enhances the provisions of s. 24CD in that s. 24CD would appear to govern the situation as at the time when the ILUA is entered into, whereas s. 24CL extends to the time right up until the registrar's decision. One consequence of this 'latecomer' provision is that an ILUA registration decision under s. 24CL may be delayed for some time if a new claim is lodged during the three-month notice period. In that case, the registrar must not make a decision on registering the ILUA until the new claim has been assessed for registration under s. 190A–F. If the new claim fails the registration test, the ILUA can be considered for registration; if the new claim passes the registration test, the ILUA cannot be registered unless the new registered native title claimant becomes a party to the ILUA.

---

879 Section 24CK(4), NTA.

880 Properly, this should be a reference to the facts mentioned in s. 24CG(3)(a) and (b), since the requirement in s. 24CG(3)(b) itself is a requirement about the inclusion of a particular statement in the registration application.

881 Section 24CL(4), NTA.

882 Section 24CL(2), NTA. The specifics of the timing and manner of acceptance for registration are detailed in s. 24CL(2)(b)(i)–(iii).

To certify or not?

This brief outline makes it possible to identify situations in which NTRB certification may be more or less advantageous than a reliance on s. 24CG(3)(b) and CL. ('Advantageous' in this context means advantageous to those persons who want the ILUA to be registered.)

In a situation where there is no great controversy about who holds native title or whether the ILUA should go ahead, the advantages of certification are clear. The ILUA parties can rely on the certainty provided by the NTRB certificate, *provided* that no objections are expected.[883] By contrast, relying on a s. 24CG(3) statement would carry the risk that the registrar may not be satisfied with the rigour of the authorisation process or with the level of detail provided in the supporting statement. Further, the registrar's decision would be expected to come sooner for a certified ILUA: as soon as the three-month notice period expires, if there is no objection the registrar *must* register the ILUA. That is likely to be a quicker decision than the more substantive decision involved in s. 24CL.

However, if any objection is made to a certified ILUA then the registrar's decision may be just as unpredictable and take just as long as that under s. 24CG(3). If the objection is not withdrawn, the registrar will still need to look behind the certification and consider the substantive merits of the authorisation process itself, based on information provided by the NTRB and the objector. There may even be further delays if the registrar considers that additional steps are necessary as a matter of procedural justice to the objector and the NTRB. (By contrast, any aggrieved person who complains to the registrar about the authorisation process for an *uncertified* ILUA is simply treated as one source of information among many, rather than a formal objector with procedural standing.)[884] This means that if there is any real risk that an objection may be lodged, the advantages of certification may be effectively lost.

This also means that NTRBs who certify ILUAs will generally need to keep records of the authorisation process that are just as detailed as if the parties were relying on s. 24CG(3). If an objection is made, substantial documentation and even anthropological evidence may be required to rebut the claims of the objector. So certification does not necessarily mean less preparatory work for NTRB staff.

One situation in which it may make sense for an NTRB to certify a claim even in the face of a probable objection is where the potential objector is likely to lodge a new but unmeritorious claim during the notice period. As mentioned, a new claim lodged within that three-month window could produce significant delays because the registrar cannot decide on the ILUA registration until the new claim has itself been assessed for registration. If the NTRB was confident that such a claim would not ultimately be registered, particularly if the potential claimants were a mere subset of the native title claim group, then the NTRB may wish to avoid the inevitable delay. Going down the certification route would make it possible for an objection to be lodged, but that objection would be determined on the substantive question of whether the ILUA was properly authorised. That substantive determination may come sooner than waiting for the outcome of the registration test on a newly lodged claim.

883 See s. 24CK(1), NTA.

884 *QGC Pty Limited v Bygrave* [2011] FCA 1457 [48].

Alternative Procedure ILUA

There is no authorisation process as such for Alternative Procedure ILUAs. The only requirement is that certain persons *must* be parties to the ILUA — namely, any RNTBCs for the agreement area plus any NTRBs for the area.[885] The legislation permits others to be parties (such as registered native title claimants for the not-yet-determined areas) but does not require this.[886]

So is the decision to enter into an alternative procedure completely unregulated? Not quite. Firstly, any RNTBC who enters into the agreement must comply with the consultation and consent provisions outlined below in Section 8.2 ('Decision-making within RNTBCs'). Secondly, any person who claims to hold native title in relation to any part of the agreement area can *object* on the grounds that registration would not be *fair and reasonable*.[887] If the objector satisfies the National Native Title Tribunal of the merits of that objection, the agreement will not be registered.[888]

Objections do not specifically relate to the NTRB's decision to become a party to the ILUA or to the RNTBC's decision to do so. They are instead general objections to the registration of the ILUA. Objections may be made by anyone claiming to hold native title — there is no requirement that they be the applicant or a member of a native title claim group, and no requirement that they be part of a registered claim group. Accordingly it would seem that an objection can be made by an individual dissident member of a claim group, or even by an individual common law holder who disagrees with the decision of their RNTBC. Although there is no guarantee that an objection would necessarily be upheld, the availability of such an open-ended right to object introduces a high degree of uncertainty into the process. Perhaps unsurprisingly, there have been no Alternative Procedure ILUAs ever registered[889] and no reported litigation about them.

Body Corporate ILUA

Of the three 'types' of ILUA, Body Corporate ILUAs are the least regulated by the *Native Title Act*, though they are regulated by the ILUA Regulations and the PBC Regulations. The *Native Title Act* itself sets out just two relevant requirements for registration of a Body Corporate ILUA:

- Each RNTBC for the agreement area must be a party.[890]
- If none of the NTRBs for the agreement area are party to the agreement, then at least one of them must be formally informed of the proposed agreement by the RNTBC.[891]

---

885 Section 24DE, NTA.

886 Section 24DE(4), NTA.

887 Section 24DJ, NTA.

888 Section 24DL, NTA.

889 See ILUA summaries produced by AIATSIS Native Title Research Unit at <http://aiatsis.gov.au/sites/default/files/docs/research-and-guides/native-title-research/IluaSummary.pdf> and <http://aiatsis.gov.au/publications/products/whats-new-native-title-june-2016>, viewed 9 August 2016.

890 Section 24BD(1), NTA.

891 Section 24BD(4)(a), NTA.

There is no objection process for Body Corporate ILUAs. The only grounds for refusing registration are if one of the *parties* notifies the registrar that they do not wish the agreement to be registered, or if the NTRB notification requirement was not met.[892]

As will be explained below in Section 8.2 ('Decision-making within RNTBCs'), an RNTBC's entry into an ILUA (whether Body Corporate, Alternative Procedure, or Area ILUA) is subject to the consultation and consent provisions of the PBC Regulations. These impose effectively the same kind of authorisation process as is required by s. 251A of the *Native Title Act*. However, the PBC Regulations create a certification process whereby the RNTBC must certify that it has complied with the consultation and consent provisions.[893] Such a certificate is *conclusive* proof of compliance and, in the absence of fraud, there is no ability for courts or the Native Title Registrar to 'look behind' the certificate and make an independent judgment about whether the consultation and consent process was adequate.[894] It appears that the only available recourse to native title holders who are dissatisfied with the way their RNTBC conducts the consultation and consent process is to vote to remove the directors, and this will not affect the registration of the ILUA. So while the consultation and consent provisions are *mandatory*, non-compliance will not necessarily prevent the registration of the affected ILUA.

7.2 Entering and authorising s. 31 agreements

ILUAs are not the only means by which native title claimants or holders may agree to future acts in their area. For future acts that satisfy the criteria in s. 26 of the *Native Title Act* and that do not attract the expedited procedure, native title claimants or holders have a right to negotiate the terms under which they may be willing to agree to the future act.[895] For convenience, future acts attracting this statutory 'right to negotiate' are called 'RTN acts' in this book.

In practice, where negotiations are successful the native title party (a term explained below) will execute a deed in which their agreement to the future act is formalised and, additionally, all parties will execute a separate *ancillary agreement* setting out the substantive terms of the deal. Although care must always be taken with the terminology, it is common to refer to the former document as the 'state deed' and the second document as the 's. 31 agreement'. In fact, only the former document is actually mentioned in s. 31 of the *Native Title Act*.

The following sections will set out the precise legal context in which s. 31 agreements are made and explain how the general concepts of authorisation apply in that context.

---

892 Section 24BI, NTA.

893 This is certainly true of ILUAs, although less clear in the case of non-ILUA native title decisions. See Section 8.2 ('Decision-making within RNTBCs') below.

894 *Gibson v Rivers-McCombs* [2014] FCA 144 [74]–[75].

895 See ss 24MA–44, NTA.

The legal mechanics of s. 31 agreements

If a proposed future act is an RTN act and it affects an area of land covered by a registered native title claim, s. 28 of the *Native Title Act* provides that the act can only be validly done if one of the following (heavily paraphrased) conditions is established:

- An agreement of the kind mentioned in paragraph 31(1)(b) is made.
- The National Native Title Tribunal determines under s. 36A or s. 38 that the act may be done (including subject to conditions) or, if the tribunal determines that the act must not be done, such determination is overruled under s. 42.

These two conditions define the basic bargaining position of the parties: if no agreement is reached under s. 31, the proponent can approach the National Native Title Tribunal for an arbitral determination.[896]

Section 31(1)(b) speaks of an agreement reached between the relevant government party, any relevant grantee party and 'each of the native title parties'. The term 'native title party' is defined to mean any registered native title claimant and any RNTBC for any part of the area to be affected by the future act.[897] A registered native title claimant, just as for ILUAs, is a person or persons 'whose name or names appear in an entry on the Register of Native Title Claims as the applicant in relation to a claim' over the relevant area.[898] So if a claim has passed the registration test under s.190A–C, then its applicant is the relevant native title party.[899]

Where a given future act is proposed for an area covered by a single registered native title claim, the person(s) whose agreement is required for a s. 31 agreement is/are the named applicant(s). (Whether the signatures of *all* named applicants are required is discussed below.) Where there is a single RNTBC for the area affected by the proposed act, the corporation is the entity whose agreement is required. And if the future act area spans multiple registered claims or registered determinations, then the agreement of all applicants and/or RNTBCs is required. Agreement is not required from applicants whose claims are not registered.[900]

The role and autonomy of the applicant in s. 31 agreements

The *Native Title Act* does not set out any particular requirements for the decision-making process of the native title party. Where the native title party is an RNTBC, its decision-

896 A search of the National Native Title Tribunal's database of arbitral decisions (as at 30 August 2016) showed that 94 contested determinations had been made. (This excludes consent determinations and cases where the tribunal lacked jurisdiction because of a failure to negotiate on good faith.) Of these, only three resulted in a determination that the relevant future act may not be done.

897 Section 29, NTA. In temporal terms, the term applies to registered native title claimants and RNTBCs as at the notification date for the future act as well as persons or corporations who become registered native title claimants or RNTBCs within specified periods after the notification date: s. 30, NTA.

898 Section 253, NTA.

899 Note that the position in *QGC Pty Limited v Bygrave (No. 2)* [2010] FCA 1019 in relation to the meaning of 'registered native title claimant' in s. 24CD, NTA appears not to have flowed through to the law on s. 31 agreements, as will be seen below.

900 This also applies to applicants for claims that are dismissed or lose their registration: s. 30(2), NTA.

making process is regulated by the 'consultation and consent' provisions of the PBC Regulations as well as the RNTBC's corporate constitution and other matters discussed below in Section 8.2 ('Decision-making within RNTBCs').[901] But where the native title party is a registered native title claimant, the power to enter into s. 31 agreements seems simply to derive from the applicant's general power under s. 62A of the *Native Title Act* to 'deal with all matters arising under this Act in relation to the application'.[902]

There is no explicit requirement in the *Native Title Act* to show that the claim group as a whole endorses the agreement. There is no equivalent to ss 24CH, 24CL and 251A regulating the making of s. 31 agreements. It seems that the conduct of registered native title claimants under s. 31 is simply left to the general regime of supervision provided by the authorisation requirements of ss 61, 66B, 84D and 251B. This means that if one or more members of the applicant propose to enter into an agreement that is opposed by the broader claim group, the relevant remedy for those opponents is to seek orders under either s. 66B or s. 84D(1). The same applies to applicants who refuse to sign agreements that are supported by the claim group,[903] although as seen below there may be additional means available for the group to proceed with a s. 31 agreement even without the cooperation of all named applicants.

If a registered native title claimant took the claim group by surprise and purported to enter into a s. 31 agreement without speaking to the claim group first, the legal consequences are not entirely clear. The legislation does not prescribe any notification process for s. 31 agreements, and s. 28 requires only that 'an agreement of the kind mentioned in paragraph 31(1)(b) is made.' I was unable to find any case dealing with such a situation but it would appear that a s. 31 agreement can have legal effect without positive proof of authorisation and could arguably operate even without actual authorisation having been given. It may be that the law of agency could operate to prevent an unauthorised agreement from being enforceable, which may in turn preclude it from giving the relevant future act validity under s. 28. Similar options may be available if the agreement could be said to have been procured by fraud.

In any case the risk of this kind of 'rogue' applicant behaviour can be mitigated by fostering good communication and relationships between the NTRB, the claim group, the relevant government body and the relevant proponent company. Government agencies will sometimes ask for evidence of group authorisation when a state deed is provided. Proponents who understand the value of doing business in the right way may be less inclined to take such shortcuts, and NTRBs who have received a future act notification can give the proponent actual notice that the applicant does not have the authority of the broader claim group, which will make it more difficult for the proponent to rely on any resulting s. 31

901 Whether a breach of the PBC Regulations or other corporate governance processes would vitiate the contract is informed by 104.1–104.10, CATSI Act. It remains to be seen whether a native title holding group could successfully challenge the validity of a future act done pursuant to a s. 31 agreement, executed by an RNTBC in breach of the PBC Regulations or its own constitution. A similar but not identical question was addressed in *Walmbaar Aboriginal Corporation v Queensland* [2009] FCA 579.

902 See *Charlie Moore & Ors (Yandruwandha/Yawarrawarrka) and David Mungeranie & Ors (Dieri)/Eagle Bay Resources Nl/South Australia* [2005] NNTTA 53 [45].

903 E.g. *Daniel v Western Australia* [2002] FCA 1147; *Holborow v Western Australia* [2002] FCA 1428.

agreement. And, of course, if the applicants have acted beyond their authority they can be removed on that basis under s. 66B.

Lawyers advising native title claim groups may wish to suggest an explicit condition of authorisation that would prohibit the applicant from entering into any agreement without an express decision of the claim group. Although this would arguably not be sufficient to *prevent* the kind of 'rogue' situation described above, it would serve to set clear boundaries around the applicant's autonomy. It would also allow preventative action to be taken via s. 66B if the claim group or NTRB gained prior knowledge of the applicant's intention to enter into a s. 31 agreement.

This kind of conditional authorisation could also be used to define certain categories of low-level agreements that would *not* require the claim group's express endorsement, such as standard heritage agreements for mineral exploration or prospecting. For claim groups facing a high frequency of applications, this kind of arrangement is fairly common: applicants are given standing authorisation (indeed, standing instructions) to sign. That, however, would be a matter for the claim group and would depend on sufficient trust and communication between the claim group and applicant.

Claim groups may choose to appoint negotiation teams (often different in composition to the applicant) to handle the negotiation of significant agreements. Given the potentially large cost of full claim group meetings, it can be more efficient for a smaller representative group to meet and discuss a proposed agreement. Once the negotiation team is satisfied with a proposed agreement, they then take it back to a full claim group meeting. Under this sort of arrangement, the role of the applicant is limited to that of a mere signatory. For purely practical reasons[904] it makes sense to limit the number of named applicants to the bare minimum that is culturally appropriate. By contrast, it can be valuable to have a more broadly representative negotiation team, including a diverse mix of skills and levels of cultural authority.

Where some of the named applicants disagree or are unavailable

As contended above, the general rules of applicant decision-making apply to the making of s. 31 agreements. This means that the previous discussion in Chapter 4 applies, such that decisions must be unanimous unless the terms of authorisation allow for majority decision-making.

The requirements of s. 31(1)(b), however, impose an additional requirement for unanimity that cannot be circumvented by a majoritarian condition of authorisation. As mentioned previously, the parties to a s. 31 agreement must include 'any registered native title claimant' for the claim area,[905] and a registered native title claimant is 'a person or persons whose name or names appear in an entry on the Register of Native Title Claims as the applicant in relation to a claim'.[906] So at first blush this would appear to mean: if an individual's name is listed as a named applicant on the register, they must be a party to the agreement for the agreement to be legally effective under s. 28(1).

904 See Chapter 4 above and further below in Section 7.2 ('Entering and authorising s. 31 agreements') in relation to signing s. 31 agreements.

905 Section 29, NTA.

906 Section 253, NTA.

But as discussed above, the case law in relation to ILUAs suggests a different interpretation of 'registered native title claimant'. It is therefore necessary to determine whether the position of s. 31 agreements is relevantly distinguishable from that of ILUAs. As mentioned previously, Reeves J in *QGC (No. 2)* considered that 'the registered native title claimant' would be a party to an ILUA if one or more members of the applicant were parties.[907] In reaching that conclusion his Honour focused on the legislative purpose of the ILUA provisions in the *Native Title Act*. In his view the ILUA provisions create 'a statutory mechanism or device by which a large unincorporated group of indigenous persons with fluctuating memberships and undetermined native title rights and interests can enter into an ILUA under the Act'.[908] His Honour regarded the detailed authorisation process set out in s. 251A as being inconsistent with the idea that the registered native title claimant had any substantive role in the contracting process.[909] These considerations do not apply to the different context of s. 31 agreements — or at least, not as clearly[910] — and accordingly *QGC (No. 2)* may be distinguished. Indeed, Reeves J distinguished two cases dealing with s. 31 on just this basis: both *Daniel*[911] and *Holborow*[912] proceeded on the basis that a s. 66B application was necessary to remove an individual named applicant who refused to sign a s. 31 agreement according to the wishes of the broader group. Justice Reeves did not consider that these cases were relevant to his task of interpreting s. 24CD.[913] Therefore, conversely, we may conclude that *QGC (No. 2)* is not directly relevant to the position on s. 31 agreements. Indeed, a number of National Native Title Tribunal cases (discussed below) have held that the assent of all members of the registered native title claimant is *generally* required for s. 31 agreements. However, there are mechanisms that can be used to circumvent the need for unanimity.

The two common situations in which problems may arise in relation to the execution of a s. 31 agreement and state deed are:

a) One or more members of the applicant cannot sign for logistical reasons or cannot be contacted.[914]

b) One or more members of the applicant do not want to sign the agreement.[915]

---

907 *QGC Pty Limited v Bygrave (No. 2)* [2010] FCA 1019 [83].

908 ibid. [69].

909 ibid. [97]–[100].

910 It is true that, like s. 24EB, s. 41 of the NTA places the rest of the native title holding group in the same contractual position as the registered native title claimant. Nevertheless, there is no equivalent of s. 24CG(3) or s. 251A that is directly applicable to s. 31 agreements.

911 *Daniel v Western Australia* [2002] FCA 1147.

912 *Holborow v Western Australia* [2002] FCA 1428.

913 *QGC Pty Limited v Bygrave (No. 2)* [2010] FCA 1019 [118].

914 Note in at least some Australian jurisdictions, government departments are willing to grant mining leases on the basis of a state deed signed only by the living members of the applicant, so long as a death certificate is provided for any deceased member.

915 *Bradley Foster & Ors (Waanyi Peoples)/Copper Strike Ltd/Queensland* [2006] NNTTA 169; [2006] NNTTA 61 [35].

In either case, the individuals in question could be removed as applicants under s. 66B, although if an agreement is required urgently that may not be an option. This course is more appropriate in situation (b) than situation (a).[916]

Alternatively, if the inability to obtain all necessary signatures was foreseen at an earlier stage then an agent could have been appointed to act on the applicant's behalf. Technically the appointment of an agent would need to be done by each named applicant individually, so this option would need to be employed at a time when all applicants are able to participate in decision-making. Further, it would be prudent for the claim group to authorise this agency arrangement, to make it clear that such delegation is within the scope of the applicant's authority.[917] If such an agency arrangement was successfully created, the agent (e.g. an NTRB lawyer) could then sign documents on behalf of all of the named applicants. An agency arrangement would not assist in the case of disagreement between named applicants — under such circumstances the agent could not claim to represent the views of 'the applicant' (unless the applicant was also appointed on terms allowing majority decision-making).

The remaining option is for the contactable members of the applicant to support a 'consent determination' by the National Native Title Tribunal under s. 38.[918] Contractually this is done by specifying in the ancillary agreement an alternative means for the native title party to fulfil its obligation to validate the future act. That way the group can still be entitled to benefits under the ancillary agreement but these benefits are provided in exchange for a consent determination allowing the future act, rather than a state deed consenting to the future act. This was the option employed in 2013 by the Mirning people.[919] In that case a proposed minute of consent determination was provided to the tribunal, relevantly signed by the solicitor on the record for the native title claim. The solicitor's affidavit stated that the claim group had resolved to allow the future act to be done subject to certain conditions contained in an ancillary agreement, but that the signatures of four out of the eight named applicants could not be obtained because of geographic dispersal and ill health. The tribunal held that this evidence was sufficient to establish that the registered native title claimant, acting collectively, had consented to the future act in question and made a consent determination accordingly.[920]

In the *Mirning* example, the tribunal's decision was based not on the fact that the *claim group* had consented to the relevant future act but rather on the tribunal's finding that persons

---

916 See *Daniel v Western Australia* [2002] FCA 1147 [54]. Also *Holborow v Western Australia* [2002] FCA 1428; *Simpson on behalf of the Wajarri Elders v Western Australia* [2004] FCA 1752 [4]; *Doctor on behalf of the Bigambul People v Queensland* [2010] FCA 1406 [71]; *P.C. (name withheld) on behalf of the Njamal People v Western Australia* [2007] FCA 1054.

917 See e.g. *N.C. (deceased) v Western Australia (No. 2)* [2013] FCA 70 [20], [23].

918 Section 39(4) provides that where all of the negotiation parties consent then the tribunal must take that agreement into account and need not take other matters into account.

919 *Western Australia/Arthur Dimer & Ors on behalf of the WA Mirning People/R A Higgins & T F Higgins* [2013] NNTTA 46.

920 ibid [12]–[17].

comprising *the registered native title claimant* had jointly consented.[921] In a different tribunal decision, this time concerning the Esperance Nyungar people, Member O'Dea said:

> The critical issue for the Tribunal is whether the native title party has given their consent. The native title party in this sense is confined to that group of persons whose names appear on the Register of Native Title Claims as the registered native title claimants, who jointly comprise the applicant for the purposes of the native title determination application.
>
> The question of whether that consent has been given is not to be determined solely by reference to the question of whether each individual comprising the applicant has explicitly expressed an endorsement of any agreement. In any particular instance the Tribunal must look to the particular facts and circumstances of the case in making its determination as to the existence of consent when all the persons who comprise the applicant have not so signified.[922]

The kinds of facts and circumstances that may be relevant include:

- the adequacy and integrity of the negotiation process;
- the provision of competent, professional and objective legal advice;
- whether the claim group has endorsed this specific agreement or previously endorsed similar agreements;[923]

---

921 ibid.

922 *James Dimer on behalf of the Esperance Nyungar People/Paul Winston Askins, James Ian Stewart/ Western Australia* [2006] NNTTA 70.

923 In *Aston Coal 2 Pty Ltd, ICRA MC Pty Ltd and J-Power Australia Pty Ltd and Anor v Gomeroi People* [2015] NNTTA 40, two of the 18 named applicants had not signed the agreement that had been agreed 'in principle' with the relevant mining company. The reason for this failure/refusal is not clear. The tribunal heard evidence that the claim group had stipulated an expectation that mining agreements would require specific group approval, but there was no evidence that the particular agreement in question had been specifically approved by the group. There was no evidence that the applicant had been authorised to make decisions by majority. Nevertheless, despite two members of the applicant being either unavailable to sign or else actively opposed to the agreement, the tribunal proceeded on the basis of a statement of 'agreed issues' presented jointly by the solicitors for the native title party, the Crown solicitors and the solicitors fot the mining company. Relying on those agreed issues, and without conducting a substantive enquiry into the matters listed in s. 39(1)(a), NTA, the tribunal determined that the future act may be done. The determination was not subject to any condition relating to the ancillary agreement, though it is possible that the parties arranged for the terms of the agreement to apply in any case. This somewhat anomalous case suggests that an arbitral determination can be made without substantive enquiry, without the explicit approval of the group, and without a unanimous decision of the applicants even in the absence of a term allowing action by majority. Such an approach, if adopted as

- whether there is evidence of dissent within the claim group or within the applicant about the proposed agreement.[924]

If the reason that some signatures cannot be obtained is simply one of unavailability (death, incapacity or distance) then there may be a relatively low threshold for obtaining a consent determination.[925] In *Foster v Copper Strike*, Member Sosso said:

> [I]f only one of the ten persons comprising the applicant has reached accord and signed a contract with the other negotiating parties, but the remaining nine are either dead or unable to be located and there is no evidence of any disagreement within the claim group over the proposed agreement, then a consent determination may be appropriate.[926]

(It seems though that at least one of the named applicants must have specifically signed or otherwise assented to the proposed agreement.)[927]

However, if one or more of the named applicants actively refuses to sign the agreement then a number of factors must be considered. The broader claim group's wishes will be extremely important,[928] although the tribunal will be cautious in 'looking behind' the applicant.[929] In an

---

general practice, could weaken the regime of authorisation as it applies to future acts under Subdivision P of the NTA.

924 *Bradley Foster & Ors (Waanyi Peoples)/Copper Strike Ltd/Queensland* [2006] NNTTA 169; [2006] NNTTA 61 [37]–[40]. See also examples collected at *Charlie Moore & Ors (Yandruwandha/Yawarrawarrka) and David Mungeranie & Ors (Dieri)/Eagle Bay Resources Nl/South Australia* [2005] NNTTA 53 [63].

925 See e.g. *Arc Energy Limited/Councillor/ Western Australia* [2004] NNTTA 88; *Councillor/ Western Australia/ Victoria Diamond Exploration Pty Ltd* [2004] NNTTA 38; *BHP Billiton Minerals Pty Ltd/Abdullah/Western Australia* [2005] NNTTA 40. See also the discussion of applicant decision-making after the death of a named applicant in Section 4.2 ('Disagreement, disability or death within the applicant') above.

926 *Bradley Foster & Ors (Waanyi Peoples)/Copper Strike Ltd/Queensland* [2006] NNTTA 169; [2006] NNTTA 61 [38].

927 *James Dimer on behalf of the Esperance Nyungar People/Paul Winston Askins, James Ian Stewart/Western Australia* [2006] NNTTA 70; *Bradley Foster & Ors (Waanyi Peoples)/Copper Strike Ltd/Queensland* [2006] NNTTA 169; [2006] NNTTA 61 [38].

928 *Bradley Foster & Ors (Waanyi Peoples)/Copper Strike Ltd/Queensland* [2006] NNTTA 169; [2006] NNTTA 61 [37], [40]; *James Dimer on behalf of the Esperance Nyungar People/Paul Winston Askins, James Ian Stewart/Western Australia* [2006] NNTTA 70 [23].

929 *Charlie Moore & Ors (Yandruwandha/Yawarrawarrka) and David Mungeranie & Ors (Dieri)/Eagle Bay Resources Nl/South Australia* [2005] NNTTA 53 [45].

arbitral decision in Queensland,[930] Member Sosso noted 'an increasing trend in Federal Court decisions' to explicitly recognise the representative role rather than personal interest of native title applicants.[931] He continued:

> However, a 'consent' determination is just that. It requires the consent of each of the negotiation parties…The core rationale of [consent] determinations is that it is appropriate to make a determination where it is clear that a commercial arrangement has the broad support of a claim group and which advances their interests. The consent determinations collectively also reject the proposition that a minority of persons who collectively comprise an applicant can subvert the interests of a claim group where the rationale for the minority in failing or refusing to execute an agreement has nothing to do with either commercial or cultural considerations.

The intramural allocation of rights may also be relevant — the refusal by one named applicant to sign an agreement will be decisive if they are found to have special traditional rights or interests in the particular land or waters that would be affected by the proposed future act.[932] The reasons for objecting will also be taken into account:[933] the tribunal will give little weight to the objections of a named applicant who refuses to sign 'for reasons unrelated to the commercial worth of the agreement, the impact of the proposed future act on claim group or the environment of the relevant area or the process adopted in endorsing the agreement'.[934] This focus on the reasons for objecting reflects a view that named applicants have a quasi-fiduciary duty and must not use their position to pursue their own personal interests to the detriment of the claim group as a whole.[935] Finally, the substance of the agreement and the

---

930 *Bradley Foster & Ors (Waanyi Peoples) & Alfie Johnny & Ors (Gangalidda & Garawa Peoples #2)/Terence John Burt, Judy-Anne Galway & Robert William Kirkby/ Queensland* [2007] NNTTA 113; [2007] NNTTA 50.

931 At [22].

932 *Bradley Foster & Ors (Waanyi Peoples)/Copper Strike Ltd/Queensland* [2006] NNTTA 169; [2006] NNTTA 61 [38].

933 *Dimer/Western Australia/Boyes* [2003] NNTTA 117.

934 *Bradley Foster & Ors (Waanyi Peoples)/Copper Strike Ltd/Queensland* [2006] NNTTA 169; [2006] NNTTA 61 [40]; *Charlie Moore & Ors (Yandruwandha/Yawarrawarrka) and David Mungeranie & Ors (Dieri)/Eagle Bay Resources Nl/South Australia* [2005] NNTTA 53 [44]–[50]; *Bradley Foster & Ors (Waanyi Peoples) & Alfie Johnny & Ors (Gangalidda & Garawa Peoples #2)/ Terence John Burt, Judy-Anne Galway & Robert William Kirkby/Queensland* [2007] NNTTA 113; [2007] NNTTA 50.

935 *Placer (Granny Smith) Pty Ltd and Granny Smith Mines Limited/Western Australia/Ron Harrington-Smith & Ors on behalf of the Wongatha People* [2000] NNTTA 75; *Charlie Moore & Ors (Yandruwandha/Yawarrawarrka) and David Mungeranie & Ors (Dieri)/Eagle Bay Resources Nl/South Australia* [2005] NNTTA 53 [44]; *Bradley Foster & Ors (Waanyi Peoples)/Copper Strike Ltd/Queensland* [2006] NNTTA 169; [2006] NNTTA 61 [39].

future act concerned will be considered: standard agreements about low-impact future acts are more likely to be given effect through a consent determination.[936]

Privity under s. 31 agreements

Section 41(1) of the *Native Title Act* provides that where the parties have made 'an agreement of the kind mentioned in paragraph 31(1)(b)' and that agreement allows a future act to be done subject to conditions being complied with, then the agreement has effect 'as if the conditions were terms of a contract among the negotiation parties'. Subsection 2 specifies that, in the case of a registered native title claim, any person in the native title claim group is taken to be a negotiation party for the purpose of Subsection 1. This means that 'an agreement of the kind mentioned in paragraph 31(1)(b)' binds the entire claim group, much in the same way as s. 24EA works in relation to ILUAs.[937] Therefore the conditions in the agreement may be enforced by the claim group even after the original signatories are deceased or no longer hold the position of applicant.

But s. 41 comes with an important caveat: it only applies to the 'state deed' — that is, the document in which the native title party's consent to the future act is formally given. Only the conditions in that document fall within the scope of s. 41(1). If the important operative provisions are sequestered away in an ancillary agreement, and particularly if the state deed specifically stipulates that no part of any ancillary agreement forms part of the state deed, then these provisions will not be affected by s. 41(1).

That means that lawyers drafting ancillary agreements must carefully consider how privity between the parties will work after the original signatories die or are removed as applicants and how the rights and obligations will be transferred when an RNTBC is established.[938]

---

936 *Charlie Moore & Ors (Yandruwandha/Yawarrawarrka) and David Mungeranie & Ors (Dieri)/Eagle Bay Resources Nl/South Australia* [2005] NNTTA 53 [65]; *Champion/Siberia Mining Corporation Ltd/Western Australia* [2004] NNTTA 26; *Dimer/Western Australia/Boyes* [2003] NNTTA 117.

937 One important difference is that s. 24EA refers to 'all persons holding native title' rather than 'a...person included in the native title claim group'.

938 Justice Reeves considered issues of privity in ancillary agreements in *Karingbal Traditional People Aboriginal Corporation v Santos GLNG Pty Ltd* [2011] FCA 1456. In that case the relevant agreement was ancillary to an ILUA rather than to an agreement under s. 31(1)(b). All five named applicants were under a joint and several obligation to nominate an entity to receive funds under the agreement. One of the five disagreed about the choice of entity. Justice Reeves held that the performance of the obligation had been satisfied by the other four named applicants and that the non-performance by the fifth was immaterial.

8. Post-determination decision-making and nominating the RNTBC

Once a determination of native title is made, the Federal Court litigation is complete and there is no longer an 'applicant' to represent the native title claim group to the world at large.[939] Instead, the *Native Title Act* provides for a compulsory system of corporate representation of native title holding groups. RNTBCs are created to act on behalf of the broader group in relation to native title matters.[940] As will be explained in this part, RNTBCs are capable of substantial autonomy in various areas of action but are subject to 'consultation and consent' requirements for some categories of decision, essentially the same as the familiar authorisation processes in s. 251A and B.

The process for creating RNTBCs is simple, though the terminology does sometimes require close attention. When a native title determination is made under ss 94A and 225 of the *Native Title Act* the court is obliged by s. 55 to make a second distinct determination[941] naming the corporation that will represent the native title claim group in the future. That second determination must be made 'at the same time as, or as soon as practicable after' the determination of native title is made.[942]

The court can make one of two types of RNTBC determination: either that the relevant corporation will hold native title on *trust* for the 'common law native title holders', or that the corporation will merely act as *agent* for the 'common law native title holders'.[943] The distinction will be explored further below in Section 8.2 ('Decision-making within RNTBCs') but for present purposes it is sufficient to note the two different sections of the *Native Title Act* that are engaged: trustee corporations are determined under s. 56 and agent corporations are determined under s. 57. The term 'common law native title holders' is necessary because, in the case of a trustee corporation, the RNTBC is technically the legal 'holder' of the native title while the people described in the native title determination as holding the native title are treated as the *beneficiaries* of the trust. This latter group of people are called 'common law native title holders' because they are the people

---

939 To be precise, there is no longer an applicant once the court file is closed; if there are outstanding issues such as appeals or costs then the applicant will retain that status. The registered native title claimant will retain its status until the relevant name(s) are removed from the register; this will only occur once an RNTBC is determined and registered. So where there is a delay between determination and the determination of the RNTBC, the applicant retains its previous function.

940 The main RNTBC functions are specified in regs 6 and 7 of the PBC Regulations. RNTBCs also have a range of functions under the future act provisions and compensation determination application provisions.

941 Technically, it seems, *two* further determinations are required in the case of 'agent' corporations — one under s. 56 stating that the native title will not be held on trust, and a second under s. 57 naming the corporation that will serve as agent: see s. 57(2).

942 Section 55, NTA. Note there have been cases where long periods have been allowed, e.g. 4 years in *Deeral (on behalf of herself and the Gamaay Peoples) v Charlie* [1998] FCA 723.

943 Sections 55–57, NTA.

who *would* hold native title under the common law; the only reason they do not is because of the intervention of the *Native Title Act*.[944]

Not just any corporation can serve as an RNTBC. The regulations set out certain criteria that a corporation must meet in order to be determined as an RNTBC.[945] Any corporation that satisfies these criteria is called a 'prescribed body corporate'. To be clear: although RNTBC and prescribed body corporate (PBC) are colloquially treated as synonyms, a PBC is any corporation that is *eligible* to be determined by the court as the trustee or agent for the common law native title holders.[946] The eligibility requirements are as follows:

- The corporation must be an Aboriginal or Torres Strait Islander corporation — that is, a corporation registered under the CATSI Act.[947]
- The corporation's objects, as stated in its rulebook, must include the purpose of becoming a registered native title body corporate.[948]
- The members of the corporation must *either* be native title holders as described in the determination *or* be persons whose membership of the corporation has been consented to by the native title holders.[949] Note that this requirement states that *only* native title holders (or their appointees) may be members; it does not require that *all* native title holders be members.
- The corporation must meet the 'Indigeneity requirement' in s. 29.5 of the CATSI Act.[950] That requirement must continue to be satisfied even if non-Indigenous persons are admitted as members with the consent of the native title holders.

Immediately after the court determines a particular PBC to be either agent or trustee for the common law native title holders, the Registrar of Native Title will enter the details of the corporation on the Native Title Register.[951] At this point, the PBC becomes known as the RNTBC.[952] In effect, the court determines that a particular PBC will be the RNTBC for each native title determination.

---

944 Sections 56(2)(a) and 253, NTA.

945 Regs 4 and 11, PBC Regulations.

946 Sections 56–57, NTA.

947 Regs 4(1) and 3, PBC Regulations; s. 16.5, CATSI Act.

948 Reg. 4(2)(a), PBC Regulations.

949 Reg. 4(2)(b) and (c), PBC Regulations. This requirement applies both at the time when the determination under s. 56 or s. 57 is made and at all times subsequently.

950 For corporations of five members or more, this requires 51 per cent of members to be Aboriginal or Torres Strait Islander people; for corporations of less than five members, the requirement is that either all or all-but-one of the members be Aboriginal or Torres Strait Islander people; and for corporations of just one member, that one member must be an Aboriginal or Torres Strait Islander person. See Corporations (Aboriginal and Torres Strait Islander) Regulations 2007, reg. 29–5.01.

951 Section 193(2), NTA.

952 Section 253, NTA.

Three points should be made about the determination of which PBC will serve as RNTBC. Firstly, the legislation allows for more than one RNTBC to be determined in respect of a single native title determination. Where more than one Indigenous group is determined to hold native title within the determination area, the court may determine a different RNTBC for each group.[953] Secondly, and conversely, it is possible for a single corporation to be the RNTBC for multiple native title determinations.[954] Thirdly, prior to the court's determination it is possible for more than one PBC to contend for the role of RNTBC even where there is only one native title–holding group.[955] That is, different factions within a native title claim group may separately decide to incorporate corporations that meet the eligibility criteria set out in the regulations, each with the intention of nominating their corporation to be determined as the RNTBC.[956] This situation gives rise to the possibility that a court may have to decide between competing prescribed bodies corporate. For all three reasons it is worthwhile examining in some detail the process by which a PBC is nominated under the legislation.

8.1 Nominating a PBC for determination

Section 55 of the *Native Title Act* requires the court to make a determination about the RNTBC at the same time or as soon as practicable after the determination of native title.[957] Sections 56 and 57 contain the substantive provisions governing the process for nominating and determining the RNTBC. Broadly speaking, s. 56 deals with trustee corporations and s. 57 with agent corporations; in either case, the process is effectively the same:[958]

a) The court must request that, within a specified time period, a 'representative of the common law holders' nominate in writing a PBC to serve as the RNTBC.

b) The nomination must be accompanied by the written consent of the nominated corporation.

---

953 *Moses v Western Australia* [2007] FCAFC 78 [376]–[386]; *Lovett on behalf of the Gunditjmara People v Victoria (No. 5)* [2011] FCA 932.

954 Section 59A, NTA; regs 4A and 5, PBC Regulations. See for example *Barunga v Western Australia* [2011] FCA 518, in which the same RNTBC was determined as for *Goonack v Western Australia* [2011] FCA 516 and *Neowarra v Western Australia* [2004] FCA 1092.

955 I am aware of at least three occasions on which this has occurred.

956 This possibility is underscored by the language of s. 57(2)(c), a paragraph stipulating how the court should proceed if the claim group fails to nominate a PBC within the required time.

957 Note s. 55 has been interpreted as requiring the court merely to *begin* implementing the procedure in ss 56 and 57 at the same time as or as soon as practicable after making the determination: *Mualgal People v Queensland* [1998] FCA 1718.

958 To be precise, s. 56 in every case requires the court first to make a determination of whether the native title will be held on trust or not. If the native title holders express their preference for a trust arrangement, the court will determine (also under s. 56) the trustee corporation as nominated by the native title holders. If not, the court moves on to s. 57 to determine an agent corporation.

c) If a PBC is nominated within the specified time and accompanied by the corporation's written consent, the court *must* make a determination in favour of the nominated corporation.

d) If not, the court must determine for itself which PBC will be the RNTBC. This 'default' appointment can only be an agent corporation, not a trustee corporation.[959] The candidates for the default corporation are limited to: (i) any corporation that has already been established for the purpose of being the RNTBC for the particular claim group, or (ii) the Indigenous land corporation (ILC).[960] Option (i) would arise in circumstances where there were multiple competing eligible prescribed bodies corporate but no consensus in the group about which one should be the RNTBC. In that situation the court would be empowered to choose between them. I could not find in the case law any example of this ever happening.

It may seem odd that the task of nominating the RNTBC is merely left to 'a representative' of the native title claim group, with no explicit requirement that the representative be a named applicant or authorised in any other capacity by the claim group. After all, all other steps in the proceedings are subject to the authorisation requirement in ss 251B and 84D, and after a determination is made the RNTBC is subject to consultation and consent requirements. (See below.) Therefore the nomination of the RNTBC may appear to be the only unregulated step in the entire claim process. It is possible that the drafters of the *Native Title Act* did not anticipate that the choice of RNTBC would be contentious between members of a native title holding group. Certainly, I was unable to identify any reported decision dealing with a contested RNTBC nomination.[961] However, there are some indications in the case law as to how courts might approach contentious cases if they should arise.

Who can nominate?

There is no explicit limitation in s. 56(2)(a) and s. 57(2)(a) on who may act as the common law native title holders' representative in nominating the RNTBC. There is no requirement that the representative be a named applicant or even a member of the claim group. It is not even clear whether the court's request for a nomination must be addressed to a *particular* representative or whether the court may simply request *any* representative to step forward. On the other hand, one could read s. 62A (which gives the applicant the power to deal with 'all matters arising under this Act in relation to the application') as applying to the PBC nomination, in which case the nomination should be made by the applicant (i.e. all named applicants acting jointly).[962]

---

959 See ss 56(2)(c) and 57(2)(c), NTA.

960 See regs 4 and 11, PBC Regulations.

961 The only slightly relevant case is *Moses v Western Australia* [2007] FCAFC 78, in which the Commonwealth objected to the determination of two separate RNTBCs for the two groups named in the determination. In that case, however, there was no argument between the native title holders themselves.

962 See Section 4.1 ('Extent of applicant autonomy') above.

In practice, some judges have named a particular person (almost always a member of the applicant) as the representative;[963] others have asked 'the applicants' to nominate a PBC;[964] and in at least one case the claimants' NTRB was requested to give the nomination.[965] Recently, a PBC nomination was made via an affidavit from the NTRB solicitor, who described the nomination decision reached at a claim group meeting. That indirect nomination, which effectively treated the lawyer as the representative, was accepted by the court.[966]

In the case of a determination that explicitly recognises more than one native title–holding group, the court will request a representative of each group to nominate a corporation.[967] That approach is consistent with s. 225, which requires a determination to indicate 'the persons, or each group of persons' who hold native title.[968] In a 2011 determination decision, the Gunditjmara people and the Eastern Maar people each nominated a separate corporation — with the result that both corporations are 'the RNTBC' for the determination area.[969] Of course, there is nothing to prevent each separate group from nominating the same corporation.[970] The Nyangumarta people and the Karajarri people obtained a joint determination for an area of shared country and each separately nominated the Nyangumarta Karajarri Aboriginal Corporation to be the RNTBC.[971]

Is evidence of authorisation or consent required?

Although there is no explicit legislative requirement that the PBC nomination be specifically authorised by the claim group, there are two reasons for inferring that such a requirement exists. Firstly, as mentioned above, s. 62A appears to apply to the nomination of a PBC as with any other step in the proceedings. As has been described previously, steps in the proceedings can theoretically be done by the applicant autonomously but in practice the court may require evidence that major decisions are done with the group's approval.[972] Certainly if the matter was contentious it may be the subject of a s. 84D(1) enquiry, either on the court's own motion or on application by a claim group member.

Secondly, a requirement of consent or authorisation may arguably be inferred from the word 'representative'. That is, one might read ss 56(2)(a) and 57(2)(a) to mean that

---

963 E.g. *Hayes v Northern Territory* [2000] FCA 671. In *Passi on behalf of the Meriam People v Queensland* [2001] FCA 697 the court had received an affidavit by one of the named applicants in which the named applicant nominated the relevant corporation 'on behalf of' the claim group.

964 E.g. *Nelson v Northern Territory* [2010] FCA 1343.

965 In *Sampi v Western Australia* [2005] FCA 777 the court ordered the Kimberley Land Council as the representative of the applicants to nominate a PBC.

966 *Bandjalang People No. 1 and No. 2 v Attorney General (NSW)* [2013] FCA 1278 [22].

967 E.g. *Lovett on behalf of the Gunditjmara People v Victoria (No. 5)* [2011] FCA 932.

968 *Daniel v Western Australia* [2004] FCA 849 [22]–[23]; approved on appeal: *Moses v Western Australia* [2007] FCAFC 78 [376]–[386].

969 *Lovett on behalf of the Gunditjmara People v Victoria (No. 5)* [2011] FCA 932.

970 See reg. 5, PBC Regulations.

971 *Hunter v Western Australia* [2012] FCA 690 [35].

972 See above Chapter 6 and Section 7.2 ('Entering and authorising s. 31 agreements').

the person making the nomination must be doing so in a representative capacity and therefore that the claim group must in some sense endorse the choice. There is support for this view in the words of s. 56(2)(a), which treats the representative's nomination as reflecting what the 'common law holders intend'. This interpretation is also supported by the decision in *Ngapil*.[973] There, the chairperson of the nominated corporation wrote to the court, both nominating the corporation and giving the corporation's consent. Justice Carr concluded that:

> [a]lthough that nomination was expressed by Mr Skeahan as 'elected Chairperson' of the Corporation I am satisfied that, at the time when Mr Skeanhan [sic] made that nomination, he was also the representative of the common law holders for the purpose of making that nomination. In that regard I rely on the evidence contained in paragraph 3 of the affidavit of Ms Krysti Justine Guest affirmed on 23 October 2002 and paragraph 9 of Ms Melbourne's affidavit affirmed on 6 May 2003.[974]

One may infer that if the evidence gave Carr J any reason to doubt that Mr Skeahan was acting in a way representative of the wishes of the common law holders, his Honour may have declined to act on the nomination.

Similarly, Merkel J in *Rubibi* considered that the court must be satisfied that the person making the nomination be a representative of the common law holders.[975] His Honour noted that the person in that case had described himself as a representative of the Yawuru community, was a named applicant and also had given evidence in the proceedings in his capacity as a senior Yawuru law man. These factors were, in the circumstances, sufficient to satisfy Merkel J about the person's status as a representative.

In the *Strathgordon* determination, Greenwood J referred to an affidavit of the claimants' solicitor which described a meeting at which the claim group had unanimously agreed to form the PBC for the purpose of nominating it as RNTBC.[976] It is not suggested that this level of evidence will be required in every case but it does demonstrate the kind of evidentiary basis that might be necessary in contested situations.

---

973 *Ngalpil v Western Australia* [2003] FCA 1098.

974 ibid. [18].

975 *Rubibi Community v Western Australia* [2004] FCA 964 [5].

976 *Malachi on behalf of the Strathgordon Mob v Queensland* [2007] FCA 1084 [41]. See also *Greenwool for and on behalf of the Kowanyama People v Queensland* [2012] FCA 1377 [31], where Dowsett J refers to the claim group's 'approval' of the nomination, as evidenced in an affidavit by the claimants' solicitor.

How automatic is the process of determination once a nomination has been made?

The last-mentioned case raises a related question: once a nomination has been made by a representative (or purported representative), how much scope is there for argument or judicial discretion?

In *Daniel* the applicants argued that the legislation does not provide other parties with any opportunity to object or otherwise make submissions in relation to the nomination of a PBC. They pointed out a number of cases in which the court had moved directly from the nomination of a PBC to the determination of the RNTBC without any intervening opportunity for argument. The applicants also emphasised that s. 56(2)(b) and s. 57(2)(b) state that the court 'must' make a determination in accordance with the nomination.

Justice RD Nicholson rejected these submissions. His Honour held that the court must satisfy itself that the requirements of the Act and regulations have been met: 'Such compliance must necessarily precondition the application of the requirement in s 56(2)(b) and s 57(2)(b) that the court must determine that a nominated PBC is to hold the relevant native title rights and interests.'[977] His Honour cited *James* as a previous example where the court heard from other parties before making a determination about the RNTBC.[978]

Similarly, in *Rubibi* Merkel J noted that a particular corporation had been nominated and that the court was therefore 'now required to consider whether it is appropriate to make a determination under ss 55 and 56' in favour of that corporation.[979] Citing *Ngalpil*[980] his Honour considered that this inquiry involved three questions:

1. Has a representative of the common law holders made the nomination in writing?
2. Is the nominated body corporate a 'PBC' as provided in the PBC Regulations?
3. Has the nominated body corporate given its written consent to be the trustee of the native title rights and interests?

These cases demonstrate that even though the process is not completely mechanical and automatic, neither is there a general discretion on the part of the court. If the criteria are satisfied then the court *must* make the determination. However, given the conclusions reached above about the meaning of the term 'representative', judges arguably have the power to seek further information from the parties in order to determine whether the person nominating a particular corporation is representative of the group as a whole. That is, the first of Merkel J's questions may imply an assessment of the degree to which the broader group supports the nomination given by the putative representative.

977 *Daniel v Western Australia* [2004] FCA 849 [38].

978 *James v Western Australia (No. 2)* [2003] FCA 731.

979 *Rubibi Community v Western Australia* [2004] FCA 964 [1].

980 *Ngalpil v Western Australia* [2003] FCA 1098 [12]–[14].

Process for nominating an existing RNTBC for a further determination

The *Native Title Act* specifically provides for the possibility of a single PBC serving as RNTBC for more than one determination: s. 59A. In addition to the standard criteria listed by Merkel J (above), this process imposes a further requirement, namely that 'all of the common law holders' consent.[981] The regulations stipulate how that consent is to be obtained:[982]

a) The existing RNTBC must consult with its common law holders and obtain their consent in the same way as if for a native title decision. (This process is explained below in Section 8.2, 'Decision-making within RNTBCs'.)

b) The incoming common law holders must nominate the existing RNTBC in the same way as any other PBC.

So although on its face the process for nominating an existing RNTBC seems to require a higher degree of involvement from the common law holders (in that the common law holders for the existing RNTBC must specifically 'consent' to the new nomination), from the perspective of the incoming claim group the process is practically no different from the standard nomination process.

Process for replacing the RNTBC

The RNTBC, once determined, can be replaced either by a decision of the native title holders or by an order of the Federal Court.[983]

Replacement initiated by common law native title holders

For replacements initiated by the common law native title holders themselves, the process is stipulated in regs 12–18 of the PBC Regulations. The applicable regulation is determined according to whether the initial RNTBC and the replacement RNTBC are trusts or agents, although the procedure is substantively similar in each case.

Table 3: Provisions of the PBC Regulations for replacing trustee or agent PBCs

Initial RNTBC	Replacement RNTBC	Regulation
Trustee	Trustee	12
Trustee	Agent	13[985]
Agent	Trustee	15
Agent	Agent	16

981 Section 59A, NTA.

982 Reg. 4A, PBC Regulations.

983 Section 56(4) and (7), s. 60(a), NTA.

984 Note reg. 13 of the PBC Regulations also applies to situations where the replacement RNTBC is the same corporation as the intitial RNTBC but where the trust is dissolved and the RNTBC now merely manages the native title rights and interests as agents.

For all of these transitions, the relevant application is made to the Federal Court by 'the common law holders'[985] and is an application 'under' the relevant regulation.[986] In each case the Federal Court application is subject to a mandatory notification process, set out in reg. 18 of the PBC Regulations. Whoever intends to make the Federal Court application must, at least 14 days beforehand, notify the existing RNTBC of (a) the intention to make the application and (b) the proposed alternative arrangement to be sought in the application (e.g. the name of the proposed replacement corporation and whether it would be trustee or agent). The application itself must be accompanied by that same information as well as the written consent of the corporation nominated as the replacement.[987]

Notably absent from these regulations is any specific stipulation as to the manner in which the applicant for replacement is authorised by the common law holders. Each of the regulations state that 'the common law holders…may apply.' But in practical terms this must be taken to refer to a representative application since the common law holders may number in their hundreds or thousands. Regulation 18 refers to 'the applicant' in respect of such applications but the term cannot be taken to mean the same applicant who prosecuted the native title claim, since the replacement application might come decades after those named applicants have passed away. There is no other definition of the term in the regulation.[988] So it is not clear on the face of the PBC Regulations just how such an application would be made.

Nor do the PBC Regulations stipulate any conditions to limit the court's discretion to grant or refuse the application — they simply provide that the court must determine the application as soon as practicable and that the court may make orders to assist any transition.[989] Nevertheless, it is fair to assume that a court, in determining the replacement application, would apply the same general principles as have been developed in relation to authorising native title claims and ILUAs. That would mean a requirement to demonstrate that either a traditional process or an agreed/adopted process had been followed, with sufficient opportunity for the entire native title holding group to be involved.[990]

---

985 See regs 12(1), 13(1), 15(1), 16(1), PBC Regulations.

986 See reg. 18(1), PBC Regulations.

987 Reg. 18(4), PBC Regulations.

988 Reg. 19 of the PBC Regulations defines the term 'applicant' for the purpose of Part 4 of the regulations, which is irrelevant to the replacement of the RNTBC.

989 Regs 12(2), 13(2), 15(2), 16(2), PBC Regulations.

990 Regs 12(2)(b) and 16(2)(b) allow the court to make ancillary orders that are 'necessary or appropriate to give effect to the common law holders' wishes'. This implies that some process of determining the 'will' of the group as a whole will be involved in the court's determination of the replacement application, which in turn implies that the applicants must be determined to be representative of the common law holders.

Replacement initiated by liquidator

The *Native Title Act* and PBC Regulations also provide for the court-ordered replacement of an RNTBC where the RNTBC has gone into liquidation.[991] Within 14 days of being appointed, a liquidator for an RNTBC must apply to the Federal Court for the determination of another body to be the RNTBC. The application will be under reg. 14 where the corporation in liquidation is a trustee RNTBC, and reg. 17 if it is an agent RNTBC. In the case of a trustee RNTBC, the court *must* determine that the trust is terminated, which produces the result that the common law holders will now hold the native title rights and interests outright until and unless a new trustee RNTBC is determined.[992] The liquidator must nominate a new corporation but there is no guidance in the regulations about which corporation can or must be chosen or what role, if any, should be played by the common law holders.

Again, the PBC Regulations do not give the court any guidance on how to determine a liquidator's application. There is no process equivalent to that in ss 56(2)(a) and 57(2)(a) of the *Native Title Act* whereby the court must request a representative of the native title holders to nominate a corporation. Nor is there any requirement on the liquidator's part to inform the common law holders and seek their view. The only relevant notification duty on the liquidator is to inform the ILC if the liquidator intends to nominate that body as the replacement corporation.[993]

Criteria for replacement corporations

All of the relevant regulations dealing with replacing RNTBCs require that the replacement corporation be a 'prescribed body corporate'.[994] This is unsurprising, since that term refers to a corporation that is *eligible* to be determined as an RNTBC. The definition of 'prescribed body corporate' is found in reg. 4 of the PBC Regulations.

Whether the replacement application is initiated by the common law holders or by a liquidator, the PBC Regulations allow the court to determine the ILC as the replacement.[995] This may be thought of as a temporary 'default option' or 'backstop', for use when no other corporation is available or (more controversially) where there is an intractable dispute between different factions of the claim group. I was not able to discover any instance in which the ILC has been determined as an RNTBC. If the ILC is determined, it must act as an agent RNTBC rather than a trustee.[996] The initial term of such determination is five years, renewable if the common law holders do not apply for a replacement.[997] It appears that the common law holders can do so at any point in time — there is no apparent requirement for the five-year term to be completed before such replacement is made.

---

991 Section 56(4)(d)(ii) and (f), s. 60(a)(ii), NTA; regs 14 and 17, PBC Regulations.

992 Reg. 14(2)(b) and (3), PBC Regulations.

993 Reg. 15(1)(b), PBC Regulations.

994 Regs 12(1)(a), 13(1)(c), 14(1)(a), 15(1)(a), 16(1)(a), 17(1)(a), PBC Regulations.

995 Reg. 11, PBC Regulations.

996 ibid.

997 Reg. 11(4), PBC Regulations.

8.2 Decision-making within RNTBCs

RNTBCs are corporations under the CATSI Act.[998] They have all of the legal capacities and powers of an individual and of a body corporate.[999] Decisions about when and how those capacities and powers are to be exercised are made by the directors, but the directors are not absolutely free to make any decision they want. There are four main sources of legal limitation on their discretion:[1000]

- the rules of the corporation and the provisions of the CATSI Act;
- the provisions of the *Native Title Act* that govern particular activities like native title agreement-making (and, similarly, the ILUA Regulations);
- the duties owed by RNTBCs in their capacities as statutory 'trustees' or 'agents' for the common law native title holders;
- the consent and consultation provisions of the PBC Regulations.

The first source does not *necessarily* impose significant constraints on the RNTBC's autonomy from the group, although additional controls and safeguards may be built in if a group wishes. The CATSI Act states that directors may exercise all the powers of the corporation unless the Act or the rules say otherwise.[1001] One such legislative exception is the stipulation that related party benefits must be approved by the members of the corporation.[1002] Another is that directors are to be appointed by resolution at a general meeting[1003] and that, if the constitution allows them to be remunerated, the amount of remuneration is to be set by resolution of a general meeting.[1004] Some corporations have rules that impose additional limitations, such as requiring constitutional changes to be approved by certain majorities of the membership[1005] or reserving certain important financial decisions to the membership. Crafting the optimum balance between rigour and flexibility, between integrity and efficiency, will be one of the most important tasks of the constitution's drafters. In some cases the added optional constraints on the corporation's

---

998 Reg. 4, PBC Regulations.

999 Section 96.1, CATSI Act.

1000 Note that traditional law and custom does not feature on this list because it is incorporated into the consultation and consent provisions. It is incorporated in two ways: in the process by which the group gives its consent, and in the determination of who is the 'affected group' for a particular decision. (See regs 8 and 3, PBC Regulations.) Traditional decision-making is also incorporated into ILUA decision-making processes and may be written into the corporation's rules also. And, obviously, traditional norms may exert an influence on decision-making even where not formally incorporated into any document.

1001 Section 274.1, CATSI Act.

1002 Section 284.1, CATSI Act.

1003 Section 246.15, CATSI Act. See also s. 246.20 for appointments by other directors in order to make up a quorum, subject to the later ratification by the membership at a general meeting. Both provisions are replaceable rules.

1004 Section 252.1(2), CATSI Act.

1005 See s. 69.15, CATSI Act. A special resolution is required in every case: s. 69.5(1)(a).

autonomy may be more significant to the practical running of the corporation than the formal requirements set out in the PBC Regulations. Note, however, that the CATSI Act contains an 'indoor management rule', similar to that in the mainstream Australian corporations law, allowing outside parties to assume that the corporation's constitution and replaceable rules have been complied with.[1006] This means that the mere specification of a decision-making procedure in the constitution will not completely protect the native title holders from the risk of unauthorised action by the RNTBC's directors.[1007]

Even where decisions are left in the hands of the RNTBC directors, the CATSI Act and common law still impose constraints on how those decisions can be made including the duties of care and diligence, the duty of good faith (also a general law fiduciary duty) and the duties not to improperly use one's position or information gained through that position.[1008]

The second source of limitation does not impinge greatly on an RNTBC's internal workings. As will be explained below, the *Native Title Act* itself imposes virtually no constraints on the corporate decision-making process for Body Corporate ILUAs, Alternative Procedure ILUAs or s. 31 agreements.

The third source of limitation derives from the fact that RNTBCs must be declared as either 'trustees' or 'agents' under the *Native Title Act* and regulations.[1009] This distinction appears to have originated as a purely formal matter intended to avoid the political or cultural sensitivities around a compulsory vesting of native title in a trustee corporation.[1010] Nevertheless, the distinction may have significant legal implications, implications that have not as yet been the subject of judicial consideration.[1011] Mantziaris and Martin point out that the native title 'trust' and 'agency'

1006 Section 104.1–104.10, CATSI Act.

1007 A notable exception to this is in relation to court proceedings involving the RNTBC, particularly those under the NTA itself. In *Walmbaar Aboriginal Corporation v Queensland* [2009] FCA 579, Greenwood J dismissed an application made by an agent RNTBC for compensation under s. 50(2), NTA. The RNTBC had not followed an applicable constitutional procedure and so was found by the court to be acting without authority. This was a sufficient basis for the dismissal of the application.

1008 See s. 265.1–265.15, CATSI Act.

1009 Sections 55–57, NTA.

1010 It seems that the original government proposal had been for all of the mandated corporations to hold the native title on trust, but the Aboriginal representatives negotiating about the Bill objected to the idea that native title holders would have no choice about their rights being taken away and vested in an artificial corporate entity. The government agreed to allow native title holders the option of not having their rights and interests held on trust by a corporation but, as the Prime Minister stated, 'There will still be a body corporate which will act as a representative body for native title holders': Australia, House of Representatives 1993, Debates, vol. HR191, p. 4541 (<http://parlinfo.aph.gov.au/parlInfo/search/search.w3p;adv=yes>). See also C Mantziaris & D Martin, *Native title corporations: a legal and anthropological analysis*, Federation Press, Leichhardt, NSW, 2000, pp. 160–161.

1011 C Mantziaris & D Martin, *Native title corporations: a legal and anthropological analysis*, Federation Press, Leichhardt, NSW, 2000, pp. 139, 157–160.

relationships cannot be equated simply and unproblematically to their corresponding concepts under the common law and equity. Because the relationship is created under the *Native Title Act* its nature must be determined by way of statutory interpretation. A statutory trust is not necessarily the same as a general law trust, and the same goes for agency relationships. Rather, the legal substance of the relationship must be derived from the text and structure of the legislation and regulations.[1012] Unfortunately these do not provide us with a great deal of detail and so there is much uncertainty.[1013] At a very general level the following seems most likely:

- A trustee RNTBC owes many of the duties of a general law trustee, such as the fiduciary duties against misusing the position or information gained from it, the duty of prudent care and the duty to account and provide information. However, any duty to administer the trust personally or not to fetter the trustee's discretion is necessarily tempered by the express statutory provisions requiring the trustee to 'invest or otherwise apply money held in trust as directed by the common law holders'[1014] and to 'perform any other function relating to the native title rights and interests as directed by the common law holders'.[1015] So while there is probably a duty for the trustee RNTBC to act in the best interest of the beneficiaries (the common law holders), there is also a clear and potentially competing duty to accept direction from them.[1016] This is reinforced by the fact that trustee RNTBCs are subject (like agent RNTBCs) to the consultation and consent requirements set out in the PBC Regulations, discussed below.
- An agent RNTBC owes many of the common law duties of an agent, such as fiduciary duties, the duty to account and the duty to exercise due care and skill. The primary duty of an agent is the duty of obedience — to obey all lawful and reasonable instructions of the principal in relation to the agent's duties. This duty is reflected in the agent RNTBC's function to 'manage the rights and interests of the common law holders *as authorised by* the common law holders' (emphasis added), and to invest or apply money and perform any other function relating to the native title rights and interests 'as directed by the common law holders'.[1017] In *Walmbaar Aboriginal Corporation v Queensland*[1018] Greenwood J found that the 'function' provisions in the PBC Regulations imposed a statutory duty on the agent RNTBC to ensure that its 'management' decisions (which included the lodgement of a native title compensation claim) had an identifiable source of authority. In that case there was an applicable provision in the corporation's rules requiring a certain procedure to be complied with, and the corporation's failure to follow

---

1012 ibid. pp. 140–6. See *Santo v David* [2010] FCA 42 [21].

1013 C Mantziaris & D Martin, *Native title corporations: a legal and anthropological analysis*, Federation Press, Leichhardt, NSW, 2000. pp. 144–6, 151.

1014 Reg. 6(1)(c), PBC Regulations, which is given binding effect by s. 57(1), NTA.

1015 Reg. 6(1)(c), PBC Regulations.

1016 See C Mantziaris & D Martin, *Native title corporations: a legal and anthropological analysis*, Federation Press, Leichhardt, NSW, 2000, pp. 52–154, 158.

1017 Reg. 7(1)(c), PBC Regulations, which is given binding effect by s. 57(3), NTA.

1018 *Walmbaar Aboriginal Corporation v Queensland* [2009] FCA 579 [55].

that procedure led to the compensation claim being dismissed.[1019] It is not clear how this decision would apply to a situation where there was no express provision in the corporation's rulebook. It is also not clear what legal consequences would follow from a corporation taking unauthorised actions that were not related to court applications under the *Native Title Act*. For example, the outcomes may be affected by the general law on agency as well as the 'indoor management rule'.[1020]

The fourth source of limitation is 'customisable' to some extent but contains certain non-negotiable constraints on the internal autonomy of the RNTBC. It is dealt with under the headings immediately below. Importantly, it only applies to certain categories of RNTBC decisions. Decisions outside those categories are only subject to the other three limitations mentioned above.

Consultation and consent requirements for native title decisions

For certain kinds of decisions made by an RNTBC, the PBC Regulations impose a mandatory 'consultation and consent' procedure that must be followed. In this context 'mandatory' means that if the correct procedure is not followed then the decision will not have any legal effect. And any agreement that 'gives effect to' such a decision 'has no effect to the extent that it applies to the decision'.[1021]

There are two kinds of RNTBC decisions that are regulated by 'consultation and consent' requirements. For the purposes of this book, these will be called 'High Level regulated decisions' and 'Low Level regulated decisions'. If an RNTBC (meaning the board of directors) intends to make a High Level regulated decision, then it must follow the procedure stipulated in reg. 8 of the PBC Regulations. For Low Level regulated decisions the RNTBC can adopt an 'alternative consultation process'[1022] or else follow the reg. 8 procedure.[1023] Decisions not falling into either category can be thought of as 'unregulated decisions' — they are not subject to any special 'consultation and consent' requirements under the PBC Regulations.

1019 ibid. [60].

1020 Section 104.1–104.10, CATSI Act.

1021 Reg. 8(6), PBC Regulations. Note that reg. 8(7) excludes registered ILUAs from this, such that registration will 'cure' any invalidity caused by a failure to comply with the reg. 8 procedure. But reg. 6, ILUA Regulations requires evidence of compliance with reg. 8 as part of the application for ILUA registration, so it is unlikely that a non-compliant ILUA would be registered in the first place. However, as is explained below, compliance with reg. 8 can be conclusively proven by providing a certificate of the kind specified in reg. 9 and neither the registrar nor the courts can 'look behind' the certificate. So an ILUA might be registered on the basis of a reg. 9 certificate without any substantive examination of the consultation/consent process that actually occurred. See further below in Section 8.2 at 'Documenting the process'.

1022 Note this alternative consultation process is entirely different from and unconnected with the 'Alternative Procedure ILUA'. It is just a coincidence in the use of the word 'alternative'.

1023 Reg. 8(1)(a) and 8A, PBC Regulations.

Note also that the regulations seem to allow for Low Level decisions to be made by way of a *general* consultation about a particular *category* of decision, with the common law holders deciding that 'decisions of that kind can be made by the body corporate.'[1024] This categorical pre-consultation and consent can be done either under a reg. 8 procedure or an alternative consultation process, so long as it concerns a Low Level decision.

High Level decisions are the following:

- a decision by the RNTBC to enter into an ILUA or s. 31 agreement;
- a decision to allow non–native title holders to become members of the RNTBC;
- a decision to adopt an alternative consultation process (which, as it happens, can only be used for Low Level decisions).[1025]

Low Level decisions are defined by reference to the concept of a 'native title decision'. A native title decision is 'a decision: (a) to surrender native title rights and interests in relation to land or waters; or (b) to do, or agree to, any other act that would affect the native title rights or interests of the common law holders'.[1026] A Low Level decision is a native title decision that is not a High Level decision.

Native title decision

Before proceeding further it is worth saying something more about the concept of a 'native title decision'. There has been little judicial guidance about the scope of this term. The main authority to date is *Walmbaar Aboriginal Corporation v Queensland*.[1027] In that case Greenwood J held that the decision to make a native title compensation application was *not* a native title decision:

> The filing of a compensation application does not extinguish native title rights and interests and is not, it seems to me, otherwise wholly or partly inconsistent with their continued existence, enjoyment or exercise. Engaging in an act of the kind described in s 226 of the Act may be wholly or partly inconsistent with the continued existence, enjoyment or exercise of native title rights and interests and may therefore have the effect contemplated by s 227 of the Act. However, a decision to file a compensation application simply seeks a compensation entitlement under the Act in respect of acts which are said to have either extinguished or significantly impaired or otherwise affected native title rights and interests.[1028]

Justice Greenwood's decision in *Walmbaar* suggests that it is the substantive rights and interests, founded in traditional law and custom, that are covered by the term 'native title decision' — not the ancillary procedural rights whose source is the *Native Title Act* itself. After all, the words in

1024 See reg. 9(1)(a)(ii), PBC Regulations.

1025 Reg. 8(1)(b)–(d), PBC Regulations.

1026 Reg. 3(1), PBC Regulations.

1027 *Walmbaar Aboriginal Corporation v Queensland* [2009] FCA 579.

1028 ibid. [53]; see also [41]–[55].

the definition of 'native title decision' must be interpreted consistently with their meanings under the *Native Title Act*:[1029] the definition of 'native title rights and interests' is found in s. 223 of the *Native Title Act* and 'affect' is defined by s. 227. Both definitions support the idea that a decision that merely affects procedural rights is not a 'native title decision'.[1030]

If that is right, then an RNTBC's decision about whether or not to exercise or enforce its legal rights will not be a native title decision. For example, heritage agreements for mineral exploration activity (at least in some Australian jurisdictions) would not involve a native title decision on the logic of *Walmbaar*. In Western Australia it is common practice for native title parties (whether applicants or RNTBCs) to give their lawyers a standing instruction to lodge an expedited procedure objection for every exploration licence notified. The native title party then has the choice whether to proceed to an expedited procedure inquiry at the tribunal or to withdraw the objection. It may decide to withdraw in return for the proponent's agreement to a heritage protection agreement. The decision to withdraw would not constitute the RNTBC *agreeing* to the grant of a licence for the purposes of s. 31 of the *Native Title Act*; it is merely a procedural choice not to object to the application of the expedited procedure. Nor would the decision to enter into the heritage agreement itself be a native title decision — it simply extracts promises from the proponent in exchange for agreeing to withdraw the objection. Accordingly, in those circumstances heritage agreements by RNTBCs would appear to be unregulated decisions.

Another example of an unregulated decision would be the decision to commence legal proceedings to vindicate or enforce native title rights. In *Santo v David* [2010] FCA 42, two common law native title holders wanted to prevent a person building on land that was subject to a native title determination. The court held that these two individuals did not have standing to sue to protect their native title rights, since the task of commencing such proceedings falls to the RNTBC under its 'managerial' function (reg. 6(1)(a), PBC Regulations). I was unable to find any case details with a fresh application subsequently made by the RNTBC, but if one had been filed, the RNTBC would probably not have been required to comply with the consultation and consent provisions in the PBC Regulations. Such proceedings would not constitute a decision to do, or agree to the doing of, an act affecting native title, since they would be directed *against* such an act. If, however, the RNTBC's own rulebook set out a mandatory authorisation procedure for such decisions then the court might dismiss the application unless that procedure was complied with, for the reasons set out in *Walmbaar*.

Finally, it would seem that an RNTBC's decision *not* to make a native title decision would not fall within the definition of 'native title decision'. For example, a decision to *refuse* to enter into a particular ILUA or s. 31 agreement would not be a decision to surrender native title rights

---

[1029] Section 13(1)(b), *Legislative Instruments Act 2003* (Cth). There is no contrary intention apparent in the PBC Regulations.

[1030] It is worth noting in passing the recent case of *Wintawari Guruma Aboriginal Corporation RNTBC v Western Australia* [2015] FCA 1053. While it does not directly concern the question of 'native title decisions' it does nonetheless illustrate the conceptual confusion that sometimes affects legal proceedings in the post-determination context.

or a decision 'to do, or agree to, any other act that would affect the native title rights or interests of the common law holders'. Such a refusal would therefore be unregulated by reg. 8 of the PBC Regulations. It is not clear whether the RNTBC's functions under the PBC Regulations could provide some basis by which the common law holders could compel the RNTBC to act as directed (in particular, regs 6(1)(e) and 7(1)(b)).[1031]

Regulation 8 procedure

As mentioned, High Level decisions must be made in accordance with the procedure set out in reg. 8 of the PBC Regulations. The reg. 8 procedure essentially mirrors the process set out in s. 251A and B of the *Native Title Act*. Paraphrased, this means:

- If there is a particular process of decision-making that, under the traditional laws and customs of the common law holders, must be followed in relation to the giving of consent for the relevant decision, the consent must be given in accordance with that process (reg. 8(3)).[1032]
- If not, the consent must be given by the common law holders in accordance with the process of decision-making agreed to or adopted by them for the proposed decision, or for decisions of the same kind as that decision (reg. 8(4)).[1033]

In the future, practitioners may wish to consider to what extent a group may be able to 'agree or adopt' a process that delegates certain categories of decisions to a smaller body of decision-makers. On one view, this may appear to contradict the statutory intention for 'alternative process' to be available only for Low Level decisions. If the drafters of the PBC Regulations made a rule specifying that reg. 8A (addressed below) applies only to a certain subset of RNTBC decisions, then a court may conclude that the intention of this rule would be frustrated if native title holders could simply use reg. 8(4) to agree or adopt an alternative process. On the other hand, the words in reg. 8(4) have a plain meaning, namely that a group lacking an applicable traditional process may agree or adopt a process for 'decisions of the same kind' as the decision in question. There are no words of limitation constraining what kind of a process can be agreed or adopted, so long as the consent can be said to emanate from the common law holders. As demonstrated earlier in sections 3.2 ('Authorisation by "all the persons" in the native title claim group') and 3.3 ('Authorisation in practice'), this is not a literal requirement for universal participation in the claims authorisation process. Justice Finn has explicitly endorsed the possibility of delegating authorisation decisions to a decision-making body for the purposes of s. 251B(b), so long as the delegation can be traced

---

1031 *Walmbaar Aboriginal Corporation v Queensland* [2009] FCA 579.

1032 Note that the language used in reg. 8(3) in relation to traditional decision-making processes is looser than its counterpart in s. 251B(a): the latter speaks of 'a process of decision-making that [...] must be complied with *in relation to authorising things of that kind*' (emphasis added) whereas the former simply refers to the giving of consent to 'a native title decision'. The different phrasing does not appear to be deliberate.

1033 Note that reg. 8(4) uses the phrase 'agreed to or adopted by', as opposed to 'agreed to and adopted by' in s. 251B. That is, agreement and adoption are treated as alternatives in the PBC Regulations, but as cumulative requirements in the NTA.

back to a valid decision of the group.[1034] Accordingly, it seems that the common law holders should be able to agree or adopt a process for making certain categories of High Level decision, such that an entire group meeting is not required each time. This option would benefit those RNTBCs who face a large number of low-value future act decisions, where the cost of the meeting would exceed any benefit to be gained from an agreement. In this book I do not propose to reach a concluded view on the question, only noting that if the PBC Regulations do not allow this sort of flexibility then such limitation may be regarded as an unjustified interference in the governance of native title holding groups. While recognising the dangers that may accompany an excessive delegation of power to RNTBC directors or another small decision-making body, it is nevertheless difficult to see why a deliberate and informed decision by a group of common law holders should not be given effect. After all, it would always be open to the common law holders to rescind the delegation later if there was evidence of abuse. Also, it is not clear why the decisions of the RNTBC in relation to low-level mineral tenements, for example, should be subject to a higher level of scrutiny than an applicant during the claims phase, especially given that the RNTBC directors are bound by the CATSI Act, the corporation's rulebook, and common law fiduciary duties, and are subject to the supervision of the Office of the Registrar of Aboriginal Corporations (ORIC) and the corporation's members.

In addition to this *consent* process requirement the RNTBC must also first *consult* with the common law native title holders. There is no guidance or specification in the regulations as to how this consultation should happen or how intensive or extensive it should be.

A third requirement (in addition to consulting and gaining consent) is that the RNTBC must 'ensure that the common law holders understand the purpose and nature of a proposed native title decision'.[1035] This must be done by first consulting and considering the views of the *NTRB* for the area (or one of them, if there is more than one) and, secondly, by telling the common law holders about the NTRB's views (if the RNTBC considers it appropriate and practicable to do so).[1036]

Where the RNTBC represents more than one 'group' of common law holders, it need only consult and obtain the consent of a group whose native title rights or interests would be affected by the proposed decision.[1037] A 'group' is defined not by reference to a determination of native title but rather as a 'tribe, clan or family, or a descent, language or other group, recognised as such in accordance with Aboriginal or Torres Strait Islander traditional laws and customs applying to them'.[1038] This means that the RNTBC is empowered to engage with the intramural distribution of rights within the broader collective; if according to traditional law and custom a decision only affects some people, there is no need to include other people in the process.

1034 *Reid v South Australia* [2007] FCA 1479 [46].

1035 Reg. 8(2), PBC Regulations.

1036 Reg. 8(2)(a)–(b), PBC Regulations.

1037 Reg. 8(5), PBC Regulations.

1038 Reg. 3(2), PBC Regulations.

Alternative consultation process (Regulation 8A)

As mentioned, some but not all native title decisions can be made by way of an alternative consultation process, potentially less stringent than the one just outlined. An alternative process can be used for any decision other than: entering into an ILUA or s. 31 agreement, admitting non–native title holders to the membership, or the decision to adopt an alternative process in the first place.[1039]

Regulation 8A sets out the requirements for an alternative process. The first requirement is that the process be contained in the corporation's constitution. This may have been done before the corporation was first incorporated (in which case it would have needed the support of 75 per cent of the initial membership)[1040] or may have been introduced as a later amendment (which, minimally, must be passed by special resolution with at least 75 per cent of votes cast).[1041] The second requirement in reg. 8A is that the 'common law holders have consented' to the alternative process.[1042] This may at first seem like a repetition of the first requirement but it is important to remember that the membership of the corporation does not necessarily overlap entirely with the membership of the native title holding group. There may be common law native title holders who are not members of the corporation. (The converse is only possible in exceptional circumstances.)[1043] And, importantly, the 'consent' required must be given in accordance with the reg. 8 process described above.[1044]

The third requirement is that the alternative process involves the RNTBC consulting with, and obtaining the consent of, the common native title holders. At first glance this appears to imply that the consultation and consent must relate to the *particular* native title decision at issue. But as mentioned above, it is open to the RNTBC to consult with the common law holders in *general* terms about a certain *category* of Low Level decision and for the common law holders to decide that decisions of that kind can be made by the RNTBC.[1045] Anecdotally, it appears fairly common for RNTBCs to obtain 'standing instructions' or 'standing consents' for certain classes of native title decisions, such as those relating to expedited procedure objections in respect of exploration licence applications.

Note that the intramural distribution of rights and interests can probably be accommodated in an alternative consultation process, although there is nothing explicit in reg. 8A to mirror the

1039 Reg. 8(1), PBC Regulations.

1040 Section 29.15, CATSI Act.

1041 Sections 69.5 and 700.1, CATSI Act.

1042 Reg. 8A(1), PBC Regulations.

1043 The relevant criteria for PBC membership is that *only* native title holders *can* be members of the corporation (not that *all* native title holders *must* be): reg. 4(2)(b)–(c), PBC Regulations. The criterion is exclusive rather than inclusive. The exception mentioned is that a PBC *may* admit non–native title holders to its membership so long as that admission is done with the consent of the common law native title holders. The admission of non–native title holders must be done in accordance with the reg. 8 process: reg. 8(1)(c), PBC Regulations.

1044 Reg. 8(1)(d), PBC Regulations.

1045 Reg. 9(1)(a)(ii), PBC Regulations.

specific provision in reg. 8(5), limiting the consultation and consent obligation to those persons whose native title rights and interests would be affected by the proposed decision.

Documenting the process

Regulation 9 of the PBC Regulations provides a means of proving compliance with the reg. 8 procedure or an alternative consultation process, by way of a document certifying that the common law native title holders have been consulted about, and have consented to, the proposed decision.[1046] As mentioned, it is open to RNTBCs to effectively pre-decide or delegate entire categories of Low Level decisions. In such cases the certifying document must state the proposed decision is 'of a kind about which the common law holders have been consulted' and that 'the common law holders have decided that decisions of that kind can be made by the body corporate.'[1047]

Note there is an additional requirement for these 'category decision' certificates that seems difficult to reconcile with the intention of allowing a flexible and efficient alternative consultation process: reg. 9(3)(a) states that a certifying document 'must, if subparagraph (1)(a)(ii) applies, include evidence of the consultation with, and consent given by, the common law holders about the native title decision'. Given that the evident purpose of reg. 9(1)(a)(ii) is to provide a way of delegating some classes of minor decisions, it seems odd that that very sub-paragraph is singled out for a *higher* level of evidence. Even more puzzling is that reg. 9(3)(a) requires evidence of consultation and consent 'about the native title decision', because surely reg. 9(1)(a)(ii) is intended to apply to situations in which the common law holders have *not* been consulted about the particular decision at hand. In light of these incongruities, it seems that one of the two following readings was intended:

a) The word 'if' is a slip and should instead read 'unless'.

b) The words 'about the native title decision' should be replaced with 'about the kind of native title decision'.[1048]

In any case, the document (whether for High Level or Low Level decisions and whether specific or categorical) must specify whether the consultation and consent occurred within a reg. 8 process or an alternative process.[1049] The document must be signed by at least five members of the RNTBC. If there are five or more people whose native title rights and interests would be affected by the decision[1050] *and* who have become members of the RNTBC,

---

1046 Reg. 9(1)(a)–(b), PBC Regulations. This certificate is referred to colloquially as a 'reg. 9 certificate'. Note, however, that reg. 9(6) deals with an entirely different type of certificate to that addressed in reg. 9(1)–(5). This reg. 9(6) certificate is briefly discussed at the end of this section.

1047 Reg. 9(1)(a)(ii), PBC Regulations.

1048 There is no case law bearing on this point and so the two interpretations suggested must be taken as purely speculative. Note that *Gibson v Rivers-McCombs* [2014] FCA 144 addressed reg. 9 but an earlier version of that regulation that did not include an equivalent to reg. 9(3)(a).

1049 Reg. 9(1)(a)–(b), PBC Regulations.

1050 See the previous discussion of intramural distribution of rights, particularly regarding reg. 8(5).

then each of the signatories must be such a person[1051] (though there is no requirement that each affected person sign). Conversely, if the number of affected common law holders who are RNTBC members is less than five, each of those affected RNTBC members must sign. (Presumably the remainder of the minimum five signatures will be made up of non-affected RNTBC members.)

There are two related issues that must be examined in relation to the legal effect of reg. 9:

a) Can or must an outside party (e.g. a state government applying s. 41(1)(b) of the *Native Title Act*) look behind a reg. 9 certificate to judge whether the correct decision-making process has been followed? Or does the certificate itself answer the question definitively?

b) Does reg. 9 impose a *requirement* to produce a certificate for every relevant decision or is a certificate an *optional* way of proving compliance with regs 8 or 8A (analogous to NTRB certification of Area ILUAs under s. 24CG(3) of the *Native Title Act*)?

The first question asks whether a certificate is sufficient; the second asks whether one is necessary. The first question was addressed in *Gibson v Rivers-McCombs*.[1052] In that case there was some disagreement within a native title holding group about whether correct consultation procedures had been followed in relation to an ILUA. A member of the group applied under the *Administrative Decisions (Judicial Review) Act 1977* (Cth) for judicial review of the registrar's decision to register the ILUA in question, arguing that although certificates had been provided the necessary consultation and consent had not in fact occurred. Justice Dowsett dismissed the application:

> If it were open to other traditional owners to dispute such a certificate, the process prescribed by reg 9 would have little purpose…In my view, in the absence of fraud, the prescribed body corporate has fulfilled the requirements of [regs 7, 8 and 9] if it is able to obtain the certificates contemplated by reg 9…The Registrar or delegate cannot go behind the certificates. The only bases upon which such person may refuse to register an ILUA are set out in s 24BI. Nonetheless it is conceivable that a court might, in the event of fraud, set such certificates aside…In my view, the delegate was obliged to act on the reg 9(2) documents which were provided to him. He had no reason to go behind them.[1053]

His Honour specifically addressed the wording in reg. 9(1), which states that common law native title holders 'are taken to have been consulted on, and to have consented to, a proposed native title decision of a prescribed body corporate if' the relevant certificate is produced. Justice Dowsett said 'I see no reason why the words "taken to have been" should be construed

---

1051 Reg. 9 applies to decisions of the kind mentioned in reg. 8(1)(a)–(d). Although reg. 9 uses the term 'native title decision' several times, this is not strictly accurate since reg. 8(1)(c) and (d) are not native title decisions. This may have been an oversight in drafting.

1052 *Gibson v Rivers-McCombs* [2014] FCA 144.

1053 ibid. [74]–[75].

as meaning something less than the word "deemed".'[1054] That means compliance with reg. 9 is *legally equivalent* to compliance with reg. 8 (in the absence of fraud). Mantziaris and Martin call this a process of 'deemed consent'.[1055] This means that there is very limited scope for the native title holders to complain about a consultation/consent process being inadequate. So long as the RNTBC directors are not acting fraudulently when they issue the reg. 9 certificate there appears to be no recourse. This is very different from the situation while the claim is still in progress, when the ILUA provisions and s. 84D allow the claim group to exert a degree of control over the applicant. Presumably the legislature intended this type of control to be exercised in the post-determination period through the CATSI Act processes of appointing and removing directors.

The second question posed above, whether the production of a reg. 9 certificate is optional or mandatory, arises because reg. 9 does not contain any explicit statement obliging an RNTBC to produce a certificate. Mandatory language is used in regs 8 and 8A, but on its face reg. 9 merely appears to be stipulating *one* manner of proving compliance, leaving the possibility open that *other* ways may also exist. In *Gibson v Rivers-McCombs* some of Dowsett J's language might suggest that his Honour took reg. 9 certificates to be compulsory. For example, Dowsett J said that 'evidence of such consultation and consent, as contemplated by reg 9(2) of the PBC regulations *had to be* provided in support of the application for registration.'[1056] (Emphasis added.) Importantly, this comment related specifically to the processes for registering Body Corporate ILUAs, governed by reg. 6 of the ILUA Regulations. That regulation mandates that applications for the registration of Body Corporate ILUAs 'must be accompanied by the documents and information mentioned in this regulation' and specifically mentions reg. 9 certificates as prescribed documents.[1057] It is clear, therefore, that reg. 9 certificates must be provided whenever an RNTBC wishes to register a Body Corporate ILUA that involves a native title decision.

So much for ILUAs, but what about non-ILUA decisions such as a decision to enter into a s. 31 agreement? In the following passage from *Gibson v Rivers-McCombs* there is some basis for interpreting a general requirement to produce reg. 9 certificates:

1054 ibid. [76].

1055 C Mantziaris & D Martin, *Native title corporations: a legal and anthropological analysis,* Federation Press, Leichhardt, NSW, 2000, pp. 143–44.

1056 *Gibson v Rivers-McCombs* [2014] FCA 144 [68].

1057 In what appears to be an inadvertent failure to update reg. 6 of the, ILUA Regulations following amendments to the PBC Regulations, reg. 6(2) refers to 'a document mentioned in subregulation 9(2) of the PBC Regulations' when the correct reference should now be to sub-reg. 9(1).

> Regulations 7, 8 and 9 provide an integrated scheme for consultation and consent and proof thereof. The functions conferred upon a prescribed body corporate by Pt 2 Subdiv 3B are to be performed in accordance with regulations made pursuant to s 58(b) [which states that regulations may make provision for an RNTBC 'to perform in a specified way any functions in relation to the native title given to it under other provisions of this Act']. For present purposes the 'specified way' is set out in regs 7, 8 and 9.[1058]

But notwithstanding that the regulations provide an 'integrated scheme', the fact that they define a 'specified way' of performing functions falls somewhat short of the kind of mandatory language that one might otherwise expect. For example, reg. 9(1) could have been drafted to stipulate that the common law native title holders 'are taken to have been consulted on, and to have consented to, a proposed native title decision…*only if*' a certifying document is produced. That would make it clear that the reg. 9 certificate is the only way of proving compliance with reg. 8 or 8A. Anecdotally, there are PBCs which do not use reg. 9 certificates, instead relying on meeting minutes and other forms of documentation. A reason given for this was explicitly to avoid the conclusive effect as demonstrated in *Gibson v Rivers-McCombs*, which could undermine good governance by removing a valuable form of oversight.

Before leaving the topic of documentation it is necessary to note that reg. 9(6) of the PBC Regulations requires an RNTBC to produce evidence of its compliance with reg. 8(2). That latter provision is the one which requires the RNTBC to ensure that the common law holders understand the purpose and nature of a proposed native title decision by consulting with at least one NTRB for the relevant area, giving notice of the NTRB's views to the common law holders (if the RNTBC considers this appropriate and practicable). Regulation 9(6) provides that compliance with this requirement can be proved by producing:

a) a document signed by at least five members of the RNTBC, stating that the NTRB has been consulted and its views considered;
b) a document signed by an authorised member of the NTRB, stating that it has been consulted.[1059]

Summary

The preceding discussion can be summed up by asking the question: what kinds of decisions can an RNTBC make by itself without going back to its membership for approval? The answer depends in many respects on the rules of the corporation. For day-to-day situations it is up to each group to establish its own limits in the constitution around corporate autonomy versus member oversight.

One of the few non-negotiable rules is that any decision that gives a benefit to a related party must be approved by the membership. Another is that the rights and interests of the native

---

1058 *Gibson v Rivers-McCombs* [2014] FCA 144 [74].

1059 Reg. 9(6), PBC Regulations. Note in this context 'authorised member' is probably meant to refer to authorised officer or employee rather than 'member' in its strict corporations law sense.

title holders must be managed 'as authorised' by the native title holders. This is a provision of potentially broad coverage (since 'management' is a flexible concept) but is also potentially shallow since the legislation and regulations do not specify how the necessary authorisation is to be obtained. Thus rules of the corporation are likely to be determinative here too.

Finally, certain kinds of decision must be taken in accordance with the consultation and consent requirements in regs 8 and/or 8A. Whether an alternative consultation process under reg. 8A can be used depends on whether a High Level or Low Level decision is involved — and if an alternative process is to be employed then it must first be adopted by the native title holders through a reg. 8 process and written into the RNTBC's constitution. For Low Level decisions, a standing consent can be used for categories of decisions, so long as the group has been consulted about that category of decision appropriately.

9. Native title compensation claims

Authorisation issues in native title compensation claims will be dealt with only briefly here, largely because there have been virtually no cases dealing with that specific issue, and indeed very few cases dealing with compensation at all.

Native title holders may seek compensation for the extinguishment or impairment of native title. Applications for such compensation are made under ss 50(2) and 61(1) of the *Native Title Act*. According to s. 61(1), a compensation application may be made by either of the following:

(1) the RNTBC (if any);

(2) a person or persons authorised by all the persons (the compensation claim group) who claim to be entitled to the compensation, provided the person or persons are also included in the compensation claim group.

9.1 Claim filed by RNTBC

An RNTBC can be the applicant for a compensation application but only if the claim is made exclusively over lands and waters for which the corporation is the RNTBC. So if certain areas are excluded from a native title determination, including because of previous extinguishment,[1060] there is no RNTBC for those excluded areas. Therefore, any compensation application must be made by named applicants rather than the RNTBC.[1061]

Where an RNTBC does make the application, there is no express requirement in s. 61(1) that the RNTBC be specifically authorised by the common law native title holders to do so.[1062] Nevertheless, the directors of the corporation are still bound by the various constraints and obligations mentioned above in Section 8.2 ('Decision-making within RNTBCs'). In *Walmbaar Aboriginal Corporation v Queensland*, Greenwood J held that an RNTBC's decision to file a compensation claim is not a 'native title decision' requiring the consultation or consent of the common law holders under reg. 8 of the PBC Regulations.[1063] His Honour found that the filing of a compensation claim could not 'affect' native title within the meaning of s. 227 and did not involve the 'surrender' of native title rights or interests, and so was not a 'native title decision' under reg. 3 of the PBC Regulations.[1064] However, Greenwood J found in *Walmbaar* that the RNTBC was bound by its own constitution to go through a particular process before making a compensation application. The RNTBC's constitution required it to give the common law holders one week's notice of all 'decisions regarding native title' and to obtain the consent of at

---

1060 See s. 61A, NTA.

1061 See *De Rose v South Australia* [2013] FCA 988 [9]–[12].

1062 Cf. Greenwood J's contrary suggestion in obiter in *Walmbaar Aboriginal Corporation v Queensland* [2009] FCA 579 [60].

1063 ibid. [54].

1064 ibid. [50]–[53].

least 75 per cent before proceeding. Justice Greenwood found that this requirement applied to the decision to lodge a compensation claim. His Honour decided that the compensation claim should be struck out according to the following (paraphrased) reasoning:[1065]

i) Section 57(3)(b), *Native Title Act* imposes an obligation on the RNTBC to perform its functions under the regulations.

ii) Regulation 7(1)(a), PBC Regulations creates the function of being the agent for the common law holders.

iii) Regulation 7(1)(b), PBC Regulations creates the function of managing the rights and interests of the common law holders 'as authorised by the common law holders'.

iv) Because the RNTBC's constitution sets out a particular process for making decisions of this kind, failure to comply with the process means that the decision is not authorised by the common law holders.

v) The decision to lodge the compensation application was 'taken without authority and in contravention of the Act' and the application should be struck out under s. 84C, *Native Title Act.*

It is not clear whether a similar result would have followed if the constitution had *not* set out a process applicable to decisions of this kind. Had the constitution remained silent, it is arguable that the corporation's plenary powers and capacities would allow it to commence the application by a simple resolution of its board. Justice Greenwood did speculate as to whether s. 251B 'may well have a role to play in determining' whether the RNTBC was properly authorised in commencing a compensation claim. But his Honour ultimately found it unnecessary to decide and furthermore conceded that the 'primary focus' of s. 251B was on the authorisation of compensation claims brought by individuals on behalf of the common law holders.

9.2 Claim filed by individual named applicants

The authorisation provisions for non-corporate compensation applications are in many respects the same as those for a native title determination application:

- The named applicants must be members of the compensation claim group: s. 61(1).
- The named applicants must be authorised by the compensation claim group: s. 61(1).
- According to a note to the 'compensation application' part of s. 61(1), s. 251B contains the relevant meaning of 'authorisation'.
- The named applicants are, jointly, 'the applicant': s. 61(2).

1065 *Walmbaar Aboriginal Corporation v Queensland* [2009] FCA 579 [55]–[61].

- The applicant may deal with 'all matters arising under [the *Native Title Act*] in relation to the application': s. 62A.

One interesting difference, though probably one without much significance, is that the compensation claim group is defined as 'the persons…who *claim to be* entitled to the compensation', rather than (in the case of the native title claim group) 'the persons…who…*hold* the common or group rights and interests comprising the particular native title claimed' (emphasis added). That is, the idea that the claim group is defined by the ultimate reality of who holds native title appears not to apply to compensation claim groups. It is not clear what difference this might make. It may be that the words 'claim to be' are intended to capture an uncertainty around the issue of *liability* rather than the issue of the identity of those people who would be entitled to compensation if liability were proven.

Another difference is that multiple compensation claims can be made by several differently constituted applicants, in respect of the same group and the same area of land. That is because the right to compensation arises in relation to 'acts' and there may be more than one compensable act in the same area of land.[1066] That means there is no issue with 'overlapping' compensation claim groups, so long as each application concerns a different act.

Note that where a compensation determination is made over an area that has not previously been the subject of a native title determination, the court must at the same time make a native title determination over the area: s. 13(2), *Native Title Act*.[1067] That means that every compensation application made over a previously un-determined area is in effect also an application for a determination of native title; in those circumstances it is unlikely that a court would treat the authorisation requirements much differently to those for a standard native title determination application.

1066 See divisions 2, 2A, 2B, NTA.

1067 Note the dismissal of a compensation claim does not constitute a compensation determination: *Jango v Northern Territory (No. 6)* [2006] FCA 465.

10. Conclusion

In general, the Australian legal system demands hard-edged decisions, with legal consequences that are concrete, final and binding rather than fluid, contextual and renegotiable. In mainstream commercial interactions between incorporated entities, corporate law and contract law deliver this certainty. Constitutional, administrative and electoral law does the same for our public political institutions. In other contexts, the law of agency and employment set the parameters for clear and predictable chains of authority.

In the native title context, the law of authorisation is intended to serve the same function. But there are obvious challenges in extracting such hard-edged decisions from unincorporated groups whose extent and composition may be unknown, open to negotiation or manipulation, or simply variable over time or context. These challenges are compounded by sociocultural environments in which decision-making processes are either fluid by tradition or have been weakened or transformed by the disruptive influence of settler society so that they are now open to contestation. Further, because the Australian legal system attempts to tailor the law of authorisation to incorporate the decision-making processes chosen or inherited by each particular native title group, the courts face a challenge in determining what the relevant processes are and whether they have been followed in the particular instance.

These challenges help to explain the sheer volume of case law on authorisation. As the length of this book demonstrates, authorisation in native title is not straightforward or capable of brief explanation. It can be conceptually complex and, in practice, can require careful planning, sophisticated organisation and considerable resources. What may appear at first as a set of dry procedural rules has emerged over two decades of native title practice as a key battleground for intra-Indigenous politics: the politics of personalities, of group identities, and of ideological choices — particularly around mining and other land-use issues. The law of authorisation is also politically significant in setting the parameters of how Aboriginal and Torres Strait Islander polities interact with the Australian legal system. By providing an interface between Indigenous and settler politico-legal systems, the law of authorisation allows (however imperfectly) Indigenous forms of political organisation to interact directly with the Australian legal system, rather than being channelled through the more familiar categories of 'individual', 'corporation', 'partnership', and the like. To conclude this book I will briefly summarise how the earlier technical, legal discussions relate to the challenges inherent in such an interface.

10.1 The scope of authority

During the claims process, because of the large and unincorporated nature of claim groups the *Native Title Act* requires the appointment of a small body of representatives — the applicant. After a determination, the *Native Title Act* requires groups to form a corporation led by a small body of individuals — the RNTBC board of directors. In both cases, there is a live question about how much autonomous authority the applicant or board should have to act on the group's behalf.

The most appealing answer, which is mostly reflected in current law, is that the delegated representatives should have as much or as little autonomy as the group chooses.[1068] As explained in chapters 4 and 5, and Section 7.2 ('Entering and authorising s. 31 agreements'), the *Native Title Act* allows great flexibility for claim groups to define the scope of an applicant's authority during the claim period. Claim groups can give the applicant a broad mandate to make decisions for the group, or specific standing instructions to act in particular ways in particular circumstances, or even stipulate that every decision must be specifically approved by the group. However, for ILUAs (whether before or after a determination)[1069] and possibly for RNTBCs, the law is more intrusive. As Section 7.1 ('Entering and authorising ILUAs') and Chapter 8 show, the *Native Title Act* (and perhaps the PBC Regulations) deprives groups of the ability to delegate certain decisions.[1070] No doubt this limitation was introduced as a procedural protection against exploitation by unscrupulous applicants or directors. But a general desire to protect a group (particularly a group without much familiarity with the details of the Australian legal system) does not explain why a group's explicit and informed decision to delegate or pre-decide certain categories of decision should not be respected.

In addition to this artificial constraint on delegation, there is also an inevitable limitation on claim groups' flexibility in deciding when and how applicants can make decisions. Unavoidably, the law must contain some 'default setting' to cover situations where a group has *not* explicitly articulated their expectations about a particular aspect of decision-making. If the group has not specified their position on questions such as the following, the law (or the court's discretion) must provide an answer one way or the other:

- Should applicants be able to act by majority or is unanimity required?
- Should applicants be capable of binding the group in contract without a decision by the group about each agreement?
- In which situations should applicants be able to give instructions about the conduct of the litigation without going back to a full claim group meeting?
- When a named applicant dies or retires, do the others lose their authorisation (because, for example, the composition of the applicant reflects a delicate balance of factional interests)?

These are not rhetorical questions and, as chapters 4, 5 and 7 have shown, the current law provides answers (albeit sometimes conflicting answers between judges).[1071] The default settings will never be completely right for all groups in all circumstances — in some cases they may be

1068 Importantly, the exercise of such autonomy would still be subject to the fiduciary duties discussed earlier in Section 4.3 ('Obligations of the applicant').

1069 Other than Alternative Procedure ILUAs, which have more relaxed rules for authorisation.

1070 An analogous situation would be if Australia's Commonwealth Constitution gave the parliament the power to make laws for the peace, order and good government of the Commonwealth but specified that any international treaty had to be put to a national referendum, no matter how minor.

1071 The answers are: (a) all living, capable and contactable members of the applicant must agree; (b) yes, but only for s. 31 agreements, not ILUAs; (c) strictly speaking, no steps in the proceeding except for originally lodging the claim, replacing the applicant and entering into an ILUA (also s. 199C(1A)

too prescriptive, formal and expensive, or conversely too lax and permissive, bestowing excessive autonomy on individuals who do not enjoy the requisite political or cultural authority. One size will never fit all.[1072] This fact, however, should not be regarded as a flaw in the legislation — given the diversity of native title groups around Australia the legislation could never be expected to get the settings right. Instead, the task of tailoring processes to the circumstances of each group must fall to the group themselves, assisted by their legal representatives. Viewed in this way, the 'clunkiness' of the default settings should emphasise to practitioners the need to learn from previous experience and prompt claim groups and RNTBCs to consider these matters explicitly at the outset. The ability for groups to impose detailed limits and mandates on their representatives is a strength of the system that should be utilised.

In my view, this flexibility should apply equally in the post-determination context to allow native title holding groups the same ability to delegate as is enjoyed by native title claim groups. As argued earlier in Section 8.2 ('Decision-making within RNTBCs'), this ability arguably exists under the current PBC Regulations via the 'agree or adopt' process in reg. 8(4). But if courts should conclude that delegation of this kind is only available for Low Level decisions covered by reg. 8A, then there is a clear case for amending the regulations. That could be done very simply by amending reg. 8(1) to allow alternative processes under reg. 8A to be used for s. 31 agreements and ILUAs. If giving the directors that much latitude was a concern for the group, the default setting could still require a full consultation-and-consent process each time.

10.2 Logical circles

The *Native Title Act* demonstrates a fairly clear intention to assign to the claimants,[1073] where possible, the task of determining (a) how the claim group is composed and (b) how the claim group makes decisions. Section 3.1 ('The "native title claim group": conceptualising the authorising constituency') dealt with the difficult concept of the 'native title claim group', Chapter 6 explained the process for changing the composition of the claim group, and Section 3.3 ('Authorisation in practice') addressed the question of what decision-making process is to be employed. By their very nature, these issues risk being embroiled in logical recursion: how does a group decide who is in the group without first deciding who is entitled to participate in the decision?[1074] And how can the group decide to agree on a particular decision-making process without

---

(c)), but for serious steps the court in its exercise of discretion may require evidence of a group endorsement; (d) not unless the evidence suggests that this was the intention of the group.

1072 See Australian Law Reform Commission, *Connection to country: review of the Native Title Act 1993 (Cth)*, ALRC Report 126, 2015, para. 10.33, including in particular the comments of Professor Marcia Langton.

1073 Putting aside for the moment whether 'claimants' in this context means applicants or native title claim groups.

1074 Essentially the same dilemma arises in international relations whenever it is claimed that a particular community has been wrongfully incorporated into a larger nation-state by historical

first making a decision about how that anterior question is to be decided? (If this sounds like a quote from Sir Humphrey Appleby or a Lewis Carroll character, that only reinforces the point.)

In the case of claim group descriptions, the law begins with the applicant (rather than the broader group, whoever they may be) and grants to them a *limited* freedom to define the group on whose behalf they claim to act. So long as an applicant is consistent about the composition of the claim group in all of their pleadings, evidence and submissions, the court will take that claim group to be the relevant authorising constituency. Of course, by the end of a contested trial with overlapping claimants, the court may determine that the applicant's version of the claim group does not represent all of the people who hold native title in the claim area. The court may ultimately make findings that are at odds with the applicant's case and make a determination in favour of a differently constituted group (or else dismiss the claim entirely). But for the purposes of authorisation, the claim group will be assessed on the applicant's *own case*. The court will not, as a general rule, attempt to determine 'objectively' whether the boundaries of the group's membership are 'correct' for authorisation purposes.

Where, however, there is any internal inconsistency in the applicant's case the court will 'look behind' the applicant's assertions about who is in the claim group and may find that the applicant is *mistaken* about the composition of the group. For example, where the applicant has pleaded certain criteria for membership and has included or excluded people inconsistently with those criteria, the court may find the applicant's authorisation to be defective. Another example is where certain membership criteria are listed in the Form 1 but the applicant's evidence suggests a different set of criteria.

So at least for the question of group composition, the courts have found a practical way out of the dilemma by focusing on the applicant and the case they bring. But things are much less clear when it comes to determining the proper decision-making process. As I concluded in Section 3.3 ('Authorisation in practice'), neither the parliament nor the courts have developed a clear or unproblematic solution to the apparent chicken-and-egg paradox. This lack of a settled position has not made the system unworkable, in large part due to the fact that so many groups have been apparently able to settle 'organically' on a given decision-making process without any explicit contestation. It seems that, for many native title groups, the choice of decision-making process must be so obvious as to go without saying, notwithstanding that the processes preferred

invasion or colonial boundary-drawing. In such circumstances, an attractive idea is to hold a plebiscite to allow the community to decide for itself whether to remain with the larger state or secede. The problem that immediately arises, however, is determining who should take part in that plebiscite. One could poll all of the people within a particular geographical area but how should the boundaries of that area be determined? In international law, the solution to this problem is to stipulate that only 'nations' enjoy a right of self-determination. Within that discourse, nations are theoretically capable of objective definition and identification. In practice, however, practitioners struggle to agree on what the objective criteria should be. I have argued elsewhere that the quest for objective criteria is conceptually flawed and that the issue should be viewed through the lens of legitimacy and political identity: N Duff, 'Negotiating political community: a constructivist alternative to self-determination', MA thesis, Australian National University, 2011.

by different groups are so different from each other. Some make decisions by the majority votes of individuals; some require a unanimous decision of families, clans or estate groups; some will go by a majority of such subgroups; others will delegate decisions outright to a group of elders or law bosses.[1075] In much of the case law there is no indication of any controversy about the choice of process and so the question of circularity never arose.

Another reason that the circularity problem has not brought the system to a halt is that the *Native Title Act* and PBC Regulations require groups to use a 'traditional' process, if such a process is applicable and mandatory. In such cases the problem of deciding on a decision-making process is avoided by stipulating that it is not up to the group to decide. Where a relevant traditional process exists, this is an objective fact about traditional law and custom, rather than a matter of choice. Of course, such an approach only works when that objective fact can be proven. Such proof will generally require expert anthropological evidence, which will in turn be informed by what members of the group do and say. Where there is disputation amongst the group about what (if anything) traditional law and custom says about decision-making in the very un-traditional context of native title claims and future act agreements, anthropologists may be unable to offer a view with any degree of certainty.

So it seems that in a great many cases, claim groups either adopt an agreed decision-making process without any real dispute or else follow a traditional process that is understood by all concerned as the appropriate way of doing things. But where such a consensus is lacking, courts (and/or the parliament) have essentially two choices:[1076]

a) They can impose some sort of default criterion for what constitutes 'agreeing and adopting' — for example taking a proposed decision-making process to be agreed if a majority (or super-majority) of individuals (or perhaps subgroups) do not object to it.

b) Or else they can adopt a fall-back position whereby any substantial opposition to the proposed decision-making process is taken to mean that the group *has not agreed to adopt any process at all.* On this approach, the lack of agreement about the decision-making process would mean the applicant is not authorised to take any step in the proceedings, and no future act agreement or ILUA is authorised (including in the case of a PBC).

At first glance, the first option seems more intrusive into the internal politics of the group while the second seems more 'hands-off'. By preferring the position of the majority of individuals, for example, the court would necessarily be 'picking winners' — using its own judgment about

---

1075 It is worth noting that what is called a 'decision-making process' here would be better described as a *criterion for a valid decision.* The process itself may involve a number of different elements like an opportunity for discussion, an attempt to reach consensus, a recommendation from respected elders, a secret or open ballot, etc.

1076 I note there is a third option open to groups and practitioners when there is a dispute about which of several decision-making processes should be used. The organisers can conduct a decision by each of the proposed methods and see if the outcome changes. For example, a decision could be made by majority of subgroups or by majority of individuals. If a vote is run both ways and produces the same outcome, then the problem of which is the appropriate method does not arise in any meaningful way.

whether a particular view shares the support of the group as a whole. But even option (b) necessarily puts the court in a position of exercising power in favour of one segment of the group over another. To refuse to recognise an applicant's authority or allow an ILUA to be registered *because* of the procedural objections of a minority would be as much of an intervention as allowing the claim or ILUA to proceed in spite of the objections of a minority. There is no way out of this — it is an unavoidable result of the power of the institutions of parliament and the Federal Court.

So if the Australian legal system's choice between (a) and (b) cannot be decided on the philosophical grounds just mentioned, perhaps there are practical policy consequences that recommend one over the other. Certainly option (a) has the greater capacity to promote the outcomes that require action on the part of native title claimants — the lodging and registration of claims, agreeing to consent determinations, making mining agreements. But the 'pro-action' bias cuts both ways — decisions to withdraw claims, or to install new applicants who will settle for a less advantageous determination,[1077] may work against the interests of claimants. Nevertheless, it is clear enough that option (b) will inevitably act as a brake on the making of claims and agreements. This could be particularly damaging in the context of the right to negotiate — where failure to reach agreement or to challenge a future act in the tribunal can result in the loss of rights without any accompanying benefits, and the failure to have a claim registered in the first place denies groups a seat at the table at all.

Taking into account the beneficial and pragmatic objectives of the *Native Title Act*,[1078] courts certainly seem to have been influenced by this consideration and have tended to prefer some version of option (a).[1079] This book does not take a final position on the question, other than to emphasise that it is a genuine policy choice that is seldom recognised as such.

10.3 Loss of procedural self-reliance?

A consequence of the court's need to understand each group's method of decision-making, and to be satisfied that the proper process has in fact been followed, has been an increasing judicial emphasis on formal and well-documented meeting processes. In the 1990s a group might have held a meeting advertised by word of mouth on fairly short notice, made decisions informally, and relied on a short affidavit explaining what had happened. However, after decades of steadily accumulating case law dealing with challenges to process, the conduct of authorisation meetings has become increasingly professionalised, institutionalised and resource intensive. Most native title claim groups are to some extent dependant on the

1077 E.g. *T.J. v Western Australia* [2015] FCA 818.

1078 Section 3 and Preamble, NTA. See *Northern Territory v Alyawarr, Kaytetye, Warumungu, Wakaya Native Title Claim Group* [2005] FCAFC 135; (2005) 145 FCR 442 at 461, [62]–[64].

1079 *Lawson on behalf of the 'Pooncarie' Barkandji (Paakantyi) People v Minister for Land and Water Conservation (NSW)* [2002] FCA 1517 [22], [25]; *Butterworth on behalf of the Wiri Core Country Claim v Queensland (No. 2)* [2014] FCA 590 [14]–[28]; *N.C. (deceased) v Western Australia (No. 2)* [2013] FCA 70 [91]–[94].

involvement of lawyers, consultant facilitators, anthropologists and logistical staff in order to make decisions that will meet the increasingly high procedural bar. The discussion in Section 3.3 ('Authorisation in practice') demonstrated the legal requirements for procedural rigour as well as the importance of learning from previous experience while planning authorisation processes. The need to ensure proper notification means meetings cannot be held at short notice and will generally require legal assistance in drafting the meeting notice. Significant resources are also needed for advertising and (often) travel assistance. The requirements as set out in Section 3.2 ('Authorisation by "all the persons" in the native title claim group') may in some cases simply be beyond the financial and organisational capacity of groups who lack the assistance and resources of NTRBs.

This development has an obvious impact on the idea of native title groups as self-reliant actors taking responsibility for their land and their heritage. It has the capacity to undermine the sense of ownership and agency to which many Aboriginal and Torres Strait Islander peoples aspire. Militating against the belief that the task of protecting their rights falls primarily on the shoulders of the claimants themselves is the contemporary reality that valid authorisation decisions are now virtually impossible without some level of external funding and administrative support. This threatens to entrench an economic and bureaucratic dependency on NTRBs, even recognising that some groups can and do go their own way without NTRB assistance. The case law discussed in this book is replete with examples of applicants whose inability to obtain funding or assistance from NTRBs has left them reliant on pro bono or discounted assistance from non-lawyers or non-specialist lawyers, often resulting in defective authorisation and consequent dismissal.

Nevertheless, these negative aspects may well be an unavoidable part of a system that seeks to incorporate Indigenous politics into the Australian legal system in circumstances of intra-Indigenous conflict. The complex and resource-intensive nature of authorisation in 2016 has come about not because of a deliberate intention by legislators or judges to create a formalistic regime. It has emerged from attempts to sort through difficult and contested disagreements between named applicants, between applicants and claim groups, between subgroups within claim groups, and between overlapping claim groups. For groups with strong traditional decision-making processes, who live in geographically concentrated areas and whose political disagreements are successfully resolved within the group, the task of organising, advertising and conducting a meeting may well be a cheap, quick and simple affair. But for large, geographically dispersed groups that are affected by conflicts over legitimacy, the case law demonstrates that the option of relying on informal, unwritten, or 'organic' processes is clearly unavailable.

There may be ways of improving the availability of funding for groups who cannot or choose not to use the services of NTRBs, and the quality of the resulting authorisation processes may be improved by increasing numbers of non-NTRB legal practitioners who are experienced in native title authorisation. Further, claimants may be partly reassured by the thought that after a determination, there will be avenues for greater self-reliance through the RNTBC. However, the often onerous requirements under the CATSI Act and PBC Regulations and the difficulties in obtaining funding post-determination mean that many groups will have little choice but to continue to rely on the assistance of NTRBs in order to make group decisions that satisfy the requirements of the Australian legal system.

10.4 Navigating in difficult territory

This short discussion of the tensions and dilemmas within the law of native title authorisation produces the strong impression that there are no absolutely right answers. Working at the interface of very different politico-legal traditions, in circumstances of frequent contestation and always with some degree of unavoidable ignorance about the cultural context, courts and legislators have sought to find flexible and practical ways of accommodating and recognising Indigenous decision-making. For their own part, Aboriginal and Torres Strait Islander peoples have had to make dramatic adjustments and concessions to the Australian legal system in order to interact successfully with it. In this situation of compromise and pragmatism, the strengths of the system are the ability for Indigenous groups to explicitly articulate their intended procedural rules, and the ability for courts to exercise discretion to avoid perverse or clearly unfair outcomes. In my view, these abilities provide the best possible chance of delivering practical justice for Aboriginal and Torres Strait Islander groups within the Australian legal system.

www.ingramcontent.com/pod-product-compliance
Lightning Source LLC
LaVergne TN
LVHW010054110826
845155LV00028B/340
* 9 7 8 1 9 2 2 1 0 2 6 1 4 *